DATE DUE

~~NV 25 '99~~		
FE 3'00		
OC 20 04		

P9-CJK-369

This revisionary study of the origins of courtly poetry reveals the culture of spectatorship and voyeurism that shaped early Tudor English literary life. Through new research into the reception of Chaucer's *Troilus and Criseyde*, it demonstrates how Pandarus became the model of the early modern courtier. His blend of counsel, secrecy, and eroticism informed the behavior of poets, lovers, diplomats, and even Henry VIII himself. In close readings of the poetry of Hawes and Skelton, the drama of the court, the letters of Henry VIII to Anne Boleyn, the writings of Thomas Wyatt, and manuscript anthologies and early printed books, Seth Lerer illuminates a "Pandaric" world of displayed bodies, surreptitious letters, and transgressive performances. In the process, he redraws the boundaries between the medieval and the Renaissance and illustrates the centrality of the verse epistle to the construction of subjectivity.

Cambridge Studies in Renaissance Literature and Culture

General editor
STEPHEN ORGEL
Jackson Eli Reynolds Professor of Humanities, Stanford University

Editorial board
Anne Barton, *University of Cambridge*
Jonathan Dollimore, *University of Sussex*
Marjorie Garber, *Harvard University*
Jonathan Goldberg, *Duke University*
Nancy Vickers, *University of Southern Californian*

Since the 1970s there has been a broad and vital reinterpretation of the nature of literary texts, a move away from formalism to a sense of literature as an aspect of social, economic, political, and cultural history. While the earliest New Historicist work was criticized for a narrow and anecdotal view of history, it also served as an important stimulus for post-structuralist, feminist, Marxist, and psychoanalytical work, which in turn has increasingly informed and redirected it. Recent writing on the nature of representation, the historical construction of gender and of the concept of identity itself, on theatre as a political and economic phenomenon, and on the ideologies of art generally, reveals the breadth of the field. Cambridge Studies in Renaissance Literature and Culture is designed to offer historically oriented studies of Renaissance literature and theatre which make use of the insights afforded by theoretical perspectives. The view of history envisioned is above all a view of our own history, a reading of the Renaissance for and from our own time.

Recent titles include

The emergence of the English author: scripting the life of the poet in early modern England
KEVIN PASK

The poetics of English nationhood, 1590–1612
CLAIRE McEACHERN, University of California, Los Angeles

Textual intercourse: collaboration, authorship, and sexualities in Renaissance drama
JEFFREY MASTEN, Harvard University

The project of prose in early modern Europe and the New World
edited by ELIZABETH FOWLER, Yale University, and ROLAND GREENE, University of Oregon

The marketplace of print: pamphlets and the public sphere in early modern England
ALEXANDRA HALASZ, Dartmouth College

A complete list of books in the series is given at the end of the volume

Cambridge Studies in Renaissance Literature and Culture 18

Courtly letters in the age of Henry VIII

Hans Holbein, Portrait of Sir Thomas Cromwell.

Courtly letters in the age of Henry VIII

Literary culture and the arts of deceit

Seth Lerer

Stanford University

CAMBRIDGE
UNIVERSITY PRESS

DICATE OF THE UNIVERSITY OF CAMBRIDGE
Street, Cambridge CB2 1RP, United Kingdom

ss

The Edinburgh Building, Cambridge CB2 2RU, United Kingdom
40 West 20th Street, New York, NY 10011–4211, USA
10 Stamford Road, Oakleigh, Melbourne 3166, Australia

© Seth Lerer 1997

This book is in copyright. Subject to statutory exception
and to the provisions of relevant collective licensing agreements,
no reproduction of any part may take place without
the written permission of Cambridge University Press.

First published 1997

Printed in the United Kingdom at the University Press, Cambridge

Typeset in Times 10/12pt

A catalogue record for this book is available from the British library

Library of Congress cataloguing in publication data
Lerer, Seth, 1955–
Courtly letters in the age of Henry VIII: literary culture and the arts
of deceit / Seth Lerer.
  p.   cm. – (Cambridge studies in Renaissance literature and culture: 18)
Includes bibliographical references and index.
ISBN 0 521 59001 9 (hardback)
1. English literature – Early modern, 1500–1700 – History and criticism.
2. Politics and literature – Great Britain – History – 16th century.
3. Great Britain – History – Henry VIII. 1509–1547 – Historiography.
4. Great Britain – Court and courtiers – History – 16th century.
5. Chaucer, Geoffrey, d. 1400. Troilus and Criseyde.
6. Civilization, Medieval, in literature.
7. Chaucer, Geoffrey, d. 1400 – Influence.
8. Courts and courtiers in literature.
9. Deception in literature.   10. Renaissance – England.
I. Title.   II. Series.
PR418.P65L47   1997
820.9′003–dc21   96–49466   CIP

ISBN 0 521 59001 9 hardback

CE

For my father

What a goddes name, haue ye a boke in your hande? let me se. Nouum
testamentum: What, thou deceiuest me / I had wend thou couldest haue
skillid of nothing but onli of flateri. But what is this in your bosom? an
other boke . . . Abyde, what is here? Troylus & Chreseid? Lord what
discord is bitwene these two bokes?

Sir Thomas Elyot, Pasquil the Playne (1533)

Contents

Illustrations

Acknowledgments

This book began as a sequel to my *Chaucer and His Readers*, and it therefore owes a debt to many of the individuals and institutions that facilitated the writing of that study. The British Library, the Huntington Library, the Bodleian Library, and the libraries of Princeton, Berkeley, and Stanford provided resources and materials. A fellowship from the John Simon Guggenheim Memorial Foundation enabled me to begin work on the present volume, while further financial support and teaching leave from Stanford helped me to complete it.

Portions of the book were presented to audiences at Berkeley, Duke, Notre Dame, the University of Pennsylvania, and Rutgers; to a meeting of the Bay Area Pre- and Early Modern Study Group; and as lectures and colloquia at Washington University, where I had the privilege of serving as the Hurst Visiting Professor in the Winter of 1996. Among those who heard or read material, I single out for special thanks: John Bender, Harry Berger, Mary Bly, Joseph Loewenstein, Patricia Parker, David Riggs, Jennifer Summit, and Steven Zwicker. For support of this project in its earliest stages, I thank R. Howard Bloch, Anthony Grafton, Stephen G. Nichols, and Brian Stock. Joseph Dane had the ability to determine precisely the moments when I was saying just the opposite of what I meant. Timothy Hampton responded fully to an early version of chapter 3 and, in the process, helped me see the larger European scope of my study. Mary F. Godfrey offered valuable commentary throughout the writing of the book. Conversations with Sean Keilen and Bradin Cormack pushed me to refine the exposition and enhance its supporting evidence. Christina Carlson and Deanne Williams secured microfilms of manuscripts. After the book was complete in draft, I had the opportunity to present some of its materials in a graduate seminar at Stanford on early Tudor literature. I am grateful to those students for showing me the implications of my interests and for forcing me to clarify my claims.

Stephen Orgel welcomed this book into the Cambridge Studies in Renaissance Literature and Culture series. But more than that, his presence as a colleague and a friend has enhanced the environment in which this publication, as well as many of my others, could productively take shape. Josie Dixon has been a model editor and Jonathan Crewe an ideal reader (whose report not only offered incisive suggestions for revision, but also managed to articulate the scope and argument of the book better than I could myself).

A small portion of chapter 2 appears as an article in *The Huntington Library Quarterly* 59 (1996). An early version of some readings now incorporated into chapters 2 and 4 appears as an essay in *The Book and the Body*, ed. Katherine O'Brien O'Keeffe and Dolores Warwick Frese (Notre Dame: Notre Dame University Press, 1996). Finally, I thank the Huntington Library, the Frick Collection, the British Library, and the Pierpont Morgan Library for permission to reproduce photographs of materials in their collections.

Note on editions and abbreviations

Unless otherwise noted, all quotations from Chaucer's poetry will be from Larry D. Benson, general editor, *The Riverside Chaucer*, third edition (Boston: Houghton Mifflin, 1987). I have, however, compared the *Riverside* edition of *Troilus and Criseyde* with Barry Windeatt, ed., *Chaucer: Troilus and Criseyde* (London: Longman, 1984), whose readings I occasionally adopt. Quotations from Wyatt's poetry will be from R. A. Rebholz, ed., *Sir Thomas Wyatt, The Complete Poems* (Baltimore: Penguin, 1978). For Skelton: John Scattergood, ed., *John Skelton, The Complete English Poems* (New Haven: Yale University Press, 1983). For Stephen Hawes: W. E. Mead, *The Pastime of Pleasure*, EETS original series 173 (London: Oxford University Press, 1928); Florence W. Gluck and Alice B. Morgan, eds., *The Minor Poems*, EETS original series 271 (London: Oxford University Press, 1974). For Tottel's *Miscellany*: Hyder E. Rollins, ed., *Tottel's Miscellany (1557–1587)* (Cambridge, MA: Harvard University Press, 2 vols. 1928–29, rev. 1965). The manuscript of Humphrey Wellys, Bodleian Library MS Rawlinson C.813, has been edited by Sharon L. Jansen and Kathleen H. Jordan, *The Welles Anthology* (Binghamton: Medieval and Renaissance Texts and Studies, 1991), and for the most part I rely on their edition (though I spell the name of its compiler as he did, Wellys). All other editions will be cited in full in the notes.

My use of these editions, however, does not necessarily imply that I accept all their readings and redactions. The literature I survey survives in manuscripts and printed books of remarkable textual variability. To some, variation is the mark of unreliability; to others, it is testimony to the creatively fluid nature of the medieval and the early modern text and to the intrusiveness (witting or unwitting) of scribes and readers. This is a book about the history of reading and rewriting, and I have often sought the manuscripts and early printed editions of many of the works I analyze. When I refer to these documents to make a point of textual criticism, or to expose the responses of a historical readership, I cite them using standard library abbreviations, shelf marks, catalogue references, *Short Title Catalogue* numbers, and foliation or pagination.

Finally, because there is a fair amount of Middle English in this book, I occasionally offer marginal translations of particularly difficult or obscure words in my quotations.

The following abbreviations are used:

EETS OS	Early English Text Society, Original Series
EETS ES	Early English Text Society, Extra Series
MED	*Middle English Dictionary*, ed. Hans Kurath *et al.* (Ann Arbor: University of Michigan, 1954 –)
OED	*Oxford English Dictionary*, ed., James H. A. Murray *et al.* (Oxford: Oxford University Press, 1933)
RES	*Review of English Studies*
SAC	*Studies in the Age of Chaucer*
STC	A. W. Pollard and G. R. Redgrave, *A Short Title Catalogue of Books Printed in England, Scotland, and Ireland and of English Books Printed Abroad, 1475–1640* (London: Bibliographical Society, 1926)
RSTC	The *STC* revised by W. A. Jacobs, F. S. Ferguson, and Katherine F. Panzer, 3 vols. (London: Bibliographical Society, 1976, 1986, 1991)

1 Pretexts: Chaucer's Pandarus and the origins of courtly discourse

Think of it as a book of lies. The courtly life had always been a show, and the literature of courtliness has always been appreciated for its arabesques of the deceitful.[1] Years before Machiavelli and Castiglione had captured the courtier's ruses in maximal form, and decades before their work had been translated into English, Henry VIII's ambassadors and poets were displaying that rich blend of sycophancy and sincerity that would mark the sprezzaturas of the sixteenth century.[2] In the first year of the young King's reign, Luiz Carroz, Ferdinand of Spain's ambassador to England, wrote that the experience of service forced him to dissimulate.[3] By the end of Henry's first decade, poets such as Stephen Hawes and John Skelton could critically reflect on the cloakings and collusions of royal service.[4] Thomas More lived among the "stage plays of the great,"[5] and Erasmus recognized that the courtier must live behind the masks of theater.[6] Such masking, as Erasmus and his peers well knew, involved not just the assumption of a voice but the transvestings of the body. The courtier becomes a creature of the *corpus*, whether it be as groom to a king, ministering to royal micturations, or as a performing self, garbed in the texts and textiles of the poet. The instabilities of courtly bodies extend to the very gender of courtiership itself. The courtier is both a pimp and prostitute: a panderer to the desires of the prince, a procurer of women, information, and advantage; but also a servant, whose needs have all the willful manipulations of the whore. As Erasmus put it, "Always be complaining and demanding, and just as skillful courtesans by various pretexts and devices always get something from their lovers, similarly let it be your endeavour always to get something from your prince."[7]

What are the sources of this life? Ovidian erotics, Ciceronian friendship, Arthurian romance, clerical pedagogy, curial service – all have been invoked as providing both the words and deeds of courtly culture. And certainly, the courtier and poet, the lover and the diplomat, have long been understood as two sides of their respective courtly coins. The currency of courtiership has been sought in those texts that meld the two:

1

treatises on the art of rhetoric that, for example, yoke together literary and political service as forms of verbal feigning; or manuals on the art of love that illustrate how the cajoleries of public *amicitia* can be transformed into the wiles of private *amor*.[8] The very terms of courtly service owe their origin to this complex of the rhetorical, the amorous, the literary, and the social. Words such as *elegantia*, *decorum*, *disciplina*, *curialitas*, *honestas*, and their many vernacular equivalents, signaled not just codes of conduct but ways of speaking and, too, ways of reading.[9] The very notion of performance itself, moreover, embraced all aspects of the self on judged display, whether it be in court, in school, or in the bedroom.

Among works of English literature that explored this blend of love and politics, few texts have stood out as clearly as Chaucer's *Troilus and Criseyde*. From its first circulation among the poet's contemporaries, through its later manuscript transmissions and reception in the printed book, the poem compelled the imagination of male love, female betrayal, power politics, and authorial responsibility.[10] Though indebted for his plot and characters to Boccaccio's *Il Filostrato*, Chaucer transformed his source through the addition of a rich Boethian philosophical texture, a uniquely English lyric sensibility, and a distinctively personal sense – born, perhaps, of years of public service – of the manipulations of the courtly life.[11] So deep was the current of courtiership in the poem, that its titular characters quickly became models for aristocratic as well as newly-emergent bourgeois lovers. Throughout the fifteenth and the sixteenth centuries, the poem functioned as a textbook for the amateur and courtly maker, "the great poem," in John Stevens's words, "in which he could study and find how 'most felyngly' to speak of love."[12] Chaucer's *Troilus* was the major source of what Richard Firth Green has called the "social and literary plunder" out of which late medieval literature was made.[13] By the early Tudor period, the social habits of reading and reciting the poem may have generated an entire "public world of courtly love," in Raymond Southall's words, a world of "love, secrecy and steadfastness" that informed the register of literariness at Henry VIII's court.[14] For Thomas Elyot's aspiring royal servant, in the passage from *Pasquil the Playne* that I have quoted as the epigraph to this book, *Troilus and Criseyde* may be carried along with the New Testament as nothing less than the bible of courtiership.

For Elyot's courtier (as well as those described by Skelton and Hawes at the beginning of the Henrician era to Wyatt and Surrey at its close) it is not, however, Troilus and Criseyde who are the models for that public world of courtly love, but rather it is Pandarus. Though his name would provide the eponym for one of the most damning terms in the English vocabulary of desire, his presence has largely been slighted by modern critics in favor of his amatory pupils.[15] Yet there is much throughout the fifteenth and the early sixteenth centuries to evidence the impact of his distinctive blend of advisory tuition and transgressive voyeurism. In manuscript excerpts and Chaucerian imitations, he appears as a model of advisory friendship and political sagacity.[16] He is here, as Gervase Matthew has argued that he was for Chaucer's Ricardian audience, "a man of cultivated sensibility, facilely expressed emotions and quick stratagems."[17] But he is also a creature of voyeurism and surreptitious-ness, an entrepreneur of the erotic, spying on Troilus and Criseyde in bed, transmitting private missives, and misreading and misrepresenting female motives and his own desires. It is this "privy" Pandarus that defines courtly poetics for the Henrician age and, more generally, that shapes the making of the early modern reader. His presence in the sixteenth century – especially after the printing of the *Troilus* by Wynkyn de Worde in 1517 and its appearance as part of the larger Chaucerian editions of Richard Pynson (1526) and William Thynne (1532) – would have addressed directly the concerns of courtiers and gentry during the reign of Henry VIII: anxieties about the interception of political and amatory letters; about the relationships between the visualization of the body and the proper codes of physical desire; about the choices offered between personal friendship and public service. Pandarus, I propose, stands at that "nexus of power, sexuality, and inwardness" that has been seen, at least since Stephen Greenblatt's *Renaissance Self-Fashioning*, as the defining condition of literary culture in the early Tudor period.[18]

This is a book about the making of what I call the Pandaric life, a book about the practices of love and politics as shaped by literary figures and, in turn, about the reading of canonical poetic texts through transgressive personal responses. It is in part, therefore, about publicity: about the makings of courtly personae, about performances of love, diplomacy, and power. But it also seeks the origins of privacy: the intimacies of the letter, the arts of secret reading, the confines of the study. In the correspondence of ambassadors, the love letters of King Henry, the commonplace books of metropolitan and provincial gentry, the courtly poetry of Wyatt and his circle, and the publications of the printshop, lie the ministrations of the voyeur and the surreptions of the surveyed. The men and women I present here read past the public discourses of power that, in early Tudor culture in particular, set the terms of institutional behavior that have long been understood as hall-marks of the modern. They locate cultural self-knowing in the rituals of theater and the impulses of spectatorship. They focus on the presenta-tions of the body and the stories of its maintenance, display, or pain.

They are creatures of the politics of ocular desire – a desire that, whether it be set before the eyes of early Tudor readers or the modern academic critic, leads us almost inextricably into Pandarus's closet.

While much has recently been made of Chaucerian reception in the formation of English literary history, and while much, too, has been done with courtly theatrics in the construction of the modern self, the nexus of the two has never fully been explored.[19] Indeed, the literary culture of the early Tudor period itself has only recently emerged as an object of study in its own right. Traditional literary history sees it as a curious interlude between the dullness of the fifteenth century and the efflorescence of the Elizabethan age. For C. S. Lewis, H. A. Mason, and John Stevens, all writing over thirty years ago, the early Tudor period was a world of pastime with good company, of stable male and female gender roles, of amorous dalliance, lyric performance, and witty exchange.[20] Much has been done, of course, to dismantle such a fantasy, especially by the New Historicist inquiries into the social politics of the early sixteenth century.[21] So, too, the literary genealogies established by the period's first chroniclers and critics (for example, the printer Richard Tottel and the theorist George Puttenham) have been challenged.[22] The defining dyad of courtly poetry has been reengineered not as that of Wyatt and Surrey but of Hawes and Skelton.[23] Texts that have long been dismissed as derivative (Hawes's *Conforte of Louers*), unreadable (the Latin panegyrics of Bernard André), obscurely topical (the documents of the Grammarians' War), or theatrically self-promoting (Skelton's *Garlande of Laurell*) are coming to be seen as central to the consciousness of English writers and readers during the first third of the sixteenth century.[24] The transition from script to print – long understood as a phenomenon both quick and irreversible, with short-term pain and long-term benefit – has, too, been reassessed as far more complicated and dilated than theorists such as Marshall McLuhan and historians such as Elizabeth Eisenstein would have one believe.[25] And the ideals of friendship and learning once unequivocally praised as the source of Western humanism – as articulated in the work of More, Erasmus, and others – have been shaded (if not shadowed) by the critical revisionism that sees an erotics to the pedagogical and that knows well the blurred line between *amor* and *amicitia* in the discourses of the letter.[26]

Though this book is indebted to this sway in recent criticism, it does not unequivocally seek to dismiss the researches of the past nor to support unswervingly the claims of current scholarship. Instead, it seeks to interrogate the cultural conditions that produced and read the literature of early Tudor England as well as the critical presuppositions that have rephrased the approaches to the period during the past two decades. This book, therefore, takes issue with a number of contemporary claims, most notably, in chapters 2 and 3, the preoccupation with the homosocial cast to Henry VIII's servants and savants.[27] At the same time, it seeks to assess anew the problems posed by more traditional scholarly methods, in particular, in chapters 4 and 5, the techniques of textual criticism as they have have been used to edit and attribute certain poems, manuscripts, and early printed volumes of the early sixteenth century.[28] As in my previous book, *Chaucer and His Readers*, my overarching goal is to restore the material text to primacy in literary study, whether that text be a canonical work of literature, such as *Troilus and Criseyde*, or such ephemera as the verse of a provincial manuscript compiler or the elusive missives of a royal ambassador. This is a book about the making of social identity through the history of reading: one that seeks to understand relationships between the public and the private, the oral and the written, the scripted and the printed, the courtly and the provincial, the educated and the popular. This may seem a tall order for a study centered on a few "major" and quite a few "minor" texts. And yet, it is precisely this relationship between the major and the minor, so ensconced in modern literary histories, that I seek to dismantle. The literature of early Tudor England is read and written in the margins of its manuscripts, the little quartos of its printers, the commonplace books of its men and women.

If the literary history of early Tudor England has languished on the byways of the non-canonical, its social and political historiography has not. For many decades, the reigns of the Henries have been central to accounts of the formation of the English nation state and its defining institutions. The patterns of legal judgment, the stratagems of statecraft, the creations of bureaucracy, the formations of political charisma – all have been located in their modern form during the early Tudor period. The history of political institutions such as the Privy Chamber has been traced by David Starkey as a phenomenon keyed to the English monarchs' personalities, as well as to the paradigms of service, class, and the acquisition of wealth in Britain.[29] Starkey's work is of immense importance, not just for its charting of the changes in a particular political institution, but for its implications concerning the ideas of intimacy and publicity in the period. In a sense, Starkey's is what we might now call of a history of the body: in Michel Foucault's terms, a reading of the royal body as the locus of force relations, where the King's corporeal form is the site of national identity formation, diplomatic intrigue, and public spectacle.[30] Henry VIII's body is, in many ways, the emblem of the Tudor body politic, a claim brought out with much subtlety by Louis Montrose in his account of Renaissance subjectivity and subjection.[31] Starkey's work has thus had great impact on the New Historicist assessment of the formation of courtliness. It stands behind many of the opening gestures of Jonathan Goldberg's *Sodometries* and it functions, in effect, as the large historical subtext of his study of writing and power in the sixteenth century, *Writing Matter: From the Hands of the Renaissance*.[32]

In addition to Starkey, one of the most influential political historians of this period is G. R. Elton, who has set forth an interpretation of the origins of Tudor constitutionality.[33] Elton argued that it was Thomas Cromwell who took the opportunity provided by the King's marital difficulties to redefine the nature of the English nation state. It was Cromwell, in Elton's reading, who renamed England as an empire, recalibrated the kingship as a constitutional monarchy ruling through bureaucratic institutions, codified and nationalized local legal customs, and galvanized Parliament into a statute-making body of government. Elton's thesis has been stated and restated many times since its presentation in *The Tudor Revolution in Government* over forty years ago.[34] Here is one succinct version of it: "By using statute – law made by parliament – to solve a variety of complicated legal and constitutional problems, and by exploiting the powers devolved upon him by the monarch, Cromwell was able to shift the burden of government from the personal servants of the royal household to properly organized departments of state."[35] Elton's work has many ramifications, and I cannot deal with all of them here. But I have singled out this particular aspect of his thesis because I think it central to this book's inquiries into the tensions between private counsel and public law in the makings of kingly power, literary taste, and courtly poetry and theater. In his later study *Policy and Police*, on which I will draw heavily, Elton limns the contours of a culture of surreptitiousness and inspection that defined the enforcement of the Cromwellian "revolution" of the 1530s.[36] The interception of letters, the taking of statements, the encouragement of informancy, the need for concealment – all are political issues that have an impact on the formation of literary subjectivity in the age of Wyatt.

Words such as "literature" and "politics," therefore, are not terms of a unique or identifiable valence, where one takes precedence over the other.[37] Instead, I posit, both emerge together from the cultural reception of certain texts and the social practices of certain groups. I argue here that Chaucer's Pandarus stands at the nexus of those texts and practices. He is the generative figure of the early Tudor age, embodying the complicated and ultimately self-baffled artfulness of courtly life[38] – what I have called the Pandaric life. In order to appreciate the texture of that life, one needs to understand the many discourses of Chaucer's poem, the history of letter-writing and the rise of silent reading, and the habits of corporeal display that shape the idioms of early sixteenth-century English literary culture. The following sections of this chapter take up these strands to sketch the pretexts of Henrician experience and my own inquiries into its forms.

The love of letters

At the heart of the Pandaric are the fabrications of the letter.[39] Scarcely has he intruded into Troilus's bedchamber – entering in "unwar" (*Troilus and Criseyde*, I.549) and deferring for nearly fifty lines his self-announcement, "it am I, Pandare" (I.588) – than he defines his counselorship of Troilus through his privy insight into Oenone's letter to Paris. "Yee say [i.e., saw] the lettre that she wrot, I gesse?" (I.656) Pandarus inquires of his friend. But how could he, or for that matter, how could Pandarus? Unlike Ovid's original, with its complaints of the young rustic girl to the imperial Paris, Pandarus quotes only her complaint that lovers cannot heal themselves. His reading of the letter, furthermore, is pressed into the service not of understanding female pain but of articulating his own status as a lover. "Right so fare I, unhappyly for me" (I.666), he avers in a curiously confused identification with the spurned girl. "And yet," he goes on, "kan I reden [i.e., advise] the / And nat myself" (668–69). This is the heart of the Pandaric dilemma. Privileged with information garnered from a private missive, he is nonetheless incapable of learning from his reading. Capable of ventriloquizing the female epistolary voice, he fails to understand the nature of female desire. And, while his store of information and proverbial lore grants him the expertise to counsel Troilus, he is still incapable of counseling himself.

When Pandarus becomes a teacher of the art of letter writing, these paradoxes are exposed for what they are: the machinations of the voyeur. In Book II, his amatory tuition of Troilus depends not just on his full command of all the strategies of *dictamen*, but on skills at subtly insinuating himself into the epistolary process.[40] Pandarus is a reader over Troilus's shoulder, a friend who watches Troilus write, fold, and seal his letter, only to have it delivered into his own hands for eventual submission to Criseyde. And when this letter reaches its addressee, it again becomes the focus of a voyeuristic reading: a text now not to be perused in private, but intruded upon by reader and messenger. This is, now, a distinctively Pandaric moment, rich with all the secretive manipulations that distinguish Chaucer's handling of the story from Boccaccio's. Pandarus draws Criseyde away from her companions with a story about Greek spies. He leads her "Into the gardyn" so that she may hear

"Al pryvely" of these events (II.1114–15). But, of course, this tale of
espionage is a ruse designed to get himself and Criseyde out of public
earshot (II.1118–19) so that he may read her Troilus's epistle. This is an
episode not of the formal manuals of love but of the stark transgressions
of propriety. It is a moment of deep surreption and barely suppressed
violence – an episode in which Criseyde reacts with anger to her uncle's
suggestion that she reply ("Scrit ne bille [i.e., write no letter], / For love
of God" [II.1130–31]), and he with indignation at the thought that he
would harm her:

> To dethe mot I smyten be with thondre,
> If for the citee which that stondeth yondre,
> Wolde I a lettre unto yow brynge or take
> To harm of yow!   (II.1145–48)

The violence that surrounds the letter here climaxes not with thunder
claps or civic acts, but with Pandarus's own physically threatening retort
and fear of being seen.

> "Refuse it naught," quod he, and *hente* hire faste,   "grabbed"
> And in hire bosom the lettre down he thraste,
>
> And seyde hire, "Now cast it awey anon,
> That folk may seen and *gauren* on us tweye."   (II.1154–58)   "stare"

This is a letter that can only be opened alone, in Criseyde's "chambre"
where she goes "Ful pryvely this lettre for to rede" (II.1173, 1176); a
letter whose reception generates a playful game of withdrawal and
surprise between Criseyde and Pandarus ("But Pandarus, that in a
studye stood, / Er he was war, she took hym by the hood, / And seyde,
'ye were caught er that ye wiste'" [II.1180–82]); a letter whose reply
demands a level of enchamberment that borders – at least rhetorically –
on imprisonment:

> And into a *closet*, for t'avise hire bettre,
> She wente *allone*, and gan hire herte *unfettre*
> Out of desdaynes *prisoun* but a lite,
> And sette hire down, and gan a lettre write,
>
> Of which to telle in short is myn *entente*
> Th'*effect*, as fer as I kan *understonde*.   (II.1215–20, emphases mine)

These lines move pointedly from Criseyde's self-absorption to the
narrator's disclosure. They point up with arresting power the shame of
Criseydian privacy, a privacy that makes us all eavesdroppers: Pandarus
himself, who just three stanzas earlier had promised to sew up and fold
the document (II.1204); the narrator, who describes what it contains; and

Chaucer's audience. This is a letter treated far differently from Troilus's. There, it was the writer himself who had folded it and sealed it with his own signet (II.1085–90). Here, all Criseyde does is "shette" (i.e., close) it (II.1226), leaving it for Pandarus to seal it up. There, for Troilus, the narrator had, in effect, paraphrased directly the content of the letter. Three stanzas narrate its progressions (II.1065–86) – a virtual transcription in indirect discourse – while Criseyde's gets only four lines (II.1221–25). And there is, too, a certain narratorial anxiety about this reportage. "Entente," "effect," "understonde" – these are the terms deployed throughout the poem to signal the surreptitiously observed or the illicitly discerned. Certainly, we have no knowledge, direct or indirect, of just what Criseyde's letter offers; nor do we have any evidence for how it would affect Troilus.

For when it reaches its intended, it does not do so in privacy. Pandarus is there to deliver it (II.1318), to hand Troilus a light (II.1320), and – we must assume – to look over his shoulder while he reads it himself. And Chaucer's narrator is there too, appealing to publicly shared observation in an odd blend of the commonplace and the erotic:

> But as we may alday oureselven see,
> Thorugh more wode or col, the more fir,
> Right so encreese hope, of what it be,
> Therwith ful ofte encresseth ek desir;
> Or as an *ook* comth of a litil spir,   "oak"
> So thorugh this lettre which that she hym sente
> Encrescen gan desir, of which he *brente*.   (II.1331–37)   "burned"

This is a curiously phallic moment for the poem. Troilus's hope and desire increase (the word shows up three times in the stanza) as an oak grows from a little sprout – a potentially disturbing application of an old saw to a new feeling. And Pandarus is there. His name intrudes again and again into Troilus's epistolary responses:

> Wherfore I seye alwey, that day and nyght
> This Troilus gan to desiren moore
> Thanne he did erst, thorugh hope, and did his myght
> To preessen on, as by Pandarus loore,
> And writen to hire of his sorwes soore.
> Fro day to day he leet it nought *refreyde*,   "grow cold"
> That by Pandare he wroot somwhat or seyde;   (II.1338–44)

And later on: "But to Pandare alwey was his recours" (II.1352). Pandarus has intruded, now, into the writing, reading, and transmission of the letters. He is, in effect, more than just postman or good friend; he is the tutor, reader, sealer, and inspirer of writing. He insinuates himself into the "verray hertes privetee" of Troilus, as he asks his friend whom he may trust to set up a liaison. "Now lat m'alone, and werken as I may" (II.1397, 1401).

I have reviewed this episode in *Troilus and Criseyde* in detail because it stands as something of the *Urtext* of Pandaric epistolary voyeurism at work in the early Tudor court. While the explicit transcript of the lovers' letters in Book V of Chaucer's poem may have had a greater impact on the amorous impersonations of the courtly lover,[41] it is this passage that speaks directly to the anxiousness of Henrician courtier intrusion and, in turn, to the kinds of surreptitious transcriptions and readings that distinguish commonplace book compilation in the first third of the sixteenth century. Book II dramatizes tensions between the public and the private in epistolary terms, marking in particular the different ways in which a man and woman read and write.[42] It also sets out the theatrics of Pandaric intrusion, offering in its figure of the go-between someone whose bold entries and lively intrusions sketch out the performative gestures of male friendship. In its broad contours and its local details, Book II of *Troilus* surfaces again and again in the early Tudor discourses of love and politics: in the pandarisms of King Henry's minions; in the manuscript assemblies of the gentry; in the Satires of Wyatt; and in the reflections on the amorous epistle that fill Tottel's *Miscellany*. Book II is thus a major "pretext" for my study, not just as a source of diction, but as structural paradigm for the defining dramas of intrusion and performance, letter-writing and illicit reading, in early Tudor courtly literature.

If letters are the lure of love, however, they are also the currency of politics. The medieval traditions of the *ars dictaminis* and the notarial development of formal correspondence generated a diplomacy that worked through letters.[43] The chancelleries of royal court or papal office developed the styles of epistolary negotiation, and throughout the Middle Ages and the Renaissance, manuals of *dictamen* proliferated, much like instructions in the art of rhetoric or guides to love. Perhaps the most complete, and yet distinctive, of such manuals is Erasmus's *De conscribendis epistolis*. Composed over a period of decades, from his first visits to England at the close of the 1490s to his return to the Low Countries in the early 1520s, his manual not only codifies the traditions of Ciceronian and notarial letter-writing; it also constitutes a topical critique of the manipulations of the courtly letter and, in turn, of the role of epistolography in the makings of human friendship and desire.[44] Historically, it exemplifies the ways in which, in John Najemy's words, "the easy confidence with which some mid fifteenth-century humanists had defined the letter form and established rules for its use had dissolved in considerable uncertainty and even confusion."[45] For me, it marks a key text in the history of the public and the private life, and I pause here to explore one telling passage in its constructs of epistolary friendship.

Towards the beginning of an early version of his treatise, Erasmus characterizes the nature of the intimacy that defines the personal epistle. In language that draws on the classical and medieval traditions of epistolary composition and the arts of *dictamen*, Erasmus recalls the familiar notion that a letter is a verbal presentation of the absent friend: a way of making almost physically present, in the markings of the hand, the voice and character of the writer. But he goes on, presenting a distinction unique both to his own formulation and, I think, uniquely descriptive of the early sixteenth-century political and social worlds in which he wrote.

For this ought to be the character of the letter: as if you were whispering in a corner with a dear friend, not shouting in the theater, or otherwise somewhat unrestrainedly. For we commit many things to letters, which it would be shameful to express openly in public.

Is enim debet esse epistolae caracter, tanq[uam] cum amiculo in angulo susurres, non in theatro clames, aut paulo etia[m] liberior. Multa enim epistolae committimus, quae coram pudet expromere.[46]

The "character" of the epistle is, of course, not just its nature as a form of discourse but the very characters in which it is composed – the markings of the hand that, as early modern readers would well know, distinctively represented the inner qualities and moral valence of the writer, in other words, the writer's "character."[47] This doubleness of meaning, this playful ambiguity between the inner and the outer, the private and the public, distinguishes the rest of Erasmus's formulation. For, by contrasting the writing of a letter with a theatrical act, he makes clear that epistolary communication is inherently anti-theatrical. Yet, as Lisa Jardine notes, there remains something "inherently theatrical" about letter writing: a performance for an audience of one, acted out not on the stages of the theater but in the corner of the chamber.[48] What can be offered in the corners cannot be exposed in public. Shame (*pudor*) here may well be said to depend precisely on the writer's calibrations of that line between the open and the closed. To commit something to the letter is, with all its etymological resonances, to perpetrate, to commit not just writing but, perhaps, a crime, a transgression, a secret (as its connotations pepper the reflections on legal and epistolary practice by Cicero, Ovid, and Quintilian).[49] So, too, the verb *expromere* recalls the depositions of the courtroom and the confessions of the confidant: the disclosures of hidden feelings, or the face-to-face announcements of a crime or an embarrassment. This is, in short, a presentation of the act of letter writing as – at least potentially – inherently transgressive: something that goes on in the closed world of the whisper, something that may well be "committed" as a crime.[50]

It is probably no accident that these lines were excised from the final, approved version of the *De conscribendis epistolis* that Erasmus permitted to be published in 1522. They survive only in a pirated edition, the one printed by Johannes Siberch in 1521, but they may well date from the earliest drafts of the treatise that Erasmus was composing in the final years of the fifteenth century.[51] Indeed, what they respond to is not so much the traditions of the medieval *dictamen* and Ciceronian forensics most modern scholars have discerned as the motives for his composing of the treatise, but, instead, to the social practices of letter-writing in the English and the European courts and, in turn, to the nascent culture of surreption and surveillance that defined the actions of the courtier and diplomat. In particular, they distill almost into aphorism those powerful tensions in the early Henrician court between the King's apparent need to theatricalize the royal body and the courtier's need to privatize diplomatic experience. The constant jousting, costuming, spectacularizing, and tournamentizing of Henry's early court has long been understood as central to the young King's penchant for self-dramatization. It has been linked to his self-definition as a monarch and, in turn, to the distinctive swerve away from the political habits of his withdrawn and distant father, Henry VII.[52] But Henry's court also moved through the surreptions of ambassadors and favorites – a habit of state secrecy that has been understood primarily as going on during the decades of Wolsean power (the 1520s) and Cromwellian control (the 1530s), but which I believe were operating from the start of Henry's rule. The act of letter writing becomes one of the central means of political self-definition; it enacts the tensions between the theater of the King and the chambers of his power.[53] It puts into play the Erasmian articulation of epistolary theater and its possible – and possibly dangerous – transgressions.

The literary legacy of Chaucer's Pandarus dovetailed with these traditions of dictaminal instruction to present a model for early Tudor epistolarity. Taken together, they offered not only the precepts for the writer but the templates for the reader of such letters. They figured as actors in the theater of both presentation and concealment, writers whose intimacy often barely crossed the line between violence and transgression. And, furthermore, they helped construct a larger social paradigm for what I call an intercessory epistolics. The condition of both the literary Pandarus and the courtly intimate is that of go-between, *interpres*, interceptor. It is a pattern of behavior that must mediate between, in Erasmus's words, *committere* and *expromere*. In these terms, the court becomes both an object of display and the subject of the voyeur's gaze. Indeed, the spectacle of the King's theatricalized body may have provoked a new sense of the private in the court: an under- standing that shouts must be discussed in whispers. Not just letter writing but letter reading takes on a newly clandestine quality – one that makes the act of reading something of a voyeuristic act, a peeping into corners where the eye should not be led.

Voyeurs and readers

This notion of a voyeuristic courtly life, and in turn, of the reader as a voyeur, may at first glance link my interests with those of a range of recent critics who have appropriated psychoanalytic theory and film criticism to historicize the habits of spectatorship and the pleasures of the act of looking. A. C. Spearing, Geraldine Heng, and Sarah Stanbury have located the voyeuristic and the scopophilic in a set of Freudian and post-Freudian texts and have applied their paradigms to the drama of vision in *Troilus and Criseyde*, in medieval romance narratives, and in the sacred and erotic lyrics of the Middle English traditions.[54] Their work has made clear the profound importance of the thematics of looking in late medieval literary culture and of how the self-representations of heroic or narrative personae often take shape in that liminal space between the secret and the open. For the most part, however, these critics have focused largely on the *writer* as a voyeur, rather than on readers or on the historical environments in which late medieval texts were trans- mitted and received. The poetry of Chaucer, Hawes, Skelton, and late Middle English romancers tend, in this critical alignment, to be read as documents of medieval writing rather than as testimonies to early modern reading. But the fact remains that these works, for all their participation in medieval literary traditions, have a precisely identifiable Tudor audience. Their fascinations with the surreptitious – especially the work of Hawes and Skelton and the romance known as *The Squyr of Lowe Degre* – possess an early Tudor topicality, a reference in the workings of the Henrician court, that grants them a historicity far more compelling than their place in a post-Chaucerian tradition. Voyeurism in these texts is not just a literary theme but a cultural condition, and the voyeuristic narrative remains the primary account in early Tudor writing of the making of the self: an account of a seeing "I" that defines subjectivity as fundamentally transgressive and that has implications for the history of private, silent reading.

Perhaps the *locus classicus* for current theory is Freud's discussion in the *Three Essays on the Theory of Sexuality* on the "perversions" that hinder or delay final sexual gratification. "Visual impressions," he wrote, "remain the most frequent pathway along which libidinal excitation is aroused." While Freud acknowledged the natural desire to behold, he considers such observance a "perversion,"

(a) if it is restricted exclusively to the genitals, or (b) if it is connected with the overriding of disgust (as in the case of voyeurs or people who look at excretory functions), or (c) if, instead of being preparatory to the normal sexual aim, it supplants it ... The force which opposes scopophilia, but which may be overridden by it (in a manner parallel to what we have previously seen in the case of disgust) is shame.[55]

The genealogy of voyeurism in contemporary theory largely derives from this passage. With its tripartite arrangement of aberrant scopophilia – genitalia, excrement, and the supplanting of the sexual function with the visual – Freud's taxonomy offers, in effect, a breakdown of the body into parts: a body eroticized, scatologized, even clinicized. Such a dismembered body is the locus, too, of shame and disgust, terms Freud uses to refer to the social governors of aberrant behavior, but which in Jean-Paul Sartre's reading, for example, become the sites of pleasure itself. In a famous passage from *Being and Nothingness*, Sartre tells his story of a childhood spent as peeping-tom: "Here I am bent over the keyhole; suddenly I hear a footstep. I shudder as a wave of shame sweeps over me. Somebody has seen me. I straighten up. My eyes run over the deserted corridor. It was a false alarm. I breath a sigh of relief."[56] Sartre's miniature narrative of voyeurism has rightly become central to contemporary theorizing. With its emphasis on shame as pleasure, Sartre's tale tells of a modern, existential Fall, a story of modesty lost, of exile from a paradise of childhood guiltlessness. But if this is an account of psychological distress, it is as well a critical interpretation. Sartre's lines do not so much affirm the "general truth" of Freud's definitions, as Spearing would have it, as they reinvent the discourse of the voyeur. With its short anaphoric sentences, its simple grammar centering on the first person, Sartre's passage mimes the genesis of subjectivity in the act of looking. What is at stake here is not what is being seen but who is seeing. In these sentences, there are no others, none save the unnamed "somebody" and the "it" of the false alarm.

Both the intensity and the grammaticality of Sartre's sentences are appropriated in Roland Barthes's commentary on the lover's gaze. Reflecting on Lacan's conception of "imaginary subjectivity," the following passage may also be appreciated as a critical ventriloquism of Sartre's childhood voice:

on the one hand, I see the other, with intensity; I see only the other, I scan the other, I want to penetrate the secret of this body I desire; and on the other hand, I see the other seeing me: I am intimidated, dazzled, passively constituted by the other's all-powerful gaze; and this panic is so great that I cannot (or will not) recognize that the other knows I see him (which would dis-alienate me): I see myself *blind* in front of the other.[57]

Brilliantly imitating the rhetoric of Sartre's story, Barthes nonetheless shifts subtly the relations between viewer and viewed. For at the close of the sequence of sentences, Barthes shifts into the passive voice as the recording "I" is passively constructed by the other. Instead of Sartre's affirmation, "I breath a sigh of relief," Barthes's narrator loses his sense of the subject: "I am intimidated . . ."

The centrality of voyeurism in this tradition of French thought, and indeed throughout much current theorizing, is not so much a concern with aberrations of the individual as it is a norm of cultural self-representation. The voyeur, as one contemporary anthropologist recognizes, "becomes a metaphor for the knowing eye who sees through the fabricated structures of truth that a society presents to itself."[58] The voyeur stands as the ethnographer or critic of the culture, and part of the broader turn in recent social anthropology has been to locate the impulse to cultural self-knowing in the spectatorial. The practice and the discourses of cultural study are imbued with images of voyeurism and spectatorship, whether it be the gaze of the fieldworker or the insight of the archivist.[59] For Natalie Davis – whose *Fiction in the Archives* remains one of the key examples of this anthropologized turn in historical research – the modern scholar is the ultimate voyeur, reading historical accounts of gruesome violence with the same degree of vicarious pleasure as contemporary newspaper stories of murder. The opening of archives, in Davis's highly self-conscious narrative, is itself a peeping at the keyhole. And such intrusions, too, are not just secret pleasures but articulations of a broadly intrusive academic institutionality. Much like the emissaries of the King, the modern archivist pulls away the curtains, opens study doors, and breaks the seals of other people's mail. In a brilliant twist on the self-centeredness of voyeuristic discourse, Davis describes her project not as a first-person inquiry but as a second-person invitation.

You will not read any quantitative estimates of, say, the kinds of weapons people used in sixteenth-century homicide, but you will hear how people described putting weapons into play. You will not read analyses of political crimes per se, but you will be asked to consider the importance of the king as a frame for all pardon tales and their role in enhancing his sovereignty.[60]

The reader of her book is made complicit in the author's inquiry – not into dry details or annalistic quanta, but into people's motives, fears, beliefs, and lives.

These are some of the current cultural preoccupations that inform a historical evaluation of the voyeuristic, and much recent work on early modern English literary culture has attended to its politics of ocular desire in examining the making of authorial identity and the production of satiric criticism. For Alistair Fox, the central narrative of Henrician life is one of personal distress coded through the fictive imagination of surveillance. Writers of poetry, tract, chronicle, and even personal letters, he argues, resorted to theatricalized dialogues to shield themselves from accusations of sedition. The inspections of courtier or historian, for Fox, represent that anxious pull between the public and the private – between the licitly observed and the illicitly performed – that distinguishes early Tudor literature.[61] So, too, for Greg Walker, the theatrical impulses of the first years of Henry VIII's reign expose the tensions between "decorum and deference." What Walker calls the "overcrowded and generally indecorous institution" of the Tudor court made every act potentially a performance.[62] Even at his most private and withdrawn, the King was surrounded by courtiers and servants, and Walker makes it clear that there could be, at times, a certain difficulty in distinguishing among those royal appearances in "public" chambers or in "private" ones. The King, in short, was always on display, whether it be as a player in masks and tournaments (described in great detail by Gordon Kipling as the legacies of a late medieval Anglo-Burgundian cultural alliance[63]), or as a ruler in the chambers of state. What Walker calls "a monarch in search of solitude" is always a monarch observed by others.[64]

Much, therefore, has been made of observation and display in Henry's court; and much, too, has been made of the new visual importance of the book and manuscript in early Tudor England. David Carlson, for example, has described the ways in which illumination, letter formation, layout, and binding all convey the cultural meaning of the printed or hand-written text.[65] In these early decades of printing, what addressed the reader's eye were new forms of the frontispiece, the preface, and the dedication: bibliographical phenomena that Wendy Wall has seen as markers of the "voyeuristic text." "Writers and publishers," she argues, "ushered printed texts into the public eye by naming that entrance as a titillating and transgressive act." The new front matter of the sixteenth-century book often "constructed a language of intrusion that designated reading as a prurient activity," and the publication – in all senses of that term – of literature that crossed and challenged boundaries of class and station also "participated broadly in constructing a concept of privacy."[66]

Such a "concept of privacy" may have its *locus* not just in the visual appearance of the printed text, but in the social practices that generated a new way of reading. Among scholars currently recovering a history of late medieval and early modern reading, Paul Saenger has been the most vocal in his view of the impact of silent reading on the cultural and social mores of northern Europe. Saenger sees the later fifteenth century as that moment when reading silently moved from a personal accomplishment to something of a social practice.[67] Together with the renewed interest in the value of private study, habits of reading silently fostered what Saenger considers as a shift in northern European ideas of the book, and these shifts also may have had an impact on late medieval theorizing on the act of reading itself. "References to the eyes and vision become more frequent in the rubrics of fifteenth-century prayers," Saenger notes, and there is a growing sense of visualization, rather than auralization, as the way of engaging with texts.[68] The sumptuousness of late medieval books, a feature Saenger finds characteristic of this new culture of the eye, may well have been matched, though, with a new sense of privacy that attended their reading. "Private reading," Saenger argues, "stimulated a revival of the antique genre of erotic art," and in fifteenth-century France, "the practice of private reading encouraged the production of salacious writing, tolerated precisely because it could be disseminated in secret."[69] The erotics of the Boccaccian tradition – through the reading, translating, and imitating of the *Decameron* – takes on, in Saenger's understanding, a distinctively transgressive force, while at the same time, "the intimacy of silent reading permitted explicit graphic representations of human sexuality to permeate religious literature."[70]

Saenger's interpretations are, certainly, not without controversy, and while I follow most of his thesis in my claims for the development of voyeuristic reading in the early modern period, his narrative needs to be qualified by situating the development of reading in the larger contexts of the cultural awareness of display. Take, for example, his account of Guillaume Fillastre's *Toison D'Or*, written in about 1470 and therefore one of the originary documents in Saenger's history of late fifteenth-century reading. Fillastre's work, the manual of Burgundian courtly ideals and the model for the English King Edward IV's ordinals of power, centered both royal display and private study in the field of vision, and his polemics on the cultivation of the sign, on the power of the written word, and on the need for literate celebrants of aristocratic honor informed the fuller development of Anglo-Burgundian humanism under Henry VII.[71] Saenger considers the following passage of Fillastre's central to his argument about the growing emphases on visualization in the period.

knowledge is not acquired by hearing alone, but also is acquired and increases by study, by reading and by subtly thinking and meditating on what one has read and studied . . . [T]he study of books is necessary in order to retain what one has learned by inquiry and hearing . . . For the sense of sight is much firmer than hearing and makes man much more certain, because the spoken word is transitory, but the written letter remains and impresses itself more on the understanding of the reader.[72]

While this text may well have some bearing, as Saenger claims, on the rise of silent prayer and the importance granted to "visual private study" in late fifteenth-century devotion,[73] it also bears directly on a new concern on the part of courtiers with cultural display and with what I would call a bodily literacy: that is, a concern with presenting the clothed courtly body as a literary text, one shaped to be interpreted and coded in the discourses of power and control. Fillastre's is the realm of Burgundian courtly humanists, the purview of the *grands rhétoriquers* who, as Paul Zumthor has shown, lived out the meaningfully sartorial condition of the public poet. What Zumthor calls the "costume of language" worn by the courtier plays on that double sense of *textus* – text and textile. The body is both dressed and readable, garbed in robes awarded for political or literary service, and yet at the same time weaving, again in Zumthor's evocative phrasing, "the fabric of a protocol . . . from ancient, exhausted feudal traditions."[74]

I would suggest that that Saenger's claims, whatever their historical validity or their heuristic value, need some cultural qualification. His is what might be thought of as a teleology of reading. He defines a progress from the public and the oral through the private and the silent, leading to a late medieval predilection for the transgressive and voyeuristic. Privacy could provide the *locus* of the meditative as well as the arena for the prurient, and while this may well be true, it needs to be refocused through the lens of contemporary cultural theatrics. The law, liturgy, and drama of the late fifteenth and early sixteenth centuries all play off these tensions between the inward and the outward, and in what follows I offer some ways of contextualizing this history of reading in the history of the body. The story of reading is not, as Saenger claims, the story of an independent social practice with a logic of its own. It is, rather, part of a larger story about representation itself.

Books and bodies

The figurations of the body and the book are central to the shaping of an early Tudor literary identity. The poetry of Stephen Hawes, for example, often narrates the confrontations of its allegorical heroes as forms of

reading.[75] The heroic lover/traveler encounters engraved objects, signs
and symbols, and pictorial displays, that instruct or guide him. Images
are "grauen" in Hawes's poetry, and the lessons of the texts and
preceptors are, variously, "impressed" or "enprynted" in the mind of the
hero. So too, in his religious verse, Hawes emphasizes the engraved,
marked, or imprinted quality of spiritual experience. The *Conuercyon of
Swerers* is described as a "lettre" offered to the reader to "prynte it in
your mynde" (lines 61–62), and in the version of this poem printed by
Wynkyn de Worde in 1509 portions of the poem are shaped as a picture
designed to arrest the reader's eye.[76] "See / Me" one shaped section
begins (lines 113–14), as it invites the reader both to meditate on Christ's
signifying wounds and to marvel at the printer's craft. At the poem's end,
Christ invites the audience to associate the body and the text, the
incisions of his wounds with the impressions of both type and seal.[77]

> With my blody woundes I dyde your chartre seale
> Why do you tere it / why do ye breke it so
> Syth it to you is the eternall heale
> And the releace of euerlastynge wo
> Beholde this lettre with the prynte also
> Of myn owne seale by perfyte portrayture
> Prynte it in mynde and ye shall helthe recure.   (lines 346–52)

This textualization of Christ's relationship to Christian, and of author
to audience, also informs the growing emphases on visualization in late
medieval legal practice. The marked and mutilated body constitutes a
document to be interpreted or a text to be read, as the signs and symbols
convey a specificity of legal meaning. The abscission of hands, ears,
breasts, and other body parts, for example, defines the surviving criminal
with all the directness and specificity of a badge. In some cases,
transgressors were even branded with a letter for their crimes: unwilling workers were branded with an F (perhaps for "felon") in mid-
fourteenth-century Yorkshire, while perjurers had the letter P burned in
to their forehead.[78] The criminal, on these occasions, becomes something
of a readable text: a walking marker not just of the crime committed but
of certain definite relationships of power between individual and community.[79]

Such relationships have long been considered to have focused not just
on maintaining corporate or state power, but on figuring the exemplary
or deterrent force of legal retribution. To terrify the criminal and frighten
a potentially transgressive populace had largely been the purpose of the
bodily mutilations of the wrongdoer; so, too, had been the purpose of the
stocks and pillory, and their later descendant the ducking stool. The

punishment for scolds in Hereford defines the function of this particular engine of humiliation as bringing the offender within the purview of the populace. "[T]he scold must stand with bare feet and let her hair down 'during such time as she may be seen by all passers-by upon the road'."[80] Indeed, the need to see the victim – to make justice a thing beheld as well as simply done – informs much of the local records and chronicle histories of late medieval England and survives well into the juridical debates of the eighteenth century. From Bishop Alnwick's need to parade his Lollard heretics bare-headed and barefoot in the market place[81] to George Osborne's recognition, three centuries later, of the exemplary possibilities of spectacular execution, the masters of judicial pain recognized that "what was seen was less the suffering of the individual than the theater of justice."[82] "The more public the punishment," wrote Osborne in 1733, "the greater influence it has commonly had," and to a large degree this tradition of theatricalized punishments and execution was what the later eighteenth-century reformers sought to bring out of the public's eye and locate privately and securely in prison walls.[83]

For late fifteenth- and early sixteenth-century England, however, such debates were far from the concerns of those who drew up and enacted the displays of mutilation in the English towns. The traditions of borough law were notable even to contemporaries for their specificities of pain. William Harrison's *History of England*, while praising the English for refusing the elaborate theatrics of the tortures of the Continent, nonetheless records in great detail the elaborate construction of a guillotine-like device for beheading witches in Halifax. With a curious blend of embarrassment and fascination, he describes the making of this "engine," its precise dimensions, its detailed workings, and its immense power, such that when the blade is released it "dooth fall downe with such a violence, that if the necke of the transgressor were so big as that of a bull, it should be cut in sunder at a stroke, and roll from the bodie by an huge distance."[84] Though writing in the later sixteenth century, Harrison gives voice both to specific surviving practices and to certain attitudes and images behind the English public sense of punishment. What he illustrates in discursive form is what the customals and borough records illustrate prescriptively or annalistically: that there is a theatrical mechanics to enacted law – that as important as the crime condemned or the judgment executed are the stagings, tools, machinery, and visible spectacle of the action. Law, much like late medieval courtiership, is something that goes on before the field of vision.[85]

So, too, does religious devotion. The powerful theatricality of pre-Reformation spiritual life has long been a problem for historians of the

English Church. The gore of the Passion, the pathos of hagiography, the bathos of that late medieval cult of childhood – all have been viewed as testimony either to the decadence of English Catholicism or to a rich aesthetics of belief.[86] In the performance of the Mass itself, the emphases on visualizing the Host, on the spectacular nature of sacramental observance, and on the "gruesome images of the Eucharistic miracle stories," all contribute to what Eamon Duffy, in a brilliantly revisionary account of this period in English religious history, identifies as the motivating visual imagination of lay piety.[87] "Seeing the Host," Duffy writes, "became the high point of lay experience of the Mass" (*Stripping of the Altars*, p.96), and to a great extent the devotional verse and public sermons of the later fifteenth century address the deep emotional response that every Christian celebrant would feel before the vision of the elevated bread and the artistically rendered or personally imagined wounds and blood of Christ. And yet, as Duffy makes clear, such a spectacularism of the Mass did not necessarily foster the passive, nonparticipatory form of worship that some scholars have attributed to it. The uses of the veil and screen in parish churches to shield the altar and the Host were, by and large, things temporary in their function. As Duffy summarizes, "The veil was there precisely to function as a temporary ritual deprivation of the sight of the sacring. Its symbolic effectiveness derived from the fact that it obscured for a time something which was normally accessible; in the process it heightened the value of the spectacle it temporarily concealed" (p.111). Such devices, redolent of the mechanics of stage-prop, costume, and scenery, form what Duffy calls "a frame for the liturgical drama" of the Mass (p.112), a drama in the course of which the congregation could be both spectators and participants.

"Spectators or Participants?" Duffy asks (p.109). This is for me the central question in discerning the relationship between the practices of social life and the representations of literary narrative. It is a question vivified in many late medieval plays, especially those centering on the mutilation and torturing of Christ's body. As in the allegorical adventures of Hawes, the public acts of execution, or the showings of the Host, "behold and see" becomes the central trope of a self-consciousness of vision in the drama.[88] The characters within the plays, together with the audience before it, both bear witness to the sufferings and mutilations of the body. At times, the plays inscribe the idea of an audience within them, as for example, in the Wakefield *Buffeting* where Caiphas stage-manages Christ's torturing. At other times, the plays dramatize the idea of literary authorship itself, as Pilate offers himself up, in the Wakefield *Scourging*, as the *mali actoris* – not just the author of evil in some

generalized, Satanic way, but the authorial agent behind the theatricalized torturings of Christ.[89]

This is, as well, a central question in locating the relationships of
power and performance in the early Tudor court. The spectacularity of
Henrician display – a feature of state politics defined as much by
Shakespeare's *Henry VIII* as by Sydney Anglo and his academic heirs –
often depends on blurring this uneasy line between spectatorship and
participation.[90] More than just a creature of pageant and staged entry,
Henry brought his courtiers (and, indeed, sometimes his family) into the
theater of his rule. On occasion, he would burst into enclosed rooms,
interrupt state banquets, or intrude upon court entertainments; performers become audience, and audience performers. As Skiles Howard has
felicitously put it, in a recent reassessment of these features of Henrician
masquerade, "Henry enacts not a 'spectacle of rule' but a spectacle of
role," an image of a king always and already imbedded in the theatrics of
state power and domestic life.[91] At such moments, Henrician theatrics
inverts the paradigmatic movement of the courtly mask. As Stephen
Orgel has defined it, for a later age, "What the spectator watched he
ultimately became."[92] For Henry's court and family, what the performer
played he ultimately came only to watch.

But if the King claimed a new place in public, he carved out a new
space in private. All things "privy" were Henry's focus of attention, not
least the Privy Chamber where he sought to redefine royal power and
personal identity. As David Starkey has delineated in great detail, one of
Henry's major administrative achievements was the centralization of
court administration in a collection of younger gentry in bodily service to
the King.[93] Grooms of the Chamber, Grooms of the Stool, Esquires of
the Body – these were the titles granted men who ministered to Henry's
private functions, and as Starkey argues, it is this new sense of intimacy
that recalibrates the English body politic into a politics of the King's
body. It is this priviness of Henry's privy chamber – and, in turn, the
nascent culture of enchamberment that would, as Patricia Fumerton has
shown, develop into the Elizabethan complex of compartmentalizing the
self – that domesticates the courtly body by progressively enclosing it in
smaller and smaller spaces.[94] The pattern of kingly reception, for
example, led the appellant into rooms sequentially smaller and more
intimate: from large receiving halls until, if so granted, the inner chamber
of the King's bedroom. Henry VIII followed up on his father's administrative plan of separating the Privy Chamber from the King's bedroom,
and, in the process, he created an even more secure and private space for
ministrations bodily and governmental.[95]

Priviness, of course, is central to the plot of Chaucer's *Troilus and*

Criseyde, and readers of the poem have long noticed how its drama of surprise and surreption hinges on the architectural specifics of the late medieval house.[96] The poem operates inside a world of rooms, of chambers, closets, and beds (in the Middle Ages, as in the Renaissance, boxed-in spaces rather than the open sleeping pallets of the modern age).[97] Its scenes of love and voyeurism, letter-writing and public reading, all transpire in spaces specially constructed for their operation. Indeed, the very principle of poetic construction Chaucer himself posits for his poem, in the famous quote from Geoffrey of Vinsauf that closes Book I, equates poetry and plotting with the making of a house. Both Chaucer and his Pandarus appeal to Geoffrey's plea to have the plumb line straight, the corners true, before embarking on their fictions (I.1065–71).[98] Pandarus, as John Fyler notes, is something of a "fabricator": a constructor of a house of the imagination, a maker of closets, rooms, and bedchambers in which he may observe the workings of his plot.[99] In short, the Pandaric room is a kind of little book, a "romaunce" in the famous double-edged term of Book III, in which Pandarus (as well as Chaucer's narrator and his reader) espy private bodies in enclosing walls.[100]

> And with that word he drow hym to the *feere*,   "fire"
> And took a light, and fond his contenaunce,
> As for to looke upon an old romaunce.   (III.978–80)

For early Tudor readers of the poem, Chaucer's literary architecture would have dovetailed with this newly fashioned social habit of enhousing. Indeed, it would have resonated with a broader understanding of the secrecy of love itself, articulated throughout many of the romances and amorous verse disputations printed during these decades.[101] It is an understanding central, as well, to the popularity of the legend of Pyramus and Thisbe – a story of lovers separated by a wall, whose midnight trysts explicitly frame themselves in terms of leaving houses of familial confinement for a new structure that both physically separates, yet brings them at the very least, linguistically together. In Chaucer's version of the story in his *Legend of Good Women* – a section of the poem that circulated separately in the early Tudor period – Pyramus and Thisbe's love moves through the built environment: from house, to wall, to Ninus's tomb, the lovers mark the landscape of their desire according to familiar structures of enclosure.[102]

Such an account marks *La conusaunce damours*, an anonymous long poem of love counsel printed by Richard Pynson in the late 1520s. Though noteworthy for its four-stanza summary of *Troilus and Criseyde*, much of the poem's bulk is taken up by a Chaucerian-flavored retelling of the myth of Pyramus and Thisbe.[103] As the poem aphorizes their condition:

> The strayter they were kept / and inclosed
> The more feruently / in loue they burned.   (Aiv r)

The lovers' response to this condition is private signifying, "signs / tokyn and lokynge" that communicate their wills. These are lovers who, after midnight meetings at the wall, "wolde . . . stele priuely to bed," lovers so possessed by desire "That they ne coude / rest in any place." Their proposed meeting at the tomb, the misinterpretation of the death of Thisbe, the eventual suicide of both, follows fairly closely Chaucer's narrative in the *Legend*. But unlike its Chaucerian pretext – pressed into the service of a string of narratives about women betrayed and the terrifying inhumation of the lover – *La conusaunce damours* considers Pyramus and Thisbe an exemplum for the sacrament of marriage and the need for parents to accede to children's love. The lovers would still be alive, the counseling Damosell of this poem notes, if the parents "had done / as reason doth require / To marry them / after theyr desyre." The point the poem makes is that marriage without such permission is outside the bonds of sacramental wedding; it is "Damnable / and eke ayenst the lawe." As the Damosell notes, "Here were two hertes / closed in one truly."

This commentary on the legend offers a new interpretation of illicit love in the environment of early Tudor domesticity. The changes in the ideals of a family structure, the shifts in parent–child relations, and the growing sense of marriage not just as a sacrament but as one sanctioned by parental control, make a legend about love into a warning about marriage.[104] That two hearts are "closed in one" necessitates, the poem argues, two people housed in one: the argument for marriage hinges on the argument for domestic control. Enclosure and confinement are the key terms of *La conusaunce damours*, and the issue raised here is one of whether such enclosure is willing or unwilling: in other words, what the relationships are between the structures of the house and the wanderings of the heart. Such relationships color, as well, the poem's briefer account of *Troilus and Criseyde*, where the key detail is Troilus's enhoused enamourment of Criseyde "As he walked within / the temple wyde." It is an interest, too, that may have shaped the poem's selection of other stories, for example, the account of Theseus' triumph over "the mase / made by Dedalus."

These features of *La conusaunce damours* are by no means original with this text, and by my emphasis I do not mean to rescue it from the critical oblivion to which it has, perhaps, been rightly assigned. This is a highly conventional poem, really little more than strung-together tropes, clichés, and tag-lines from the heritage of Chaucer, Lydgate, and Hawes. But in its selections and emphases drawn from those clichés, it does represent an early Tudor fascination with enclosure and enchamberment. And, in its constellating of the story of Pyramus and Thisbe with the tale of Troilus and Criseyde, it may well have had an influence on later, and much more canonical, poetic treatments of both amorous and literary identity. Its narrative and imagery can be discerned in Surrey's poem, titled in Tottel's *Miscellany*, "Complaint of a dying louer refused vpon his ladies iniust mistaking of his writyng" (Rollins, *Tottel's Miscellany*, pp.16–18). Coming upon a suicidally lamenting lover, this poem's narrator hears a lament and witnesses the death of one whose love has spurned him. Seeking a place to bury this man, the narrator finally decides to entomb him "Where Chreseids loue, king Priams sone, ye worthy Troilus lay" (p.18.12). The poem ends with bloody death and burial: relocates, in other words, the narrative dramatics of the tale of Pyramus and Thisbe on to *Troilus and Criseyde*. So, too, Surrey's eulogy to Wyatt closes with a synthesis of Troilan and Pyramic loss:

> Honour the place, that such a iewell bred,
> And kisse the ground, whereas thy corse doth rest,
> With vapord eyes; from whence such streames auayl,
> As Pyramus dyd on Thisbes brest bewail.[105]

These poems draw on the legacy of *La conusaunce damours* not simply to reiterate the forms of Middle English writing in Renaissance contexts, but to relocate the lyrical, writing self in an inheritance of secrecy and surreption – in the chambered worlds of missed trysts and misunderstood epistles. Surrey's allusions to Troilus and Criseyde and to the story of Pyramus and Thisbe reveal the close association of both narratives in early sixteenth-century culture, and they constitute something of a subtext for the poet's confrontations with the literary politics of late Henrician England.[106]

La conusaunce damours and Surrey's poems do not offer the only ways of reading Chaucer's lovers through Pyramus and Thisbe. Francesco de Rojas's closet drama, *La Celestina*, pointedly introduces its young lovers as contemporary figurations of the mythological pair, and it, too, needs to be understood as both a provocation to and product of the early Tudor Chaucerian reception of literary voyeurism. First printed in Spain in 1499, and reissued in a revised version a year later, *La Celestina* came to England with the courtiers of Katherine of Aragon in 1501, and it soon established itself as one of the most compelling of documents in Anglo-Spanish literary relations. With its dramatic preoccupations with bawdry and surreptition, its rich fantastic lectures on the magic of female anatomy, and its thematic attentions to the power of language and the commerce of deceit, *La Celestina* would have addressed pointedly the cultural fascinations of the early Henrician court. It went through many editions in the first third of the sixteenth century, and was known in the More circle, most likely through the influence of Juan Luis Vives (who knew and commented upon the play).[107] Its Spanish idiom may well have influenced the language of such diplomatic documents as Luiz Carroz's 1510 letter to Ferdinand of Spain concerning the gravid status of his daughter and the pandering machinations of what he calls Henry VIII's *privado*, the groom William Compton.[108] And, in its English abridged adaptation, *Calisto and Melebea*, published by John Rastell sometime in the second half of the 1520s, it entered into a vernacular discourse on bawdry and courtiership already formed by Chaucer's *Troilus and Criseyde* and Skelton's *Phyllype Sparowe* and *Magnyfycence*.[109] Indeed, Chaucer and Skelton so inform the verbal texture of Rastell's play that we might see it not so much as an appropriation of the Spanish work as a domestication: an attempt to rephrase its key moments and its claims in a familiar literary language. *Calisto and Melebea* signals the deep impress of the Pandaric in early Tudor literary culture: an impress that molds an imported work to the contours of vernacular social satire and moral pedagogy.

Though it was probably not written for performance, *La Celestina* also confronts in both comic and disturbing ways the theatrical qualities of courtly service, commercial exchange, and feminine display. And, while it addresses some of the most sordid aspects of what Roberto Gonzáles Echevarría calls "sex, corruption, violence, and general human depravation," it does so in sophisticated ways that call attention to the role of linguistic signification in the makings of social identity.[110] The work's eponymous heroine – the old bawd who uses sorcery and surgery to restore women's hymens and, in turn, pass them off as virgins to unsuspecting customers – is a creature who trades in the female body; one who deploys a skill with words to make her money, one whose status as go-between or mediatrix illustrates the fact that what is truly bawdy about this work – and in turn, what is truly erotic in all literary narrative – is not so much action but talk. Gonzáles Echevarría summarizes her "genius" in ways, too, that may well speak for Pandarus himself, and in a manner that suggests to me some of the broader early Tudor contexts in which her play and his poem may have well been understood in tandem. "Celestina's genius lies not only in her acute sensitivity to the desires of her fellow human beings, but in her recognition of the fact that human desire – physical, sexual, metaphysical – is in large part a hunger for words, a hunger which seeks not only to express itself, but also to satisfy itself verbally."[111] In short, Celestina is a great talker, and in her appearance in Rastell's *Calisto and Melebea* her garrulousness helps shape the governing dramatics of the interlude. Scenes that in Rojas's original transpire in the many voices of disparate characters are, in Rastell's abridgment, told as stories by Celestina. Her opening self-presentation offers what she calls "a prety game" (line 319), an exemplum of her "craft of bawdery" (line 329). Her tale is of Crito and Elicea: drinking together in her house, they are almost caught unawares by Sempronio, the lover of Elicea. Celestina hides Crito in her "chamber among the brome" (line 331), Celestina and Elicea pretend to be spinning, and Sempronio enters to find his beloved accusing him of negligence and betrayal (lines 342–45). Crito is heard rumbling in the broom closet, Sempronio inquires about the noise, and Celestina intervenes to avoid the confrontation, patch things up between the lovers and leave the cuckolded Crito laughing (lines 353–73).

This opening narration, for all of its fidelity to the gist of the Spanish original, lies, in its English literary context, as a wild burlesque of Pandarus's hidings and manipulations of Troilus and Criseyde. Indeed, for Celestina herself in this passage, the language of the Pandaric is essential to her self-definition. Much like Chaucer's go-between, she sees her task of bawdry as a game, and when she interrupts her story to announce its denouement, she cries, "But now hark well, for here begynnyth the game" (line 352). Such a remark recalls directly Pandarus's triumphant announcement of control over his friend. Watching Troilus redden with desire and embarrassment in Book I, he exults: " 'A ha!' quod Pandare: 'Here bygynneth game.' " (I.868). Rastell's text is shot through with such allusions to Chaucer's poem. Melebea's concern with "the entent of thy conclusyon" when addressing Celestina's plan for her to sleep with Calisto (line 780) recalls directly *Troilus and Criseyde*'s preoccupations with intentions gone awry and, in particular, Pandarus's account of Criseyde's actions: "Yet for al that, in hire entencioun / Hire tale is al for som conclusioun" (II.258–59). Calisto, too, sounds at times more like a character from Chaucer than his Spanish original. His apostrophes to his absent beloved at the interlude's beginning,

> Lo, out of all joy I am fallyn in wo,
> Uppon whom advers Fortune hath cast her chauns
> Of cruell hate, whych causyth now away to go
> The keper of my joy and all my pleasauns   (lines 73–76),

and

> A woman! Nay, a god of goddesses   (line 156),

resonate with Troilus and Criseyde's concerns about their "pleasance" and his "joie,"[112] and with Troilus's opening debate within himself about Criseyde: "But wheither goddesse or womman, i-wis" (I.425).

Taken in tandem, these verbal echoes constitute evidence for the association of the Troilan paradigms of love, bawdry, and betrayal with the plot lines and character figures of Rojas's play. They augment not only the ambiance of *La Celestina*'s reception and domestication into early Tudor literary culture, but they point, as well, to some of the dramatic strategies of what one might call Celestinesque theater that would be deployed by Skelton in his interlude of courtly excess and royal pimpery, *Magnyfycence*. The figures of Courtly Abusyon and Counterfet Countenaunce – with their acts of sexual procurement, their fixations on the meretriciousness of both female lovers and male courtiers, and in the case of the latter character, an almost creepy fascination with the possibilities of counterfeiting virginity by resewing the hymen – represent a synthesis of the Pandaric and the Celestine. Read in the context of the diplomatic and the literary discourses of the 1510s, Skelton's play illustrates the powerful theatrics of courtiership and, in the process, it exposes for satiric view the erotic subtexts of political, amorous, and literary service in the first decade of Henry's reign.

Such stories as the tale of Pyramus and Thisbe, and such venues as *La conusaunce damours* or *La Celestina*, would have meant something quite specific to an audience preoccupied with the pitfalls of courtiership, the nature of private correspondence, and the institutionalization of surveillance as a mode of political control. The rise of surreption and informancy as social acts during the 1530s – propelled by what G. R. Elton has called the "willingness of gentry and aristocracy to report what they heard" and by "the readiness of neighbours, friends, enemies and acquaintances to denounce . . . supposed traitors"[113] – shifted the meaning of the literary tropes of seeing, reading, writing, and printing. So, too, would have the many acts of Parliament that, throughout the decade, regulated the book trade, and made "writyng ymprintinge [and] cypheringe" potentially seditious acts. The old language of impression and the image of the seal – in Hawes, a way of defining the affirmations of the lover or the meditation on the wounds of Christ – take on new political resonances at a time when forging the King's signet and the Privy Seal was a treasonable offense.[114] The Parliamentary statutes of the decade, as well as the rhetoric of propaganda and control issuing from Cromwell's aegis, return again and again to the acts of writing, reading, and iconic presentation as the marks of fealty or treason. By the time of the Act of Proclamations of April 1539, for example, the King's anxieties about the possible "democratization" of biblical interpretation and the threats of subversive preaching codified themselves in to the demand that "such as can and will" read the Scriptures may "quietly and reverently read the bible and New Testament quietly and with silence by themselves secretly at all times and places convenient for their own instruction and edification."[115] Similarly, in 1542, the Act Touching Prophesies upon Declaration of Names Arms Badges, &c, prohibited "any persone or persones [to] prynte or wryte" false prophecies against the King, especially those based on readings of "badges or signetes, or by reasone of lettres."[116]

If the evidence for heresy and treason lay in these visible representations of the letter, the practicalities of discerning the agents of such representations were often impeded by the concealment of the traitor or his work. "Concealment," Elton notes, "was the bane of the government's police work" (*Policy and Police*, p.346), and throughout the Cromwellian period a central question arose as to the nature and motivations of those who would hide the traitor. Elton discusses this matter in terms of motivation: "The concealing of a treason was not always the fault of the first accuser" (p.348), and he notes how the delays of epistolary exchange and the processing of letters of admission or accusal may have led to false imprisonment and charges soon to be dropped. Muriel St. Claire Byrne notes the "anxieties and distress" felt by members of the Lisle family throughout the 1530s concerning the preservation and destruction of potentially seditious letters. As she states, "the destruction of private letters could become yet another count in an indictment for treason. To burn letters on receipt . . . might be dangerous. To have no letters to produce could be as fatal as to have indiscreet letters. Their absence could be interpreted as evidence that one had something to conceal."[117] Indeed, the Lisle letters are replete with injunctions to save or burn, to strike out or read carefully, to hide or to come forth. Concealment – as an act, a rhetoric, a process – had become not just, in Elton's terms, a bane of political work but a controlling theme for literary writing and reading.[118] It will be, as I argue later in this book, the motivations of the personal anthologist and the fears of the courtly advisor. It will, in fact, become the dark side of the Pandaric, as secrecy becomes no longer the privilege of courtier or poet. "You must," as Francis Bryan advised to a friend in 1534, "keep all things secreter than you have used."[119]

Preview

This review of these Henrician political and social issues reveals not just a mode of power politics or doctrinal enforcement but a cultural condition. The tensions between observation and withdrawal – and, in turn, the emphasis on the iconic nature of political representation, with the language of the seal, the impression, and the printed text all pressed into the service of controlling public information and private feeling – dovetail with both the literary figuration and the social practice of epistolary interception. They construct a culture of the go-between – a state Pandarism, as it were – that sustains what I see as the political ocularism of the Henrician court. Cromwell's culture of surveillance is not some newly conceived technique of repression but an outgrowth of the spectatorial and epistolary impulses of the early Tudor age.

The image of the intercepted letter thus controls each account of Henrician writing in this book, and each of its following chapters locates that nexus of display and surreption in a set of secret or illicit documents. Chapter 2 apposes Pandaric theatricality against ambassadorial deceit in a review of Henry's minion politics and the makings of courtly literature in the first years of the King's reign. For Luiz Carroz, Ferdinand's ambassador, the transmission of the diplomatic correspondence is of such importance, and its contents so delicate, that the writer himself is compelled to disavow its contents. The surreptitions of the ambassador and the manipulations of the panderer are the very subject of Carroz's mission, and they may inform, as well, a political environment for the reception and translation of Rojas's *La Celestina*. Carroz's missive, together with Edward Hall's accounts of Henrician play, constitute the base texts for a study of the courtly poetry of Skelton, Hawes, and the *Squyr of Lowe Degre*. Read in tandem, they define the literary politics of Henry's court – a politics of the Pandaric emblemized in the play "Troilus and Pandar" that was performed at Henry's court on Twelfth Night, 1516.

The impulses of the early decades of the court traced in this chapter – the feints of *amicitia*, the ruses of procurement, the performativity and interception of epistles – find their refractions in Henry's illicit correspondence with his new mistress and future Queen, Anne Boleyn. Chapter 3 charts the power of the King's hand as manipulator of the letter and controller of both love and politics in the late 1520s. The barely suppressed violence of his letters to Anne makes the act of kingly writing into a performance of, and on, the body of the lover. So, too, the reconfiguration of the royal secretariat shifted the relations among King and counselors in the scripting and signing of royal correspondence. Henry's letters to Anne are the only sustained correspondence wholly in his own hand, and the impress of that hand becomes, I argue, something of an icon not only of royal power but of royal authorship during the period. These letters, too, were intercepted, and the King's fears of illicit reading, together with what I take to be one contemporary set of poetic allusions to the letters, illustrate the cultural impact of royal epistolography.

Such intercepted letters are the stuff of commonplace books, and chapter 4 argues that the rise of this social habit and this literary genre responds to the voyeurisms of desire and the temptations of surreptition. Commonplace books present themselves as compilations of intercepted texts, and one might say that the controlling fiction of the commonplace book is that it is a book of intercepted letters. Nowhere is this clearer than in the compilation made by Humphrey Wellys. Here, verse epistles of an often powerful eroticism and male scopophilia stand side-by-side with documents of seditious political content. Wellys constructs his own Pandaric persona through his compilation, and his poems by and about women, in particular, bring out the violence that inheres in such literary techniques as the *blazon* and the Chaucerian poetry of Hawes. Wellys's work also provides a foil for studying that more familiar anthology of early Tudor family surreptition, the Devonshire Manuscript, whose closing pages fill themselves with excerpts culled from Thynne's Chaucer edition of 1532. Here, the work of Thomas Howard and Margaret Douglas offers an exchange of verse epistles modeled on that of *Troilus and Criseyde*. But more than showing off the virtuosity of literary imitation, their work illustrates the ways of reading in an age of monitored interpretation: the social and political anxieties of loving, letter writing, and book-making in the decade of Cromwellian control and state surveillance.

Wyatt's verse epistles, the central subject of chapter 5, figure forth the pitfalls of Pandaric courtiership and enact the voyeurisms of illicit readership. They explicitly draw on Chaucerian formulations of deceit and service, while at the same time framing those formulations in uniquely topical environments. The Satire to Francis Bryan – as rich a Pandar to King Henry as there ever lived – constitutes a summa of the poet's readings and reframings of the Chaucerian inheritance. It also stands, together with the Satires to John Poyntz, as a defense not just of courtiership but of courtier poetry, and read together with Wyatt's political defenses (those texts prepared for his treason trial in 1540), they give voice to a concern with linguistic and literary instability that is both theme and textual condition of the verse itself. Wyatt's poetry, too, is the subject of certain styles of voyeuristic reading, and this chapter also reexamines one of the main venues for its transmission, Tottel's *Miscellany*, in order to show how public printers could construct the court as subject of the intruding eye. Tottel's volume offers to its readership the chance of buying into the experience of the courtly compilation. It grants a glimpse into the workings of aristocratic manuscript assembly and, in printed form, provides such readers with a model for their own construction of the personal anthology and their own writing of courtly verse. But Tottel's *Miscellany* also stands as something of an epitaph to an earlier age: a Tudor book of the dead, where epitaphs become epistles, letters eulogies, and allusions to *Troilus and Criseyde* recall the dead and buried lovers and their loss.

A major implication of this study, therefore, is a new appreciation of the verse epistle as the constitutive mode of early modern subject formation. In *Troilus and Criseyde*, as well as in the spate of shorter ballads circulating under Chaucer's name, letters are the vehicle for authorial self-presentation, pleas for patronage, or marks of *amicitia*. For Wyatt, in particular, this inheritance enables him to use the genre as the place to confront the burden of a literary heritage and the boundaries of public writing. But more generally, the verse epistle is the means by which the manuscript compiler and the early English printer defined literariness itself: the place where canonical authorship and courtly discourse take shape. The idea of the English lyric voice, as codified by Tottel, is inescapably epistolary. These are texts read not just by the intended recipients but by intruders. They are poems viewed over the shoulder, personal missives approached by invited and uninvited readers.

If the power of the Pandar lies in the ability to intrude into private correspondence, it lies, too, in the will to dismember the corpora of the letter and the writer. From Chaucer's own Pandarus through the commonplace-book makers of the age of Wyatt, reading is an act of separation and dismantling: letters are taken out of context, poems broken down for use as private centos, narrative personae cobbled out of literary allusions, scraps and shards of manuscripts pasted together to form personal anthologies. The ways of looking at a woman and the ways of looking at the book are similar. For the former, the literary genre is the *blazon*; for the latter, it is the cento. Pandarus or Carroz, Stephen Hawes and Humphrey Wellys, may break the woman down into her separate parts and make those parts into the precious objects of visual delectation. But they may also take the text in such a way. The literary corpus may be broken up and reconstructed for anthologies of private use or public sale. The fate of Chaucer's poetry is to be subject to such selective dismembering – what I would call a literary *blazonerie*. The sixteenth-century encounter with a fourteenth-century text is the moment when the early modern reader may emerge. If this is a book about that reader as a voyeur, it is as well a book about the scholar as an intruder. Reading the past – the confrontation with the texts of distant, dead, and displaced writers – remains the task not just for Chaucer's Pandarus or

Henry's courtiers, but for ourselves. In a surreptitious age, technologies of information become, almost as soon as they are made, the tools of our transgressions. Though this book hopes to shape new understandings of an earlier age, it also hopes to refract something of this current light. Its study of transgressive reading and the arts of surreption – the study of Pandaric lives – exposes those historical habits of behavior and those modern currents of criticism that define our roles in making meaning out of medieval and Renaissance literary history.

2 The King's Pandars: performing courtiership in the 1510s

> But here, with al myn herte, I *the biseche*   "beg of you"
> That nevere in me thow deme swich folie
> As I shal seyn: *me thoughte* by thi speche   "it seemed to me"
> That this which thow me dost for *compaignie*,   "friendship"
> I sholde wene it were a *bauderye*.   "pandering"
> I am nought *wood*, al if I lewed be!   "crazy"
> It is nought so, that woot I wel, parde!
>
> But he that gooth for gold or for ricchesse
> On *swich message*, calle hym *what the list*;
>   "such an errand"   "what you like"
> And this that thow doost, calle it gentilesse,
> Compassioun, and felawship, and *trist*.   "trust"
>
> *(Troilus and Criseyde*, III.393–403)

Twelfth Night, 1516, and the King would have his show. William Cornish, a Gentleman of the Chapel Royal and a familiar figure from the masques and disguisings of Henry VII's court, was master of the revels, and he led the children of the Chapel Royal in a performance of "ye storry of troylous and pandor." According to the Revels Books of Richard Gibson, whose account remains the fullest of this lost play, the characters performed "rychely inparelled," especially "all so kallkas & cryssyd inparylld lyke a wedow of onour in blake sarsenet and other abelementes for seche mater dyomed and ye grekes inparylld lyke men of war." Gibson goes on to describe several of the other stagings and devisings for the Twelfth Night celebrations, and his record ends with a list of items ordered for the plays. As far as we can tell from his accounting, the characters of this Chaucerian disguising were all played by children: "oon of ye chappell chylldryn yt playd eulyxes"; "ii chyllderne tryollus and pandor." Yet, Cornish himself played Calchas, "in a mantell and a bechopes surkoot," and while we may assume that one of the boys of the chapel played Criseyde, he did so in the "aparell" provided "by ye dyscrecyun of ye ladyes of ye koort."[1]

This brief report of Henrician revelry has long been used by historians of the theater to exemplify the various relations among Chapel, court, and outside entertainers in providing for the King's enjoyment.[2] Such revels, too, have been appreciated for their political as well as their recreational function. The 1510s and 1520s were, as Greg Walker has recently reiterated, decades of "heightened political and diplomatic activity," and the plays presented at the time – what he christens "a golden age for court drama" – often refracted the concerns of power politics through allegory and allusion. Cornish and his company of children were occasionally pressed into the service of propagandistic playing, and the political messages behind these plays were clear both to the audiences in attendance and to later chroniclers, such as Edward Hall.[3] Nonetheless, Walker finds no "especially political burden" to "Troilus and Pandar" – nothing to separate it from the run of revelries that were, in Richard Gibson's words, the "pastym" of the "feest of crystmes."

Yet "Troilus and Pandar" has, by its very choice of title, a powerful political association. This is a story not of lovers but of friends. Its heritage lies not with tales of desire and betrayal, but with maxims of male companionship. It stands in a tradition of amicitial dramatics drawn from Chaucer's *Troilus and Criseyde*, a tradition that does more than write out advisory dialogues between the poem's friends (as, for example, in John Shirley's copy of the whetstone stanza, titled "Pandar to Trojlus," or in the later lyric interchanges of the clandestine lover–scribes of the Devonshire Manuscript), but that recognizes a distinctive performativity to the Pandaric. Pandarus is a stager of entries, an intruder into private spaces and closed rooms. There is at times a wild theatricality to Pandarus's speeches and his actions – a theatricality that transforms him from wise counselor to boon companion, and that, in his later literary afterlife, shifts him between the poles of "trusty friend" (as in *La conusaunce damours*) and "Troylus baud" (as in Skelton's *Phyllyp Sparowe*). Pandaric bawdiness and bawdry have a powerfully performative aspect, not just in Chaucer's poem, but in the poetic and dramatic texts that constitute his early Tudor reception. It is a bawdry of surprise *and* surreptition, where the bearing of the lover's letter, in particular, becomes the venue for elaborate intrusions, games, and costumings. Pandarus stages the erotics of the letter, as he takes the privacies of writing out of the lover's closet and plays them before an audience of friends.

Of all Chaucer's Tudor readers, perhaps John Skelton recognized most clearly this distinctive blend of pimpery and play.[4] In *Phyllyp Sparowe*, he has Jane Scrope rehearse the events of *Troilus and Criseyde* from a distinctively Pandaric perspective, one that frames the story of the poem by named references not just to the poem's lovers but to their intercessory agent.

> And of the love so hote
> That made Troylus to dote
> Upon fayre Cressyde,
> And what they wrote and sayd,
> And of theyr wanton wylles,
> Pandaer bare the bylles
> From one to the other,
> His maisters love to further.   (lines 677–84)

Jane Scrope's is an account of gifts exchanged, of letters read and written, songs sung, loves betrayed, and sullied reputations. Criseyde is "disparaged," Troilus is alone, and:

> Pandaer, that went betwene,
> Hath won nothing, I wene,
> But lyght for somer grene;
> Yet for a speciall laud
> He is named Troylus baud;
> Of that name he is sure
> Whyles the world shall dure.   (lines 717–23)

This version of the *Troilus* offers what would become the controlling early Tudor reading of the poem: a reading that plays out all the ambiguities between bawdry and friendship encoded in Troilus's own lines to Pandarus in Book III (393–403), and that recognizes, too, the anxious ambiguities of Pandaric desire itself.[5] Pandarus here is more than simple intercessor. He is the controlling fabricator of the story, a figure with, at times, even an erotic life of his own. Skelton hints as much, in another reference to his wiles, in the *Garlande of Laurell*. Here, Pandarus wants something of the woman too. For all his seeming devotion to Troilus, he is nonetheless drawn to Criseyde: "Goodly Creisseid, fayrer than Polexene, / For to envyve Pandarus appetite" (lines 871–72).[6]

The social memory of this eroticized friend, this Pandarus who trips the line between *amor* and *amicitia*, informs not just the literary patterns of Chaucerian reception but the politics of royal desire in the early years of Henry VIII's reign. From his first months on the throne, Henry was famous for engaging in illicit affairs, stage-managed by Pandaric confidants. Men such as William Compton, Henry Norris, and Anthony Denny were among the King's most trusted Grooms of the Chamber. Their position granted unique intimacy in the early Tudor court and, as David Starkey has amply illustrated, it linked the preserves of political

privacy with the ministrations to the royal body in its most personal –
indeed literally privy – functions.[7] And yet, in spite of all the secrecy
attending their illicit missions, the panderings of these figures were widely
known. In May of 1510, the Spanish ambassador, Luiz Carroz, remarked
on Henry's use of Compton as his *privado* (favorite or confidant) in a
household intrigue centered on the Duke of Buckingham's sisters. Two
decades later, Compton's successor, Henry Norris, was thought to be
"du roy le mieulx aimé," and it was rumored that he had served as
"bawd" between the King and Anne Bolyen before their marriage.[8]

Such men are creatures of the Privy Chamber, and the drama of
Henrician bawdry often depends on breaking down the barriers between
the private and the public, the domestic and the diplomatic. Ruses, lies,
and dramatic irruptions are the currency of early Henrician power. The
disguised King breaks into private bedchambers, interrupts local tournaments incognito, and exits state banquets only to appear again, garbed
with his friends as exotics from other lands. He boldly intrudes into
spaces usually reserved for social intercourse or sexual encounter. As
Chaucer's narrator had put it, blessing Pandarus's first insinuations into
Criseyde's private chambers: "Now Janus, god of entree, thow hym
gyde!" (*Troilus and Criseyde*, II.77). These words may stand as something
of an epigraph to Henry's energetic invasions: "royal entries," as it were,
of a distinctively erotic order, as the King and his minions burst upon the
Queen or secrete themselves into the rooms of women destined for illicit
affairs. The early Henrician court constructs a theatrics of the intrusive, a
condition of domestic invasion and sexual predation that define courtier
service, diplomatic inquiry, and regnal self-display.

The theatrics of minion politics finds its expression in a clutch of
documents from the first years of the King's reign. Luiz Carroz's letter of
1510 to King Ferdinand, detailing both the erotic adventures of the King
and the menstrual cycles of the Queen, provides a master narrative of
political pandarism. It offers a phenomenal account of voyeurism and
spectatorship, a complex blend of Erasmian political counsel and
popular literary burlesque that affords a peep-show into the intrigues of
both the King's libido and the Queen's uterus. Read in conjunction with
the chronicles of Edward Hall, the courtly makings of John Skelton and
Stephen Hawes, the English reception of *La Celestina*, and the popular
romance verse of *The Squyr of Lowe Degre*, Carroz's letter writes the
narrative of intimacy and exposure behind the amatory diplomatics of
the King's first years. These texts present the chamber world of *Troilus
and Criseyde* – the world of enclosed rooms, of unmade beds, of letters
written, intercepted, and mistaken, and of the "espyinge" of Pandarus's
ruses – translated to the household politics of Henry's reign.

This is a chapter, then, about theatricalizations of the intimate. The private ruses of the King or the inspections of his courtiers are made public in elaborate performances and circulated correspondence. The stories of Henry's great vigor in disguisings and his boundless energy for play articulate the two sides of the Pandaric: one, a surveillant privacy, an *amicitia* grounded on male advisory rhetoric and surreptitious bawdry; the other, a public courtly and performing self, rich with the comic show of feigning and the witty, at times self-ironizing, awareness of duplicity in action. For Richard Gibson, "Troilus and Pandar," is not the "litel trageyde" of Chaucer's poem but a "Comedy."[9] Seemingly unconcerned with love and pain, the revel speaks directly to the playfulness of male display and public friendship. And in its audience would have been ranged the King's own Pandars, actors in a theater of intimacy, favorites who make public the world of the *privado*.

Such a theatrics of the intimate also fosters a corresponding theatricalization of the narratives of public and private conduct. For Edward Hall, dramatic recreation of events often takes precedence over mere narrative historiography. Hall vivifies life at the Henrician court, frequently lavishing his attentions on descriptions of costume, scenery, and public spectacle; transcribing, if not inventing, public speeches and private letters; and, in general, providing what Alistair Fox has called "semi-dramatic recreations" of events.[10] For Hawes and Skelton, too, court life is scripted out of the traditions of the drama: for the former, the domestic interludes that structure the *Conforte of Louers*; for the latter, the language of the cycle play moralities that shapes the characterizations of *Magnyfycence*. And for the *Squyr of Lowe Degre*, the drama of intrusion resonates profoundly with one of the most familiar images of medieval religious theater: Joseph's discovery of the pregnant Mary. These are, I argue, the defining moments for an early Tudor literary culture in which courtly and authorial identity takes shape.

This chapter charts the transformations of a Chaucerian moment into paradigms of royal behavior, measuring the literary structures of Pandaric *amicitia* and voyeurism against the performances of Henry and his men, his diplomats, and his poets. Courtly verse, much like courtly life, takes as its self-defining moment the confusion of the secret and the open, and if "Troilus and Pandar" seems a unique theatricalization of Chaucerian narrative, it is not alone. The literary products of its period expose confusions and conflations among poetry and drama, private letters and public performances. The Twelfth Night revels speak directly to the workings of a courtly minionism, where the private acts itself before a spectatorial community, and where even the King's chamber or the Queen's bed could become the stages for the play of service.

The pimp and the ambassador

The career of William Compton is a case study of the politics of intimacy in the Henrician court.[11] Born to a small landholder in Warwickshire in about 1482, Compton became a ward of the crown on the death of his father in 1493. He became a page to the younger Prince Henry and rose rapidly in royal service after the Prince's accession as King. At Henry VII's funeral, he was Groom of the King's Chamber. Soon after, he became Groom of the Stool, Gentleman, and then Chief Gentleman of the King's Chamber. Well known were his responsibilities as spy, go-between, and pimp. Whether investigating the Earl of Northumberland's plans for marrying off his son, bearing important diplomatic correspondences, or permitting the use of his own house for one of Henry's liaisons, Compton functioned as a public bearer of the private. It is as if he had lived out the paradigm of Pandarus: in Skelton's words, bearing "the bylles / From one to the other," furthering "His maisters love," and serving as a "baud" (*Phyllyp Sparowe*, lines 682–84, 721). And yet, unlike Chaucer's unfortunate figure who, "hath won nothing," Compton won it all. He was, in the words of Polydore Virgil, "primus minister in regis cubiculo," and when he left this position in 1526 it was to become usher of receipts in the exchequer.[12] Along the way, Compton managed to amass a fortune in lands and stipends to become, by his death, what G. W. Bernard has characterized as "one of the wealthiest men in early Tudor England."[13]

Compton's main role early in the young King's reign, however, was as public companion and private confidant. They appeared first together in a jousting tournament, held as part of the Christmas celebrations at Richmond, on 12 January 1510.

And the xii. daie of Ianurie, diuerse gentlemen freshely appareled, prepared them self to Iuste, vnknowen to the kynges grace, whereof, he beyng secretly informed, caused hymself and one of his priuie chambre, called Willya[m] Compton to bee secretly armed, in the litle Parke of Richemond: and so came into the Iustes, vnknowen to all persones, and vnloked for: The kyng ranne neuer openly before, and there were broken many staues, and greate praise geuen to the two straungers, but specially to one, whiche was the kyng: howebeit, at a course by misfortune, sir Edward Neuell Esquire, brother to the Lorde of Burganie, did runne against Master Cumpton, and hurte hym sore, and was likely to dye. One persone there was, that knew the kyng, and cried, God saue the king, with that, all the people wer astonied, and then the kyng discouered hymself, to the greate comforte of all the people.[14]

Edward Hall's version of this story highlights pointedly the tensions between revelation and disguise, voyeurism and intrusion, that are central to the formations of early Henrician discourse. His is a narrative not so much of a public tournament but of a private play. This is a story of information secretly obtained, a story of the networks of informancy already in place in the first months of the King's reign. It is a story, too, of surreption answered by disguises. The secret information and the secret arming provide a new context for the priviness of the Privy Chamber. Compton and Henry share in the intrigues of power – here the power to intrude and interrupt. Unknown and unsuspected, Henry literally breaks in on the jousting match. The violence of Henrician intrusion spills over to the near-death of his friend. In Hall's narrative, what follows upon this accident is not, however, friendly grieving but royal unmasking. The King does not reveal himself over the body of his injured friend, but rather discovers himself after the recognition by a courtier. What comforts all the people, in this telling, is the simple fact that it is not the King himself who has been injured.

The theatrics of *amicitia* were not limited to displays of public splendor. Soon after the return to Westminster, such a theatrics burst in on the Queen's chamber, and Hall immediately follows his account of Henry's jousts with this story of the king's intrusion.

And on a tyme beyng there [i.e., Westminster], his grace therles of Essex, Wilshire, and other noble menne, to the nombre, of twelue, came sodainly in a mornyng, into the Quenes Chambre, all appareled in shorte cotes, of Kentishe Kendal, with hodes on their heddes, and hosen of thesame, euery one of them, his bowe and arrowes, and a sworde and a bucklar, like out lawes, or Robyn Hodes men, whereof the Quene, the Ladies, and al other there, were abashed, as well for the straunge sight, as also for their sodain commyng, and after certain daunces, and pastime made, thei departed. (*Chronicle*, p. 513)

In the following days, Hall continues, Henry left an ambassadorial banquet with Essex, Wiltshire, and others, only to return dressed as Turks, Prussians, and Moors. They left again, only to return with fifes and drums and newer, fashionable garments. And, on another occasion, Henry showed off before the Spanish diplomatic corps, riding for a brass ring in a game that displayed the King armed for the first time before these ambassadors. Here, Henry himself caught the ring, and gave the badges and devices sought for to the Spanish diplomats. He commanded each of them, Hall concludes, "to take therof what it pleased them, who in effect toke all or the more parte: for in the beginning they thought that they had bene counterfait, and not of golde" (pp. 513–14).

The point of these disguises is not just to illustrate the King's penchant for play in the first months of his reign; nor is it simply to vivify his status, in J. J. Scarisbrick's formulation, as a "stupor mundi," a player in "a world of lavish allegory, mythology and romance."[15] The point is that

the King disguises himself as figures from literature and politics. Chivalric knights and Robin Hood stand side-by-side, as it were, with
emissaries from exotic polities in Henry's costumery. These performances
exemplify his understanding of the theatrical nature of both love and
politics: his recognition that the court remains a world of masks.

Friendship had always been a ruse. In pursuing the arts of love, Ovid
had counseled that *amicitia* could be a cover for *amor*: a device for
initially securing the attention and trust of the desired. In the *Ars
Amatoria*, Ciceronian friendship forms the role or costume for the lover,
a name as in a play or masquerade: "Let love make his entrance
concealed beneath the name of friendship" ("interet amicitiae nomine
tectus amor," I.720).[16] *Amor* and *amicitia* are garbs, as when Ovid
advises the man "to put a hood over your shining looks" ("palliolum
nitidis inposuisse comis," I.734). These strategies of amicitial deceit have
long been seen as central to medieval traditions of courtly loving, and
their literary heirs lie in a line from Pamphilius, through Andreas
Capellanus, Jean de Meun, and Chaucer.[17] Pandarus works precisely in
this lineage when he advises Troilus to put on the masks of love, and in
particular, when he counsels Criseyde:

> Swych love of frendes *regneth* al this town;   "governs"
> And *wre you in that mantel* evere moo.   "conceal yourself in that cloak"
>   (II.379–80)

But what Pandarus does here, and what is central to Chaucer's appropriations of Ovidian advice, is to conflate the issue of disguise for matters
both amorous and diplomatic. Pandarus translates the dissimulations of
the arts of love into the deceits of courtly politics. He makes advisory
rhetoric apply equally to sex and service and, in the process, he provides
later readers with a paradigm for public action. Friendship, in Pandarus's
terms, remains a style of feigning, and later advisory treatises on courtiership appropriate this advice precisely in these terms. As Erasmus had put
it, voicing what would become one of the great commonplaces of
Renaissance courtiership, in a model letter of advice from *De conscribendis epistolis*:

Arrange your facial expression beforehand at home, so that it may be ready for
every part of the play and so that not even a glimmer of your true feelings may be
revealed in your looks. You must plan your delivery at home, so that your speech
suits your looks and your looks and the bearing of your whole body suit your
feigned speech. These are the rudiments of courtly philosophy, for which no one
will be fitted unless he has first wiped away all sense of shame, and leaving his
natural expression behind at home, has put on a mask, as it were.[18]

Prius igitur domi vultum componito, vt is tibi paratus sit ad omnem fabulae partem, ne quid veri affectus in facie subluceat. Meditanda domis est actio, vt oratio vultui, vt vultus ac totius corporis gestus, orationi fucatae subseruiat. Haec sunt aulicae philosophiae rudimenta, ad quae nullus erit idoneus, nisi prius omnem pudorem absterserit, ac vultu natiuo domi relicto, quasi personam sumpserit.[19]

Erasmus's advice, much like Pandarus's, is to wrap oneself in the mantle of friendship: to put on the mask of *amicitia*, whether it be to secure a beloved or a patron. The rhetoric of friendship is, both in love and politics, the rhetoric of disguise, and this is precisely what Hall understands about the King's mumming. He shows Henry not secreted in privy counsel with his minions, but performing on a public stage. He shows them not in the private spaces of their true selves, but always elaborately costumed as aliens, be they "outlaws" of the forest or emissaries from the ends of the earth. But if Hall's Henrician court is full of masks, he recognizes that only the King may take his off. The pleasure of disguise lies in the stripping off of costume. The power of the King's theatricality lies, in the end, in the theatrical self-reflection that he is the King. What Henry enacts in these performances, as Skiles Howard puts it, is not a "spectacle of rule" but a "spectacle of role."[20]

As in all playings of a role, there may be times when actors lose their place, when they forget not just the script but confuse the artifice of acting with the practices of everyday experience. Such a confusion provoked public anxieties about the King's men. At issue was not just that these minions had attained great wealth and power disproportionate to their social degree or formal office – though certainly this bothered Wolsey and his faction.[21] Rather, what bothered many in the King's Council was how their behavior transgressed the norms of role-playing, especially the norms of heterosexual male behavior. Hall captures the tenor of the debates in May 1519, as Wolsey was planning to displace the King's young men, in the familiar terms of xenophobic sexuality. The men had spent time at the French court, riding with the French King "disguysed through Paris, throwyng Egges, stones and other foolishe trifles at the people." And when they returned to England, they "wer al Frence, in eatyng, drynkyng and apparell, yea, and in France vices and bragges" (*Chronicle*, p. 597).[22] Just what precisely these "Frence vices" were is spelled out in Hall's subsequent account of the Council's deliberations of May 1519: "In whiche moneth the kynges counsaill secretly communed together of the kynges gentlenes & liberalitee to all persones: by the whiche they perceiued that certain young men in his priuie chamber, not regardyng his estate nor degree, were so familier and homely with hym, and plaied suche light touches with hym that they forgat themselfes" (p. 598). This critique of the minions rephrases the relations between intimacy and performance that had shaped Henry's displays of public friendship. Instead of sharing in the costume changes of Henrician power, these men participate in the rude incognitos of the French. Such gallicized disguisings are now foolish trifles rather than the strategies of politics. And when the men return, their theatricalized intimacy crosses boundaries of sexual decorum. The actions of familiarity impinge upon the body of the King (the "light touches" of which the men are accused). That such men may forget themselves implies that what they have forgotten is the role assigned to them: in short, that these are actors in a play of royal power who have crossed the line between performance and reality. They have forgotten their roles, in both the social and the dramatic senses of that term. In turn, Hall's language reenacts the very processes of voyeurism and spectatorship defined by Henry's public *amicitia*. He takes the reader into both the "secret" Council and the Privy Chamber. He reenacts the "perceiving" of council members – a term that, in early sixteenth-century usage, connoted intrusive or penetrating inspection, associated with spying, as in Thomas More's phrasing: "here is it ethe to spye and *perceyue* his iuglyng well inoughe."[23]

Hall's rhetoric, together with the actions of the King and the intrusions of the Council, recall the powerfully intrusive quality of Pandarus's behavior. Pandarism centers not only on the solitary voyeur, but on the hearty intruder, someone who shares in the opening of locked doors and the entries into chambers. In Chaucer's poem, Pandarus's uninvited entries are, from their initiation, ceremonies of intrusion, literary acts subject to the invocation of the "god of entree." But just what "entree" is Pandarus considering, especially so soon after his dream about the swallow Procne?

> and evere lay
> Pandare abedde, half in a slomberynge,
> Til she so neigh hym made hire cheterynge,
> How Tereus gan forth hire suster take,
> That with the noyse of hire he gan awake.   (II.66–70)

This barely suppressed vision of the violence against Procne's sister, Philomela, by her husband Tereus – and behind it the whole legend of Philomela's rape and mutilation and the consequent dismembering of Tereus's own son – constitutes the pretext for Pandarus's first entry. There is a profoundly disturbing quality to these mythic pretexts and, in turn, to Pandarus's brusque intrusions into private spaces: be it here, in his interruption of Criseyde and her friends reading in their parlor (II.80–112), or later in Book II when he comes "lepyng in atones" to

Troilus's bedchamber (II.939), or most dramatically, when he delivers to Criseyde the first of Troilus's letters.[24] Faced with Criseyde's demurral to accept it, Pandarus says to her, "Refuse it naught," and the narrator goes on: "[he] hente hire faste, / And in hire bosom the lettre down he thraste" (II.1154–55). It is this glib intrusiveness that marks the Pandar both for Chaucer's poem and King Henry's court. Disguise and theater inhere in the nature of male friendship, and the tropes of heterosexual identity often devolve to scenes of interruption and intrusion. Pandarus breaks into the bedchamber and, if not into Criseyde's body, then at least her bodice. In turn, it is essential, in Hall's telling, for Henry and his men to intrude, invade, break in, and interrupt occasions of domestic decorum or state control in order to affirm the male-ness of the King. The King and his friends burst in to Katherine's bedchamber; they leave the ambassadorial banquet only to return disruptively in disguise. It is essential, too, for Henry to affirm both his prowess and his friendship with Compton by coming incognito at the joust, interrupting the ceremony – even to the point of Compton nearly being killed – and only then revealing who the players really are.

This paradigm of interruption and intrusion stands at the opposite end of voyeurism as a strategy of male behavior. Indeed, one might consider it the anti-type of voyeurism: not the unnoticed insinuation of the viewer but the unannounced invasion of the actor into privy scenes. If voyeurism makes the public private, interruption makes the private public. It takes personal relations or diplomatic negotiations – both activities of the chamber – and sets them on the stage. The theater of intrusion, therefore, is a theater of "entree," a drama that affirms not just royal prerogative but potency. It is a strategy of affirmation necessary to the maintenance of that great public narrative of Tudor rule: that Henry sire children and the Queen bear them.

That Henry's potency was subject to the public's gaze is a well-known facet of royal self-presentation. The King's codpiece was a familiar item of what Louis Montrose dubs his "personal iconography," and in a subtle reading of the Holbein mural for the Privy Chamber, Montrose calls attention to the thrust of Henry's phallic self: "the size, strength, and carriage of his body."[25] Holbein's painting, Montrose goes on, "manifests the inseparability of sexual and political potency, virility and kingship."[26] Though this portrait dates from late in Henry's reign, commemorating as it does the birth of Prince Edward, it nonetheless may stand as a visual gloss on these earlier Henrician irruptions, a mirror in which we may see the King's self-image. But, if it is a mirror, what it reflects back is now the image of the younger King's exploits. For here, we see no image of the boon companion but the picture of the royal father; no vision of intrusions into marital or extramarital chambers, but a tableau of secure and securing paternity. Holbein's portrait seals off the early history of Henry's exploits and shuts off for future questioning the status of the King's member. What it celebrates is the long-awaited successful siring of a male heir – the very issue (in all senses of the word) that was central to the King's marriage to Katherine of Aragon years earlier and that, soon afterwards, became the talk of court and country.

Luiz Carroz's letter to King Ferdinand of Spain, written on 29 May 1510, brings together these concerns with voyeurism and theatrics, potency and politics, in ways that reflect both on the theoretics of courtly behavior and the practices of courtly literature.[27] Carroz's letter, while ostensibly concerned with the account of Henry's infidelities, is also a testimony to his father-in-law about his potency. Written only weeks after the Queen's first miscarriage (and only two days after Katherine herself had written to her father about it), it bears witness to the King's libido and the Queen's receptiveness. Carroz's story of the intrigue with Compton plays off against the rumors circulating about the homosociality of the King's minions, while at the same time brushing them aside to stress the King's male needs. It reenacts that masterplot of Renaissance preferment: "male pleasures all depend upon the exchange of women."[28] And it does so, not only in its story of Henry and Compton, but in its medical account of Katherine. For what Carroz has done is offer up himself as something of a Pandar to the Spanish King. He makes himself the agent in the exchange of a woman, here Ferdinand's daughter – a creature who had, for the previous decade, been one of the key items in the uneasy truces forged between the Spanish and the Tudor monarchs. Married to Henry's deceased brother Arthur in 1501, she was, for a brief time, even considered by Henry VII as a possible mate after his widowing in 1503.[29] Prince Henry got her almost by default. Now, in the gynecologized account of the ambassador, she stands as one more item in the preferment of royal power.

The force of Carroz's missive, again, is preferment – in this case, his own preferment as official representative over that of the "real" ambassador, Diego Fernandez, whom Carroz calls the Friar, and who was Katherine's confessor retained from the time she was betrothed to Arthur.[30] Carroz's letter begins with a lament over the dissimulations necessary to control and cajole the Friar – this holdover from an earlier court and this shadow informer for Ferdinand. It then moves through the stories of the court and the descriptions of the Queen. Carroz ostensibly concerns himself with proffering information. What he delivers in the end is a woman's body. He is, then, as much a procurer as Compton: as much concerned with securing the preferment of his King by trading in the body of a woman. The story of Henry's infidelities, in this light, throws added shadow on Carroz's own devices. Carroz plays pander for his own King. What is so bizarre is that he offers not someone's sister but the King's daughter herself.

Carroz's version of events centers on the intrigues of the chamber, on the passings back and forth of sexual ambassadors in what could only be described as a parodic version of the diplomatic embassy. His account reads like a burlesque of Chaucer's own bedroom scenes in the *Troilus*, or, for that matter, of the brothel comedy of *La Celestina*. And yet, the story of the King's intrigues is but one part of Carroz's whole communiqué. For this is, in effect, a miniature essay in the arts of courtly deceit: a letter that begins by complaining about the diplomatic failures of the Friar and that ends by revealing, in great gynecological detail, the status of Queen Katherine's pregnancy. Carroz's Spanish draws on the vocabulary of courtly dissimulation: *discreto* (discreet), *encobrir* (to conceal), *receloso* (suspicious) (Bergenroth, ed., *Supplement*, p. 37). It offers maxims on the courtier's job: "to praise him as much as is necessary, but not overmuch, that he may not suspect that there is any deceit in it" (*ibid.*). To the evils of the Friar, Carroz notes, "we are forced to dissimulate with him" (p. 38). And yet, such dissimulations are as much a part of the ambassador's own charge as they are a response to intra-courtly tensions. Every day, he states, "occur numberless things which it is well for me to know" (pp. 38–39) – and one of those things is the affair managed by Compton. The King, he writes, "has shown great displeasure at what I am going to tell" (p. 39); but this, of course, does not stop Carroz from telling.

This Conton [i.e., Compton] carried on the love intrigue, as it is said, for the King, and that is the more credible version, as the King has shown great displeasure at what I am going to tell. The favourite of the Queen has been very anxious in this matter of her sister, and has joined herself with the Duke, her brother, with her husband and her sister's husband, in order to consult on what should be done in this case. The consequence of the counsel of all the four of them was that, whilst the Duke was in the private apartment of his sister, who was suspected [of intriguing] with the King, Conton came there to talk (*fablar*) with her, saw the Duke, who intercepted him, quarreled with him, and the end of it was that he was severely reproached in many and very hard words. (p. 39)

Favorites, servants, and relations – both by blood and marriage – mix and meld in this account. With its long sentences, its strings of subordinate and relative clauses, and its concatenation of relational terms (for example, the chiastic string of nouns joined by the copula, "su hermano y a su marido y al marido de la hermana"), Carroz's narrative effectively mimes the serpentine maneuvers of the favorites in the chambers of the palace. This is a world of talk. Carroz's word for what Compton does here is *fablar*, not just to talk but to tell a story, to confect a narrative. Compton is Carroz's *alter ego*, a go-between among the rival factions of the court, much as the Spanish ambassador is the interlocutor among deceiving diplomatic rivals.

For Henry, too, this is a world of mutual intrigue and surreption, a world in which the King himself fears that the Queen has favorites "insidiously spying out every unwatched moment, in order to tell [her stories]" (p. 40). And Carroz, as he makes clear, moves for his own King with a similar insidious attention to detail. His language links his own procurement of information with the procurings of Compton in the sexual arena: "And this knowledge I have procured, and I write it" ("y esto he yo procurado saber y lo escribo," p. 41). In the end, what is procured is knowledge of a pregnancy and details of a physical specificity so intimate, that the nineteenth-century editor of the *Spanish Calendar* was reduced to translating Carroz's language not into the English of the volume, but into the Latin of the medical manual.[31]

In brief, the central problem for Carroz is to determine whether Katherine is pregnant. The Queen had been delivered of a stillborn daughter on 31 January 1510.[32] Her miscarriage was kept a great secret, not just from the court but from King Ferdinand, to whom Katherine did not communicate until 25 May, in a letter written by Fernandez. The Friar, eager both to mollify the Spanish King and to affirm his own ambassadorial status, writes: "The last day of January in the morning her Highness brought forth a daughter . . . [T]he affair was so secret that no-one knew it until now except the King my lord, two Spanish women, a physician and I."[33] The secret of the miscarriage was kept, however, because the physician believed that Katherine "remained pregnant with another child and it was believed and kept secret." Two days later, on 27 May, Katherine herself wrote to her father about the dead child. Thus, when Carroz writes to his king on 29 May, he is in effect playing catch-up with the court. His charge is thus to offer information proffered neither by the Queen nor by Fernandez – that she, in fact, is pregnant again.

His story of the Queen's pregnancy, like the tale of Henry's infidelities, is filled with innuendo and suspicion. First, Carroz notes that "eight days ago" (i.e., 20 May), the Friar came as emissary to the Queen to tell the King's ambassador that Katherine had not been pregnant for more than nine weeks. Katherine makes clear that she does not want Carroz to include this information in his letter, for she wishes to wait until her pregnancy is well established and can please her husband with it. But then, Carroz notes, the Queen intends to write it herself. "I do not know what will be done," the ambassador writes, "but before this letter is closed I shall know and make mention of it" (p. 42). And yet, Carroz notes that he "knew it already before the friar had spoken to me" (*ibid.*). Clearly, Carroz has informants of his own, and what they tell him is that Katherine menstruates so irregularly, that it is difficult to discern when she is pregnant and when she is not. Again, he notes to Ferdinand, "Before this letter is closed I shall know and write it" (p. 43). What is this knowledge? First, that Katherine's irregular menstrual cycles may be caused by her irregularity in eating and the indigestion caused by food at court. This seems, to Carroz, like good common sense: a common sense in contrast to the "thousand extravagant follies" provided by the Friar about the Queen's pregnancies. And in the end, having prepared the King for information by the letter's close, he tells Ferdinand that the Queen is truly pregnant; that he does so in spite of the King's confusion over what to say and of the Queen's final decision to write. He closes: "It must not be known here that I have written ought of these affairs, because I have said that I do not write of them" (p. 44).

This closing passage of Carroz's letter dazzlingly recasts the inspections of the first part. The Queen's apparent inability to bring a child to term contrasts sharply with the King's sexual appetite. Her life within the chamber contrasts, too, with the King's ruses among rooms and houses. Katherine, in this letter, is a creature of her room: a woman who does not go out, and who is, by the letter's close, "confined" in the anticipation of her pregnancy. Carroz, too, functions as a kind of surreptitious Compton here. He, too, insinuates himself into the chamber of the lady – indeed, he enters, at least informationally, the inner chambers of her body. Like Compton, he is a fabulator: the verb "fablar" describes his conversations with Henry much as it had described Compton's ("he fablado con el Rey," "I have spoken with the King," p. 44). What we are left with is a weird intrusiveness into the chamber of the Queen: a secretive account of letters deferred and, then, of information withheld and then finally released. Carroz's letter offers more than just the maxims of the courtier's dissimulation. It presents a concise essay on voyeurism: an account of male inspections of the female form, a fascination with the workings of the woman's private parts, a clinical inspection of the fluids that determine health and pregnancy.

But what it also does is to narrate and theatricalize those observations. There is a suspense to the letter, a waiting for withheld or as-yet-undiscovered information, and the miniature chamber play of this epistle may owe much to the gynecological theatrics of *La Celestina*.[34] Certainly, Carroz's Spanish is replete with the key idioms of Rojas's text. The verb *procurar*, so central to the ambassador's mission, appears again and again in *La Celestina* to define that nexus of commerce, sex, and personal diplomacy that is the motivating center of the play (Celestina likens herself to "el buen procurador," *Calisto y Melebea*, p. 282). So, too, the emphasis on *fablar* as the verb of telling situates both Compton's and Carroz's actions in that world of talk that defines the sexual magic of Celestina herself: a world in which, as several recent critics have averred, language comes even to replace sex.[35] Compare, for example, Carroz's remark that the Friar has told him "a thousand extravagant follies" with Celestina's claim that the girl Elicia will tell her lover Sempronio (in the evocative English of the seventeeth-century translator Joseph Mabbe), "A thousand flimflame tales" (Mabbe, *Celestine*, p. 131, translating the phrase, "Dira mill locuras," *Calisto y Melebea*, p. 236). *La Celestina* works in the same backdoor world as Carroz's court: doors are thrust open or surreptitiously listened through; staircases are the venues for illicit eavesdropping. When Carroz notes that the Queen has favorites "such as go about the palace insidiously spying out every unwatched moment in order to tell the Queen stories" (*Supplement*, p. 40), he may as well be rehearsing the plot lines of the Spanish play. Eyes and ears are central here (indeed, what Carroz actually writes in the last clause of this remark is "para presentarlo a los oydos de la Reyna," in order to present the information to the ears of the Queen). So, too, in *La Celestina*, Melebea's servant, Lucrecia, will observe things surreptitiously, and Sempronio will announce – in a phrase whose now clichéd quality has denatured it of its early modern sexual and courtly power – "the walls have ears" (Mabbe, *Celestine*, p. 133, translating the phrase, "las paredes han oydos," *Calisto y Melebea*, p. 238). In a tragicomedy about spying and eavesdropping, about procuring women, selling them, repairing them, and constantly interrogating their physical and sexual status, everyone has a sordid part to play.[36] And perhaps, too, this is what Carroz has in mind when he rehearses the dialogue between himself and Diego Fernandez. He said, he told, I said, I spoke – each sentence here recreates secretive diplomacy as theater. "Porque en esto entiendo saber mi parte": I think, in this matter, I know my part. Carroz now speaks as an actor in the drama of courtiership and inspection, a figure in a play of gynecological politics as rich as *La Celestina*, a *persona* in Erasmus's script for the *vita aulica*.

The discomfort of Stephen Hawes

At the same time Carroz was writing to his King, Stephen Hawes was attempting to return to courtly service. A former groom of Henry VII's chamber, and an aspiring courtier poet during the first years of Henry

VIII's reign, Hawes sought the resources of print technology to offer up a vision of love poetry as anxious and acute as anything in Carroz's official correspondence. From the *Pastime of Pleasure* (composed during the last years of the reign of Henry VII and printed by Wynkyn de Worde in 1509) to the *Conforte of Louers* (written, so the title page says, in the second year of Henry VIII's reign and published, also by de Worde, probably in 1515), Hawes's texts write out narratives of secret correspondence and illicit love.[37] They figure forth anxieties about the visualization of the body and the proper codes of physical desire, while at the same time dramatizing the choices offered between personal friendship and public service. Hawes's work takes as its theme the confrontation of the public courtly body with the private reading self, and in the *Conforte of Louers* the pitfalls of courtier performance inscribe themselves on the body of a book and on the book of the body. The *Conforte* is a poem about the dangers of illicit desire and the consequences of poetic rivalries and the whims of patronage.[38] Read as a landmark in the tired topography of Chaucerian impersonation – as it almost is – it reeks more of Lydgate than of life, and, indeed, its characteristically self-deprecating prologue sets its literary and political agendas more securely in the nostalgias for Hawes's predecessor poets and the golden age of Henry V than in the courtly realities of his competitors and Henry VIII. But, read in the environment of its precisely contemporary texts, the *Conforte* presents a complex, troubling assessment of the courtly body and its poetic representation. With its sly barbs against Hawes's more successful courtier poet, John Skelton, it stands as a document of that competitive self-fashioning that, as David Carlson has recently observed, defined the early Tudor coteries of Skelton and Alexander Barclay, Bernard André and Thomas More.[39] Hawes's work provides the lens in which the reader could discern, not just the inheritance of Middle English verse but the intrigues of Henrician literary politics. Hawes's poetry narrates the very condition of such kingly Pandars as Luiz Carroz and William Compton: tensions between birth and opportunity, concerns about the rise of a professional courtier class, and insecurities about the blurred line that often fails to separate the erotic from the political.

From its first lines, the *Conforte* writes itself upon the literary body. After reviewing the accomplishments of Gower, Chaucer, and Lydgate, and after lamenting that Hawes himself has not attained either their own level of literary fame or the level of current political sanction of a "hystoryagraffe nor poete laureate" (line 20, a clear reference to Henry VII's patronage of Bernard André and John Skelton),[40] the prologue closes with the vision of the dead and buried *auctores* of the vernacular past.

> But syth they are deed / & theyr bodyes layde in chest
> I pray to god to gyue theyr soules good rest.   (lines 27–28)

Here, in an obvious allusion to the Clerk's eulogy of Petrarch in the *Canterbury Tales*, Hawes locates the authorial body in its grave.

> He is now deed and nayled in his cheste;
> I prey to God so yeve his soule reste!   (*Canterbury Tales*, E, lines 29–30)

The force of this allusion makes the act of literary imitation – whether for Chaucer's Clerk or Hawes himself – a confrontation with the inhumed corporeal form of the *auctor*. Indeed, to be an *auctor* here is to be buried – to be laid or nailed into a "cheste," to be irrevocably removed from the converse of the maker. Hawes's Chaucerian quotation here frames his own book within the body: offers up a paradigm of authorial identity keyed to the various locations of the author's corpus.

If such corporealizations link Hawes to the literary past, they also place him squarely in the political present. Even before these opening lines, the title page of the *Conforte* locates its author in the workings of the courtly body. This is a poem "made and compyled by Steuen Hawes sometyme grome of the honourable chamber of our late souerayne lorde kynge henry ye seuenth." Hawes had elsewhere been identified as a groom of Henry VII's chamber – for example, in the colophons to the editions of the *Conuersyon of Swerers* and *A Joyfull Meditation* – and this information constitutes a plea for preferment in the new King Henry's court.[41] But it also presents Hawes as a figure in the early history of the Privy Chamber, that locus of royal trust that, under Henry VIII, would transform personal attendance into personal diplomacy. Hawes, in effect, becomes a kind of proto-minion, someone who in his advertisements in his printed texts would seek to carry with him what David Starkey has called "the indefinable charisma of monarchy."[42]

Hawes's status as a *former* groom reduces whatever monarchical charisma he may have earlier possessed, and such a public status dovetails with one of the *Conforte*'s major private themes: the poet in exile. The true subject of this poem is not the success of courtiership but its failure. It is a story of books unread, of lost opportunities, transgressive actions, and crushing rivalries. As Alistair Fox has recently argued, the *Conforte*'s seemingly deliberate confusion of erotic and political levels of signification is central to Hawes's critique of the courtly poetic career. Fox presses his reading of the poem into a larger claim about Hawes's unrequitable love for Henry VIII's sister, Mary Tudor, and about the political consequences of his early poetry devoted to her. He argues that Mary is the Pucelle of the *Pastime of Pleasure*, and he claims that

Hawes's whole poetic career encodes an infatuation with a princess far above his station. For Fox, Hawes's status as a former groom signals a public dismissal, and the *Conforte*, in his aggressively biographical reading, becomes a new plea for preferment and an act of public contrition.[43]

We need not purchase all of Fox's topical allegory to recognize with some assurance that Hawes is preoccupied with one of the central issues of courtier service – social mobility – and that he does present himself as someone painfully excluded from the workings of the courtly patronage system. But I would argue further that the controlling issue of this poem is not just the status of the courtly poet but the place of illicit desire in what Jonathan Goldberg has recently seen as the role of sexuality in "the formations of courtly literariness."[44] Goldberg defines the story of preferment as the story of exchanging women. Courtly advancement depends on the courtiers' ability not just to serve or love, but to dissimulate in both roles. "How are courtly makers made?" he asks (*Sodometries*, p. 54), and one answer he offers – and one raised by Hawes in the *Conforte* – is that they are made upon the body. Hawes offers up a courtly body on display: a body readable and knowable, but also subject to the pains, dismemberments, and mutilations of thwarted desire and ambition.

With its repeated emphases on visionary apprehension, and its deployment of familiar Hawesean devices of engraved *blazons*, meaningful mirrors, and significant inscriptions, the *Conforte* tells its story somewhere between the dark allegories of "dyuers bokes" made "Full pryuely" and the everyday activities that "all persones . . . openly espyeth" (lines 93–94, 105). These bodily anxieties frame pointedly the pandarisms of both amicitial advice and amorous desire in the *Conforte*. The goodly lady who appears in the narrator's vision sounds curiously like Pandarus himself, offering maxims that recall the latter's advice to the lethargic Troilus. Her string of saws, for example, at lines 148–61, recalls explicitly Pandarus's advice to the bedridden Troilus in Book I of Chaucer's poem.[45] With its rhetorical appositions and its overarching philosophical commitment to the mutability of earthly wills, these lines from the *Conforte* expose that tense blend of Boethian advice and courtly pragmatism that distinguishes Pandarus's discourse. Such a discourse, too, governs Hawes's critique of courtiership, as he takes the Pandaric condition of the beguiler beguiled and the figurations of the blind man to apply to politics, as well as love. When the poem's narrator approaches one of the many inscribed texts presented to him on his journey, he finds written there a set of maxims that may be appreciated as a critique of the courtly life itself.

> it is openly sene
> That many a one / full pryuely dooth wene
> To blynde an other / by crafte and subtylnes
> That ofte blyndeth hym / for all his doublenes.   (lines 361–64)

All the key terms of the *Conforte*'s anxieties are here, and all have a Chaucerian pretext. The contrast between open appearances and private knowledge, the union of craft and subtlety in construction of a "doublenes" of courtier behavior, and the imagery of moral blindness – all derive from the amicitial paradigms of *Troilus and Criseyde*.

And yet, throughout the *Conforte*, these tidbits of Pandaric advice are framed in confessions of great bodily distress. True, Troilus had been ill with love, and Pandarus had come to cure him. But the poem's characters had also been preoccupied with greater pains. Both Troilus and Criseyde, as well as Pandarus, have dreams of arresting physical violence: dreams of dismemberment and mutilation that stand in for castratory and rapine fears.[46] Criseyde's dream of the eagle tearing out her heart (II.925–31), Troilus's nightmare of the boar with its threatening "tuskes grete" (V.1233–46), and Pandarus's own uneasy and allusive early-morning fantasy of Procne and Tereus (II.64–70) all signal a profound set of anxieties about the body of the lover and the friend. In the *Conforte*, Hawes displaces these threats to bodily integrity onto the narrator himself. His own brutal dismemberment resonates with these Chaucerian moments, as they make the narrator into an uneasy blend of Troilan lover and Orphic poet:

> Aboue .xx. woulues / dyde me touse and rent
> Not longe agone / *delynge* moost shamefully   "treating [me]"
> That by theyr tuggynge / my lyfe was nere spent.   (lines 163–65)

This is a literary body that, as Hawes puts it a few lines later, "had but lytell rest" (line 173), where "subtylte" and "cruelte" (lines 169, 171) are joined as the conceptual and rhyming pairs of courtly anxiety. The lover–poet here is constantly subjected to bodily constraints: his right hand is bound (line 135), in what is perhaps an allusion to Hawes's own censure at the court, and later on that hand will grab the magic sword: "I felte the hande / of the stele so fyne / Me thought it quaked / the fyngers gan to stretche" (lines 582–83). In the central portion of the poem, Hawes paraphrases Psalm 129, a canticle rich with the imagery of violence to the body. The poet's courtly enemies now take on the appearance of the enemies of Zion, as Hawes notes how they have "expugned me," "shytte me in a cage," and "Vpon my backe synners hath fabrysed [i.e., built]" (lines 562, 565, 568). Though this was not one of the Psalms later transmuted into Thomas Wyatt's painful paraphrases, it does stand at the nexus of bodily pain and courtly dominance that was a central feature of Henry VIII's control almost from the day of his ascension. What Stephen Greenblatt finds so characteristic of Wyatt's Psalmistry – its obsessions with steadfastness in the face of bodily vulnerability, its transformation of the politics of torture into the poetics of desire, its underlying equation that "power over sexuality produces inwardness"[47] – all distinguish the world of Hawes's *Conforte*. A generation before Wyatt, he exposes the machinery of inspection and discovery that defines the rhetoric of Henrician power. His appositions between openness and privacy resonate with Carroz's maximal readings of ambassadorial intrigue, while at the same time looking forward to the tone of Edward Hall's account of minion politics and the "perceivings" of the Council.

If Hawes's poem frames the anxiousness of the courtier's body in a world of courtly wills, it also shares in the early Henrician anxieties about the female form. If the male body is exposed to pain, the woman's body is the object of a powerful desire. Early Tudor poetry is, *par excellence*, the poetry of the *blazon*, that rhetorical device that catalogues the woman's body parts and, in the process, makes her not so much a sum of those parts but, rather, a collection of free floating members – corporeal signifiers that are the object of the courtly poet's gaze. Hawes is a master of this *blazonerie*. Though owing much to Chaucer's earlier descriptions of the female form (say, in the presentations of the dead Lady White in the *Book of the Duchess* or in Troilus's fantasy encounters with Criseyde), Hawes's go beyond those of his master in length and detail. Hawesean *blazons*, here as well as in the *Pastime of Pleasure*, are, in fact, more akin to the tours de force of contemporary French *rhétoriquers*, and the *Conforte* offers, in his dazzling account of Pucelle's body, a description that could rival anything of Clément Marot.[48] From her forhead "Vnder her orelettes [i.e., head-dress]," down through "the vaynes blewe / in her fayre necke well tolde," to her arms, her waist, and her "longe trayne" upon the floor, Pucelle is a creature of fetishized parts (lines 722–48). This is woman as the synechdochic self, a woman broken up into her parts, yet also textualized through her clothes. As in his figurations of the male body, Hawes offers up a woman as a *textus*: a body dressed and readable, covered in text and textiles, "knytte," as he puts it, all together (line 748).

Hawes's anatomizing of the woman's body, much like Carroz's gynecologized description of the Queen, articulates a central principle of early Renaissance literature: a fetishizing of the body parts into objects of erotic attraction. Such a device, both cultural and poetic, has been famously defined for the Petrarchan lyric by Nancy Vickers, and

Lawrence Kritzman has developed this critical interpretation to describe that blend of writing and desire for the later *rhétoriquers*.[49] Though writing on sixteenth-century French literature, Kritzman's remarks attend precisely to the features of Hawesean description, and I quote him here not just to characterize the poetry but to anticipate some larger points I will make later in this study about the place of the woman's body in the culture of Henrician violence.

In the *blason anatomique* the female body becomes consubstantial with the body of writing; the representation of the woman depicts that of the poet's imaginary projection of the reality of his desire onto an object that is narcissistically subjectivized ... What is ostensibly symbolized here is a phenomenology of desire that entails a dismemberment of the female body, one that conjures up detached body parts or fetishized objects, whose wholeness is entirely phantasmatic.[50]

What is "entirely phantasmatic" in the *Conforte* is not just the wholeness of the woman's body but the wholeness of a body politic and the unity of courtly life. The poem takes the pandarisms of the Chaucerian legacy and textures them through violence and desire. It presents courtly writing not as normative and faithful, but as transgressive and seditious, while presenting – in however adumbrated form – a species of male desire that crosses boundaries of class and literary decorum. The *Conforte* presents, in other words, the dark alternative to the brightly lit theatrics of Henrician performance.

   To this point, I have argued for a pattern of bodily representation in the *Conforte*: a pattern of figurations that define the courtly self as something of a body on display, caught between openness and priviness. This tension is subtly coded, too, in a complex set of wordplays on the titles of Hawes's own works, and these wordplays associate inextricably the body of the author with the body of his work. In the process, they make him into something of a living version of the authorial bodies buried in their chests. One of the key themes of the *Conforte* is the reading and reception, not just of Chaucer and his heirs, but of Hawes's own *Pastime of Pleasure*. From the very first lines of the poem, Hawes creates a complex structure of self-reference that puns on the titles of both of these works. The "gentyll poetes" to whom he appeals in line 1 are themselves writers of "fables and storyes" that are "pastymes pleasaunt / To lordes and ladyes" (lines 8–9). Such pastimes constitute the currency of public courtiership, and throughout her moral lectures, Hawes's visionary tutorial lady plays on the idea of the "pleasure" courtly books in general, and "your bokes" in particular, may generate (lines 193, 191).[51] Before she departs, she enjoins the poet:

> *Passe* ye *tyme* here / accordynge to your lykynge
> It maye fortune / your lady of excellence
> wyll *passe* her *tyme* here / soone by walkynge.
>
> (lines 247–49, emphases mine)

And when she leaves, the poem's narrator laments:

> My herte doth blede / now al totorne and rent
> For lacke of *conforte* / my herte is almost spent
> O meruelous fortune / whiche hast in loue me brought
> Where is my *conforte* / that I so longe haue sought.
>
> (lines 256–59, emphases mine)

These lines echo precisely the iterations of the previous stanza. By repeating *passe . . . tyme* and *conforte* in exactly the same positions – in alternating lines, with both terms placed before the marked caesura – Hawes brings the two terms together not so much as moral or sensory conditions but as titles of his books. The "conforte" that is sought is to be found in the making of the *Conforte of Louers* itself.

Such bibliopsychiatry is central to the Hawesean project. As he avers only four stanzas later:

> Two thynges me conforte / euer in pryncypall
> The fyrst be bokes / made in antyquyte
> By Gower and Chauncers / poetes rethorycall
> And Lydgate eke / by good auctoryte.   (lines 281–84)

Here, in an obvious return to the literary historiography of the poem's prologue, Hawes makes the act of reading more than just a "pastyme pleasaunt," but a "conforte": in other words, not an activity of public courtly life, not an activity performed by "lordes and ladyes" but rather one of private meditation, one performed by the author alone. So, too, are books an act of "conforte" in the second point he raises. Hawes's narrator looks forward to those inscribed texts set in the walls or signs along his journey. "Letters for my lady"; "letters for me"; all these are "Agreynge well vnto my bokes all" (lines 291–93). Books and letters are the source of physical well-being: the maintenance of the intact private body depends on the reading and writing of texts. "Conforte," in this vocabulary of lisible health, comes to mean quite explicitly the ways in which the courtly body privatizes itself through the act of reading. And yet, not all writers may be granted such a gift. As Hawes says later in the poem, "Many one wryteth trouthe / yet conforte hath he none" (line 558).

"Conforte" and "pastime" are the two poles of the courtly self and the two ways of reading and writing in courtly society. As Hawes puts it again, the courtly lover woefully seeks out "only suche pastyme / here for to repayre," and must ask, "Where is my conforte / where is my lady fayre" (lines 627–28). Where, indeed? The narrator becomes progressively a creature of his own texts: his lady is "fayrest and moost swete / In all my bokes," he notes how she greets "Also my bokes full pryuely," and he concludes, "The more I wryte / the more my teeres dystyll" (lines 633, 636, 643). Allusions continue to build as Hawes concatenates these terms. Finally, when La Belle Pucelle appears, she explains to the lover–narrator, and to his reader, just what these cryptic references mean. The lover seeks her "swete conforte" (line 784), and she responds:

> Of late I sawe aboke of your makynge
> Called the pastyme of pleasure / whiche is wondrous.   (lines 785–86)

Her remark here is of a piece with the encounters of Hawes's hero of the *Pastime* itself, Grande Amoure, as he comes upon visions of graven scriptures. She sees this book as if it were an artifact, and like Grande Amoure she conflates its physical journeys and its verbal pathways. "I redde there all your passage daungerous" (line 789), she notes, in an ambiguous allusion to the possible censurable passages Hawes had written and/or to the dangerous passage of his fictional hero. At such a moment, Hawes is inseparable both from his literary personae and his bibliographical productions. The body is the book.

Finally, at the poem's end, when the lover awakes from his literary dream and seeks to take up the pen and write it down, Hawes turns again to his own works. "Go lytell treatyse," he announces (line 932), in an obvious allusion to the close of *Troilus and Criseyde*. And yet, Hawes's own book seeks submission not to the canons of classical poets. This is not a text that will kiss the steps of Virgil, Ovid, Homer, Lucan, and Statius; not a book that, as with Chaucer's, will be submitted for the correction of such learned friends as Gower and Strode. This is, instead, a book that has survived its rivals and its author's exiles. It is a book that has been made in spite of courtly dismissal, in spite of the barbed satires of his literary rivals and the "snares and nettes" of courtly intrigue. It is a book that goads its reader to return to Hawes's own body of work. Its envoy beseeches readers, "From daye to daye theyr pastyme to attende" (line 937). Not only are these ladies to appreciate the workings of this author. They are enjoined to return to Hawes's signature text, the *Pastime of Pleasure*. To attend their pastyme means to reread his book, now through the lens of the apologetics of the *Conforte* and the explanations of La Belle Pucelle.

The minion theater of John Skelton

If Hawes's *Conforte of Louers* shuffles in the dark recesses of erotic fantasy, Skelton's *Magnyfycence* revels in the bright halls of fawning dissemblance.[52] If Hawes's poem is about the pitfalls of the personal, then Skelton's drama is about the dangers of the public. It takes the paradigms of royal performativity and sets them up against the kinds of Pandaric theatricalisms of which Henry's minions had been accused in 1519. Skelton's play is now widely understood to be specifically located in the minion controversy of that year. Alistair Fox and Greg Walker have found striking similarities between its characterization of the courtly vice figures and Edward Hall's accounts of Henry's Frenchified young men, and both critics, too, have illustrated in detail how Skelton transmutes the familiar tropes of morality play allegory into a pointed critique of the dissembling of courtiers and politicians.[53] But Skelton's play is also a commentary on the theatrics of *amicitia* itself: a play that reflects on its own dramatic techniques and, in turn, on the illusory nature of both the court and stage. Sex, service, and epistolarity – the defining *loci* of Pandaric life – are brought together not just to script a satire of politics but to interrogate the politics of satire. Much like *Conforte of Louers*, *Magnyfycence* queries the effectiveness of the very genres it enacts. If Hawes's poem ends by rejecting the possibilities of courtly making, Skelton's play closes by dismissing the interlude and, in the process, drawing a clearer line between the "pretences" of play and the responsibilities of power.

Almost from their first entrance, the crafty courtiers that surround Magnyfycence reveal themselves as masters in the arts of feigning. Fansy comes first, irrupting into the King's conversation with Felycyte, denouncing their "langage" as "vayne" (line 251), and introducing himself under the pseudonym of Largesse (line 270). So, too, when Counterfet Countenaunce, Crafty Conveyaunce, Clokyd Colusyon, and Courtly Abusyon enter, they define themselves through modes of physical disguise, deceptive self-naming, or confounding wordplay. Though seemingly defined by the transparency of personification allegory, these creatures are, in fact, anything but transparent. They represent, instead, allegories of disguise, shifting illusions of courtier pandering. Clokyd Colusyon, in particular, plays on the power of dissimulation, and his entry marks itself through an elaborate set of sartorial and linguistic ruses. "Knowe you not me, syrs?" (line 593), he inquires of his cohorts, and Crafty Conveyaunce recognizes him only after some inspection:

> Crafty Conveyaunce. Abyde. Lette me se. Take better hede.
> Cockes harte! It is Cloked Colusyon!   (lines 595–96)

But the identity of this courtier still remains in doubt. He is so elaborately garbed – probably in two layers of clothing – that he appears less as a disguised figure than as a figure of disguise itself. His instability is only

enhanced in the rich rattle of colloquial oaths and confusing puns that
greet debate on his identity.

> Crafty Conveyaunce: What is this he wereth? A cope?
> Clokyd Colusyon: Cappe, syr, I say you be to bolde.
> Fansy: Se howe he is wrapped for the colde
>   Is it not a vestment?
> Clokyd Colusyon: A, ye wante a rope.
> Counterfet Countenaunce: Tushe! It is Syr Johnn Double-Cope.
>
>   (lines 601–5)

This play on the particularities of vestment (a cope, a cape, or a cap) is
but one moment in a larger burlesque of the vesting of the courtly
body.[54] As in Hawes's *Conforte*, such a body is a dressed display, and the
courtier of words, be it a poet or a counselor, is a creature of his *textus*,
what Paul Zumthor has called his "costume of language." Clokyd
Colusyon is, in essence, not just a parody, or even a burlesque, but a
travesty, a creature who puts on another's habit.[55] The linguistic
instability that surrounds his appearances reflects this courtly shape-
shifting, as well. "Cokes arms," "Cockes harte," "Cockes bones" – the
vulgar oaths that greet his entry and that resonate with the deviltry of the
cycle and morality plays – are here, as throughout Skelton's drama,
symbols of a vulgarized, dismantled divine body, a divinity that is itself
mocked by the possible ecclesiastical flavor of Clokyd Colusyon's "vestment." "God gyve you confusyon!" (line 597), he states as his benedic-
tion upon this house of vice, and He certainly does.

The textilic imagery of courtiership extends beyond the garb of fealty
or dissimulation to embrace, too, the ruses of sexuality. Sex-work
demands a cloak of public propriety under which the vices of desire may
go on, and the travesties of *Magnyfycence* go way beyond the amicitial
impersonations of Pandarus, who would but "wre" (i.e., wrap) himself in
the "mantel" of friendship to procure a love. For Skelton, it embraces
the explicit sex trade of *La Celestina*. Here, prostitution is arranged
behind the front of businesslike respectability. "Her first trade," says
Parmeneo in his review of Celestina's wiles, "was a cloak to all the rest,
under color where many young wenches" came to her house (Mabbe,
Celestine, p. 135; *Calisto y Melebea*, p. 242). Celestina herself is an
embodiment of such a cloaking, not just in her public ruses but in her
private magic. As a creature who, among other things, repairs virgins,
Celestina sews up female parts, much as if she were repairing clothes or
leather goods. Stitching and sewing are her primary activities, and not
just in the purely surgical realm. As Mary S. Gossy has shown in great
detail, the stitchery of Celestina is, by the late fifteenth century, already
deeply imbued with "the strong sexual double entendres that are a

mainstay of contemporary bawdy literature." "To stitch," Gossy goes on, "is to bring together, which is the office of a go-between,"[56] and Celestina's patching up of hymens works in tandem with her patching up of relationships. Her secret acts on women's bodies have their counterpart in her public actions in the body politics. As Sempronio states, selling her skills:

For her arte in recoueringe decayed virginityes, and mendinge of lost maydenheades, some she healpt with her bladders, and some of them she stitcht vp with Needle and threede. She had a little Cabinett or painted worke box, certeine fine small needles, such as your glouers sowe withall, and threedes of the slenderest and smallest silke she could possiblie gett, which threedes were waxed all ourer. She had also lyinge vppon a little table manie rootes, all of them servinge for this purpose: . . . O! She would worke miracles with theise! When the french ambassader came this waye, she made sale of one of her wenches three seuerall tymes for a virgin.[57]

These are as much the machinations of the bawd as they are the dissimulations of the courtier. By fixing, sewing, painting, and waxing, the bawd transmutes the plain or the plainly used into the brilliant and the new. Her marvels, in the end, are pressed into the service not just of male pleasure but political deceit, here selling off a woman to the French ambassador.

Magnyfycence is vividly alive to these Celestinesque gestures, nowhere perhaps as much as in the figure of Counterfet Countenaunce. His opening speech, much like Celestina's, is a catalogue of all the fakeries of politics and power, and he notes in particular his power to counterfeit not just letters or expressions but virginity itself.

> Counterfet maydenhode may well be borne,
> But counterfet coynes is laughynge to scorne;
> It is evyll patchynge of that is torne.
> Whan the *noppe* is rughe, it wolde be shorne.   "nap"
> Counterfet *haltynge* without a thorne;   "limping"
> Yet counterfet *chafer* is but evyll corne.   "merchandise"
> All thynge is worse whan it is worne.   (lines 445–51)

This stanza offers up a veritable lexicon of the obscene: a vision of the bawdry of *La Celestina* now transmuted into English courtiership. Its language seems to speak directly to those aspects of the Spanish play that made it so condemnable by Vives as one of those *pestiferis libris*.[58] Counterfet Countenaunce explicitly mimes Celestina's role, and in this context of patched maidenheads, torn body parts, pubic hair (the rough nap that is shorn at line 448), one may well find at least a double if not a triple entendre in the reference to "counterfet coynes": false coins, false coyness (as Paula Neuss suggests[59]), and perhaps even false "conys," that term of almost obscene endearment that appears in Skelton's *Elynour Rummynge*.[60] So, too, Skelton's character brings together Celestina's surgery with the commercial aspects of her craft. This is a statement about "counterfet chafer," faked goods, bad merchandise, a "thynge" (now read, as Neuss does, as "privy member") worn out, yet patched up for resale.[61]

At such a moment, Counterfet Countenaunce is the ultimate panderer, one who like Pandarus or Celestina revels not just in the making but the selling of the lie. His trade lies in the commerce of the bogus, where counterfeited "kyndnesse," "letters," "weyght," and "langage" are all, as he states, the "proper bayte" to lure the unsuspecting.

> A counte to counterfet in a *resayte* –   "receipt"
> To counterfet well is a good *consayte*.   (lines 443–44) "device, trick"

Skelton's character is something of a mock accountant, offering up falsified receipts.[62] The very meaning of his name inextricably yokes together money and manipulation, and recalls both the sexual economics of Celestina and the erotic barter of Pandarus. Counterfeiting is, too, part of the stock of the Pandaric, an elaborate blend of what R. A. Shoaf calls the "narcissism and false coining [that] are inseparable from his *auctoritas* in the story."[63] Counterfet Countenaunce's long speech extolling his dissimulations – much like Celestina's – is a model of narcissism and false coining, and it is significant (as I had noted earlier) that when Celestina's Spanish is adapted for English performance in Rastell's *Calisto and Melebea*, she speaks in the language of Pandaric self-promotion and ludic exchange. As Parmeneo puts it in the English play – distilling these complex associations of sex, money, and dissimulation – the ruses of Celestina's minions are "smoke" in the eyes (*Calisto and Melebea*, line 465): "Nothyng but for lucre is all theyr bawdry" (line 471).[64]

If there is, though, a character in *Magnyfycence* whose bawdry is all for lucre it is Courtly Abusyon. Here is someone who is explicitly the King's bawd, a Compton-like creature seeking preferment by presenting his ruler with an idealized female limned according to the very techniques of late medieval *blazonerie*, but destined not for the distant longings of the unrequited courtier but for the immediate gratification of the King himself.

> To fasten your fansy upon a fayre maystresse
> That quyckly is envyved with *rudyes* of the rose,   "ruddiness"
> *Inpurtured* with fetures after your purpose,   "adorned"
> The streynes of her vaynes as asure Inde blewe,
> Enbudded with beautye and colour fresshe of hewe,

> As lyly whyte to loke upon her *leyre*,   "countenance"
> Her eyen relucent as carbuncle so clere,
> Her mouthe *enbawmed*, dylectable and mery,   "fragrant"
> Her lusty lyppes ruddy as the chery –
> How lyke yow? Ye lacke, syr, suche a lusty lasse.
>
> (*Magnyfycence*, lines 1550–59)

Taken out of context, this *blazon* could come out of Hawes's *Pastime of Pleasure*, or out of any of the many early sixteenth-century descriptive lyrics modeled on his aureate excesses. Indeed, the characteristic idioms of such descriptions – the ruddy lips, the comparisons with the rose, the blueness of the veins beneath the skin, the exquisiteness of the mouth – inform, too, Calisto's first description of his love in *Calisto and Melebea*. Compare his lines with Skelton's:

> Her gay *glasyng* eyen so fayre and bryght,   "glass-like"
> Her browes, her nose in a meane no fassyon faylys,
> Her mouth proper and feate, her teeth small and whyght,
> Her lyppis ruddy, her body streyght upryght,
> Her lyttyl tetys to the eye is a pleasure.
> O what joy it is to se such a fygure!
>
> Her skyn of whytnes endarkyth the snow,
> Wyth rose colour ennewyd – I the ensure –
> Her lyttyll handys in meane maner – this is no trow –
> Her fyngers small and long, with naylys ruddy most pure,
> Of proporcyon none such in purtrayture,
> Without pere, worthy to have for fayrenes
> The apple that Parys gave Venus the goddes.
>
> (*Calisto and Melebea*, lines 235–47)

These two quotations illustrate the ways in which the language of the courtly *blazon* stands but a hair's breadth away from whoredom. For Calisto, his love will all too soon become the sex goods of the bawd. For Courtly Abusyon, it already is. Bawdry is all for lucre here, and when Magnyfycence asks, "Where myght suche one be founde?" (line 1568), Courtly Abusyon can only answer, "Wyll ye spende ony money?" (line 1569). Money replaces sex here, as the courtier and the King discuss for some twenty lines the value of desire and the ways in which women become commodities in political action (lines 1570–86). And, in a Latin proverbial line that brilliantly sums up the confluence of money, sex, and dissimulation in this play, Courtly Abusyon finally avers, "omnis mulier meretrix si celari potest": every woman is a whore if it can be hidden.

If every woman is, under it all, a whore, then every man is but a pimp. Certainly, *Magnyfycence*'s courtiers embrace the spectrum of the go-between, from the counterfeiter and the pander to the diplomatic messenger, and perhaps this play's most explicit engagement with the ruses of Henrician courtiership lies in its sub-plot of epistolary transmission. The forged letter of introduction at its opening – a letter written by Counterfet Countenaunce for Sad Cyrcumspeccyon and presented by Fansy to Magnyfycence – stands at the nexus of early Tudor ambassadorial intrigue and Chaucerian epistolarity that defines the politics of the Pandaric. Fansy brings in the letter, a "wrytynge closed under sele" (line 312). Its contents are as yet unknown to the monarch, and when he gets the chance to "knowe" what "this letter doethe contayne" (line 324) he reads it silently. "Hic faciat tanquam legeret litteras tacite," read the stage directions ("Let him act as if he were reading the letter silently"). Though an apparently minor part of the dramatic action, the letter is the nodal point of privacy and power, diplomacy and desire, for the play. It places Fansy in the role of the go-between; gets him accused of being a spy (line 352); and, in its final revelation as a counterfeit document, brings together the Chaucerian literary tradition and the Henrician political present into a powerful critique of courtly epistolarity.

At the play's end, the masks are stripped away and forgeries revealed for what they are.

MAGNYFYCENCE:	Sothely to repent me I have grete cause;
	Howe be it, from you I receyved a letter sent,
	Whiche conteyned in it a specyall clause
	That I sholde use largesse.
CYRCUMSPECCYON:	Nay, syr, there a pause.
REDRESSE:	Yet let us se this matter thorowly ingrosed.
MAGNYFYCENCE:	Syr, this letter ye sent to me at Pountes was enclosed.
CYRCUMSPECCYON:	Who brought you that letter? Wote ye what he hyght?
MAGNYFYCENCE:	Largesse, syr, by his credence was his name.
CYRCUMSPECCYON:	This letter ye speke of never dyd I wryte.

(lines 2434–42)

Here, at last, all is clear. The impersonations of Fansy are stripped aside, as "Largesse" is revealed to be his role. The counterfeiting and the cloaking of the play drop away to show not just the truth of this bogus document, but the true nature of kingship and, in turn, the heart of the play's constructive satire.

But is it really all that constructive? Is Skelton's goal political reform, as Greg Walker has argued, of a not terribly threatening variety? At stake in such a question is not just the set of topical resonances that locate this play in the minion controversy of 1519. Rather, it is a confrontation of the very idea of topical literature itself – a querying of the effectiveness of moral drama and political satire. If, in the course of my analysis, I have appeared to slight the direct topical allusiveness of this play in favor of its literary resonances, it is not for any lack of textual evidence. *Magnyfycence* is full of scenes of topical critique: for example, when the courtiers ape the dress and dandyisms of the court of France (lines 748–51, 877–88), or when they display their vast knowledge of the terms of tilting (lines 1179–85).[65] Like Clokyd Colusyon's entry, they have been interpreted as specific moments of social satire against the excesses of King Henry's minions. And yet, it seems to me, that what is at stake in such episodes is more than just the transparency of topical allusion. Rather, *Magnyfycence* defines the quality of minion politics in scenes of otherness. Episodes of Frenchified performance, exaggerated theatrical gesturing, wild costuming, and travesties of courtly and religious language all remind the modern reader, and perhaps the historical audience, of similar theatricalizations of alterity in Henry's court, as when he burst upon the Queen or interrupted the state banquet with his men dressed as outlaws or rare exotics. These are the moments when the courtiers define themselves as alien to the conventional discourses of a social life: when they define themselves, in other words, as courtiers.

For Edward Hall, such figures needed to be purged from Henry's world and be replaced by what he called the "sad and aun.cient knightes, put into the kynges priuie chamber" (*Chronicle*, p. 598). In Skelton's play, such figures are placed by characters such as Sad Cyrcumspeccyon, and it is precisely this quality of *sadness* that defines not just the political but the literary response to minion theatricality. In the sixteenth-century English of Hall and Skelton, *sad* does not mean simply dour or sober. It refers explicitly to moral qualities of steadfastness, stability, and truth. It signals, too, sobriety of countenance and dress, and it stands as a key term in the language of moral pedagogy.[66] To be sad is to be laconic, plain, and clear. It is to be everything Pandarus is not. The word, so much a part of Chaucer's moral vocabulary, never appears in *Troilus and Criseyde*. Rather, it is the purview of such creatures as patient Griselda of the *Clerk's Tale*, whose sadness signals an acquiescence to the power of adverse paternal figures. By the early sixteenth century, sadness is the goal to which didactic works move, in particular, didactic works for children.[67] To "Walke by the wey verry sadly" and to watch one's "array" are the injunctions of the so-called "Poem to Apprentices" transcribed into a commonplace book of the early 1500s: injunctions that recall the conventional teachings of such treatises as John Lydgate's *Testament*, John Russel's *Book of Nurture*, and the collections of maxims in such early printed volumes as the *Boke of St. Albans* (1486). Hall's "sad and ancient knights," then, are not just old and sober. They are figures drawn from the inheritance of pedagogic literature, paternal instructors for the young King, creatures cobbled out of the familiar raw materials of maximal advice. As Magnyfycence recognizes when Sad Cyrcumspeccyon enters with Perseveraunce and Redresse, "Well, I perceyve in you there is moche sadnesse, / Gravyte of counsell, provydence, and wyt" (lines 2475–76). Such lines, for all their historical allusiveness to Henry VIII's recognition of the "sad and ancient knights," are, too, a signal that the theatrics of politics and play are at an end.

The word *sad* thus signals a quality of staid demeanor and veracity of word and deed that counteracts the glib performativity of courtliness. Figures of sadness, whether in Hall or in Skelton, are therefore figures of anti-theatricality. They strip away the ruses of courtier performance, reassert familiar stable gender roles, and teach the young King and the lapsed Magnyfycence that the ideals of power lie not in the spectacle of rule but in a "processe" and the "treatyse" of instruction. Those are the words used at the play's close to define its generic and moral status (see lines 2481, 2482, 2510, 2538). It is now, as Sad Cyrcumspeccyon himself states, "A myrrour inclerd is this interlude" (line 2524), a *speculum principis*. And as Magnyfycence himself states at the play's close, "This mater" has been offered "under pretence of play." The ruse of roleplaying is the momentary entertainment and illusion of the stage. But the business of governance should be far removed from the theatrics of the minions or the playful counterfeitings of a Pandarus.

The romance of intrusion in *The Squyr of Lowe Degre*

Though Hawes and Skelton spoke directly to the machinations of the courtier and the relations between openness and privacy in love, few poems of the early sixteenth century describe these problems with such detail and such drama as *The Squyr of Lowe Degre*. Printed by Wynkyn de Worde around the year 1520, and republished by William Copeland a generation later, the poem circulated among early Tudor readers under the title "Undo Youre Dore," a reference to the episode when the young squire tries to gain entry into his beloved's chamber.[68] This poem, recently the focus of much critical inspection of the role of voyeurism in late Middle English narrative and of the place of royal patriarchy in the formation of courtly *ethoi*, resonates explicitly with many of the Henrician gestures of display and intrusion I have been discussing, and it may stand as something of a popular verse commentary on the kinds of courtly performances that distinguished the first decade of Henry's rule.[69] It offers a complex range of allusions to contemporary events, Chaucerian themes, and medieval English religious drama. It also offers, in its surviving early prints, associations among Skelton, Hawes, and Chaucer that locate it squarely in the literary afterlife of *Troilus and Criseyde*.

Its elements of plot are drawn from the familiar staples of the Middle English romance. A young squire of low degree is in love with the daughter of the king of Hungary.[70] The lady overhears his lament, counsels him to keep their love secret, and sends him off on a seven-year mission of chivalric probation. The king's steward, also in love with the princess, overhears this conversation and plans revenge against the squire. In an encounter before the lady's chamber, the squire kills the steward and some of his men; he is subsequently taken prisoner, while the dead steward is dressed in the squire's clothes. As the princess laments what she believes to be the death of her beloved, the squire finds himself released through the largesse of the king. Eventually, the king overhears his daughter's laments, tells her the truth, brings the squire home, and marries them.

This is a poem about chambers and their opening; a poem about the surveillance of possible traitors and about the various devices of collecting courtly information. It is a poem concerned also with the rituals of courtly power: with the spectacle of knightly investiture and the jousts and tournaments that celebrated courtly prowess. Whole sections of the poem read like little more than catalogues of early Tudor ostentation, comparable to Edward Hall's descriptions of the food, clothes, ornaments, and entertainments of the Henrician court.[71] And in its replays of familiar gestures of chivalric service, the poem recalls such displays of official theatrics as the Winchester Pageant of 1511 celebrating the birth of Henry's first, but short-lived, son (the child, by the way, with whom Katherine was pregnant at the time of Carroz's letter). The vision of a monarch who can imprison or release the suitor knight is a cliché exploited in both poem and pageant, while the latter's representations of Queen Katherine echo the romance figure of the lady fought over by her suitor knights.[72]

The Squyr of Lowe Degre is also acutely sensitive to those relations between wealth and social status that informed the rapid rise of men such as William Compton, and, perhaps, the equally rapid decline of Hawes. Though the story of a man of lesser rank in love above his station is a chestnut of romance, this poem gives it a specifically topical edge. In response to the steward's claim that the young squire is unworthy of the princess, the king responds with a statement of Henrician fealty:

> Hath he be so *bonayre* and benynge,   "debonaire"
> And serued me syth he was yinge,

> And redy with me in euery nede,
> Bothe trewe in worde and eke in dede. (W, lines 357–60)

Commonplaces, yes, but this king may as well be Henry speaking of a man like Compton, in service since his youth and ready in "euery nede." The king of Hungary goes on, too, to report that marriage may become the means by which a "page" may elevate himself to gentleman.

> Then it is semly to that squyer
> To haue my doughter by this manere,
> And eche man in his degree
> Become a lorde of ryaltee,
> By fortune and by other grace,
> By herytage and by purchase. (W, lines 375–80)

This reference to lordship attained "by purchase" clearly would have spoken to the anxieties surrounding men such as Compton, whose actions, in G. W. Bernard's words, "point vividly to the attractions of the noble way of life to a successful and ambitious man in early Tudor England." Purchase, indeed, was Compton's mode, for while he was never actually ennobled, it may well have been due to his greater attention, in Lord Herbert of Cherbury's words, "to his profit, then publique affaires."[73]

But in addition to its topical allusiveness, *The Squyr of Lowe Degre* remains a poem of great narrative power, and the episode that gave the text its early Tudor title may recall directly the intrusive and theatricalized gestures of the King that Hall felt necessary to recall towards the end of his reign. Here, in a telling rich with *double entendre*, the squire stands armed before the lady's locked door,

> his drawen swerd in his hande,
> There was no more with him wolde stande:
> But it stode with hym full harde,
> As ye shall here nowe of the stewarde.
> He wende in the worlde none had be
> That had knowen of his pryvite. (C, lines 507–12)

With his hard weapon standing in for the erect phallus, it may be little wonder that we now know all about this squire's "pryvite," a term that here, as throughout later Middle English, connoted both the secret intents of the agent and the private parts of the person. To know, as in Chaucer's *Miller's Tale*, "Of Goddes pryvetee" or of that of a man's "wyf" (A, line 3164) is to know about the very parts of generation – the parts, as Laura Kendrick has recently argued in a powerful explication of this Chaucerian line, that are the very object of social anxiety about the sexuality of Christ.[74] This squire's "drawen swerd" *is* his "pryvite," and his poem is a story of such threatened private parts. Men are killed and mutilated, shut up or sent away, returned in disguise and uncloaked. The story of the steward and the squire, rivals for the princess, is the old romance plot of the mutable male body now filtered through the politics of Henrician service and of early Tudor sumptuous display.

If the male body in the poem is constantly subject to the wiles of king or rival, the woman's form is arrestingly stable. One might think, then, that the *locus* of the theatrical in the poem lies with the actions of its men, with scenes such as the one quoted just above. And yet, the real drama of this poem lies not so much with the movements of the man but with the immobility of the woman – a drama that recalls pointedly one of the key scenes of the popular medieval religious stage. "Youre dore undo," "Undo," "Undo thy doore," "Undo your dore," "Undo thy dore" (C, lines 534, 535, 539, 541, 545): this phrase becomes the plea of the supposedly protecting squire. And yet, the lady replies:

> For I wyll not my dore undo
> For no man that cometh therto.   (C, lines 551–52)

Porta haec clausa erit. In a remarkable rephrasing of the biblical injunctions of Marian virginity, the lady bars not just the portal of her room but the entry into her body. As Gail Gibson has explained, the image of the locked door was a central figure of the female body inviolate in the late medieval English drama, and this episode recalls explicitly the scene in the N-Town play when Joseph discovers the pregnant Mary:[75]

> JOSEPH: How dame how . *vndo ʒoure dore vn-do*
>   Are ʒe at home why speke ʒe notht
> SUSANNA: Who is ther why cry ʒe so
>   telle us ʒour herand wul ʒe ought.
> JOSEPH: Vn-do *ʒour dore* I sey ʒow to
>   Ffor to come in is all my thought
> MARIA: it is my spowse þat spekyth us to
>   *On-do þe dore* his wyl were wrought.
>   well-come hom myn husbond dere
>   how haue ʒe ferd in fer countre.[76]

Gibson considers this scene "a remarkably inventive translation into dramatic action of the medieval exegetical commonplace of Mary's virginity as the porta clausa, the locked door in Ezekiel's vision of the new Temple (Ez. 44:1–2)."[77] What it also represents is the recognition of the inherently dramatic quality of Joseph's entreaty, and in turn, of the possible resonances with the scene in the *Squyr of Lowe Degre*. In its anaphoric requests to "un-do" the door, this episode prefigures the iterations of the squire. And with its calm allowance of Mary to "on-do" the door to her spouse, it offers something of a subtext to the uninformed resistance of the princess in the poem – a resistance broken only when she recognizes the squire for who he is, and then, too, broken only to announce that she will keep "my maydenhede ryght" until he proves himself virtuous (lines 574–75). Much of the humor of this passage for an early sixteenth-century reader would have come precisely from its burlesque of the dramatic tradition of exegetical Marianology. As Gibson notes, "the porta clausa was so omnipresent a symbol for the Virgin Mary's miraculously inviolate participation in the Incarnation that a medieval audience would scarcely have needed [a] reminder."[78] In short, even by titling this poem "Undo Your Dore," de Worde and Copeland already invest in the allusions to this image. The poem's wild mockery of this epicentral scene – with its appearance of a symbolically phallicized suitor read against the comically impotent Joseph – thus constitutes a comic commentary, not just on the image itself, but on the traditions of popular theatrics that had made it part and parcel of the public literary imagination.

These patterns of theatricalization and burlesque take on added political meaning when read against the courtly incursions into Katherine's bedchamber. The condition of the chambered woman, her gravid status behind the closed door, was a defining concern of the early Henrician court. It shaped both the insinuations of Carroz and the invasions of the King; it may have stood behind the obscenities of Skelton's Counterfet Countenaunce. Indeed, one may well ask, with Skelton's character, if one *could* counterfeit a pregnancy. "Undo youre dore," in this environment, becomes a plea for evidence, a cry for the dissimulations of the courtier and the woman to be stripped aside, for chambers to be opened, and for female form to be revealed. In Hall's account of Henry's sudden entry into Katherine's bedchamber we may find, now, something of a wild inversion of this moment in *The Squyr of Lowe Degre*. In Hall's *Chronicle*, Henry does not ask but comes in "sodainly." He is not garbed as King or husband, but as outlaw in a play of intervention. And, of course, the Queen *was* pregnant – in mid-January 1510, visibly so, perhaps as much as thirty-three weeks into her term, and she was to miscarry less than three weeks after this episode.

The Squyr of Lowe Degre has as its underlying topical anxieties this clutch of royal personal and social issues. To read of the eagerness of the young squire or to witness the burlesque of Joseph is, at this moment in Henry's reign, to share in the theatricalizations of a profound public unease. To confront this poem at the moment of its printing – at the close of a decade marked by intrigue and surreption, where the politics of minion governance had raised for critical inspection the very problems of social mobility and royal service that are this poem's themes – is to confront not the decadence of a late medieval literary tradition but the vigor of contemporary Tudor satire. The deceptions of the amorous and political life are central themes for this text almost from its opening. The princess alerts the squire at their first encounter that the king's steward will "deceyve" and "bewraye" him (W, lines 162, 164). When we first see the steward, he is overhearing this entire conversation, vowing to "bewraye" the princess (W, line 288). And when the squire appears at the princess's door, his appeal for entry relies not just on honor or desire, but on espionage. When he yells out, in a desperate plea, "I am beset with many a spy" (C, line 536), he voices the concern of courtiers and poets throughout the 1510s. For Carroz and his kings, for the narrator of Hawes's *Conforte of Louers*, and for the courtier Fansy in Skelton's *Magnyfycence*, physical entry and epistolary politics work in a world where, as the *Squyr of Lowe Degre* avers in this episode, "treason walketh wonder wyde" (line 520). And, as in all these texts, it is telling, not just knowing, that locates power. As A. C. Spearing phrases it, the steward and the squire "are not rivals in knightly prowess but rival storytellers," and he goes on, in an analysis that captures both the gist of this poem and the climate of early Tudor literary culture generally:

The power to tell is closely connected with the power to spy on behaviour intended to be private, and whereas the Princess overhears the Squire, the Steward establishes his superiority by overhearing them both. He then carries his story, suitably amended, to the King, is set by him to continue spying, and steps treacherously outside the limited narrative role that the King specifies for him, thus apparently incorporating the King in *his* narrative and becoming the poem's champion storyteller.[79]

The power to tell is the power to spy. Carroz's verb "fablar" and his preoccupations with the act of diplomatic writing had signaled both his Spanish rivalry with Diego Fernandez and his English rivalry with Compton. Carroz fashions himself his King's champion storyteller, beating his rivals both with better information and with greater skill. Read in the context of the literary fabulations of the *Squyr of Lowe Degre*, the texts I have discussed here may be said, for all their differences of form and tone, to share in the romances of the voyeur. In each, a quest for knowledge finds itself dilated through intercepted letters, royal dismissals, coterie rivalries, and the cloakings of political and amorous deceit. In the end, courtiers and lovers, diplomats and poets, kings and pimps, seek out the lady's door and, either bursting in or surreptitiously eavesdropping, seek the truth of the woman.

The wiles of a woodcut

In sum, "Undo Youre Dore" – for that is what I think this poem rightly should be called – reflects as much on Henry's minion politics as *Magnyfycence* does, and it attends as much to courtly privacy and class anxiety as Hawes's *Conforte*. But it survives, too, in a literary world defined by Chaucerian trope and Skeltonic allusion, a world limned not only by the poem's verbal texture but by the pictorial environment that would have signaled, to its earliest readers, its place in the inheritance of the Pandaric. In its first printing by de Worde, as well as in its subsequent republication by Copeland, readers would have seen a familiar picture on its frontispiece.[80] The woodcut of a woman giving her ring to a man (Hodnett, *English Woodcuts*, no. 1009) was part of de Worde's stable of courtly illustrations.[81] It appeared in the 1509 and 1517 prints of the *Pastime of Pleasure* introducing the discussion between Grande Amoure and La Belle Pucelle (figures 1 and 2),[82] and de Worde used it subsequently as the frontispieces to four volumes: the 1517 *Troilus and Criseyde* (figure 3) (where it appears, too, on the penultimate leaf of the volume [figure 4]); *The Conforte of Louers* (figure 5); *The Squyr of Lowe Degre* (figure 6); and the anonymous and only conjecturally datable religious love poem, the *IIII Leues of a Truelove* (figure 7) (a slightly modified version of the fourteenth-century alliterative Middle English *Quatrefoil of Love*, preserved in two fifteenth-century manuscripts).[83] Even though this may appear to be a standard picture, there are differences in placement and in detail that imply some thoughtful critical reflection on the printer's part and that may associate these publications as a kind of literary group. Examined in this way, this woodcut comes to stand as the emblem of courtly converse for the early Henrician period, and it returns me to the contexts of the early sixteenth-century reception of the *Troilus* with which I began this chapter.[84]

When it first appears, in the 1509 *Pastime* edition, no accompanying text or denotative names fill the ribbons above the figures. In fact, it seems odd that this woodcut should illuminate the *Pastime*'s text at this point, for unlike many of the other woodcuts in de Worde's editions of the poem, this one does not bear on any of its actions.[85] Though the conversation between Grande Amoure and La Belle Pucelle transpires in a "garden fayre" (*Pastime*, line 1976), there is no mention of a ring or any other gift exchanged between them. So, too, the woman's dress in this woodcut bears little resemblance to the verbal description offered in the poem (note, in particular, the absence of "A payre of gloues / ryght sclender and soft," which Hawes states were "On her fayre handes," (*Pastime*, lines 2042–43). What this picture, then, is doing in the *Pastime* is unclear. But what it does in *Troilus and Criseyde* is obvious. Here, it appears to illuminate the exchange of rings described in Book III. Criseyde had asked Pandarus to convey a "blewe ryng" to Troilus (III.885), and later – in a scene rich with both narrative and doctrinal confusions – the lovers played at exchanging "hire rynges" (III.1368), perhaps in imitation of the marriage rite. But Troilus and Criseyde are, by this moment in Book III, in bed, not in a garden, and only Criseyde offers up a present to her lover here. Something is clearly amiss here, and something certainly is strange that de Worde should present this picture both as frontispiece and endplate to his edition – as if this moment were the most important for his readership; as if it were, in other words, the emblem of the poem as a whole.

But why would this scene, among all those of the poem, be considered emblematic? I suggest it is because it represents not what the lovers really did but what Pandarus did for them, and, in particular, what John Skelton said he did for them. Certainly, for Jane Scrope, the ring is central to Pandarus's adventures.

> Pandaer bare the bylles
> From one to the other,
> His maisters love to further,
> Somtyme a presyous thyng,
> An ouche or els a ryng,
> From her to hym agayn;
> Somtyme a pretty chayn
> Or a bracelet of her here,
> Prayd Troylus for to were
> *That token for her sake;*
> *How hartely he dyd it take.*
>
> (*Phyllyp Sparowe*, lines 682–92, emphases mine)

Jane does not recount precisely what had happened in the text of *Troilus* as much as she conflates a series of events that center on Pandarus's activities as go-between. As John Scattergood recognizes, in his note to this passage, Skelton "seems to have confused" the episodes in Book III.[86] But, as Susan Schibanoff has argued, in a study of the poem acutely sensitive to what she calls Jane's "gender-selective recollection" of the books she has read, Skelton does not so much confuse as select and rewrite.[87] "Jane's experience as a reader," Schibanoff shows, is the experience of personally rewriting the canonical texts of the medieval literary tradition. The attentions that control her literary interests, her envisioning of herself "as a sexually aware, bawdy woman," help shape her recastings of Chaucerian moments: the close reading of the Wife of Bath, say (lines 618–27), or her fascinations with the "lyght" and

Of Ouncell and J than rose full quyckely
    And made vs redy on our way to walke
Jn your clenly wede apparayled proprely
What J wolde say J dyde vnto hym talke
Tyll on his boke he began to calke
How the sonne entred was in gemyne
And eke Dyane full of mutabelyte

Entred the crabbe her propre mancyon
        Pleasure,   G.iij.

Figure 1   Stephen Hawes, *The Pastime of Pleasure*, 1509, Sig. Giii r.

Ouncell and I/than rose full quyckely
And made vs redy/on our waye to walke
In your clenly wede/apparayled proprely
What I wolde saye/I dyde vnto hym talke
Tyll on his boke/he began to calke
How the sonne entred was in Gemyne
And eke Dyane/full of mutabylyte

Entred the Crabbe/her propre mancyon
Pleasure.   G.iii.

Figure 2   Stephen Hawes, *The Pastime of Pleasure*, 1517, Sig. Giii r.

Figure 3   Geoffrey Chaucer, *Troilus and Criseyde*, 1517, frontispiece.

Figure 4   Geoffrey Chaucer, *Troilus and Criseyde*, 1517, penultimate
leaf.

Figure 5 Stephen Hawes, *The Conforte of Louers*, n.d., frontispiece.

Figure 6   Anonymous, *The Squyr of Lowe Degre* [*Undo Youre Dore*], n.d., frontispiece.

Figure 7   Anonymous, *IIII Leues of a Truelove*, n.d., frontispiece.

"wanton" women of romance (lines 628–73).[88] In Jane Scrope's reading of the *Troilus*, Pandarus stands as the controller of the lovers, a bearer not just of the letters but of gifts and tokens of desire. He, more than those lovers or the poet, is the agent of the poem's actions, and Jane's capsule rendering of Chaucer's narrative concludes not with a reference to the afterlife of Troilus or the reputation of Criseyde, but with "Pandaer" named as "Troylus baud" (lines 717–23). This is a poem retold through the ministrations of that "baud," a poem retold by a woman who figures herself a player in the wiles of amorous desire, epistolary surreption, and intrusive gift-exchange.

In his edition of the *Troilus*, de Worde presents an icon of this Skeltonized Chaucer: an image of tokens proffered and accepted, where not just the actions but the very language of Jane Scrope's account must have been in the printer's mind. When he sought to put words into the mouths of these figures, the printer drew directly on this version of the *Troilus* from *Phyllyp Sparowe*. In the frontispieces to the *Conforte of Louers* and the *IIII Leues of a Truelove* – poems that, at first glance, appear to have nothing to do with Chaucer's text or Skelton's notion of it – the characters' names are replaced by a pair of rhyming couplets. Above the woman, as she gives the man the ring, it says "Holde this / a token ywys," and the man responds, "for your sake / I shall it take."[89] They echo Jane Scrope's lines, and I believe them to be pointed references to Skelton's poem. If so, they make these editions share in one of the most enigmatic, yet clearly most virulent, of early Tudor literary rivalries, and they suggest as well that de Worde had a hand in sustaining a public interest in this literary competition.

Hawes and Skelton have long been understood as conducting an oblique set of attacks on each other's positions, tastes, and poetic accomplishments.[90] Each poet knew the other's work well. Hawes had borrowed from the *Bowge of Court* and from a poem known as *Woffully Afraid* (which he may have thought was Skelton's) elsewhere in his work. Skelton had taunted Hawes in *Phyllyp Sparowe*, borrowing the phrasings of the *Pastime of Pleasure* to describe the prolixity of Lydgate (Hawes's admitted literary model) and to poke fun at his elaborate praises of La Belle Pucelle.[91] Hawes got back at Skelton at the close of the *Conforte of Louers*. After narrating in some detail the plights and pains of the exiled courtly poet, Hawes's narrator notes,

> Surely I thynke / I suffred well the phyppe
> The nette also dydde teche me on the waye
> But me to bere I trowe they lost a lyppe.   (*Conforte*, lines 890–92)

Since the Skelton edition of Alexander Dyce in the mid-nineteenth century, these lines have been perceived as a direct attack on Hawes's rival poet. The word "phyppe" has been interpreted as a familiar name for a sparrow, a contraction of Philip, and the allusion to *Phyllyp Sparowe* seems clear.[92] Hawes's mention of the "nette" in this passage, as well as his reference to the "snares" and "nettes" and "gynnes" set out to catch him (lines 904–6), are also taken to be part and parcel of the language of bird-catching, drawing the reader's mind back to the image of the sparrow caged in Skelton's poem. In fact, it would appear that during the early 1510s, Skelton was known primarily for this work, and the "phyllyp" or the "phyppe" had come to stand as something of a metonymy for his work as a whole. In Alexander Barclay's *Ship of Fools*, the author disapproved of Skelton's literary "wantonness" by noting that "It longeth not to my science nor cunning, / For Philip the Sparowe the Dirige to singe." And, in response to the "flytyng" between Skelton and Christopher Garnesche in 1513 or 1514, Barclay had included further rejoinders to this "Poete laureate" in his *Eclogues* (published by de Worde, probably in 1514 or 1515).[93] In fact, the Eclogues have been read as shot through with allusions to both Hawes and Skelton: the former, alluded to in the figure of the rustic Godfrey Gormand (taken to be a play on the figure Godfrey Gobeleve from the *Pastime of Pleasure*, who had also been mocked as Skelton's "gorbellyd Godfrey" in the second poem *Against Garnesche*); the latter, attacked as "Poete laureate, / When stinking Thais made him her graduate."[94]

These multiple allusions, barbs, and critical attacks were, as David Carlson has recently argued, the common coin of early Tudor literary self-promotion. It was through such articulated rivalries and, furthermore, through the manipulations of printers and booksellers, that writers of the period defined their social roles and pleaded for royal patronage and public readership. Writing about the competition between Thomas More and Bernard André in their Latin poems, Carlson voices a condition of literary culture that may also bear on the vernacular rivalry of Hawes and Skelton, and in turn, de Worde's role in its propagation.

That the early Tudor humanists should have attacked one another from time to time is to be expected, in light of the ongoing struggle to win reputation enjoined by the dominant system of literary exchange, of literary labor for patronage. Ridiculing others, as objectionable as it was pretended to be, was a tactic acknowledged in practice to be an effective means of self-promotion.[95]

In this environment, for Hawes to have "suffred well the phyppe" is to have lost out to his rival for response and patronage from the newly crowned Henry VIII. Such an allusion complements the laments at the opening of the *Conforte*, where Hawes notes how positions such as historiographer and laureate have been denied him, and in turn, where his status as an ex-groom places him as the odd man out in the first years of Henry VIII's reign.

De Worde's participation in these literary rivalries and self-promotions is of a piece with his long-standing commitment to Hawes's work and literary reputation. Hawes and de Worde had early on established a distinctive, and perhaps, unique relationship of poet and printer.[96] De Worde was Hawes's sole publisher, printing all of the poet's works from the *Pastime of Pleasure* through the *Conforte of Louers*. He reprinted several of the poems throughout his lifetime, and even after Hawes's death sometime in the late 1520s, he continued to print works (such as Thomas Feylde's *Louer and a Jay*) and employ editors and correctors (such as Robert Copeland) who would sustain Hawes's reputation.[97] De Worde's incorporation of Skeltonic lines in his woodcut must thus constitute a kind of in-joke for the knowing early Tudor reader. As the words that introduce the *Conforte of Louers*, they would provide a precise textual analogy to Hawes's own competitive response to Skelton at the poem's end. They make the printed volume of the *Conforte* not just a medium of poetic transmission, but a cultural artifact itself, one whose meaning takes shape within the climate of authorial self-definition and courtier competition that is the defining quality of the early Tudor literary system.

If de Worde's woodcut has a precise place in the *Conforte of Louers*, it may signal a more complex and more general set of literary relationships in the other volumes where it appears. The picture with the Skeltonic lines appears as the frontispiece to the *IIII Leues of a Truelove*, a poem that has seldom been discussed as part of the printer's canon and that – in its relations both to its earlier fourteenth-century sources and its later sixteenth-century dissemination – may stand at the nexus of medieval literary convention and early Tudor critical response.[98] Indeed, one may well question why de Worde had published such a poem in the first place. On the one hand, its content appears all too familiar: the narrator enters a beautiful orchard on "a mornyng of may" (Ai r; 1); he hears the laments of a young woman ("I was ware of a may that made mornynge," Ai r; 7); and then the advisory lecture of a turtle-dove sitting on a nearby tree ("Then spake the turtyll on a tre with care," Ai r; 22–23). He learns, in the course of that lecture, about the Christological meanings of the four leaves of the truelove herb and, as a consequence, about the nature of the moral life and the true meaning of the Passion. On the other hand, the *IIII Leues* seems out of place in its contemporary literary setting: it was unusual for de Worde to reprint Northern alliterative poetry for his London readership;[99] and the poem itself, for all its resonances to the religious allegory of the *quatrefolium amoris* and the traditions of medieval preaching, has in fact little to do with the more popular associations of the truelove as an item of exchange in the secular relationships of love – associations that, in fact, fill a good deal of late medieval and early Renaissance English verse.[100]

The meaning of de Worde's frontispiece needs to be sought among these paradoxes. For while it has no resonance to the doctrinal allegorics of the poem's narrative, it speaks directly to the commonplaces of truelove verse and, in turn, to the commercial motives of capturing the imagination of this volume's potential reader. As a token in the encounters of desire, the truelove figures prominently in literature stretching from fabliau bawdry – the effete Absolon of Chaucer's *Miller's Tale* bears a "trewe-love" under his tongue[101] – to courtly erotics. It is a central image for *Sir Gawain and the Green Knight*, appearing on the knight's embroidered clothing,[102] and in several sixteenth-century texts the truelove appears as both the plant with its four leaves and as wrought objects fashioned in imitation of the *quatrefolium*.[103] Such objects often took the form of brooches, necklaces, and rings, and in the *Pastime of Pleasure* La Belle Pucelle creates a gift out of the truelove plant itself.

> She maketh a garlonde / that is veraye shene
> With trueloues / wrought in many a coloure
> Replete with swetenes / and dulcet odoure
> And all alone / withouten company
> Amyddes an herber / she sytteth plesaunty.   (lines 1991–95)

The truelove here is both the symbol of love and the component of an artifact. The scene clearly resonates with the opening section of the *IIII Leues of Truelove*, and it is significant that this episode in the *Pastime* is the very moment introduced by the woodcut of the man and woman. For now we see, I think, that what the woman offers to the man in this Hawesean woodcut is not just a ring but, more likely, a truelove gift: a love knot, worked into the shape of the four-leafed herb and presented on a ring of some kind. The meaning of this picture in the *Pastime*, then, concerns the habits of truelove exchange and the details of locale: what the *Quatrefoil / IIII Leues* would describe as the orchard full of bright trees and flowers.

This picture and its captions now address the eye of the reader expecting a poem on the secular truelove.[104] Just such a reader has left us a mark of expectations in the copy of the *IIII Leues* preserved in the Huntington Library. Upside down on the frontispiece, an early owner of this book has written, in a clear but unprofessional early sixteenth-century hand, the following remark: "Thre leues of yo[r] true loves, which is very plesant to the herers & profytable also as you shal p[er]sow no less in the good matter."[105] Aside from the miscounted minims in the poem's title, and aside from the garbled grammar of the inscription's second half, this little bit of marginalia nicely expresses the tastes of the kind of reader de Worde sought to reach. It is a book both pleasant in the hearing and profitable in its matter; a book whose profit is to be pursued, much like the truelove flower itself. It is a poem, in the end, that would have addressed directly some of the most popular images of early sixteenth-century love verse, and with its frontispiece in de Worde's printing, one that would have been associated with the moral allegories and love pursuits of the *Conforte of Louers*, the *Pastime of Pleasure*, and not least *Troilus and Criseyde*. For this, too, is a poem, much like the *Troilus* and the *Conforte*, about amorous betrayal and the transitoriness of worldly goods and desires. Another early reader of the poem has marked out these very issues on its pages, too. In the copy now preserved in the British Library, a bracket appears in the left margin beside the lines, "There is no loue that lasteth aye / Without treason or traye" and the word *traye* is underlined (Aii r; 24). This couplet could well stand as an epigraph for the entire clutch of de Worde's prints, and it returns the reader to the Troilan world evoked by the poem's frontispiece. Such marked lines offer additional evidence for a complex set of relations among the literary history of Chaucer's poem and the literary politics of poetic rivalries. They resonate with the thematics of betrayal among lovers, courtiers, and romance heroes shared among these texts.

And, finally, shared too in *Undo Youre Dore*. To see this poem, now, in the environments of early Tudor literature, politics, and bibliography is to see it not as the late printing of a decadent Middle English romance, but to understand it as a pointed commentary on the politics of courtiership in the first years of Henry VIII's reign. To view its frontispiece would stimulate associations among the books of love and surreption that shared it. The complex visual and textual allusions of these woodcuts offer evidence, not only for de Worde's critical and commercial instincts, but for the climate of reception and interpretation of his volumes. Carol Meale has suggested that the "visually compelling" features of de Worde's editions – their illustrations, layouts, designs, and typefaces – "are revealing about the ways in which the needs, or preferences, of the reader could be satisfied by the printer – perhaps even before they were fully articulated."[106] De Worde's anticipation of his reader's interests, his ability to shape and to respond to the interpretive communities of early Tudor England, may be matched in the fictive world of readers by one of the very sources of his shaping: Jane Scrope. Read against the work of the printer, Jane becomes not only what Susan Schibanoff has illustrated as a figure of the reader, but as an emblem of literary reception itself. Jane may well select pointedly what she wishes to read; but she is also, in Schibanoff's words, "as much the product as the producer of her reading."[107] For the early Tudor readers of de Worde's books, such mutual self-fashioning creates not just an individual response but a climate of literary understanding: an aesthetic of reception that links certain texts and characters together in ways that are only barely visible to the more modern reader.

What makes such historical associations visible is evidence such as de Worde's woodcuts. By the close of the 1510s, when the *Pastime, Troilus, Conforte, IIII Leues,* and *Undo Youre Dore* were all in print (either for the first time or in new editions), the picture of the man, the woman, and the ring would have helped to associate them in thematic, cultural, and literary ways. It would have placed these poems in the frame of a Skeltonic retelling of the *Troilus*, and, as such, would have provided early Tudor readers with keys not just to their contents but their contexts. It offers up a signal that reminds us of fealty and betrayal, of the secrecies of exchange, of rivalries both courtly and amorous, of spying and inspections that, taken together, constitute the Pandaric life in early Tudor England.

"Of that name he is sure / Whyles the world shall dure" (*Phyllyp Sparowe*, lines 722–23). For Henry's Twelfth Night revels of 1516, the name of Pandarus would certainly have resonated with the bawdry of his legacy. From the matrix of diplomatic pimpery, Hawesean anxiety, Skeltonic theatrics, and romance burlesque, we may extract a meaning for the play of "Troilus and Pandar" and, more broadly, a new understanding of the shapes of early Tudor courtliness. In the early years of Henry's reign, courtly performance was structured around problems of inspection and display, theatricalization and voyeurism. In each case, it is the status of the woman's body that is questioned, and in each case, it is the figure of the Pandar (pimp, ambassador, merry companion, or even the King himself) who deploys the ruses of *amicitia* and the dissimulations of diplomacy to gain entry, either literally or figuratively, into the Queen's chamber. The texts I have discussed here refigure the various relations between voyeurism and advice defined by Pandarus for *Troilus and Criseyde*, and they articulate the literary culture in which "Troilus and Pandar" could be performed and understood. At the local level, the text of this lost play may very well have dramatized that distinctive conversation on bawdry and friendship from Book III of Chaucer's poem: a conversation whose key moment stands as an epigraph to my own chapter and whose ambiguities fueled the reception of the poem in the early sixteenth century. But, at the global level, the subject of "Troilus and Pandar" is Henry himself. From the beginning of his reign, the King had already been acting out a play like this one. With his theatrical entries into the Queen's chamber, his disguised joustings, and his use of men such as Compton for surveillance and procurement, Henry was living through the paradigms of the Pandaric. That the Spanish ambassador should frame his story of the King's pimp in a profoundly self-reflective narrative of diplomatic procurement and intrusive deception only heightens our appreciation for the pandarisms of the court. That he should write his King of rivalries and competitions may remind us that the ins and outs of courtly life affected diplomats as well as poets, Carroz and the Friar as well as Hawes and Skelton. Together with the evidence for the reception of the *Troilus*, *La Celestina*, and the popular romance, these writers fill in the contours of a community that was both audience and subject for the King's makers and his "Troilus and Pandar."

3   The King's hand: body politics in the letters of Henry VIII

> For what is a man the better
> For the kynges letter?
> For he wyll tere it asonder!
> Wherat moche I wonder
> Now suche a *hoddy poule*   "simpleton"
> So boldely dare controule
> And so malapertly withstande
> The kynges owne hande,
> And settys nat by it a myte!
> He sayth the kynge doth wryte,
> And writeth he wottith nat what.
>
> (Skelton, *Why Come Ye Nat to Courte?* lines 669–79)

What *man* indeed? The King loathed writing, hated even signing his own name. Unlike his father – who, under the pressure of increasing demands for the royal signature, developed what has been described as a "cursive HR, formed with one long, flowing movement of the pen" – Henry VIII never seemed to bow to clerical pressure.[1] He signed only when he was in the mood, and the volumes of the *Letters and Papers* devoted to his reign are rife with stories of excuses, moments of impatience, or protests of indisposition that got Henry out of the task of writing, reading, or signing official documents.[2] "He sayth," wrote Skelton, ventriloquizing Cardinal Wolsey, "the kynge doth wryte, / And writeth he wottith nat what." Perhaps Henry did not know what was passing under his signature. As the secretariat moved more and more under the aegis of the grooms, as the keeping of the seal itself became entrusted to men such as William Compton and Henry Norris, and as Henry signed in the odd moments between eating or attending mass or (one assumes, since these men *were* grooms of the stool) privy ministrations, it was quite possible that documents passed under his hand of which "he wottith nat what."[3] True, Henry did attend to certain correspondences himself. He did seem, on occasion, to summon the interest to review, correct, and recast certain official proclamations or ambassadorial exchanges in his own hand.[4]

And he did write to Wolsey, at times bypassing his secretary because, as he wrote in July of 1518, there were "things . . . which be so secret that they cause me at this time to write to you myself."[5]

But again, what man? Only in Wolsey's case (and once, late in life, to Cuthbert Tunstall, Bishop of Durham) did Henry personally write to other men.[6] The modes of social converse, textually calibrated through what Lorna Hutson has called "the intimacy of shared reading and writing," seem to have escaped Henry's purview.[7] Rather than acts or tokens of familiarity, letters for Henry were occasions for intrusion, surreption, or violence. Indeed, the very subject of those secret things Henry wrote to his Cardinal was the pregnancy of Katherine of Aragon and the travel restrictions placed on her because of what he calls "her dangerous times."[8] And, a decade later, writing in rebuke to Wolsey over the appointment of a new abbess of Wilton Priory, the King attends repeatedly to the dissemblances of courtiership that impede his relations with the Cardinal. Wolsey, he notes, has sought "to cloak your offence," and borne only "the cloak of kindness," in his dealings with his lord and master. "These things," Henry writes, "bear shrewd appearance," and this language of dissimulation, this throwing off by Henry of the cloaks and feints of faction politics, makes the otherwise familiar language of his affection ("Written with the hand of your loving Sovereign and Friend,") sting with an almost acid irony.[9] Reading these missives, one must see beyond the King's own cloak of amicitial rhetoric to the only barely suppressed power of his anger.[10] In the satiric verse of the decade, such power turns to violence in the Cardinal's hands. Wolsey tears up the correspondence that displeases him, withstands, as Skelton says, "the kinges owne hand." The violence of the letter that emerged between the two men in the 1520s is again the subject of another anti-Wolsey satire (largely influenced by Skelton's work), printed in 1528 and titled *Rede Me and Be Nott Wrothe.*

> His power he doth so extende
> That the kyngis letters to rende
> He will not forbeare in his rage.[11]

The stories of the King's hand, whether they be phrased in the official euphemisms of the secretary or the subversive satires of the critic, are stories of isolation, violence, and disdain. We are far from the world of epistolary bonding limned in Holbein's portraits of the 1520s, where Erasmus, More, and Gilles appear as readers and writers of letters that, in Lisa Jardine's words, demonstrate "the compelling yet illusory ability of graphic representation to capture the individual."[12] The letter in the sitter's hands, notes Jardine paraphrasing More, "identifies the sitter more securely than his physical traits . . . The sender of the letter is only 'plain' for someone who can recognize the handwriting."[13] At the center of the great humanist friendships lie these recognitions. Books are inscribed and signed, letters are passed among their readers before publication, printed volumes are annotated by the hands of favored readers. Hands make the man, whether they be figured in the portraits, epistolae, or personal seals and tokens that authenticate the writer as a man of letters.

For Henry VIII, the intimacies of the letter were not to be the purview of other men. As far as we can tell, the only sustained correspondence in the King's own hand was the series of letters (seventeen of which survive) written to the woman who would become his second Queen, Anne Boleyn.[14] Written during the years 1527 to 1529, these letters remain the most famous illicit correspondence of early sixteenth-century life. In their acute shifts from deftly erotic French to bluntly corporeal English, they offer a kingly twist on the traditions of the post-medieval verse epistle and the lessons of Erasmian post-classical *dictamen*. They show the King as lover, author, ruler, killer; reveal him as a reader of contemporary English poetry; and display a range of verbal feints, puns, and wordplays that rival those of his early tutors, John Skelton and Bernard André. They are unique, yet emblematic, as revealing of the writer and the time as is Carroz's epistle to his king. And yet, like that diplomatic missive, they are fraught with fears of interception. Illicit texts, they were illicitly read, perhaps stolen by the Papal embassy, and known to groups as diverse as the French ambassadors and the London gentry.

It is their status as transmitted, intercepted documents that grants these letters a place in my history of the Pandaric. As texts borne between two lovers, they emblemize, together with the gifts that occasionally accompanied them, Henry's participation in a Troilan scene perhaps not too far different from the one he witnessed at the Twelfth Night revels a decade before. But if "Troilus and Pandar" figured forth the public feints of courtiership, it is *Troilus and Criseyde* that writes the script for private love. The King's letters are shot through with the shards of late medieval Chauceriana: phrases, idioms, allusions, and wordplays that place his letters in a literary trajectory traceable from the late medieval lyrics copied into manuscript anthologies to the Petrarchan sonnets of Sir Thomas Wyatt. If Henry, in some sense, saw himself as Troilus to Anne Boleyn's Criseyde, it was not only as the suppliant letter writer of Book II of Chaucer's poem, but as the betrayed epistolarist at the close of Book V. And yet, this Henry/Troilus outlives his betraying lover to write what he called his own "tragedy" of their affair – a tragedy that lives on not in any surviving example of his writing, but in a courtly anecdote, another story of the King's hand.

Henry's correspondence also has a place in my narrative for the way in which it transforms the corporeal poetics of the letter central to the Chaucerian tradition. His preoccupations with the body stand in a line of direct influence from the Ovidian narrators of love treatises to Pandarus himself. Their instructions that lovers write in their own hands, that they mark their missives with the fluid impress of the body (be it from wet tears or moist lips), and that they personally sign and seal it up, all make the letter into something of a body. Stories of lover's letters from the *Metamorphoses*, the *Amores*, and the *Heroides* are distilled into the early scenes of epistolary composition in *Troilus and Criseyde*, and some of their details will resurface in Henry's letters to Anne.[15] "Ne scryvenyssh or craftyly thow it write," Pandarus counsels Troilus (II.1026): avoid the mannerisms, indeed, the very look of the professional scribe. If I were in your place, he announces, "I wolde outrely / Of myn owen hond write hire right now / A lettre" (II.1004–6). Bypass the conventions of formal correspondence; eschew the scrivener, use your own hand, and, even, "Biblotte it with thi teris ek a lite" (II. 1027). In these instructions, the letter and body stand as one, as both mark out the contours of the writer's power. Letters construct a subjectivity of the corporeal, and the love letter in particular always takes as its subject the human body, whether it be the body of the writer or the subject of his gaze. And, if that writing is successful, the response will come in kind. "I hope," Pandarus urged the anxious Troilus, "of it to brynge answere anon / Of hire hond" (II.1054–55).

But if Henry seems to eschew the tropes of *amicitia* for the those of *amor*, and if his letters seem, at first glance, to fit into the framework of a Troilan epistolography, his correspondence with Anne also subverts many of these first impressions. Henry does deploy the traditions of epistolary friendship, and he does evidence a profound awareness of the deeply ambiguous language of male writing. Letters are loving things, and Lisa Jardine sensitively unravels the language of love in letters between men. Discussing the representations of the written text in Quentin Metsys's diptych of Erasmus and Peter Gilles, she brings out what she calls the "bodily" and "textual trace" of friendship in letters between friends. She quotes and translates, too, Thomas More's poem on the portraits:

The Painting Speaks

I represent Erasmus and Gilles as close friends as once were Castor and Pollux. More, bound to them by as great a love as any man could entertain for his own self, grieves at his physical separation from them. So the measure they took, in response to the yearnings of the absent friend, was that loving letters should make their souls present to him, and I [the painting] their bodies.[16]

The classicizing vision of male friendship in this poem loca[...] the desires of the friend. There is a sense here (not express[...] reading of the text) of the possibilities of deep affection[...] almost (I stress almost) a physical relationship.[17] Erasm[...] declared that "A friend is one soul in two bodies," and t[...] pictorial presentation of Erasmus and Gilles, together [...] reference to the letters making present the two men's "soul[...] [s]uggests that the diptych visually realizes this maxim (ultimately drawn, in fact, from Cicero and Pythagoras).[18] The imagery of "loving letters," and the grief at physical separation may resonate, too, with Erasmus's own vivid expressions in his letters to a young protégé, Servatius Rogerus. "Since we are seldom permitted to talk face to face," he wrote upon receiving one of Servatus's letters, "your letter is my consolation; it brings me back to you when I am absent, and joins me with my friend though he be away."[19]

Henry takes this profoundly corporealized imagery of epistolary friendship and recasts it to articulate a powerful, and at times violent, love for Anne. Crucial to the rhetoric of his epistolary erotics is the way he places Anne not in relationship to other women but to other men. He defines her political and personal role with reference to minion service and male counsel. Anne is invited to share the world of the Privy Chamber, of grooms to the royal body, of secretaries, ministers, and servants all of whom are men. One may well claim that Henry is enacting the transference of a generic association devised by Erasmus himself. Letters of friendship are defined, in *De conscribendis epistolis*, as "letters exchanged between young men, boon companions, and lovers."[20] To read the letters of the King is, in a way, to seek the place of the third category in a world governed by the first two.

Admitting Anne into the chambers of male service or male friendship brings to mind again Erasmus's maxim on the theatrics of the letter. Henry's letters are, to a large degree, whispered in corners, and a close reading of their rhetoric – and of the cultural artifacts that surround them – demonstrates how the King makes literal and physical Erasmus's simile. To speak *cum amiculo in angulo* is to withdraw to a precise physical locus. Epistolary intimacy takes form in what was fast becoming a uniquely private and domestic space. There is an architecture to the intimate in early Tudor England, a housing of the writing, reading self in the small rooms of mental concentration. The early sixteenth-century semantic shifts in such words as "study," "chamber," and even "hand," reveal a new preoccupation with enclosure and control.[21] The very structures of Henrician administration concerned themselves with this enchamberment of power. Henry VII had already gestured towards this pattern of enchamberment by separating the household apartments devoted to sleeping, receiving, and writing.[22] His son extended these developments in personal administration. Nonesuch Palace, begun in 1539, replaced the structures of public rooms with intricate arrangements of small chambers surrounding the King's private apartment.[23] In words that vivify Erasmus's image of friends whispering in corners, it was said that at Nonesuch, "sundry noblemen, gentlemen and others, doe much delight and use to dyne in corners and secret places, not repairing to the king's chamber nor hall, nor to the head officers of the household when the hall is not kept."[24] The theater of Henrician power is now played out not on the stages of the great, but in the corners of the counselors. Friendship finds its enactment less in the intrusions of a young Henry and his grooms, than in the secret machinations of the chamber and the writing desk.

The correspondence with Anne Boleyn, long read for its supposed sincerity of feeling and the vigor of its royal desire, is a study in this intimate performativity of kingship.[25] For Henry, it is not so much the rhetorical feignings of the lover that preoccupy him as it is a kind of dressing and undressing of the body that the letters help perform. These are texts centrally about the human hand: as comforter or killer, as marker of gender and power, as recipient and maker. The hand stands as a personal extension of the body, the means by which Henry makes present to the absent reader kingly form and royal claim. It is in many ways what his missives are about. More than just the means by which he writes, the King's hand is the subject of the text and subject to the will. It displaces the text of love on to the body of the King, the body of the reader, or the body of the gift (be it a mute picture or dead animal) accompanying the epistle.

Henry VIII's letters are essays in the erotics of the hand. They translate the tropes of love into expressions of royal power, and in the process, construct an epistolary identity for the King and a social identity for his beloved. Many of these letters are preoccupied with naming and re-naming: Henry as lover, servant, scribe, and secretary; Anne as beloved, mistress, and potential Queen. They also are preoccupied with bodies: with their health, their beauty, and their change. The body's wholeness is in constant threat from disease or dismemberment, and throughout Henry's texts there lies a governing tension between the need for whole-ness and the desire to dismember. More than metonymies for love or power, body parts are almost fetishes of force, as in the now-famous colloquial English letter where the King breaks down Anne's body into the arms that hold him and the "dukkys" (breasts) he longs to "cusse."

Before exploring in detail some of these strategies of manual erotics, it is necessary to review some of the conundrums that surround the correspondence. The first point is that no one really knows the precise order in which the letters were written. They are not dated, nor are they (except occasionally) fitted to specific events in the history of court or political life. It is generally assumed that, of the seventeen surviving letters from the King, the nine French ones were written first; that the correspondence transpired from sometime in the late spring of 1527 to the fall of 1528; and that the shift from French to English signals either a new level of intimacy with the future Queen or a relaxing of security precautions after Henry's love for Anne became public in the summer of 1528.[26] The letters are now preserved in the Vatican Library, most likely because they were stolen from Anne (either from her rooms at Hever Castle or from her London apartments) and smuggled to Rome by someone wishing to present the Pope with evidence of Henry's misbehavior during his divorce proceedings with Katherine of Aragon. Their interception was immediately known, and both Henry and his French ambassador were anxious over the publicity resulting from their possible dissemination. But, as with the dating and the order of the letters themselves, we have no sure evidence about their interception and their theft – although at this chapter's close I argue that their interception (or, at the very least, rumors of their existence) influenced a strain of courtly poetry inscribed into manuscript anthologies of the 1530s.[27]

Second, it is important to remember that Henry's aversion to writing speaks not just of personal dislike or administrative reorganization but of literary subjectivity as well. The early modern construction of such a subjectivity finds evidence in Henry's letters to Anne, and in particular, in the unique signature with which he closed them. Only in these texts does he sign himself "H Rx." Elsewhere, his signature is uniformly "Henry R." Even in a handwritten coda to a letter to his then-wife, Katherine Parr, written towards the end of his life, he closes, "Written with the hand of your loving husband, Henry R."[28] Nearly three decades earlier, in the most personal of correspondences to Wolsey, he is "Henry R."[29] Indeed, if there is one constant in the King's reign and his writing it is his signature. "Throughout his life," Muriel St.Clare Byrne writes, it "remains as uniform and constant as the rest of his handwriting . . . Whatever the size of the writing, whatever the nature of the pen used, the constancy and conformity of Henry's signature is as remarkable and as characteristic of the man as is the constancy of his purpose."[30]

The King's unique signature in the letters to Anne thus represents something apart from the political identity formed by the "Henry R" of other correspondence (though I see it not through Byrne's admittedly romanticizing lens that reads it as the mark "kept for the woman he loved").[31] Rather, I see it as an issue in the formation of an authorial subject. "What is 'personal'," Jonathan Goldberg notes, "has to do with the passage of the signature." But the meaning of that signature – that is, the construction of the "personal" – emerges only in the system of named signifying of the early modern period. "The individual is authenticated within a system in which he copies himself within the simulative order of divided practices of writing," Goldberg notes in a Derridean vein.[32] Writing on the literary culture of the Wyatt circle, Stephen Merriam Foley makes a corollary observation that the writing subject emerges not out of the physical presence of the author but out of the displacement of that presence "onto the social processes that authenticate his sign, among them the emergence of human letters as a cultural field in the elite culture of early Tudor England."[33]

When Henry breaks with personal habit and institutional practice he establishes himself as a writing subject. Nearly all of the letters to Anne close with the avowal that they are written in the King's own hand. "Written by the hand of the secretary who in heart, body, and will is your loyal and most assured servant" (Ridley, *Love Letters*, V), is a characteristic final line – characteristic, not just in that Henry avers that the hand is his, but that in the very act of writing he becomes no longer King but secretary (in the French, *secretere*) and servant (*serviteur*). These are the tropes of love transformed into the ministrations of the courtier and diplomat. They give voice not to Henry as the King and master, but as servant and subject. These are, then, acts of what I would call figured intimacy: role-playings of a distinctively Erasmian type that expose an inherent paradox of Henrician power. In one sense, by bypassing the superstructure of official secretarial dissemination, Henry makes the letters truly personal. His acts of writing are thus acts of self-authentication: displays of individuation that, to paraphrase Foley, center not on the presence of the writer but on the "social processes that authenticate his sign." The King's signs are those emblems of identity that mark the makings of the hand: a miniature portrait, a killed beast, and the signatures themselves, especially those signatures that yoke the initials of the man and woman into a symbolic corporealization (for example, the letters HR and AB inscribed into a crudely drawn heart). But in another sense, Henry is not writing the self but scripting a performance. By adopting the name of secretary, he takes on the mask of servitude. By ventriloquizing the language of love, he appropriates the stance of the male lover conjured out of the clay of post-Chaucerian lyric, minion politics, and homosocial play. This is, in short, another of the King's great roles, and as in all of them, the force of kingship lies for Henry in the final unmasking of the boon impersonator to reveal the King manipulating (in the root senses of the word) the subjects of his hand.

The kynges letter

In what has long been taken to be the first of the letters to Anne, Henry introduces the governing corporeal trope of the whole correspondence.[34] "I and my heart put ourselves in your hands" ("moy et mon ceur se mestet en vous mains"), he begins, and he closes: "This by the hand of your loyal servant and friend" ("C'est de la main de vostre loyall serviteur et amy," Ridley, *Love Letters*, I; Stemmler, *Die Liebesbriefe*, V). The hand holds both the heart and its writer, and the framing of this first epistle makes it clear that what is central to the Henrician project is the making of identity and the representation of the forms of power.

. . . et voiant que personellement ni puis estre en vostre presens, chose le plus appartiant a cella qui m'est possible, au presant je vous envoye, c'est a dire: ma picture myse en braselette a toute la device que deia savés, me souhaitant en leure plase, quant Ill vous pleroit.

[. . . seeing that I cannot be present in person with you, I send you the nearest thing to that possible, that is my picture set in bracelets, with the whole device which you know already, wishing myself in their place, when it shall please you.]

Henry asks that his picture replace his lived presence, a conventional enough wish. A letter's depth of feeling brings writer and recipient into a kind of physical embrace. As in the missives of the More–Erasmus circle, letters become the vehicle for grief or pain at absence. Loving letters, as in the Metsys diptych, bring friends together, much as the painting restores the bodies to proximity. Such missives are the testament of feeling, and Henry's letter draws on the lexicon of the epistolary emotions: affection (*affection*); pain (*painne*); great pity (*grande pitié*); intolerable suffering ("que par force faute que je suffre, il m'est presque intollerable"). Henry has hope not simply of Anne's "unchangeable affection," in Ridley's translation, but of her "indissoluble affection vers moy" – an affection that is indissoluble, one that will not dissolve the bonds of amity he seeks to establish in this letter. The written text, and the bracelet that it accompanies, are bonds: verbal and physical links that articulate and represent the hope for an affection that will not dissolve. Henry's language of emotion and physicality gives voice to what

Erasmus would call "real feelings," the essential quality of letters. "If letters lack real feelings," Erasmus wrote to Beatus Rhenanus in a letter which prefaces the 1521 edition of his *Epistolae ad diuersos*, "and fail to represent the very life itself of a person, they do not deserve the name of letters."[35] In these terms, Henry's letter brings the man and woman into something of a surrogate physicality, and it does so in a way that not only defines the nature of their relationship but defines the very medium of their communication. For if this is in fact the inaugural missive of their correspondence, what it inaugurates is the very idea of letter-writing. It grants the addressee a specificity of title (*mestres et amye*); deploys a vocabulary of intense feeling; and, in the process, earns what Erasmus would call the name of letters.

If this letter carefully deploys the inherited conventions of friendship, it also invokes the contemporary innovation of diplomacy. Henry's picture is far less important than the place it bears and the handwritten text that sends it. It is, significantly, a picture in a bracelet, and this moment of Henrician gift-giving stands as an example of the new politics of ornament in the late 1520s. What Henry offers Anne is a miniature, a limned gift of the kind that soon would become central to the practices of early Tudor self-defining. The English miniatures generated in response to Flemish and Burgundian courtly practice were, in Stephen Foley's words, "a typical locus for the operative confusion of personal and political power."[36] These function as markers of official identity and social role. They distill the "character" of the sitter into what Foley calls "official iconological status markers," and in the process, they initiate the very means of recognition for the members of the court.[37] Henry's gift of the bracelet, and his attentions to his own hand and handwriting, share in the makings of a new form of political and personal representation, and it is worth pausing briefly to detail some of these influences on what would become his personal symbolism.

Henry's first miniaturist, Lucas Hornebolte, had begun to limn his tiny portraits in the middle of the 1520s.[38] By 1525, he was receiving a regular annuity from Henry, and in 1531 he is referred to in the records as the King's Painter. These miniatures, it has recently been argued, were commissioned by the King in response to a gift from Madame d'Alençon, François I's sister, in the late autumn of 1526. Inviting Henry to intercede in a familial diplomatic tension with the Emperor, the French Princess sent the English King two elaborately crafted lockets, one containing a picture of François I, the other a double portrait of his two sons, held as prisoners in Spain. The gift, by all accounts, caused a sensation at the English court, and Roy Strong, in a recent reassessment of this moment in ornamental diplomacy, argues that it prompted Henry to recruit

Hornebolte as his miniaturist. By the summer of 1527, Henry could send portraits of himself and his daughter, Mary, to François I, in what Strong believes to be a direct response to the French royal family's initial gift. And it is during this same summer that the King begins his correspondence with Anne Boleyn and presents her, in the letter, with the miniature-containing bracelet.

This gift, then, has a precise meaning in the constructions of Henrician artistic diplomacy during the latter 1520s. Within the structure of political gift-giving, Anne holds the same place as the members of the French royal family – not just because the King had found a new means of engaging in the arts of negotiation and wished to display it, but because Henry clearly thought of such limned ornaments as distinctively French. Certainly, Hornebolte himself had found his models in the miniatures of François I's court painter, Jean Clouet, and the idea of making Hornebolte King's Painter may well have been Henry's emulation of French courtly practice. Indeed, Henry's own writing desk is an assembly of such francophilic miniatures. It is an elaborately decorated piece of artifice, rich with the iconography of mythological desire and classical imperialism. That it still offers the symbolic union of the King and Katherine of Aragon – the H and K, the pomegranate and the sheaf, the portrayal of Mars and Venus – dates this work before 1529, and Strong would attribute it to Hornebolte himself.[39] If so, it signals not just an identifiable origin for this object, but also a notion of what private royal writing is: itself an act of miniaturism, a reproduction by the King's own hand of the hand-limned depictions of character and power by his painter. To write in the King's hand on such an object is to play the miniaturized King and place the royal self in the dynamics of ornamentary exchange and pictorial presentation.

Whoever made the writing table, it is clear that by the time Holbein arrived in England for his first stay (1526–27) the idea of courtly miniaturism had come of age, and the representations of the King and his courtiers as creatures of the hand was well established. Hornebolte's miniature of Katherine of Aragon (probably from these very years), showing the Queen's hands dandling a pet marmoset on a chain while proffering it food,[40] anticipates in many ways the finely modeled hands of Holbein's little limnings. Consider that of Margaret Roper with her book (c.1536) or that of the five-year-old Charles Brandon (1541), precociously displaying pen and paper.[41] As Stephen Foley puts it, summarizing this development in manual representation,

[The hands in Holbein's portraits] – clasped, grasping a collar, playing lightly over a book or clutching it, debating, like Henry Wyatt, between the crucifix and the memorandum – provide a technical vocabulary for the representation of social codes and professional traits.[42]

As Lisa Jardine has shown in great detail, the paintings of Erasmus, More, Gilles, and many of the other merchants, scholars, and ambassadors that shaped Anglo-Flemish relations in the 1520s and 30s, all define the character of their sitters in the hands.[43] The figure reading, writing, or manipulating the instruments of his profession (as in the remarkable portrait of Nicholas Kratzer, the King's astronomer, of 1528) sits, for Holbein, absorbed in the manual dexterities of craft.[44] These are professionals as writers, merchants opening letters of correspondence, scholars making books. Look at Cromwell, in the 1532 portrait that stands as the cover illustration to this book, with the foregrounded clasped volume, scissors, pen, and papers of the man charged with procuring information on dissent.[45] Even King Henry's falconer, Robert Cheseman, in a painting of 1533, is a character defined by handlings, as his prominent right hand touches the mottled, hooded bird not so much in an act of calming and stroking, but in something of a manual performance of identity. Cheseman's falcon replaces the letters and books of Holbein's other sitters, as it, in effect, becomes the text through which the falconer displays himself.[46]

Henry's attentions to the hand address directly this constellation of manual representations in the early sixteenth century. His letters to Anne translate social codes of French diplomacy, Holbeinian portraiture, and Erasmian epistolary friendship into performances of personal desire. In short, he transmutes *amicitia* into *amor*, powerfully eroticizing the tradition of handwriting and hand-reading that had centered itself as the public venue for political and scholarly identity. He makes the writing hand the instrument of intimacy, and throughout the letters, signatures and mottoes reify what Henry poses as the linking of the lovers' hands and bodies. In several of them, his initials link themselves with Anne's in crudely drawn hearts.[47] In one, he offers up a motto for them both, written in cipher.[48] These signatures represent the power of Henry's own hand to bring his mistress into the kingly identity. They bind her to the King, and one may well imagine the transgressive power of such signatory acts. Writing in what he claims to be the privacy of isolation, without scribe or secretary, Henry must have penned these letters on his writing desk, an artifact itself embellished with the linked initials of the King and the yet-still Queen Katherine. The little hearts of Henry's letters – with the letters AB set inside, the whole written between the H and Rx of Henry Rex – read like a curiously privatized transgression of the official iconography of the writing desk. And with its many tiny cases, its keyed inner lid, and its inner drawers, the writing desk itself becomes the very emblem of the etymon of "secretary": the bearer of the secret. The *secretaire* that Henry apes is more than just the taker of dictation. It is also the physical chamber, what citations from late Middle English reveal as the "place of privyte or cowncel," the repository of things hidden. Flee, says one text, "into þe secretary of þin herte."[49] Such an idiom may well inform the private writings of a king who would find his illicit lover in what he calls his "racine en coeur," and whose initials would stand in the royal signature not as the H and K of intertwined allegorical politics – as on the outer lid of the writing desk itself – but in the very secretary of his heart.

Anne's status in these cryptograms of love shifts, too, as Henry seeks not just to reinscribe her in his personal iconics but, in essence, to rename her. From the first letter, Henry preoccupies himself with just what to call Anne Boleyn: mistress, friend, lover, or prospective queen. Another letter (Ridley, *Love Letters*, IV; Stemmler, *Die Liebesbriefe*, III) devotes itself to the interpretation of Anne's own missives and, as a consequence, to the interpretation of her social identity. This early text in French essays the arts of epistolary hermeneutics, as it meditates on the meaning of authorial intention and the logic of response. "Th'entente is al," Criseyde had memorably written, "and nat the lettres space" (V.1630), and Henry's own letter expounds on this maxim of epistolography.

En debatant d'apper moy le continu de vous lettres, me suis mis en grande agonye, non shachant command les entendre: ou a mon desavantage, comme en aucunne lieu le munstrés, ou a mon avantayge, comme en des aucunes aultres je les entende; vous suppliant de bien bon ceur me voloire certeffyere expressement vostre intention entiere tochant l'amoure entre nous deux: Car nécessité me contraint de purchasere ceste responce, ayant esté plus que vng anné attaynte du dart d'amours, non estant assuré de faliere ou trover plase en vostre ceur et affection çartynne. Lequel dernyre point m'en a gerdé depuis peu temps en ça de vous point nomere ma mestres, avec ce que, si vous ne me aimés de aultre sorte que d'amoure commune, cest nome ne vous est point appropriee: Car ill denote vng singularité, lequel est bien longné de la commune. Mes si vous plet de faire l'offyce de vngne vray loyal mestres et amye, et de vous donner corps et ceur a moy, qui veus estere et a esté vostre tres loyal serviteure (si par rigeure ne me defendés), je vous promes, que non seullement le nome vous sera du, mais ausi vous pranderay pur ma seulle mestres, en reboutant tretoutes aultres auprès de vous hors de pensé et affection, et de vous sellement servire; vous suppliant me faire entiere responce de ceste ma rude lettre, a quoy et en quoy me puis fiere. Et si ne vous plet de me faire reponse per escripte, assiné moy quelque lieu, la ou je la pourroy avoire de bouce, et je me j troueray de bien bon ceur. Non plus de peur de vous annuyere. Escripte de la main de celluy, qui voulentiers demoureroyte vostre –

H Rx

(Stemmler, *Die Liebesbriefe*, III)

[My turning over in my thoughts the contents of your last letters, I have put myself into a great agony, not knowing how to understand them, whether to my disadvantage, as some passages indicate, or to my advantage, as I interpret other passages. I beseech you now, with all my heart, to let me know your whole intention as to the love between us two; for I must of necessity obtain this answer from you, having been, for more than a year, struck with the dart of love, and not yet sure whether I shall fail, or find a place in your heart and affection; and this last point has prevented me recently from naming you my mistress, which would be inappropriate if you do not love me with more than ordinary affection, as it denotes a special relationship which is far from ordinary. But if it pleases you to play the part of a true, loyal mistress and friend, and to give yourself body and heart to me, who will be, and has been, your most loyal servant (if your rigour does not forbid me), I promise you that not only will you deserve the name, but also that I will take you for my only mistress, casting all others, that are in competition with you, out of my thoughts and affections, and serving only you. I beg you to give an entire answer to this my uncouth letter as to what and on what I may depend. But if it does not please you to answer me in writing, let me know some place where I may have it by word of mouth, and I will go thither with all my heart. No more for fear of annoying you. Written by the hand of him who would willingly remain your

H Rx]
(Ridley, *Love Letters*, IV)

Henry positions himself, first, as reader. How can he understand (*entendre*, *entende*) the text he has received; what are the meanings of its passages (*lieu*); what is the *intention* of the author? Struck by love's arrow, Henry seeks a place (*plase*) in Anne's own heart, and this point (perhaps of the argument as well as of the arrow) introduces the whole question of the appellation of the lover. Anne's status as a mistress is, at least at first, contingent upon something more than ordinary care. It denotes something singular, and here Henry shifts from the reader of a text to something of a lexicographer of love. Denotation is central to his inner argument. For the central question that he asks really is one of lexicography: what do the words *mestres*, *amye*, or *serviteure* denote? Do they define conditions of social and personal identity, or do they suggest something else? Are they essential qualities or are they as names in the *dramatis personae* of love? Let me know some place (*lieu*) where I may have it orally, if not by letter, Henry writes. By this letter's end, Henry and Anne are now no longer writers, readers, and interpreters. They are play-actors in the stagings of desire. Anne is invited not just to write or love, but to "play the part" ("faire l'offyce"), an averral of courtly acting that recalls both Erasmus's announcement that the courtier adopts a persona and, too, Luiz Carroz's avowal to his King, "saber mi parte." And Henry, too, imagines himself now in a new role: the loyal servant who will serve only her. To seek out some place where they may play out these roles, not *per escripte* but *de bouce*, is to recall the literary theatrics of love. He invokes the trysts of Pyramus and Thisbe, the staged meetings of *La Celestina*, and for that matter, the hopes of Troilus and Criseyde, who by the close of Chaucer's poem are exchanging missives about meeting face to face (see *Troilus and Criseyde* V.1424–28, 1583–86).

This is a brilliantly crafted document. Its verbal repetitions – its chiasmi, echoes, interlacements – make it far from the "rude lettre" Henry claims it to is. It moves from reading to writing, from texts to lives, from hands to mouths and back to hands again. Its sense of place shifts from the *lieu* of a written passage, to the *plase* in the heart, the *lieu* of a tryst. It is a letter that verbally reenacts the argument it makes: to bring Anne deep into the fold of Henrician power, to be transformed from a subject of mental *agonye* or verbal disputation to the physical presence of someone who can offer up the word of mouth. What is now written in the King's hand, at the letter's close, is not just the text of the missive but the script of love.

Such literary self-construction has a multitude of sources, and in writing out the subjectivity of love or the renamings of the beloved Henry draws on the traditions of corporeal representation central to the *blazon* poetry of late medieval and early sixteenth-century England. Anne is, like many of her literary counterparts, defined by body parts. She is the hand, the mouth, the heart, and perhaps most famously in one of the English letters, the breasts. Beset by the pains of loneliness and by some pain in his head, Henry imagines himself "comyng toward yow."

me thynkyth my painnys bene halfe relesyd, and allso I am ryght well comfortyd in so muche that my bok makyth substancially for my matter, in lokyng wheroff I have spente above IIII ours thys day, whyche causyd me now to wrytte the schortter letter to yow at thys tyme bycause off summe payne in my hed; wyschyng myselfe (specially an evenyng) in my swethart harmys [i.e., arms], whose prety dukkys I trust shortly to cusse. Wryttyn with the hand off hym that was, is, and shal be yours by hys wyll –

HRx
(Stemmler, *Die Liebesbriefe*, XIV)[50]

Such intimacy is not just a project of the unrestrained Henrician libido. It is a crafted literary ploy, one that displaces onto arms and breasts the comforting of love. And such comfort, of course, is necessary due to the work of the King's hand: now, the hand that writes "my book." This book is Henry's *Glasse of Truthe*, a treatise that assembled theological arguments proving the nullity of his marriage to Katherine of Aragon.[51] But more than that, it is the book of pain itself, an act of writing that demands comfort from the new woman who replaces the old. In what may well be a wild, personalized twist on Hawes's *Conforte of Louers*, Henry shifts the relationships between writing and bodies that characterized that work. "Two thynges me conforte / euer in pryncypall," Hawes wrote: "The fyrst be bokes"; "The second is . . . Lettres for my lady . . . / And lettres for me . . . / Agreynge well / vnto my bokes all" (*Conforte*, lines 281–93). The author Henry, like the author Hawes, beset with physical and emotional pain, seeks out the *conforte* of a lady limned in letters: a lady who, in the case of Henry, takes him from "my book" and sets him in the arms and breasts.[52]

This vision of Anne Boleyn as but arms and "dukkys" makes her heiress to the *blazonerie* of poems such as Hawes's – a creature, to recall Lawrence Kritzman's words, in whose "*blason anatomique* the female body becomes consubstantial with the body of writing."[53] Rhetorical dismemberment "conjures up detached body parts or fetishized objects,"[54] and for the English writers working in the wake of the *blazon* tradition, such parts were invariably arms, or hands, and breasts. In Hawes's *Pastime of Pleasure*, La Belle Pucelle is anatomized into these constituent parts:

> Her pappes rounde / and therto ryght praty
> Her armes sclender / and of goodly body
> Her fyngers small / and therto ryght longe
> Whyte as the mylke with blewe vaynes amonge.   (*Pastime*, lines 3863–66)

Such fascinations with the female form – with what Kritzman calls the "architecture of the breast" – sustain themselves throughout late Middle English poetry. Resonant with Hawes's description are these lines from a late Middle English poem preserved in the manuscript anthology of the early Tudor Staffordshire lawyer, Humphrey Wellys (Bodleian Library MS Rawlinson C.813):

> hur fyngers be bothe large and longe
> with pappes round as any ball
> no thyng me thynke on hur ys wronge
> hur medyll ys both gaunte and smal.   (4.17–20)[55]

Much of the poetry preserved in Wellys's manuscript – compiled during the late 1520s and early 1530s and thus precisely contemporary with Henry VIII's courtship of Anne – echoes the King's epistolary gestures, and we may see its contents as representative of the vernacular sources on which Henry drew. Several of this manuscript's items are centos cobbled together out of the *Pastime of Pleasure* and the *Conforte of Louers*; one is similarly crafted out of nine stanzas of *Troilus and Criseyde*; another is a long excerpt from Skelton's *Why Come Ye Nat To Courte?*; and several refer directly to political and social events of the early 1520s in ways that reveal this compiler's knowledge of the intimacies of Henrician politics and courtly discourse. To read this manuscript (as I do in greater detail at the close of this chapter and throughout the next) is to be struck by the familiarities of its phrasings. Its poems' conventions of the salutation and the signature, the pleas for understanding, the complaints of pain, the excuses for "rude" writing – all recall bits and pieces of Henry's epistolary prose.[56]

The thirteenth item in this manuscript, a cento drawn from stanzas of the *Pastime of Pleasure*, emerges as a font of diction for the King. In this newly constructed poem, Hawes's romance narrative becomes a verse epistle to a distant lover.[57] It deploys the language of the hunt, with the lover's "hart" caught in a net (Wellys 13.2–4) and in a snare (13.44). It refracts the idioms of Chaucerian desire, with its reference to the lover's "hart Roote" (13.70, a term Henry would attempt to translate into the neologism "racine en ceure"[58]). It emphasizes the servitude of the lover and his fascinations with the "priuete" of his mind (13.16–21). It addresses a departed beloved, "gone . . . yn hur owne cuntrey wher she dothe abyde" (13.141–42). It prays that the lady "remembre all þat I wryte vnto you ryght nowe" (13. 155–56). Finally, it anatomizes the beloved's body into the *blazon* of optical desire. Here, a long catalogue of body parts ends with the stanza on the breasts and arms that I had quoted earlier (*Pastime*, lines 3863–66, corresponding to Wellys 13.123–26). But in the following line, Wellys has elided two more of Hawes's stanzas of description to move directly to the central image of the cognitive vocabulary: "Thys yn my mynde . . . I had engrauyd" (13.127).

This is the kind of poetry that stands behind the language of the King. It represents the possibilities of reconstructing amorous epistles out of old familiar narratives, while at the same time organizing the clichés of English verse into a powerful preoccupation with the lover's mind and heart, his privacies and public life, his focus on the body and the hand. This poem not only addresses body parts in fetishized or disembodied form. It makes them texts "engrauyd" in the mind. It places them within the ambiance of amatory writing, in the inscriptive processes that make the delectations of the hand the cuttings into memory.

Tere it asonder!

Perhaps nowhere in Henry's correspondence are these images of bodily dismemberment, remembrance, and inscription brought together with such passion as in the early French letter offering the present of a buck to

Anne. This letter's power has compelled many modern readers to place it among the earliest of Henry's missives. E. W. Ives and Theo Stemmler put it first for its playful deployment of the "conventions of courtly romance."[59] But there is little that is truly conventional about this letter. If anything, it is a text that transforms the conventions of desire into a personal account of masculinized politics and royal power.

Toutefois, ma mestres, qu'il ne vous pleu de souvenir de la promesse, que vous me fites, quant je estoy dernirrement vers vous, c'est a dire de savoire de vous bones novelles, et de savoire responce de ma dernire lettre, nenmains il me semble, qu'il appertient au vray serviteur voiant que autrement il ne peut rien savoir, d'envoiere savoire la salute de sa mestres. Et pur me acquitre de l'office du vray serviteur, je vous envoye cest lettre, vous suppliant de me avertire de vostre prosperité, lequel je prye a dieu qu'el soite ausi long comme je voudroy la mien. Et pur vous faire encorps plus sovant sovenire de moy, je vous envoye per ce porteur vng bouke tué her soire bien terde de ma main, esperant que quant vous en mangerés, il vous sovendra du chaseur. Et ainsi, a fault de espace, je fray fin a ma lettre. Escripte de la main de vostre serviteur, qui bien sovent vous souhait ou lieu de vostre frere –

HRx

(Stemmler, *Die Liebesbriefe*, I)

[Although, my mistress, you have not been pleased to remember the promise which you made me when I was last with you, which was that I should hear good news of you and have an answer to my last letter; yet I think it is fitting for a true servant (since otherwise he can know nothing) to send to inquire about his mistress's welfare; and to acquit myself in the office of a true servant, I send you this letter, begging you to inform me that you are prospering, which I pray God you may continue to do, as I hope I will; and to make you think of me more often, I send you by this bearer a buck killed late last night by my hand, hoping that when you eat it, it will remind you of the hunter; and thus, for lack of space, I will make an end of my letter. Written by the hand of your servant, who often wishes you were in your brother's place.]

(Ridley, *Love Letters*, X)

It is a letter rich with puns and power, a document not only to the King's apparent ardor for his mistress, but a testament to his command of the resources of literary French and his knowing twists on the traditions of the romance hunt. It is in many ways, too, a letter of the body. Explicitly, it makes inquiries into Anne's health, wishing her to stay as well as Henry himself. Implicitly, however, it displaces those inquiries onto a vocabulary of knowledge and ingestion, of understanding and remembering, of servitude and desire. Henry's French plays on the familiar double meaning of the Latin etymon *sapere* for French *savoir* (to know) and *saveur* (to taste), and in the process it works through a remarkable set of twists on words beginning with the morpheme {s + vowel + v}.[60]

First, he writes of a remembrance (*souvenir*), and then a string of references to knowledge (*savoire* / *savoire* / *savoir* / *savoire*) gained by the servant (*serviteur*) of love. Knowledge and remembrance are paired again, when Henry makes his own intention the acceptance of the animal ("plus sovent sovenire de moy"). And when the animal is eaten, it will cause the hunter to be remembered (*sovendra*) – the hunter who remains the servant (*serviteur*) who desires (*sovant*) something of his own. Remembering is knowing, knowing is eating, and eating is embodiment: ". . . et pur vous faire encorps plus sovant sovenire de moy." Finally, Henry's unique French spelling of *encore* as *encorps* etymologically corporealizes remembrance.[61] "Again," is "in the body"; what is done "de ma main" is what one can "mangerés."

These puns and soundplays have an almost Rabelaisian quality about them – a revelry in the resources of a highly artificial language, a consciousness of etymology, a pleasure in riding the knife-edge between courtliness and death.[62] If the King's hand is the instrument of love, it is also a tool of violence. The buck it kills and offers to Anne stands, as the product of the hand, alongside the very letters (proudly written with that hand) as gifts of love. Surely, what is at least in part occurring here is the displacement of the lover's body on to the stricken animal. By denoting himself as the hunter, Henry, of course, makes Anne into the hunted. He makes the very letter she receives not a document of affection but a treatise on violence.

Such violence, too, inheres in the act of writing. As Jonathan Goldberg has illustrated, the associations between knife and quill inform some of the earliest manuals on the art of penmanship.[63] The knife cuts the quill, trims it to make it speak, such that, by the close of the process, the cut quill's sharp edge resembles nothing else but a knife. Goldberg summarizes:

My comparison of the penknife to a butcher's would hardly be an overstatement were the writing surface vellum . . . whose hairy backside as well as imperfections and markings remind the writer of the slaughtered animal upon whose skin he inscribes, repeating (in however displaced a fashion) an act of violence. But, even when paper is the surface, as was more often the case, the pen point frequently is described as if it were a knife . . . in which case the materiality of the page lends itself to a reading that writes the world.[64]

If Henry writes the world, he does so on the multiple bodies of letter, buck, and lover – a wild constellation of corporeal materialities that reflect not only on the King's love of Anne, but on the literary and political landscapes in which that love may be inscribed.

That literary landscape is the hunt of love, the paradigm of medieval and Renaissance amatory narrative that displaces the violence of the kill

onto the chase of the bedchamber.[65] Its familiarity to Henrician readerships would have been shaped by the traditions of Old French romance,
by English versions of the Gawain story, and furthermore, by the
Petrarchan idioms most famously translated into English in Sir Thomas
Wyatt's "Whoso list to hunt." This poem has long been located in the
historical moment of Henry's courtship of Anne, a courtship that
displaces Wyatt as her (supposed) lover and that makes the sonnet's
speaking subject the rejected poet.[66] Its presumed topical allegory makes
Anne the hunted and the King the hunter/Caesar. Its acknowledged
literary referent, Petrarch's "Una candida cerva sopra l'herba," is
similarly figured in a displacement of power and authority: a transferal of
sonneteering subjectivity from the pursuing lover to what Jonathan
Crewe calls the "envious loser," and in turn, a transformation of the
Italian of Petrarch's version of the motto into the Latin of explicit
biblical citation. This is, as many critics have defined it, a poem that sets
the terms for early Renaissance male subjectivity, one that defines the
literary history and the psychological dynamics of the lyric voice in
English.[67]

And yet, by reading it against Henry's French letter, Wyatt's sonnet
also becomes something of an essay in the iconographies of kingship.

> Whoso list to hunt, I know where is an hind,
> But as for me, helas, I may no more.
> The vain travail hath wearied me so sore,
> I am of them that farthest cometh behind.
> Yet may I by no means my wearied mind
> Draw from the deer, but as she fleeth afore
> Fainting I follow. I leave off therefore
> Sithens in a net I seek to hold the wind.
> Who list her hunt, I put him out of doubt,
> As well as I may spend his time in vain.
> And graven with diamonds in letters plain
> There is written her fair neck round about:
> '*Noli me tangere* for Caesar's I am,
> And wild for to hold though I seem tame.'
>
> (Rebholz, *The Complete Poems*, XI)[68]

Like Henry's letter, this too is a souvenir of love. Like the King's French,
Wyatt's English plays on the multiple associations of its key vocabulary.
And yet, of course, the differences are striking. While Henry's letter is a
testament to royal impatience, Wyatt's poem is a disquisition on courtier
impotence. Time is of the essence for the King: does Anne remember, will
she write back, will she think of him more often, will she accept the buck
killed late the previous night? The King concludes, in the end, "a fault de

espace." The speaker of the sonnet, however, languishes in the afterwards: he is continuously weary, coming behind, possessed by the vanity
of the pursuit. Wyatt's is time spent in vain, and when we reach the
sonnet's final lines the lover's necklace stands as a sad counterpoint to
the inscribed and lettered gifts the King had sent to Anne. This is a
souvenir "graven . . . in letters plain," not the cryptic or symbolic gifts of
the King's letters. The bracelet of the first French missive, or the cryptic
sign-off of another of the early French texts (possibly decipherable as a
necklace motto reading the names of both Henry and his love), or the
buck itself – these are the icons of royal power, textualized objects that
functioned in Henry's amorous diplomacy of ornament. Artifacts of rich
surfaces, they have but one clear meaning in the logic of Henrician gift-
giving. By contrast, there is nothing "plain" about *Noli me tangere*. It is a
complex and ambiguous inscription, one whose meaning goes beyond
biblical allusion, classical reference, or Petrarchan subtext to embrace
Henry's manual iconography: the power of the touch to heal or harm,
the vision of a loving hand fresh from the bloody kill and rushing to the
writing table.

Wyatt's poem and the King's letter also function within a complex of
Christological images signaled by the Latin phrase. To render unto
Caesar what is Caesar's defines the desired creature as the subject of the
imperial will. But Henry's version of the literary hunt further ambiguates
its meaning. By offering an animal to be ingested, and by claiming that to
eat is to remember him, Henry effectively equates himself not just with
Caesar but with Christ. Here, Anne is not the hunted in an allegory of
love, but the celebrant in an allegory of the Eucharist. Henry is not the
hunter/Caesar but the seemingly self-sacrificing servant who offers a
surrogate body for ingestion. He is, in short, both Caesar and Christ.
There is, then, nothing that is not his, nothing that does not belong either
to *rex* secular or sacred.[69]

If Henry absorbs Christ and Caesar into the symbolism of his gift –
that is, if he conflates the religious and the political – he also conflates the
political with the libidinous. Anne now replaces not another woman but
her brother, George, in the bodily ambiance of royal power. For George
Boleyn was, himself, a member of that minion circle who had a unique
and privileged access to the King's private body. He was the King's page
as a young man, and after over a decade of service Henry appointed him
Esquire of the Body on 26 September, 1528, a position that granted him
unique access to the King's person.[70] As defined in the *Liber Niger* (the
manual of household management that structured royal organization
from the time of Edward IV through Henry VIII), the job of Esquire of
the Body was to be "attendant upon the king's person, to array and

unray him, and to watch day and night." The Esquire was to be ready at
all times, day or night, and as the *Liber Niger* states, "no man else to set
hands on the king."[71]

Anne's brother thus represents the political intimacy shared by the
members of the Privy Chamber, and, in Henry's letter, Anne replaces
George in the most private and intimate of bodily ministrations. In this
desire, Henry signals an important shift in the theatrics of intimacy. He
articulates a move away from the homosociality of the Privy Chamber
and towards a privatized heterosexuality of conjugal relations. Henry, in
essence, invites Anne into the group male world of the Privy Chamber.
But in so doing, he must banish all others (represented by her brother
George) and make now a chamber shared by just the one. By renaming
himself servant to the woman, Henry also renames her, in essence, not as
lover or as Queen (not yet anyway) but as page to the royal body –
member of the Privy Chamber, potential Esquire of the Body, one who is
uniquely empowered to "set hands on the king."

What is significant about this letter, and what is significant about
Anne's comparative status in all the letters, is that she is always defined
in relationship to other men. There are no other women in the letters, no
reflections on the King's marriage, his purported affairs, his appetites or
appreciation of the female form. These letters are full of men: the bearers
of the documents, the named and unnamed counselors with whom the
King consults, the friends with whom he consorts. In a French letter
datable to late June 1528 (Ridley, *Love Letters*, III; Stemmler, *Die
Liebesbriefe*, IX) he defines Anne's susceptibility to the sweating sickness
by listing the men who had been taken ill: "for when we were at
Waltham, two ushers, two grooms of the Privy Chamber (*deux verles de
chamber*), your brother and Mr Treasurer fell ill." And in an English
letter of the next month (Ridley, *Love Letters*, XIII; Stemmler, *Die
Liebesbriefe*, XI), he lists the men who fell from the sweat and refers to
his Lord Cardinal, that is Wolsey, in "the matter of Wilton." This is, in
fact, the only letter that refers to other women, in this case, to the Abbess
of Wilton and the conflict between Wolsey and the King concerning her
successor. And yet here, the context is not one of women in the court of
love but women in the ruses of a power politics that centered on the
sexual transgressions of the candidates for Wilton's successor.[72]

It is remarkable here to compare the measured tone and almost
patronizing quality of this epistle with the elaborate feints and protestations of two of the letters in Henry's hand to Cardinal Wolsey, written at
the same time. Those texts – the subtle rebukes that refer to Wolsey's
cloaking and dissimulation – are full of all the rhetoric of male affection.
Henry signals again and again "the great affection and love I bear you";

he remarks on the "rude, yet loving letter" he must send, a letter in which
there remains "no spark of displeasure towards you in my heart." And
he concludes both letters with the avowal that they are "written in the
hand" of a sovereign and friend who is "loving."[73] For Anne, the King
closes: "writtyn with the hand de vostre seulle" (Stemmler, *Die Liebesbriefe*, XI; Ridley, *Love Letters*, XIII). If Wolsey gets the full court
treatment of epistolary *amicitia* and personal affection, Anne gets the
signature in French. And when Wolsey gets his own letter from Anne
(sometime in the summer of 1528), he gets it with a postscript by the
King himself that announces, "The writer of this letter would not cease
till she had caused me likewise to set to my hand."[74]

My point here is that Anne is measured against men, that her place in
the King's circle is as replacement for the minion friends and courtier
servants who share in the unique access to his body and his counsel.
Henry invites Anne to share in the theater of privy politics, to play a role
in the drama of the chamber, and we may reread his French letter of the
summer of 1527 in this political light. For now, when he invites her to
"play the part of a true, loyal mistress and friend," he is providing for
her something of a role in the stage-play of courtiership. Anne is invited
to "faire l'offyce," as if the appellation "mestres et amye" were something of a designated office on a par with page, groom, or esquire.
Henry's letters, here and in the letter on the buck, are letters about roles
and offices, letters that meditate upon the line between the public and the
private, the official and the personal. That line is often blurred, and when
Henry promises, in this same letter, to cast "all others, that are in
competition with you, out of my thoughts and affection" ("hors de pensé
et affection"), he may contribute to a blurring among lines of gender
roles, as well. Are these others merely other mistresses, or are they others
more generally, those in competition for the King's thoughts and
affection? Are they, in short, men like Wolsey who had been the very
subject of epistolary "affection" in the King's own hand; does Anne's
status as friend (*amye*) challenge the King's status as sovereign and
friend in his letters to other men?

And what about the hand? Anne stands here in the circle of those men
who were creatures of the hand, men who, in Edward Hall's words,
"were so familier and homely with hym, and plaied suche light touches
with hym, that they forgat themselves."[75] Jonathan Goldberg has made
much of this remark, and he has apposed it to Henry's closing request
that Anne replace her brother in order to query the boundaries between
the homosocial and the homosexual in Henry's court and to raise up the
specter of a sodomitical George Boleyn.[76] I think, however, Henry's
rhetoric is more about the problematics of the role than the specifics of

sex. What the minions "forgat" was, I argued in my previous chapter, the role of companion, friend, advisor. Hall's critique of the minions is, as I suggested, a critique of the performativity of service, one that needs to be read in the contexts of Erasmus's notions of the personae of courtiership and the metatheatrics of Skelton's *Magnyfycence*. Here, I suggest that Henry has rewritten the script of service, replacing the performances of companions, with their "light touches," with the "office" of Anne Boleyn. It is a script full of the markings of the stage, a script concerned essentially with proper place and stance. "[Wishing] you were in your brother's place [*lieu*]"; "wishing myself in their [i.e., the bracelets'] place [*plase*]"; to "find a place [*plase*] in your heart." This is as much a vocabulary of stagecraft as it is a language of the body. It concerns itself with placement, stance, and office – with the roles of service and the service of the role. In each, the placement of the hand functions in an elaborate theatrics of intimacy: a set of gestures that defines relationships of power in terms of the intimacies of the privy chamber and the bedroom.

And, finally, what about the *bouke*? The English word itself intrudes upon the King's French to recall yet another literary referent.[77] Not just the deer of Wyatt's sonnet nor the *cerf d'amours* of French romance, it also brings to mind that animal whose afterlife was chronicled in one of the most telling, and perhaps the oddest, of early Tudor poems. In "The Testament of the Buck," the slaughtered animal describes its hunting, killing, and dismemberment in ways that reflect the deep tensions of the courtly servant. The poem was deemed popular enough to be printed by William Copeland sometime in the middle of the century, and it survives, as well, in two earlier sixteenth-century manuscripts, one of which is the anthology of Humphrey Wellys.[78] As Edward Wilson has demonstrated, this text stands in the Wellys anthology not just as witness to its compiler's "taste for the ceremonial solemnities of the chase," but as part of a larger sequence of political and courtly verse.[79] Nestled in a set of topical poems on the early Tudor court – elegies on Henry's fool, Lob, on the courtier Sir Griffyth ab Ryse and his wife, and on Edward Stafford, Duke of Buckingham – this poem gives voice to a conception of the transitoriness of courtly fealty and, in turn, to the responsibilities of poetry itself in bearing such a witness.[80] As the buck says to the hunter who has just slain it,

> then take vpe your houndes and sett yow downe and wrytte
> what I to yow say and how I shall me quytte   (20.13–14),

an injunction altered in Copeland's printed text to, "Then take penne & Inke, & sett yow down and wrytte."

The testament of the buck becomes the testament of public service: an account of the bequeathals of the hunted body to the merchants, courtiers, king, and queen, who will find use for him. It stands, too, as a disturbing foil to Henry's letter and to Wyatt's sonnet. In its narrative of death and dismemberment, it enjoins us both to read and write the violence of the court. As its named beneficiaries eat the animal – the right shoulder to the vicar, the left to the parker, the tongue to the lady, the grease to the cook, the sweetbread to the king, the lungs to the hounds, the "steykes for your brekefast," and so on – we must, I think, recall too what the King asked of his mistress. When you eat it, it will remind you of the hunter. But when we eat this animal, it forces us to think of the hunted. *To serve* in this poem becomes the overarching pun of courtly life. To serve is to serve up, perhaps resonant, too, with the French idiom for killing the stag in the manuals of venery: *servir le cerf*.[81] As the buck says about his bones: "loke when ye them serve þat small ye them hewe" (20.35).

As the dead courtiers who populate Wellys's manuscript would testify, and as Anne Boleyn herself would later learn, service at Henry's court was but a fleeting thing. Their bodies will die in battle or on the block. The King's hand gives way to the soldier's or the executioner's. And, like the talking buck of this strange poem, they will be hewn to feed the maw of power. To return to Henry's letter, now, is to return not to the complex of religion, politics, and love of Wyatt's sonnet but to the unalterable violence of the King's hand. What we see is a hunter who takes up the injunction of the slaughtered animal, sits down and writes, and serves up an account of what it means to *servir* in all senses of the word.

Light handlings

If the body's touch was carefully controlled, the handling of the letters was not. Missives came and went by others' hands, and the illicit reading, if not interception, of both personal and official correspondence had, by the late 1520s, become the primary means of diplomatic leveraging in the English and the European courts. The French ambassador, Jean du Bellay, wrote to Montmorency in August, 1528 about the fact that Cardinal Wolsey knew the intimacies of the French court. "It is," he noted, "certainly not owing to anything that has passed through my hands, but I know many things leak out from thence in the packets of my lord of Bath, and I assure you nothing is said or done at the French court but they soon know it here." Du Bellay then remarks: "Mademoiselle Boulan has returned to court. The intercepted letters that you sent me

about this matter have disquieted them."[82] These intercepted letters, it is
now assumed, must have been Henry's missives, and the King himself, a
month or so before this diplomatic correspondence, wrote to Anne that
he suspected someone else was reading their mail.

Darlyng, I hartely recommande me to yow, assertayneyng yow that I am nott a
lyttyl perplexte with suche thynges as your brother shall on my part declare vnto
yow, to home I pray yow gyffe full credence, for it wer to long to wryte. In my
last letters i wrotte to yow that I trustyd shortly to se yow, whyche is better
knowne att London than with any that is abowght me, weroff I nott a lytyll
mervell. But lake of dyscrette handelyng must nedes be the cause theroff. No
more to yow att thys tyme, but that I trust shortly our metynges shall nott
depende vppon other menys lyght handyllynges but vppon yor Awne. Wryttyn
with the hand off hym that longyth to be yours –

HRx
(Stemmler, *Die Liebesbriefe*, XIII; Ridley, *Love Letters*, XV)

Here, in one of his last letters, Henry sums up the idioms and images of
masculinized power that controlled the early French texts. He plays on
the idea of the letters being handled, on the lack of "dyscrette handelyng," on the "lyght handyllynges" of other men, and on the hand itself
that writes the letter and desires to be handled by the woman. His
phrasings recall pointedly the earlier debate about the minions: the "light
touches" that had seemed so unseemly, and so French, to the King's
Council. George Boleyn is here, too, in terms oddly unstated. What he
will say to Anne, and what the King has not the time to write about, may
well have been the interception of the letters: a phenomenon that has
"perplexed" the King, or as in du Bellay's interpretation, "disquieted"
the court. In this context, "light touches" or "light handlings" suggests
something other than transgressions of the homosocial. They imply acts
of interception, risks of security at both the personal and national levels.

But what is central to the King's disquiet here is not his fear of French
involvement in the romance, nor his anxiousness about the letters'
transmission to Papal or Imperial hands and their use in the alliance
politics of the late 1520s – a fate they were destined for when they were
actually stolen, perhaps by Campeggio, in 1529.[83] What concerns him is
the possibility of a domestic knowledge of the letters, a loss of national
control over an issue that, as the contemporary historian Nicholas
Harpsfield would describe it, was eventually "tossed in every man's
mouth, in all talks and at all tables, in all taverns, alehouses, and barbers'
shops, yea, and in pulpits too."[84] Such commentary offers more than just
a witness to the rumors that would spread about the King and his
prospective Queen. It translates his love from hands and writing to
mouths and speech. We are no longer in the Erasmian corners of

whispering friends. We are, instead, seated in the open spaces of the tavern and the pulpit. In spite of Henry's efforts, Anne rapidly became not just the node of rumor but the subject of a literature, and by the time of her downfall in 1536 she was inscribed into the popular ballads and courtly poems preserved in the personal anthologies of London and provincial gentry. It is in these manuscript contexts, rather than in the popular imagination, that I wish to locate the immediate legacy of Anne's presence and the King's hand. The afterlife of Henry's love lies in the habits of epistolary interception, and I turn now to a text that refigures, in a complex and possibly transgressive way, the tropes of Henrician fealty and the discursive traditions that informed them.

I have already suggested that the poetry collected in the manuscript anthology of Humphrey Wellys might emblemize the kind of writing that informed the King's epistolary diction and direction. Though deeply indebted to the post-Chaucerian traditions of the verse epistle and the lover's lyric, the manuscript offers a range of topical, satirical, and elegiac verses that testify to its owner's intimate awareness of the details of Henrician courtly politics. At the intersection of the traditional and the topical lies item thirteen, Wellys's cento of stanzas drawn from Stephen Hawes's *Pastime of Pleasure* – a text, like several others in the manuscript, that constructs freestanding verse epistles out of longer narratives. Set in a sequence of four poems cobbled together out of Hawes's verse (a sequence that introduces the topical narratives including "The Testament of the Buck") this cento speaks directly to the broader personal and political interests controlling Wellys's compilation.

In his selections, annotations, and verbal recalibrations of canonical Middle English verse, Wellys relocates his poetic inheritance in the new environment of surreption and surveillance governing English life in the 1530s.[85] His appropriations of the poetry of Chaucer, Lydgate, and especially Stephen Hawes, bring out those idioms of visualization, engraving, printing, and embossing that had characterized these authors' amatory epistemology. Throughout Wellys's book, the body of the lover is a marked, fettered, or inscribed thing. In turn, its lovers often dare not speak or sign their names; and Wellys himself has transcribed poetry and prose of such seditious power – anti-Henrician prophecies, Skeltonic satires, and pro-papal verse – that the very writing of his manuscript would, if it were known, have condemned him to imprisonment or death as a traitor. Wellys is a creature of the surreptitious, and his volume is a testimony to possibilities of both amorous and political transgression. His revisions and excerpts transform the clandestine meetings of courtly poetry into the policings of sedition. For his Middle English sources, the lover's letter is a bill of feeling; for Wellys, it is a document of treason.

I believe that Wellys recasts the poetry of Hawes in order to reflect on the issue of manual authority in the making of royal power. His unique alterations to the text of the *Pastime of Pleasure* suggest an awareness of the shifts in secretarial control during Henry VIII's reign, and they suggest, too, an awareness of the King's own correspondence with his future Queen. In the last stanza of his poem, Wellys rewrites Hawes's lines to locate this new verse epistle in the secretariat of Henry's rule.

> Thys fare ye well þer ys no more to Sey
> vnder my signett yn þe *courte Inperyall*
> of Aperell þe nyen and twenty day
> I closyd thys lettur and to me dyd call
> desyre my frend Soo dere and espetyall
> cummandyng hym as fast as he myght
> To my swete lady to take ytt full ryght.   (13.162–68, emphases added)

In the *Pastime of Pleasure*, Hawes's corresponding stanza closes a long letter, not from the male lover, Grande Amoure, but from his female beloved, La Belle Pucelle. She responds to his missive (titled "The supplycacyon" in Hawes's poem) with a text titled "The copy of the letter," and she commands Cupid to deliver it.

> And fare ye well there is no more to say
> Vnder our sygnet in our *courte ryall*
> Of Septembre the two and twenty day
> She closed the letter and to her dyde call
> Cupyde her sone so dere and specyall
> Commaundynge hym as fast as he myght
> To labell pucell for to take his flyght.
> (*Pastime*, lines 4084–90, emphases added)

Wellys's poem has recast these lines to make them consistent with his male speaker; he has elided the classical reference and changed the date, perhaps, as the poem's editors suggest, to adapt Hawes's poem "for a particular occasion."[86] But there is more at work here than the simple changes in the topicality of courtly verse. The poem in the Wellys anthology sends the letter under the signet of the "courte Inperyall," a reference to the new idea of Henry's court as the seat of an empire. The 1533 Act in Restraint of Appeals had declared, "this realm of England is an empire . . . governed by one supreme head and king having the dignity and royal estate of the imperial crown of the same."[87] This imperialization of royal power – this location, in the language of the Act, of sovereignty in both the "body politic" and in the "imperial crown" – has long been appreciated as the signal achievement of Henry's political revolution, and Anne Boleyn's role in this imperialization may date from her first public presentation to the London populace. Two days before her official coronation on 1 June, the Londoners were treated to a spectacle that was as much an education in the iconographies of power as it was an affirmation of the King's new Queen. In the pageant at Leadenhall on 29 May, a mechanical white falcon appeared from a cloud, landed on a bed of roses, and was then crowned with what Edward Hall called "a close crowune of golde": the imperial diadem. As Nicholas Udall's script for this pageant put it, "an Angel descending crowned the empire-worthy bird."[88] The imagery of the pageant may well inform another poem preserved in a manuscript of the 1530s, the ballad "In a Fresh morning among flowers" found in the commonplace book of the Londoner John Colyns. Here, in a poem allegorically narrating the Queen's rise and fall – with Anne figured as a falcon, Henry as a lion, and the house of Tudor as a rose – the fallen Queen laments:

> I am com in at þis lytell portall
> so lyke A quene to Resseve A Crowne ymperiall
> but now am I come to Resserue A Crowne inmortall
> suche ys fortune![89]

The "Crowne ymperiall" recalls the "courte Inperyall," and courtly love – whether for the balladic clichés of Colyns's poem or the Hawesean substrate of Wellys's cento – now lives in a precisely limned political environment. The private world of desire becomes the public world of power. The old tropes of Cupid find their meanings in an empire of love.

And for the King himself. Once Henry's body and his body politic had been declared imperial, it was but a short step to make the signings of his hand the marks of empire. By 1536, it was considered a treasonable offence to forge "the kinges signe manuell signet and prevye seale."[90] Imperial control and domestic surveillance are both centered in the markings of the hand. Royal writ takes on an almost spiritual quality, while personal texts came under the purview of official inspection. The rise of surreption and informancy as social acts – propelled by what G. R. Elton has called the "willingness of gentry and aristocracy to report what they heard" – shifted the public connotations of the old, literary tropes of clandestine love, as did the many Parliamentary statutes concerning writing, reading, and iconic presentation as the marks of fealty or treason.[91] "Writyng ymprintinge [and] cypheringe" could all be seditious acts.[92] By 1542, the Act Touching Prophesies upon Declaration of Names Armes Badeges, &c, could prohibit "any persone or persones [to] prynte or wryte" false prophecies against the King, especially those based on readings of "badges or signetes, or by reasone of lettres."[93]

Wellys's Hawsean cento takes place in these specific realms of Henrician power. His manuscript's overarching fascination with withdrawal, secrecy, encryption, and signature find their articulation in this clutch of recast stanzas from the *Pastime of Pleasure*. Instead of calling upon courtly servants for delivery of the letter, as in Hawes's original (where Venus commands "Cupyde her sone so dere and specyall," [*Pastime*, line 4088]), this letter relies on a trusted friend for its successful transmission ("desyre my frend Soo dere and espetyall"). In Wellys's manuscript, there is a "finis" after these last lines, and a phrase appropriated from the motto of the Order of the Garter: "Si troue Soit hony Soit qui mal y pense" ("If this is discovered, evil to him who evil thinks"). The force of this annotation is far more complicated than a simple injunction to secrecy. Its meaning lies both inside and outside the poem's fiction. On the one hand, we may take this motto as inscribed on the closed cover of the letter. Its injunction refers to the fear of interception, and as such, it sustains the narrative of an epistle surreptitiously delivered by a knowing friend. But on the other hand, the motto speaks directly to the governing concerns of Wellys's book. It is of a piece with Wellys's own encrypted *ex libris* to the volume, written in a Latin letter substitution code and enjoining the finder of the book to return it to Wellys himself.[94] It is, too, of a piece with the injunctions to secrecy and anonymity that fill many of the anthology's verse epistles: claims not to reveal the name of the writing lover, claims to keep silent about who is saying what to whom.[95]

What Wellys has done here is inscribe himself into the fictions of epistolary writing and return that shape his manuscript. He has, in essence, written out his own assembly of intercepted letters, and his version of the Garter motto offers an illuminating gloss on early Tudor contexts for defining the tensions between private desire and public shame in the construction of the male reader. It signals not a pleasure in the text but almost an embarrassment at fantasy: a vision of the reader now subjected not only to the judgment of an imaginary woman but to the censure of a judging public. Wellys's cento, and its unique rewritings of its source stanzas, may thus be appreciated as the literary version of the social practice of the intercepted letter, and in turn, as a possible refraction of the Henry/Anne exchange. As someone with close family ties to the Henrician service, who had been educated at the Inns of Court, who owed his professional standing to the complex networks of patronage spun out from Henry's circle, and who evidenced an ongoing connection with the court, Wellys would have been well poised to hear of Anne Boleyn. Certainly, as a recusant during the early 1530s, he would have been part of that broader community of dissidents of whom Henry would have been, to say the least, "disquieted" to know.[96]

Wellys's work thus offers information both about the kinds of sources for the King's epistolary language and about the ways in which those sources could be reread and rewritten in the years following the romance. It also illustrates the possibilities of a transgressive reading of those sources. In an age when forging the King's seal was treasonous, when ciphering could be grounds for sedition and when even the very writing of the Pope's name could bring arrest, when intercepted letters were the means of seeking out the traitor, when gentry friends and neighbors could be counted as informants – in this age, the very making of Wellys's manuscript is criminal. His poem now, in this environment, performs an act of both literary and political impersonation: on the one hand, ventriloquizing one of the key sources of an early Tudor amorous diction; on the other, miming the royal salutation and imagining the impress of the King's signet.

If there is a Henrician subject – or at the very least, a Henrician subtext – to Wellys's cento, it lies in the power of the King's hand to authenticate the transgressive. It takes the Erasmian tension between intimacy and theatricality full circle, transforming a pre-text of amorous desire not into the product of the King's own hand but into a document of the royal writing chamber, and offering a version of epistolary love that replaces the King's hand with an imaginary signet and a nervously signed afterward. What remains in Wellys's own hand is the personalized Garter motto and the plea for surreption. What we read here is the product of an impersonated Imperial court, a book of intercepted letters transcribed in the whispered corners of the study that, in its distinctive way, plays out the tensions between what may be committed to the page and what may be expressed in public. The afterlife of Henry's amorous epistolarity lives not in the confines of the writing desk or in the archives of royal control. The letters survive in a library far away; their discourse and discussion is the subject of foreign ambassadorial intrigue; and, at home, they stand at the center of the King's anxieties and, perhaps, at the seditious peripheries of courtly verse and of the secret compilations of the traitorous reader.

In the end, the rhetoric of Henrician kingship is the rhetoric of the hand: of marking with the touch, of keeping minion politics or private love under the impress of the manual. The verbal, plastic, and cultural artifacts that I have studied here, each in their own way, attempt to form a containable identity. Whether they offer wrought gifts or a bloody kill, they show the grasp of kingship on the form of love. They transform the public tropes of politics into the private codes of love. "Lyght handyl-lynges" of the woman replace the "light touches" of the minions; a French-educated woman displaces Frenchified grooms. Henry's letters make her the sole object of the royal touch and, in turn, make the royal body the exclusive purview of the woman's hand. It is as if they offer in epistolary terms what Wyatt saw in his Petrarchan sonnet: that holding on not just to love but to the privacy of correspondence is as futile as attempting "in a net . . . to hold the wind." The body of the letter, like the body of the woman, sealed and signed, marked with the signet or the dead beast of desire, stands as a badge of love: a badge that, more than royal motto or brute gift, should say *noli me tangere*.

A tragedy in his own hand

Years later, after she was ready for the block, the King still made Anne subject to his hand. In a dispatch dated 19 May 1536, the very day of her execution, Eustace Chapuys noted Henry's joy at having done with her. The royal barge, he noted, "was actually filled with minstrels and musicians of his chamber," and the celebrations reflected, in Chapuys homely simile, "the joy and pleasure a man feels in getting rid of a thin, old, and vicious hack in the hope of getting soon a fine horse to ride – a very peculiarly agreeable task for this king." Chapuys goes on to tell the story of Henry's response to Anne's arrest. Reporting what the Bishop of Carlisle had told him, Chapuys quotes what he takes to be Henry's words and deeds:

'For a long time back had I predicted what would be the end of this affair, so much so that I have written a tragedy [*une tragedie*], which I have here by me.' Saying which, he took out of his breast pocket a small book all written in his own hand [*ung petit livret escript de sa main*], and handed it over to the Bishop, who, however, did not examine its contents. Perhaps these were certain ballads, which the King himself is known to have composed once, and of which the concubine and her brother had made fun, as of productions entirely worthless, which circumstance was one of the principal charges brought against them at the trial.[97]

This wild blend of quotation, hearsay, and speculation, redefines the King's relationship to Anne as centered on the writings *de sa main*. The public demonstration of royal understanding marks itself, here, in the presentation of a book – a tragedy, as Henry is reported to have called it, written in a little volume and kept concealed in his bosom. His transmutation of the love affair into a literary form has little impact on the Bishop, who declines to read it, but much on Chapuys, who could not have. His speculations say not so much about Henry himself as they do of Chapuys's own conception of the King as author and the personal importance of that authorship to his public and private status. The poetaster Henry is the butt of humor, the writer of what Chapuys calls "chose inepte [et] gouffe," whose humiliation at the fun made of his writings by Anne and her brother is a cause of their arrest.

Henry is figured in this anecdote as the inept manipulator of the literary form. A book that is not read, a set of poems mocked, his "tragedy" epitomizes his failures as husband to a cultivated, French-educated woman and her circle. His failure here is not so much as king or husband, but as author – though the account of his alleged impotence, reported by Chapuys earlier in this letter, only contributes to the sense that Anne was believed to have thought Henry "inepte" with both the penis and the pen. Indeed, this narrative association paints as brutal a portrait of Anne as Chapuys, long her antagonist, could have wished. For now the mockery of Henry rests in the productions of the hand: the very hand that had been both the tool of violence and the instrument of love in those letters of nearly a decade before. The King's articulations of royal power through rhetorical control – his displacements of sexual conquest onto dead animals and crafted letters – find their bathetic anticlimax in Chapuys's story. In this account it is not so much what was in this little book as the fact of its making that is noticeable. We have no idea, in spite of Chapuys's speculations, what the book contains. Nor is there any response offered from the Bishop of Carlisle, who perhaps recalls what price Anne and her brother paid for literary criticism of the King.

Just what was Henry's "tragedy"? Greg Walker is inclined to take Chapuys at his word, noting that narratives such as Chaucer's *Monk's Tale* and Lydgate's *Fall of Princes* were considered tragedies by medieval literary parlance and figuring, by implication, that the "certain balades" of the Ambassador's letter must have meant something like these. And yet, Walker holds out the specter of the theater in his reading: "Even if this document was not the dramatic text which the term 'tragedy' suggests to the modern reader, it nonetheless provides a striking further illustration of the degree to which literary forms were seen as suitable vehicles for even the most important of political expressions."[98] But what is centrally at stake here is not our modern understanding of a term, but that of Henry's – and Chapuys's – early Tudor audience. The *Fall of Princes* and the *Monk's Tale* are collections of tragedies: compilations of *de casibus* accounts of famous men and women falling from their fame. The one text of the Middle English period that would have circulated as a single tragedy, and from which later imitators would appropriate the term, was *Troilus and Criseyde*. In the concluding stanzas of the poem, Chaucer sends his book off to his readers with lines that would become the defining node of imitation and authorial self-definition for a century of vernacular makers:

> Go, litel bok, go, litel myn tragedye,
> Ther God thi makere yet, er that he dye,
> So sende myght to make in some comedye!
> But litel book, no makyng thou n'envie,
> But subgit be to alle poesye;
> And kis the steppes where as thow seest pace
> Virgile, Ovide, Omer, Lucan and Stace. (V.1786–92)

The tragic quality of *Troilus and Criseyde* lies not just in the turns of Fortune's wheel but in the transformation of that narrative into a little book. The tragedy of Chaucer's poem measures itself against other poetry, and sees itself subject to the canonical *auctores* of the classical tradition. And both the poem's titular protagonists imagined themselves in the afterlives of little books. For Troilus, reflecting on the "processe" by which Cupid has made war upon him, "Men myght a book make of it, lik a storie" (V.582–85). And for Criseyde, acutely conscious of her own impending literary reputation:

> Allas, of me, unto the worldes ende,
> Shal neyther ben ywriten nor ysonge
> No good word, for thise bokes wol me *shende*. (V.1058–60) "disgrace"

For Henry – who had witnessed "Troilus and Pandar" at Twelfth Night twenty years before and who, in 1532, received the dedication of Thynne's Chaucer – the tragedy of Troilus and Criseyde could well have been the text of his allusion. Could the King have taken Troilus at his word, making a book of his affair with one who emblemizes the betrayals of the woman? As documents from Chapuys's letter to the ballad preserved in John Colyns's commonplace book testify, of Anne as well as of Criseyde, "Shal neyther ben ywriten nor ysonge / No good word." And in the King's theatricalized gesture of display, drawing the little tragedy out of his bosom, may lie the resonances to another story of a secreted volume. Recall, now, Thomas Elyot's Pasquil who finds in the aspiring courtier's hand a copy of the New Testament.

But what is this in your bosom? an other boke . . . Abyde, what is here? Troylus & Chreseid? Lord what discord is bitwene these two bokes?[99]

What discord, indeed. For here, in Elyot's colloquy on the wiles of courtiership, Chaucer's poem appears as the hidden text. It is drawn out from its barely secreted spot in the elaborate dress of the courtier Gnatho; it displaces the New Testament as the true manual for one, as Pasquill says, who knows "nothing but onli of flateri." It is, in short, the bible of the courtier.

Such verbal resonances dovetail with the arc of literary making in the King's letters to Anne Boleyn and to the possible reception of those letters in the personal anthologies and public missives of the time. Taken in tandem, they provide a strong case for a Troilan quality to Henry's tragic making. At the very least, they contribute to an appreciation of the Anne Boleyn affair as charged with the literary fashioning of Henry himself as an author, whose writings were read – or not read – by the licit and illicit subjects of the King's hand.

4   Private quotations, public memories: *Troilus and Criseyde* and the politics of the manuscript anthology

> And with that word he drow hym to the feere,
> And took a light, and fond his contenaunce,
> As for to looke upon an old romaunce.
>
> (Troilus and Criseyde, III.978–80)

Just what was Pandarus looking upon? Readers of this passage, almost from its earliest circulation, have been puzzled by its ambiguities, not least the status of the "romance" Pandarus withdraws to see. Is he observing Troilus and Criseyde in bed, secreting himself in a corner of the room to witness this romance in progress? Or, is he removing himself from the action just to read: to look upon a book, perhaps, much like that other "romance" that he found Criseyde and her friends reading at the opening of Book II of the poem ("This romaunce is of Thebes that we rede," II.100)? Or, too, is it a situation far more complicated than either interpretation admits? A. C. Spearing has remarked on how the "contrast between love as really experienced and love as read about in books is underlined" in Chaucer's verbal ambiguities, and he finds in this episode the *locus classicus* of Pandarus's voyeurism.[1] His presence at a moment of deep privacy; the motives of his "look"; the status of his own "contenaunce" – all come together to define Pandarus as voyeur, and to raise the specter of his own arousal at his observations. For Spearing, Pandarus "has gained and is still gaining a vicarious sexual pleasure from the encounter between his niece and her lover," and he is not alone among modern interpreters of Chaucer's poem to find something of an anxious ambiguity in the go-between's actions the following morning.[2] When Pandarus returns to Criseyde's bed, he dallies with her playfully and then, as the narrator characteristically allows:

> With that his arm al sodeynly he thriste
> Under hire nekke, and at the laste hire kyste.
>
> I passe al that which chargeth nought to seye.   (III.1574–76)

If, as the narrator obliquely implies, "Pandarus hath fully his entente" (III.1582), we may well wonder just what that "entente" has been.

122

Skelton, it would appear, had little doubt about the possibilities of an aroused, or at least sexually conscious Pandarus, in his remark in the *Garlande of Laurell*: "Goodly Creisseid, fayrer than Polexene, / For to envyve Pandarus appetite" (lines 871–72) – a remark cited approvingly by Spearing as a "perceptive" early interpretation of Chaucer's lines.[3] And even earlier in the reception of the poem, Pandarus's behavior was subject to review. For fifteenth-century scribes, the ambiguities surrounding these passages resulted in competing readings and interpretations. One manuscript, for example, alters the word "fond" in III.979 to "feyned," and also changes "romance" to "remembrauns" in the following line – changes that shift radically Pandarus's observation of, or participation in, the bedroom scene.[4] For him to *feign* his countenance is, in this version, to mask his engagement with the lovers: to present himself as passing off a role. In turn, to look upon an old *remembrance* is to place him now not as the reader or observer of the lovers, but as the reflector on the self: to remove him from world of books to the landscapes of memory.

These ambiguities surrounding Pandarus shape not only the role he plays in Chaucer's poem but in the environment of his reception and, in turn, in the constructions of a literary readership in early Tudor England. While his fascination with the surreptitiousness of love and the manipulation of the amorous epistle had a deep impress on the many of the courtly and political discourses of the Henrician era, they take on a new and quite specific import in the age of Thomas Cromwell. As its definitive chronicler, G. R. Elton, has illuminated in great detail, this was a time in which codes of national loyalty, religious belief, and personal affinity were irrevocably recast; in which the interception of personal correspondence had become a tool of government; in which informancy and arrest terrorized the gentry; in which concealment had become the byword of the populace and their police.[5] The development of an elaborate machinery of information gathering, together with a string of Parliamentary Acts concerned with the proprieties of writing and the dangers of textual interpretation, might well be said to mark the rise of a state Pandarism: a condition of official life that sought to look in on the products of the writing desk, the conversations of the study, and the personal romances of the chamber.

Chaucerian reception in this period could not but be affected by these broader social moves. Familiar set pieces of Pandaric advice – the counsels against false speech and the lessons in the "priuite" of love that circulated in the excerpts found in fifteenth-century manuscripts – came to be understood in the highly charged climates of public courtiership and private eroticism.[6] The arranging of affairs, the transmission and interception of letters, and the eavesdropping on scenes of passion bore with them an excitement all their own. The anxiousness of courtly service that informed the allegories of Hawes and the satires of Skelton, that stood at the core of Erasmus's vision of the *vita aulica*, and that ran as a subtext throughout the debate on the minions and the love letters to Anne Boleyn, also came to shape the appropriations of the *Troilus* in the personal anthologies of early Tudor gentry and aristocrats. The contexts of Chaucerian quotation here are those of surreption and sedition. Poetic excerpts stand not as static maxims of advice, but as voiced outbursts in the closet dramas of epistolary love or the *debat d'amours*. More than just testimonies to the reception of Chaucer's poem, these manuscripts show literary culture in an age of monitored interpretation. Personal desire, family relations, and political anxieties are all subject to the voyeur's gaze, as acts of reading and rewriting come to operate not at the centers of the courtly space but at the margins of the provincial or the peripheries of imprisonment. Such volumes stand, in essence, in the very space cleared by Chaucer's early scribes: a space between "romance" and "remembrance," between finding and feigning, between public books and private memories.

Two major manuscripts of the 1530s exemplify these habits of Pandaric reading. The anthology put together by Humphrey Wellys – an anthology I have already discussed as bearing witness to the literary percolations of Henry VIII's amorous epistolarity – reveals the personal responses to the possible intrusions of the state. His is a manuscript rife with the anxiousness of surveillance, voyeurism, and the fear of being caught. Containing vulgar verse, satiric prose, and politically seditious poetry and prophecies, it represents the private compilations of a man close enough to the workings of political control to keep them secret. There are texts dangerously pro-papal and anti-Henrician. One I have already mentioned vigorously crosses out the word "pope," while others – notably the elegies on the deaths of courtiers and servants of the early 1520s – reflect on the dangers of royal service and the punishments for treason. Such political concerns inform the larger project of this manuscript: one governed by the secret thrill that attends transgressive correspondence, that hinges on the suppression of identity, and that generates the charge of surreptitiously observing and participating in potentially felonious activities. Several of its love poems, for example, cross the boundaries of textual and sexual decorum. Women are subject to derision as untrustworthy dissimulators; they are objects of erotic fantasy, the subjects of lyrics that revel in both a fearful anonymity as well as in a glib eroticism. There are female verse letters of both a popular and courtly nature, poems characterized by an appropriation of

Chaucerian and Lydgatean amatory service as well as those more in tune with the good gossips and Alewife poetry of the Skeltonic kind, possessing what Edward Wilson has called a "fireside vulgarity" that "resists summary."[7] Wellys's collection brings together texts that, in the words of Skelton's own conception of Pandaric pleasure, would "envyve" the appetite of the observer and transcriber. To look upon his manuscript is to look upon the "old romaunce" of epistolary love and courtly desire. This is a document of personalized Pandarism, made through the ministrations of the interloping postman and manipulative peeping tom. And when this reader comes to Chaucer's text itself, it is as an intrusive epistolarist of the imagination, as Wellys's cento of stanzas from *Troilus and Criseyde* writes a bill of complaint, introduced and passed on in the voice of Pandarus himself.

The work of Humphrey Wellys is not so much a record of transcription or of imitation as it is of impersonation: the knowing adaptation of a literary voice that, in the process, both identifies and masks the subjectivity of the impersonator. In the Devonshire Manuscript, such literary impersonations take on a more complex set of resonances. Devonshire has long been valued as a witness to the reading habits of the early Tudor gentry.[8] Apart from its large offering of Thomas Wyatt's poetry, the manuscript contains excerpts from Middle English texts drawn, it is now known, from works printed in Thynne's Chaucer edition of 1532.[9] Such selections have been largely understood as commentaries, of a sort, on the personal relations among several of the many contributors to the manuscript, notably Thomas Howard, Margaret Douglas, and Mary Shelton. Much scholarly energy has been devoted to matching the many hands of the assembly with known historical figures from the Howard/Shelton circle – almost as much energy, perhaps, as to the identification of the authors of its many poems and the codification of the canon of Wyatt's verse it represents.[10] Superficially, Devonshire may seem vastly different from the Wellys anthology. It is the work of many hands, writing over a period of time; it is the product of readers and writers intimately close to the hub of Henrician power; and it contains the identifiable transcriptions, if not compositions, of both men and women. And yet, much like Wellys's collection, Devonshire is possessed by those "concerns for love, secrecy, and steadfastness" that have long been appreciated as controlling both its most personal and enigmatic entries and its most famous and canonical selections from the poetry of Wyatt.[11] Like Wellys's work, it dwells on the imprisonments of love, on the enchainments of desire and the social consequences of illicit longing. It focuses, too, on the difficulties of letter: on the limitations of the pen, the insecurities of misinterpretation, and the fears of interception. And it is preoccupied with privacy and public life. Whether recounting the love and imprisonment of Thomas Howard and Margaret Douglas, or recording the political and amorous affairs of Wyatt, Surrey, and other known and anonymous poetasters of the period, the lyric sequences of Devonshire tell stories of voyeurism and intrusion. The manuscript's selections from Thynne's Chaucer (long considered relatively random excerpts from a handy published volume) are, in fact, carefully calibrated selections from a literature concerned with love and loss, observation and advice. Devonshire's own cento of stanzas from *Troilus and Criseyde* matches, too, that of Humphrey Wellys, as both draw on the same episodes of Chaucer's poem and as both begin their new narrations in the voice of Pandarus.

But more than bearing witness to the circulations of Chauceriana, these manuscripts also illuminate the ways in which courtier literacy constructs itself out of the canons of late medieval English verse. Both draw on the conspectus of familiar authors, genres, and poetic voices. Both illustrate the historical range of English writing, from fourteenth-century narrative, through fifteenth-century allegory, to early sixteenth-century political satire and love lyric. And both, to some degree, center their assemblies in the cultural authority of a known author. For Wellys, it is Stephen Hawes; for Devonshire, it is Wyatt. Hawes and Wyatt constitute the benchmarks for literary writing in their respective anthologies. It is not just that they take up more space than any other author in their manuscripts; rather, it is that their works take the measure of all other things. They offer up the idioms, the voices, and the idea of a courtly poetry through which the other entries in their compilations may be read. The Wellys and Devonshire manuscripts are thus anthologies of *literature*. They define ways of reading and not just by transcribing circulating texts from memory or manuscript but by incorporating passages from printed books into the compilation. Whether they be the products of the de Worde circle (in the case of Wellys) or the edition of Thynne (in the case of Devonshire), the published canons of late medieval English verse find themselves personalized in the manuscripts of early Tudor readers. These manuscripts present the privatizations of public literature, the transformations of the familiar into the intimate, of the commodities of the press into the artifacts of the hand.

Before examining these manuscripts in detail, and before exploring their precise relationship to courtly literary culture and Chaucerian impersonation, it is important to locate them in the larger social moment of the personal anthology. Early Tudor literary culture is in many ways defined by the rise of the anthology, be it the commonplace book made piecemeal over a lifetime or the manuscript collection written throughout as a fair copy. Bodies of inherited and canonical texts were personalized into manuals of pedagogy and repositories of delight. The practice of gathering selected passages and framing them in moral or thematic contexts goes back, of course, to the earliest anthologies and florilegia of the Greek and Roman periods, and throughout the English Middle Ages the construction of vernacular anthologies (whether individually transcribed or commercially commissioned) often served to fashion publicly the social status of their readers and the canonical status of their authors.[12] The early sixteenth century witnessed not only an increase in the number of commonplace books and anthologies produced, but also a new social function for such personal assemblies. The principles of selection, memorization, and application that were the core of humanist *imitatio* could only stimulate the rise of commonplace book-making. In turn, the circulation of such paradigmatic humanist works as the collection of personal correspondence or the assembly of adages – both of which Erasmus had brought to a high art in his editions of the 1510s and 20s – also contributed to the social moment of this kind of volume.[13] As Mary Crane has phrased it, in a recent reassessment of these intellectual and literary traditions, "gathering and framing were, in sixteenth-century England, the basis for a theory and practice of reading, writing, education, and social mobility that developed alongside and in partial resistance to the individualistic, imitative, and aristocratic paradigms for selfhood and authorship that we tend to associate with the English Renaissance."[14] In her view, the assembly of philosophical and literary fragments became a way not just of imitating ancient or canonical authors, but also a manner of imitating humanists as well. What Crane calls the "middle-class subject" could enact these practices of selective incorporation to construct books that, in themselves, constituted public literary identity. Gathering and framing, in this account, share in the rivalries of "aristocratic and humanist versions of subjectivity and authorship in the period."[15]

But if the practices of assembly and organization helped make the public man (or woman), they also fostered a new view of privacy in reading and writing. If they helped in the constructions of social class or personal identity, they also abetted the destruction of literary texts. The commonplace book not only makes new wholes out of old parts; it makes new parts out of old wholes. The project of the personal anthology is one preoccupied with fragmentation and dismemberment. By its very nature, the anthology performs an act of interception and ventriloquism. It removes texts from their originary contexts, breaks them up, reassembles and reorders them. Selections from canonical writers – Chaucer, Lydgate, Skelton, Hawes, Wyatt, and Surrey – take on new voices and new meanings when set in personal manuscripts. Lyrics or verse epistles ranged in sequence tell a story different from the narratives implied in their original environments (or, for that matter, in their modern placement in critical anthologies or editions of complete works). The literary corpus finds itself dismembered in the personal collection: a body of desire transformed into bits and pieces of idealized or delectated beauty. Long texts may find themselves transmuted into brief centos – assemblies of lines or stanzas designed to make new texts wholly out of previously written parts. The cento is the defining genre for the early Tudor compilation: an anthology writ small, a distillation of the voices, idioms, and arguments of the inheritance of Middle English literature into compact, memorable form.

If the cento is a kind of miniature anthology it is, as well, a kind of metaphorical *blazon*. The selective dismembering of the female body that is the *blazon anatomique* has its textual parallel in the fragmenting of the literary corpus into individuated lines or stanzas, objects of visual (or scribal) delectation. Reading is *blazonerie* from the compiler, and it is no accident that many of the passages selected for inclusion in the early Tudor personal anthology concern themselves with bodily description and ideals of female beauty. To read the work of Humphrey Wellys or the contributors to the Devonshire Manuscript is to enact again the visionary journey of the early Tudor poetic hero. The lover/narrators of poetry from Hawes's *Pastime of Pleasure* to the derivative Chauceriana of Thynne's edition trace their educations through inscribed texts, engraved announcements, and pictures offered up with cryptic or explanatory captions. The experience of loving for such heroes is inseparable from the life of reading, and what early Tudor readers learned from this life goes beyond local appropriations or adaptings of a verbal legacy. They learned, I posit, a habit of compilation, a conception of the private and the public, and a notion of literary subjectivity, that depends directly on the confrontation with brief, disembodied texts. To love, in short, is to anthologize.

"A quotation," notes the musicologist Charles Rosen, "is, of course, a memory made public."[16] The Chaucerian quotations of the Wellys and Devonshire manuscripts write out the private memories of very public figures. And yet, what are remembered here are not just the occasions of desire but the history of English verse. Publicity itself becomes the centerpiece of literary excerpt and quotation. Political sedition or illicit love are, in these texts, inscribed into the masterplot of Troilan love and Pandaric advice. Reading remains a form of voyeurism here, for, in the end, the audience for Chaucer's writing is not so much the intended addressee as it is the inquiring go-between: the Pandarus who tutors in the arts of love, who bears, transmits, and interprets the letters of desire, and who, in the end, becomes the implied reader of the early Tudor verse epistle. Lyric anthologies are books made up of intercepted texts. In the sequences of love or the *debats d'amours* constructed out of Chaucerian voices lies the personalizations of a public literature: a making private and transgressive of a literary body that is, at this historical moment, coming to stand as the canon of officially sanctioned English writing.

The Wellys anthology

From its very opening, Wellys's manuscript evidences a preoccupation with the intercepted letter and the visualized body. It begins with a Hawesean bill of complaint, beseeching the recipient, in lines adapted from the *Pastime of Pleasure*, "to gyffe audyence" to the love letter (1.1).[17] The lover is constrained by love, "fetteryd" by her beauty (1.6), and this image of imprisonment sustains the second poem in the volume. Here, in an odd conflation of Promethean legend and Criseydean erotic dream, its narrator imagines himself taken prisoner in a beautiful bower, where a "bryde" – read either "bird" or "bride" – "wholly fro me my harte hathe take" (2.6). This is a poem of the riven and the fettered body, bare of solace, chained in prison yet enclosing, too, a heart that moves from coldness to fire. Each stanza's painful images and blunt repetitiveness concatenate the clichés of love lyric into an arresting statement of physical pain. In poem 3, the imprisonments of love are now metaphorized into the knottings of the truelove and the lockings of the chamber of the heart. This text, also a verse epistle, introduces what will become another of the governing themes of the Wellys's anthology: the anonymity of the letter writer and the secrecy of love itself.

> froo whens ytt cummethe ytt hathe no name
> but frome hym þat ys nameles
> and whyder ytt shall ytt sayethe the same
> by cause they shulde be blameles.   (3.45–48)

Surreption and anxiety become the motivating features of this poetry. The *blazon* of the following poem has about it all the excitement of the Hawsean extracts: an excitement that provokes not just the reflection on the lady's body but on what it means to read and write erotic poetry.

> hur lyppes are lyke vnto cherye
> with Tethe as whyte as whalles bone
> hur browes bente as any can be
> with eyes clere as crystall stoune

> hur fyngers be bothe large and longe
> with pappes round as any ball
> no thyng me thynke on hur ys wronge
> hur medyll ys bothe gaunte and small.   (4.13–20)

There is a sense here of the virtual impossibility of inscribing the beauty of the lady, a sense of the innumerability of love itself.

> wherefore as many tymes I grete yow
> as clarkes can wrytte with papur and ynke
> and as monye moo as *gressys* grewe   "grasses"
> or tonge can tell or harte can thynke
>
> noo more I wryte to yow at thys tyme
> butt wher euer ye be on lande or watter
> crystes dere blessyng and myne
> I sende yow yn grettyng of thys letter.   (4.49–56)

Read in the light of the familiar tropes of medieval literary love, these stanzas may seem trite. They are, as the anthology's most recent editors have shown, rife with the proverbs of the popular advisory tradition.[18] And while their violence and eroticism may seem, at first glance, more acute than that of the well-known anthology pieces of the Middle English lyric legacy, theirs is not unique to the scope of what P. J. Frankis had long ago identified as erotic dream vision.[19] There is, it has been argued, too, a certain Wyatt-like anxiety about these poems – an apprehension about social censure, an obsession with the disillusionments of love.[20] But I believe this poetry is richer and more powerful than such historical or literary appositions may suggest. It exposes the potentially transgressive violence of the tropes of love, drawing its eroticism not from the delights of female company but from the pains of separation and the markings of the body. It attends so explicitly to fetterings and chainings, to the physical condition of imprisonment and pain, that they may well be seen as personalized literalizations of the metaphors of verse. Even a poem as seemingly unimaginative as the fifth one in the manuscript takes an odd violent twist midway through its accounts of longing:

> yf þat ye come I wyll yow mete
> betyde of me what Soo euer may
> what thoughe I shulde be well I-beytte
> noo thyng shall *lett* me nyght nor daye.   (5.9–12)   "prevent"

Though I might be completely beaten ("well I-beytte"), nothing shall prevent me from meeting you by night or day.[21]

These first few poems constitute an *ordinatio* of amorous excitement that addresses the anxieties, pains, pleasures, and scriptorial conundrums of the lover's life.[22] They constitute, as well, a kind of *accessus* to the anthology, a summary account of its key themes and verbal interests, a compilation of clichés and extracts that will fill out the entire volume. Indeed, their imagery controls not just the sixteenth-century texts unique to it, but the inheritance of earlier Middle English documents as well. Poem 6 is a widely circulated poem, probably composed in the first half of the fifteenth century, and rich with the language of late medieval penitential verse.[23] But this is a poem too that resonates with Wellys's idioms. "All crysten men that walke me by / beholde and See thys dylfull syght," it opens – now, offering in its "behold and see" phrasing the invitation to regard the sinner's body as something of a peccatory text. We move now, from the prisoner of love to the imprisoned sinner; from the body fettered or "I-beytte" to one now

> lappyd all abowte
> with todes and snakes as ye may see
> they *knawe* my bodye throughe owte.   (6.33–35)   "gnaw"

The poem's speaker abides in a "cage . . . of euerlastyng fyre" (6.61); he lies "fettered with Fendes Fell / and as a beest bounden In a stalle" (6.65–66).

So, too, in the selections drawn from Hawes's poetry, the most erotic and most violent passages are selected and juxtaposed for powerful effect. Poem 13 draws on those passages that describe the lover's "fetteryd" heart, bound "with brennyng cheens" (13.19–20). The lover's heart is caught in a snare (13.44); his is a body "pale and wanne" (55); her love "hath percyced my hart Root" (70); and again, his heart is "perst" with the "stoke of loue" (100). Such declarations of distress, here, work not as the strings of lament scattered as they are through Hawes's *Pastime of Pleasure*, but as a concentrated voicing of a palpable physical pain. That they introduce the *blazon* drawn from the *Pastime* – one of the most explicit and extended of Hawes's physical descriptions – only affirms his yoking together of pain and physical desire. Such is the pattern for all four of the major Hawsean centos of the volume: bodily pain coupled with the ocular delectation of the woman, and framed in letters of complaint that call attention to the difficulties of epistolary writing. "Remembre all þat I wryte vnto yow," poem 13 enjoins towards its conclusion; "pardon me of my Rude wryttyng" closes 14; the "byll ys presentyd" in 15.

What is the overall effect and purpose of this poetry, and how does it relate to the broader environments of courtly Pandarism I have been describing? These are, at a basic level, fantasies of male desire. They transform earlier narratives of courtly education or of moral travel into tales of scopophilia. They rewrite the *Pastime of Pleasure*'s concern with gentlemanly fashioning and courtly performance into a contemporary courtier's anxiety about discovery. The catalogues of female beauty in the Wellys anthology have, in the mid-Henrician period, all the ripe intensity of the Skeltonic burlesque. Read now the *blazonerie* of poem 4 (lines 13–20, quoted above) against Courtly Abusyon's parade of his wares in *Magnyfycence*:[24]

> As lyly whyte to loke upon her leyre,
> Her eyen relucent as carbuncle so clere,
> Her mouthe *enbawmed*, dylectable and mery,   "fragrant"
> Her lusty lyppes ruddy as the chery –
> How lyke yow?   (*Magnyfycence*, lines 1555–59)

And, to Magnyfycence's own query, "Where myght suche one be founde?" (line 1568), it is as if Wellys's pained narrator has already given an answer:

> for I haue gone throughe englond on euery syde
> brettyn flanders with many an oder place
> yet founde I neuer non yn these ways wyde
> Suche on as she ys to my purpasse.   (4.25–28)

So, too, in the excerpts from Hawes's *Pastime* and the *Conforte*, Wellys's poems draw out those descriptions that echo these Skeltonic theatricalizations of the *blazon* – selections, it would seem, designed to pick up Skelton's imagery and pick up Hawes's pace. Poem 13 lifts out the *blazon* from the *Pastime* (lines 3839–3866, corresponding to Wellys 13.99–126) and elides the meditation on the woman's uniqueness or on her inner virtues that follows it in Hawes's original (*Pastime*, lines 3867–80) to move directly to the line, "Thys yn my mynde when I had engrauyd" (13.127; *Pastime*, line 3881). This excerpt, too, has a Skeltonic resonance about it; certainly Hawes's awkward repetitions, "With vaynes blewe in which the blode rane inne," and "Whyte as the mylke with blewe vaynes amonge" (lines 3862, 3866), represent the kind of writing parodied in Courtly Abusyon's hawking words, "The strains of her veins are azure indy blue" (*Magnyfycence*, line 1554). Skelton would also parody this portrait of La Belle Pucelle in *Phyllyp Sparowe* (lines 1170–76), in a way that tells us about the possibilities of reading, and recasting, Hawesean erotic in newly charged political or satiric environments.[25] For Skelton, the excesses of the *Pastime* are just that: excesses to be mocked and played with, strings of what appear to be *non sequiturs* of beautiful description, culminating in the bizarre question,

> Wherto shuld I disclose
> The garterynge of her hose?   (*Phyllyp Sparowe*, lines 1174–75)

For Wellys, such chunks of verse are building blocks of an ocular erotics, a way of looking at the woman that almost defies transcription. What is humor in Skelton is almost torture in Wellys:

> I behelde hur *chere* and louely countenaucne   "demeanor"
> hur garmentes Ryche and hur proper stature
> I regesterd well yn my remembrance
> that I neuer Sawe Soo fayre a creature
> Soo well fauouryd create by nature
> þat hard ytt ys for to wryte with ynke
> all hur hyghe bewtye or any hart to thynke
>
> hur feete were proper She garteryd well hur hose.   (14.120–27)

Here, Wellys has brought together disparate stanzas from the *Pastime* to voice, again, the pains of love.[26] Unlike poem 13, the courtliness of this cento lies not in the scriptorializations of the "courte Inperyall" but in the public halls of "musyke with all hur mynstralsye" (14.37), where the dances, songs, and chatter of good company only increase the burnings of desire (14.61–70). Love here burns with a "persyng vyolence" (14.7), and the lover, once again, lies "fettered yn cheyens" (14.141).

Nearly every line of these poems comes from the *Pastime of Pleasure*; yet there is little that is purely Hawesean about them. Stripped of their allegorical narrative, reconfigured as epistles, located in the pastimes or the surreptitions of the court, focusing repeatedly on vision, bodily distress, and the details of female beauty, and resonant with the idioms and imagery that would become the butt of Skelton's satire, these poems transform the romances of the age of Henry VII into the fantasies of the era of Henry VIII. To witness Skelton's handling of this same material, whether in the theatrics of *Magnyfycence* or the burlesques of *Phyllyp Sparowe*, is to see how he exposes the erotic topicality of Hawes's verse: shows its excesses, makes it ribald, risible, or rife with political potential. Wellys's poems are as much essays in excess as Skelton's are; yet for Wellys, the excesses are private, personal, and pained. Indeed, one might well say that the name Courtly Abusyon befits both Skelton and Wellys in their own distinctive ways. Both appear as figures who abuse courtly literature for powerfully transgressive ends, as readers of courtly texts who take the stories of desire and make them exemplars of rude pimpery or private angst.

I have already reviewed some of the environments in which Wellys read and wrote this poetry. His status as a recusant, his close ties to the circle of the Duke of Buckingham, his political service in Staffordshire, all placed him at the crossroads of political infighting throughout the middle of the sixteenth century.[27] He was admitted to the Inner Temple, married the daughter of William Chatwyn (an esquire of the body to both Henry VII and VIII), was elected to Parliament, and held a good deal of the Chatwyn lands in Staffordshire. Several of the poems in his manuscript on specifically courtly topics may have derived from exemplars in Chatwyn family manuscripts. His transcriptions of prophecies against the King would have been just the kind of treasonous action that local acquaintances informed against and which the Parliamentary acts of the 1530s and 40s were designed to legislate against. His writing, and then crossing out, of the word "pope" in several of the poems exemplifies what G. R. Elton has characterized as "Sedition or disaffection short of treason . . . the sort of resistance manifested in failure to erase the pope's name from books."[28] And Wellys's own encrypted statement of possession at the close of the manuscript preserves precisely the kinds of "cypheringe" that Henry VIII's acts defined as treasonous.[29] Even late in life, the smoke of sedition hung about him. During the Parliamentary election of Buckingham's grandson, Henry Stafford, in September 1553, Wellys clearly botched the campaign he was charged to manage. Stafford turned on his managers, among them Wellys, "who did as much as they could to have made sedition in that great assembly."[30] And, finally, the inventory of his will – with its record of a "settle to laye bokes in" and its account of "certen bokes" presented under the heading of "In the studye" – locates his reading matter, and, as Wilson has suggested, this very manuscript itself in the enclosures of the private space of reading: in the "studye," a place of secretive withdrawal, and in the "settle," a bench with a locker for secreting books.[31]

The privacies and surreptitions that control this manuscript's externals, and that are revealed in its familial coterie allusions and its defining accouterments of secrecy, encryption, and withdrawal, become the subject of the poetry it offers.[32] Throughout, love is a secret and a surreptitious thing. "Vnto you I nede nott to wryte my name," announces one of the verse letters, and another claims:

> from whens ytt cumethe ytt hath no name
> and whydder ytt shall yt sayethe þe same
> Then passe forthe the letter thorowȝ þis prese
> and save þi mastur shameles.   (47.65–68)

In this environment of anonymity, in a world of secretive unsigned missives and potentially dangerous encounters, the logic of sense impression takes on a new energy. To imprint in the mind – the language of Chaucerian impression and Lydgatean mnemonics filtered through the imagistic obsessions of Hawes – becomes one of the key tropes of these poems. What is inscribed, imprinted, or engraved, though, are not names but forms; not identifiable persons as such but the bodies of the lovers. Hearts and minds, too, are locked up: set deeply away in the recesses of the memory.

> my loue ys lockyd vnder your lace
> my body ys bereyd withyn your bowere.   (34.15–16)

And yet, the lover is not simply a prisoner, but I believe, more akin to one of the seditious books secreted in the settle of the study. As poem 45 puts it, announcing the injunction "prynte þis yn your mynde,"

> for yn your confydence my worde I haue closyde
> bothe locke and kay ye haue yn your gouernance
> and to yow my mynde I haue *sayllyde*   "sealed"
> Of very pety exyle me nott owt of remembrance.   (45.7–10)

The writer's word is locked up, much like a book closed in the clasps of binding or hidden under the lock and key of the *arca libraria*. Closed in the lover's remembrance, the writer's words now take on something of the status of Chaucer's "olde bookes" which, in the well-known equation from the *Prologue* to the *Legend of Good Women*, are the "keys to remembrance."

For Humphrey Wellys, the romance of remembrance lies precisely in these moments of epistolary surreptition and poetic allusion. As we read through his collection, we see strings of unnamed lovers exchange verse epistles that lament the losses, or endure the pains, of separation. Wellys's is a book of remembrances – of elegies on dead courtiers, of letters on departed loves. But it is, too, a book of literary reminiscences: of centos, quotations, and fragments drawn from the repositories of Middle English verse. Not only Hawes, Lydgate, and Skelton, but Chaucer shares a place in this chronicle of literary borrowings. "Exyle me nott owt of remembrance," writes the anonymous lover of Wellys's poem 45; but as we read on, we soon see that this is a woman writing:

> Thys I doo fynyshe my symple byll
> at owr metyng ye shall knowe more of my wyll
> vnto yow I nede nott to wryte my name
> for she þat louethe yow best send yow þis same.   (45.11–14)

The promise of the meeting invokes once again (as it had for the missives of Henry VIII) the trysts of Pyramus and Thisbe or, for that matter, of Troilus and Criseyde. Indeed, the language of imprisonment and bondage, so compellingly erotic in the Wellys anthology, may well have its Chaucerian source in Criseyde's own first effort at epistolary making.

> And into a closet, for t'avise hire bettre,
> She wente allone, and gan hire herte unfettre
> Out of *desdaynes prisoun* but a lite,   "the prison of disdain"
> And sette hire down, and gan a lettre write.   (II.1215–18)

And she, and Chaucer, go on: she will not "make hireselven bonde" to
Troilus, but will keep him at an arm's length (II.1222–23); she never did,
she says, anything "with more peyne / Than writen this, to which ye [i.e.,
Pandarus] me constreyne" (II.1230–31).

What Humphrey Wellys remembers in his book, I would suggest, are
moments such as this one: scenes of letter writing interlarded with the
language of imprisonment and pain. The locks and keys, the bonds and
fetters of the lyrics and epistles copied in his manuscript make literal the
psychic angst of Criseyde writing at this nodal point in Chaucer's poem.
And they raise, too, the compelling question of both Chaucer's and
Wellys's books. What does it mean to be a woman and be read by other
men? "Th'entente is al, and nat the lettres space" (V.1630), Criseyde
announced in closing her last letter, and with this remark she queries
what the proper space of letter-writing is: what are the boundaries of
personal decorum; how can the brief space of the folded paper contain
all the feelings of the writer?

> I dar nat, ther I am, wel lettres make,
> Ne nevere yet ne koude *I* wel endite.
> Ek gret effect *men* write in place lite.   (V.1627–29, emphasis mine)

The logic of Criseydean epistolarity centers on the impediments to self-
expression posed by male-defined epistolary form. To write letters as a
woman is – as she herself and Oenone could testify – by nature to be
misread by men.

For Humphrey Wellys, all women are potentially Criseyde. "Womans
sayinges trust noot to trulye" (57.16); "doo nott euer beleve the womans
compleynte . . . harlottes can collour bothe gloyse and paynt" (57.23,
25). Wantonness, harlotry, deception, elusiveness – all fit the women of
these texts, as in the poem with the refrain line "She þat hathe a wantan
eye" (21) or in the prose piece distinguishing between a harlot, a hunter,
and a whore (29). These are not simply the received tropes of a generalized anti-feminism, but a language specifically linked to Chaucer's
heroine. It is a language that descends directly from the portrait of her
limned by Lydgate; by the references to her in the fifteenth-century
Chance of the Dice and the *Pastime of Pleasure*; and, of course, by
Henryson's *Testament of Cressid*, a work that would have been widely
available to Tudor readers in its publication in Thynne's 1532 Chaucer
edition.[33] This is the fickle Criseyde, the exemplar of women who are, in

the words of Hawes's Godfrey Gobelieve in the *Pastime of Pleasure*, "so subtyll and so false of kynde / There can no man wade beyonde theyr mynde" (*Pastime*, lines 3568–69). Such a creature, to continue Hawes's paradigm, is not just adventitious or duplicitous, but also surreptitiously observed, as for example, when Godfrey, a little further on, describes Aristotle's desire:

> For to haue remedy of his sore sekenes
> Whan he her spyed ryght secrete alone
> Vnto her he wente and made all his mone.　　　(*Pastime*, lines 3579–81)

This is precisely the recalibration of the Troilan dilemma that informs Wellys's stance: the woman, now, as creature "spyed ryght secrete alone"; the woman who potentially would control the man; the woman who, while loving in private is humiliating in public. As Godfrey finishes his story:

> And so a brydle she put in his mouthe
> Vpon his backe she rode bothe northe and southe
> Aboute a chambre as some *cherkes* wene　　　[sic] "clerkes"
> Of many persones it was openly sene.　　　(*Pastime*, lines 3606–9)

Now, it is neither Troilus nor Diomede who would lead Criseyde by the bridle, as in Chaucer's poem, but this nameless woman who would turn philosophers into horses and reveal the privy power-plays of the beloved's chamber to the many in the open.

This is the context of Chaucerian reception that defines Wellys's transcriptions of women at their most vulgar and humiliating. When they are not the creatures of male delectation, they are powerful insulters of the male body. When they write their own letters of love and friendship to each other, they dismantle the male body into its scatologized, if not castrated, private parts. One of the most powerful of such articulations of female–female intimacy in the Wellys anthology is poem 7, titled "A lettre sende by on yonge woman to anoder, which aforetyme were ffellowes togeder." Here, we find not the courtly rhetoric of female love, nor do we find the finely-tuned elaborate stanza patterns of the Chaucerian and Lydgatean inheritance. Instead, the reader is subjected to rough couplets and rough intimacies. Traditionally associated with the genre of Good Gossips or Alewife poetry of late medieval England, this poem raises questions central to the construction of the female epistolary persona and the surreptitious male reader. It is a poem full of local detail, yet also one rich with broader literary implications. Its importance lies not simply in the family intrigues of the Staffordshire inhabitants it names, but more pointedly in the historical conundrums of the man who reads – or even intercepts – the writings of the woman.[34]

My loving ffrende, amorous bune,
I cum *ambelyng* to you by the same tokyn   "ambling"
That you and I haue be togeder,
And settyn by the ffire in colde wether,
And wyth vs noo moo but our Gullett,
Wyth all the *knakes in hur buggett*;   "trifles in her bag"
Hur trumpett and hur merye songe
Nowe ffor to here, I thinke itt longe.
Come amble me to hur, I you praye,
And to Agnes Irpe as bright as daye.
I wolde you were here to lokke our gates,
Butt alas itt ys ffare to the jakes.
Ffarewell, ffaire Agnes Blakamoure,
I wolde I hadde you here in stoore,
Ffor you wolde come with all your harte.
Ffarewell, ffarewell, my ladye darke.
Commande me to Wyllyam, I you desyre,
And praye hym to *wyshe vs* some of his ffyre,   "lead us to"
Ffor we haue non butt a coole or a stykke,
And soo we dryve awaye the *weke*.   "weak" or "week"
And commande me also to the roughe Hollye
That turnethe *itt* ofte into Godes bodye,   [i.e., bread; in the Mass]
And to all your oder ffelowes besyde
As well as I hadde ther names *discryed*.   "declared"
And praye John Cossall to be goode and kynde,
Ffor the nexte yere he wyl be blynde.
And bydde *Humffrey* doo hym noo shrowed turne,   [Humphrey Wellys?]
For then Sir John muste hym *wor[n]e*.   "restrain"?
Ande commande me to Thomson, that talle man,
Whiche shulde have a *lather* to pisse in a can;   "ladder"
And also to Nicholas with the blake berde,
On whome to loke itt makes me a-fferde.
My vncleȝ and my aunte be merye and glade.
And, thankes be to God, I am nott sadde,
And Christoffer, your ffrende, ys off good cheere
And many tymes he wissheth hym ther.
Ffaire tokens I wolde haue sende,
Butt I lakked money ffor to spende.
And thys, ffare you well, this goode Newe Yere
I pray you be merye and off good cheere;
And, ffor the love of swete Seynt Denys,
Att thys my letter thinke noo vnkyndnes,
Ffor to make you all merye I doo ryme,
And nowe to leave I thinke itt tyme.
Att nyne off the clokke thys was wrytten;
I wolde you were all *beshetyn*.   "shit upon"

Rhetorically, this poem seems to violate all the conventions of formal epistolary discourse set out in the literary models of Criseydean writing and the many manuals of *dictamen* proliferating in the fifteenth and the sixteenth centuries. From its first line, it establishes a personal relationship between the women that exceeds conventional amity. It begins, "My loving ffrende, amorous bune," and later addresses its recipient as "my ladye darke" (line 16). The anonymities of writer and reader contrast with the proliferation of the names in this text, so many "names discryed" that scholars have been able to reconstruct the precise social ambiance in which it must have circulated among the Wellys and other families of Staffordshire of the early 1530s.[35] But the whole point of this missive lies in the contrast between the identified circle of locals and the unidentified correspondents. Writer and reader stand as anonymous girls in a world of named, parental and authoritative figures. And while it is quite pointed in its dating ("Newe Yere") and even its timing of composition, its concluding lines confirm the correspondents in a playful mockery of social and epistolary decorum (lines 42–46).

This is a letter that just barely skirts the line between *amor* and *amicitia*, between the everyday conventions of epistolary friendship and the innuendoes of intimacy. Who is this "lady darke" and why is she unnamed? What is the force of the scatology that closes the letter, and for that matter, of the couplet in the middle of the poem: "I wolde you were here to lokke our gates, / Butt alas itt ys ffare to the jakes" (lines 11–12)? And just who is the "amorous bune"? Lexicographically a puzzle, *bune* is a proper name to Edward Wilson, who confesses in his study of the manuscript: "not recognized by previous editors as a surname, but I have not identified her."[36] The editors of the recently published edition of the *Welles Anthology* are similarly baffled, and reduced to finding in the *OED* a meaning of "squirrel" and conjecturing a term of endearment.[37] But we need no great proficiency in lexicography or onomastics to see *bune* as just what it appears to be. The *OED*, in fact, does define *Bun* in northern dialect as "the tail of a hare, also transf. to human beings," and the *Dictionary of the Older Scottish Tongue* concurs (and offers *bune* as an alternative spelling). Both cite a quotation from the Scots poet Sir David Lyndsay, *c.*1538, contemporary with Wellys's poem: "I lauch best to se ane Nwn, / Gar beir hir taill abouve hir bwn." *Bune* means "buns," and this expression of anatomical intimacy is on a par with the poem's overarching preoccupation with the scatologized body: for example, the use of the familiar Tudor sexual innuendoes of horsemanship in line 9, "come amble me to hur, I you praye"; the blunt insult about Thomson, "that talle man / Whiche shulde have a lather to pisse in a can" (lines 29–30); the concluding wish to shit upon all those named in the letter; and what I believe to be the innuendoes of lines 14 ("have in store"), 18 (the fire of Wyllyam) and perhaps the puns on the name Gullett (line 5) and rough holly (line 21).

This is a poem that does not simply violate social decorum and epistolary convention through its "fireside vulgarity." It is a poem that defines the male and female body as the sum of their genital and excremental parts. Its catalogue of attributes, its coterie allusions, even its specificity of dating, make it the vulgar antitype to the Hawesean compilation of poem 13. This is not a poem of the "courte Inperyall" but verses of the jakes, a poem that appeals not to the erotics of the courtly gaze but to the voyeurisms of the provincial interloper. It is, in essence, an anti-*blazon*, a poem written from the woman's view, one that dismembers human forms not into items of erotic delectation but, instead, into the objects of a voyeur's gaze. For the key point is that, irrespective of its historical composition, its survival in this manuscript makes it a poem written down by a man's hand. Read in the context of its scribe's preoccupations with discovery and shame – and with his parallel predilections associating sexual and political transgression – this text becomes a textbook of voyeurism. It is a poem, then, that makes its reader privy to the privy. Its transcription into Wellys's volume renders it a spectacle of the transgressions of the female voice and body. It functions, I believe, in Wellys's book as something of an intercepted document: a letter found and transcribed by the very "Humffrey" who is there inscribed within it.

Such an environment of epistolary transmission and transgression provides the contexts for the cento of stanzas from *Troilus and Criseyde* that constitutes item 38 in Wellys's manuscript.[38] Like the Hawesean poems of the volume, it represents an attempt to transform narrative poetry into amorous epistle. Moreover, in its rewritings of Chaucer's lines, the poem seeks to place the *Troilus* not in the Lydgateanized moral calibrations of the fifteenth century, but in the Hawesean preoccupations with engraving, etching, memory, and courtly secrecy that articulate the early Tudor literary condition. Wellys's poem begins with Pandarus's voice paraphrasing Troilus's first letter to Criseyde (II.1121–27). In Chaucer's poem, this is a moment rich with all the secretive manipulations that distinguish the English figure from his source in Boccacio's Pandaro. Pandarus draws Criseyde away from her companions with a story about Greek spies. He leads her "Into the gardyn," so that she may hear "Al pryvely" of these events (II.1114–15). But, of course, Pandarus's tale of espionage is itself a ruse designed to get himself and Criseyde out of public earshot (II.1118–19) in order that he might read to her Troilus's letter. This is the setting for Pandarus's performance and for the opening of Wellys's poem: a narrative prehistory of surreption and epistolary secrecy that surrounds the announcement of the letter. And in the text of Wellys's manuscript, the stanza's last two lines are altered to enhance this sense of secrecy. Instead of Pandarus's claim that Troilus might die unless Criseyde responds, the Wellys poem voices the fear that the lover might never see her beloved again.

> or Soo helpe me god the truthe to sayne
> I thynke ye shall neuer See hym agayne.   (38.6–7)

Instead of offering the Chaucerian original, in which Pandarus appears to inaugurate the love affair, this stanza creates the impression that an affair has been going on. In other words, what we read here is an intercepted missive in an ongoing exchange of surreptitious meetings and exchanges.

What follows this stanza in Chaucer's poem is Criseyde's blunt answer, "Scrit ne bille . . . that toucheth swich matere / Ne bryng me noon" (II.1130–32). Yet, that is just what Wellys's poem does, as its following two stanzas offer something that looks very much like a traditional lover's epistle. Their source in *Troilus and Criseyde*, however, is not a written letter but a song: the "Cantus Antigone" from earlier in Book II (corresponding to II.841–47 and 869–75, respectively). Here, again, each of these stanzas ends with lines that radically depart from Chaucer's text. Stanza two ends with a conventional lover's plaint, complete with the prayer, "Iesue preserue yow wher So euer ye be" (38.14). Stanza three reaffirms the impediments to the lovers' meeting: "for she hathe answeryd me that we tweane / shall neuer mete as louers a gayne" (38.20–21). Each of these stanzas also shifts subtly the focus of their Chaucerian original – or, to put it more precisely, what modern editors have construed as that Chaucerian original. Compare line 10 of Wellys's poem with II.843 of *Troilus and Criseyde*:

> of wytt apollo stoune of Secretenes   (38.10)
> Of wit Apollo, stoon of sikernesse   (II.843)

Wellys's line shares the reading "secretnes" with the scribally manipulated Harley 2392 text (Windeatt's sigla H4) as well as with Caxton's 1483 printing (and those of de Worde, 1517, and Pynson, 1526, that derive from it). At line 18, Wellys's poem shares another Caxtonian reading (II.872):

> In whome my harte grauyn ys Soo faste

All the surviving manuscripts of Chaucer's poem read "growen" for "grauen" in this line, and yet Caxton's phrasing was retained by de

Worde and Pynson in their editions. Not until Thynne's edition of 1532 was this line restored (as was the reading "sikernesse" at II.843).[39]

At one level, these seemingly minor variations (together with several others)[40] have a bibliographical importance in that they point to a pre-Thynne source for Wellys. The other identifiable extracts in the manuscript – poems made up of stanzas culled from the poetry of Hawes, as well those that incorporate lines from Lydgate's *Temple of Glas* and *The Churl and the Bird* – were all drawn from texts originally printed and reprinted by Caxton and de Worde, and significantly not included in Thynne's volume. Taken together, these selections and the evidence of their printed transmission imply that Wellys's Chaucerianism was not stimulated by the publication of Thynne's edition, as was that of the contributors to the Devonshire Manuscript. Nor do his transcripts and appropriations testify to what Paul G. Remley has called, writing of that manuscript, "the *immediate* impact of printed texts on the reception of medieval poetry in the Tudor period."[41] Instead, Wellys's selections look back to the older lineage of Caxton and de Worde, of Hawes and Skelton, to show us a reader of a previous generation's literature. In this context, the Hawesean flavor of Wellys's own revisions to Chaucer's text take on a thematic as well as a bibliographical significance. The exhortation that begins the second stanza of Wellys's *Troilus*-cento, "O my swete harte . . . of truthe the grounde myrrour of godlyhede" (83.8–9, corresponding to *Troilus and Criseyde* II.841–42), resonates with the imagery of the *Pastime of Pleasure*, with its attentions to the grounds and mirrors on whose surfaces the lover sees inscriptions of his love. Speech transforms itself into texts, and the trajectory of *Troilus and Criseyde*, much like that of the Wellys anthology itself, presents its lovers finally as distant readers of transmitted letters.

Such a thematizing of the documentary informs another of Wellys's revisions to his Troilan poem, one not traceable to a textual source. After a stanza drawn from Troilus's lament (stanza four, corresponding to IV.561–67), stanzas five and six turn to Criseyde's speeches (V.1072–78 and II.778–84, respectively). Criseyde's address in Book V ends with a line in the narrator's voice:

> And with that word she *brast* anon to wepe.   (V.1078)   "burst"

In Wellys's poem, the line reads:

> thys for to wryte my harte doeth *brest* to wepe.   (38.35)   "burst"

"Word" becomes "wryte," speech becomes text, and what the lover writes, in stanza six, are lines from Criseyde's inner thoughts from Book II. Here, too, the lines are recast slightly to displace them from their local reference in the poem and make them appear more pointedly the laments of the lover in the manuscript. The poem then proceeds, in stanza seven, to return to Pandarus, now in a maximal mood (from I.708–12), while the stanza concludes with two lines drawn from Diomede's explanations to Criseyde (V.139–40). Finally, in the last two stanzas, Troilus's voice appears again in the laments of Book IV, though of course the spoken names of Troilus and Criseyde in his speech are effaced behind the anonymities of the first- and second-person pronouns and an apostrophe to "dere gode" (38.50–63, corresponding to IV.266–73).

If we step back from this analysis of local variations and contextual allusions, we may see not the garbled awkward compilation read by the Wellys anthology's most recent editors but a creative attempt to distill the entirety of Chaucer's narrative into a brief exchange of voices, letters, and anxieties. Its sequence is precise, offering a stanza-by-stanza epistolary dialogue and commentary: Pandarus (1), female lover (2, 3), male lover (4), female lover (5, 6), Pandarus (7), male lover (8, 9). Its stanzas are voiced texts, not disembodied fragments. Its imagery is consistent with the controlling interests of the manuscript as a whole. And its drama is to be located not just in the laments of the lovers but, I think more powerfully, in the reader's own experience of their laments. For, in the end, this is, like so many of the lyric sequences of Wellys's volume, an act of poetic ventriloquism. To read the sequences of love epistles alternately voiced as male and female; to turn from the girlish intimacies of "amorous bune" to the paternal maxims of the letter which follows to the young apprentice; to read the poems spoken by the dead Sir Gryffyth, his wife, and the slaughtered buck in their sequence – these are experiences that reveal not just that Wellys had, in Edward Wilson's words, "an order and a purpose" to his *compilatio*.[42] It is to recognize that something of that order is the drama of impersonation. Wellys's poems often shift from male to female speakers like a homespun *Heroides*. They write little dramas of epistolary exchange or debates on love and public service. And they provide, in the large, the model for his Troilan cento: a distillation of the voices, characters, and views of Chaucer's fictional creations. His miniature dramas take place in the small space of the literary letter. They speak the language and reflect the reading of the Pandaric postman and counselor in love.

The Devonshire Manuscript

The poems of the Devonshire Manuscript have long been understood as testimony to the personalizations of the Middle English literary inheritance. Interlarded among selections from Wyatt, Surrey, and other known and anonymous versifiers of the Shelton–Howard circle, are excerpts from poetry now known to have appeared in Thynne's Chaucer edition of 1532. One piece, copied towards the beginning of the manuscript, brings together four stanzas from Troilus's lament from Book IV of Chaucer's poem (lines 288–308, 323–29), introduced by a couplet drawn from the narrator's proem to that book (lines 13–14), in order to create a new verse epistle in a sequence of exchanges believed to record the illicit love of Thomas Howard and Margaret Douglas. Midway through the anthology, Pandarus's advisory remarks from Book I (lines 946–52) punctuate an assembly of short lyrics on the fickleness and deceits of love. The final leaves of the anthology are filled with stanzas culled from Thynne's Chaucer volume: from Hoccleve's *Letter of Cupid*, the anonymous *Remedy of Love*, Sir Richard Roos's *La Belle Dame sans Merci*, Chaucer's *Anelida and Arcite*, and on its last two leaves, five stanzas taken from Book II of *Troilus and Criseyde*.

Yet, while the sources of these excerpts have been known for decades, and while much scholarly energy has been devoted to identifying the different hands that wrote them, they continue to be discussed *as* excerpts: that is, as gobbets of Chaucerian sentiment that, stanza-by-stanza, reflect the emotional condition of the Devonshire Manuscript's scribes. This "plundering" of medieval poetry tends to be understood as something of a slack ventriloquism, a recourse to familiar texts to voice the personal experience of the lovers associated with the volume's compilation.[43] Furthermore, the critical interpretation of these selections has been inextricably linked with the paleographical identification of the individuals who wrote them – as if literary meaning were inseparable from scribal action; as if literary voice were identical to scribal hand.

Ever since Kenneth Muir printed the unpublished selections from the manuscript, three blocks of writing have been recognized as appearing in the same hand: poems numbered by Muir as 7–14, 31, and 43–54.[44] These are sections that incorporate or are made up of the Thynne selections, and it is clear that they represent narrative and lyric sequences. Their handwriting has long been thought to be that of Thomas Howard, a view challenged recently by Paul Remley, but (without knowledge of Remley's work) powerfully reasserted by Helen Baron. Remley argues that these poems are in the hand of Mary Shelton, and that her selections of Chauceriana represent not passive copyings but acts of literary composition. Shelton, he claims, "interacts with the medieval texts she copies in the Devonshire Manuscript" in order to "find a voice for her indignation at the treatment of women of her time by hypocritical lovers."[45] Baron, however, offers a different picture of Chaucerian appropriation. Her systematic disentanglement of the nineteen or so hands that appear in the collection points not to Mary Shelton as the author/compiler of the Thynne texts, but instead to Thomas Howard. Moreover, Barron argues that the poems between Howard and Margaret Douglas are not, as Remley thinks, sequences transcribed by Mary Shelton after the imprisonment of the lovers but are, instead, poems of courtship entered in Howard's own hand.[46]

My purpose here is not to adjudicate among these various interpretations of the scribal hands (though I believe that the logic of the Chaucerian centos does imply, if not a male hand, at least a male literary agency behind them). The emphasis on Troilus's voice, on Pandarus's counsel, and on the drama of Book II of the poem all point to a ventriloquist of Chaucer's masculine anxiety, someone who appropriates, and at times bluntly rewrites, the touchstones of Troilan love in order to articulate a new literary persona. My goal, instead, is to assess this poetry as lyric sequences, to read the mix of voices in the single scribal hand, and to understand how literary imitations or poetic excerpts can write voiced dramas. These passages from Devonshire are much like their contemporary entries in the manuscript of Humphrey Wellys: acts of impersonation that cautiously and, at times transgressively, tread the line between public life and private memory, between romance and remembrance. Yet such passages, male script notwithstanding, are testimonies to the woman's role in love, and in the course of my analysis, I illustrate the ways in which Margaret Douglas is inscribed as Criseyde in this family Chaucerian performance – not just in the Devonshire Manuscript itself, but in the many documents that offer us a vision of her life sketched out along literary lines.

The first set of poems in what may be Thomas Howard's hand (Muir 7–14), show the lovers separated by "pryson stronge" (7.5).[47] Some of these verses are clearly in the man's voice, some obviously in the woman's, and read in sequence they chart a rhetorically conventional epistolary exchange centered on the angst of courtly love. Whether they chronicle the historical imprisonment of Thomas Howard, or whether they simply deploy the conventions of amorous metaphorical incarceration, one thing they do stress is the physicality of writing and, in particular, the importance of the pen in transcribing love. In poem 8, the narrator declines "To wryte off them that dothe dysdayne / Faythfull louers that be so truew," thus in the process denying himself something of the obvious relief for the pains he suffers. And yet, writing alone does not grant unequivocal release. Poem 9 depicts the paradoxes of the writing lover:

> Yff I shuld wryte and make report
> What faythfulnes in yow I fynd
> The terme off lyfe yt were to short
> Wyth penne yn letters yt to bynd:
> Wherfor wher as ye be so kynd,
> As for my part yt ys but due
> Lyke case to yow to be as true.   (Muir 9.8–14)

Here, the poem's narrator plays on the many connotations of writing in both its legal and its amorous contexts. To "wryte and make report" is drawn directly from the language of the law, as if these poems now were offering a testimony to the love: a wild inversion, say, of the proceedings that placed these lovers in jail and that tested a "faythfulnes" not to the lover but the crown.[48] So, too, the phrase "terme off lyfe" connotes the sentence granted (the life term of prison) as well as the more familiar literary phrasing drawn from the conventions of Middle English love poetry.[49] The pen and letters, here, are not a release but a further fettering. What is bound in line 4 of this stanza is both the bond of love between the man and woman and the sentence, the life term, of line 3. The final couplet of the stanza further develops these legal and amorous ambiguities. What is "due" in the penultimate line is the report that must be written, and the "case" of the final line is both the situation of the lover (asking for written reply) and the legal case that has placed them in prison.[50]

Poem 11 similarly takes the image of the pen and presses it into the service of a binding. The beloved is "firmly set" in the lover's heart "As tonge or penne can yt repet," that is, as anyone could speak or write about it. Poem 13 develops these images to meditate on the practice of amorous epistolary exchange itself.

> To yowr gentyll letters an answere to resyte,
> Both I an my penne there to wyll aply,
> And thowgh that I can not your goodnes aquyte
> In ryme and myter elegantly
> Yet I do meane as faythfully
> As euer dyd louer for his part,
> I take god to record whych knowyth my hart.   (Muir 13.1–7)

Here, the overlay of legalism which had characterized poem 9 is transmuted into the patina of poetry. The lover's apology here repeats precisely the humility topos so familiar from post-Chaucerian verse-making: the appeal to intention in the face of limited ability, the association of the writer with the agent of writing, and the sense, too, that the epistle is really a kind of envoi offered for the delectation, and possible correction, of the reader. "For terme of lyfe thys gyfte ye haue," the poem's final stanza opens (echoing the idiom of poem 9) and it concludes with what has long been understood as Thomas Howard's initials, in effect, signing this poem much as Chaucer's Troilus and Criseyde would close their missives of Book V as "T" and "C."

This poetic self-consciousness – this sense of an identified author (T. H.) miming the tropes not just of love but of late medieval literary authorship – extends to the final poem in this sequence, the stanzas from Book IV of *Troilus*, prefaced by the couplet from that book's proem:

> And now my pen, alas, wyth whyche I wryte,
> Quaketh for drede off that I must endyte.
>
> (Muir 14.1–2; *Troilus and Criseyde*, IV.13–14)

These lines from Chaucer's proem to Book IV would provide one of the central idioms of authorial anxiousness throughout the fifteenth and early sixteenth century. They became, in fact, so widely used by Lydgate that they stand as something of a signature for his own post-Chaucerian protestations of inadequacy. In the *Troy Book*, *Fall of Princes*, the *Life of Our Lady*, and other widely circulated works, Lydgate appropriates the image of the quaking pen to signal his anxieties about the literary task ahead.[51] But it is, perhaps, in the *Temple of Glas* that the phrase becomes the touchstone for the visionary lover in a bind. When the narrator beholds the sorrow of the poem's lover, chastised by the goddess of love, he states:

> For rouþe of which his wo as I endite,
> Mi penne I fele quaken as I write.　　(*Temple of Glas*, lines 946–47)

These lines were clearly singled out by later readers for their personalized power and, perhaps, Chaucerian referent. An early reader of the 1477 Caxton edition of the *Temple* (in the copy now in the Cambridge University Library) placed an X in the left margin next to this couplet, and the line – more akin to Lydgate's version than to Chaucer's – shows up later in poem 34 of the Wellys anthology, a poem cobbled out of pieces of the *Temple*.

> Swete harte vnto yow thys letter I Sende
> my peyne I feele quake as I doo yt wryte.　　(Wellys 34.22–23)[52]

Much like the poem in the Devonshire Manuscript, these are the lines of a lover in a prison, and they are lines, like the ones that follow, modeled on Lydgate's amorous incarceration.

> Thys I most lyue bothe yn hoppe and drede
> lyke as a prisoner wayttyng his lybertye
> bowndon yn cheens lyke to be dede
> nott yn parradyse butt yn purkatorye.　　(Wellys 34.29–32)[53]

These excerpts illustrate the ways in which the stance of authorship could be transferred to the anxieties of love. They chart the passage of a Chaucerian idiom through the amorous fantasies of Lydgate to the shorter verse epistles of the Wellys and Devonshire manuscripts, and, in the process, reveal not just the influence of Chaucer but the mediations of Chaucerians. To select these lines from the prologue to Book IV of *Troilus and Criseyde* is, in a sense, to read Chaucer through his later imitators. It is to appropriate the language of authorial reflection for the processes of amorous epistolarity. It is to enact what may be a pervasively Lydgatean reading of Chaucer, and the image of the prisoner of love, together with the more complex associations of amorous writing and authorial self-definition that characterize Lydgate's work, make these entries from Devonshire less the unique personal articulations of sixteenth-century identity and more the voicings of a tradition of late medieval poetizing.[54] Chaucer's stanzas from the *Troilus* thus stand at the close of a poetic sequence in the manuscript. They return us to the *Urtext* of love's penmanship and to the Troilan longing that stands verbally and tonally as the controlling subtext to poems 7–13 in the manuscript.

This couplet also stands as something of an epigraph to the selection of stanzas that makes up Muir 14. Such a selection now is less a lyric or a letter than it is an inscription on a tomb. Troilus's lament on fortune from Book IV is abbreviated and excerpted here into a species of "enditing." The voiced complaint from Chaucer's poem – with its image of the errant "goost" flying out of Troilus's body and following Criseyde – becomes in Devonshire an incised epitaph. "Thy ryght place ys nowe no lenger here" (IV.308). In Chaucer's text, this line is followed by two further stanzas on the loss of Criseyde, on the pain of Troilus, and on the central imagery of sight and light that makes the woman the absent object of Troilan vision. In Devonshire, we move directly to the stanza in which Troilus imagines himself dead and buried, and in which he addresses all future lovers visiting his tomb.

> But whan ye comen by my sepulture
> Remembre that yowr felowwe resteth there,
> For I louyd eke, thowgh I vnworthy were.
> *(Muir 14.28–30; Troilus and Criseyde, IV.323– 29)*

Now, in this sequence, Troilus's earlier line comes to mean not only that the soul would flee the body after the beloved, but that the "ryght place" of the lover is not in the "here" of living speech but in the "there" of sepulchral writing. What the pen "endites," in this poem, is the lover's own epitaph.

This poetic sequence may be understood not only in relation to its source in Chaucer, but in apposition to its analogue in Wyatt. The first poem of the second grouping in the manuscript[55] is Wyatt's "My pen, take pain a little space" (Rebholz, *The Complete Poems*, CCVIII), a poem that sets out the key relations between writing and desire so central to Devonshire's Chaucerian sequences. The set of prison poems offers clear verbal resonances to Wyatt's text, and both develop a controlling pun on "pen" and "pain." Wyatt apposes both words in his first line, and his subsequent stanza subtly refigures the relations – semantic, metrical, and sonic – between the two words. Stanza two places "my pains" and "my pen" in precisely the same metrical position in their respective lines (7, 10), while stanza four chimes out a sequence of internal rhymes and assonances:

> To love in vain whoever shall,
> Of worldly pain it passeth all
> . . .
> Alas, my pen, now write no more.
>
> (Rebholz, *The Complete Poems*, CCVIII.21–22, 25)

And, as the poem's final stanza recapitulates the first, the pen and pain vie for the "space" retained for the beloved in his heart. This is a poem about the ability of writing to recapture loss; about how the act of personal inscription replaces the space left by the lover's pain. The sequence of anxieties, culminating in the decision for the pen to "write no more," describes a movement not from voice to silence but from full to empty page. So, too, for the lyrics of the Devonshire Manuscript, the pen and pain are linked in acts of amorous writing. To read poem 9, for example, against its analogue in Wyatt is to see now the puns and pains in its first stanza:

> What thyng shold cawse me to be sad?
> As long as ye rejoyce wyth hart
> My part yt ys for to be glad:
> Syns yow haaue taken me to yor part
> Ye do relese my pene and smart
> Whych wold me very sore insue
> But that for yow my trust so trew.
>
> (Muir 9.1–7)

"Ye do relese my pene and smart" – a line redolent of Wyatt, a line that sonically (as well as orthographically) associates the "pain" and "pen" that is released. For, as the second stanza of this poem will aver, it is the "penne yn letters" that will "bynd" the term of life – not just a "pen" in letters but a "pain in letters." This space between the pen and pain informs, too, not only the wordplay of Wyatt or the orthography of

Thomas Howard, but the scribal readings of *Troilus and Criseyde* itself. Indeed, the confusions between the two words may have led to the scribe of the manuscript Durham, Cosin MS V.II.13 (Windeatt's MS D) to rewrite those lines from the prologue to Book IV that generated the procession of images I have been tracing:

> And now my *pein*, allas, with which I write,
> *O waketh* for drede of that I moste endite.[56] (emphases mine)

Such fascinations with the graphology of love govern the Devonshire scribe's reading of his Thynne, and it would have directed his eye to the stanza from the *Remedy of Love* that is transcribed into the closing sequence of Chaucerian stanzas in the manuscript.

> Yff all the erthe were parchment scrybable
> Spedy for the hand, and all maner wode
> Were hewed and proportyoned to pennes able
> Al water ynke, in damme or in flode,
> Euery man beyng a parfyte scribe or goode,
> The faythfulnes yet and prayse of women
> Cowde not be shewyd by the meane off penne.   (Muir 45)

The Devonshire scribe has departed from the original in Thynne by rewriting the stanza's penultimate line in praise of, rather than in condemnation of women. In Thynne, it was "The cursydnesse yet and diceyte of women" that could not be shown by means of the pen, and this stanza had fit into the *Remedy*'s sustained misogynist diatribe. It is a benchmark of anti-feminism familiar from much of early Tudor printed poetry on love, and it recalls, too, many of the biting poems in the Wellys anthology, as well as the string of stanzas in Devonshire attributed to Richard Hattfeld.[57] This stanza's small revision has been noted ever since its source was first discerned. As Elizabeth Heale has put it, summarizing much of the scholarship on this section of the manuscript and voicing, too, some of the current critical desires of the modern reader:

It would be pleasant to be able to claim that these stanzas were copied by a woman, . . . but it is entirely possible that they were noted and copied out by Thomas Howard or another man, whether to amuse and please their female acquaintances, or as a source of poems of their own. The content of the stanzas does, however, make clear that the copyist was particularly interested in a rhetoric spoken in a woman's voice of defence against misogynist attack . . . In a system of manuscript copying, appropriation, and adaptation, the question is perhaps less one of the name or gender of an originating author than of the kinds of voices and gestures the available discourses make possible to copiers and readers of both sexes.[58]

I think this is precisely what is going on in the revisions to the *Remedy of*

Love and to this stanza's place in the concluding *ordinatio* of Chauceriana in the manuscript. At stake is not, necessarily, the gender of the scribe or author but what Heale describes as the available "voices and gestures." What I would argue, however, is that such voices and gestures have both an historical and literary meaning – or to put it more precisely, that the line between the literary and the historical is meaningfully, if not deliberately, blurred by those voices, gestures, and discourses. We cannot fruitfully distinguish between the "real" Thomas Howard and the personage presented on the page. Nor can we truly assume that the audience for these poems corresponds to the historically recoverable men and women of the Howard/Douglas/Shelton circle. What we can do, however, is locate more precisely the poetic contexts for the voices on the Devonshire manuscript's last leaves. Such contexts, I propose, are to be found not simply in the individuated stanzas culled from Thynne's volume, but in the new poetic sequences they are assembled to create: sequences that are modeled on the poems found in Thynne itself. This is a new sequence that enacts the very charge of the *Remedy*'s stanza: namely, to show by means of the pen the power of love and love verse; to show, quite pointedly, through the pen what the printed text did not.

This emphasis on pens and writing frames these Chaucerian appropriations against their source in a published volume and helps effect what I consider as the transformation of this public, published literature into private writing. In effect, this scribe has constructed a miniature epistolary exchange, a set of alternating male- and female-voiced stanzas, that mime the dialogues and the *debats d'amours* that shape such poems as *La Belle Dame sans Merci*. The characters in that poem, Lamant and La dame, speak, in essence, in the Devonshire Manuscript in words appropriated from the most explicit of late medieval amorous debate texts. In turn, the self-conscious epistolography of these selections may also reenact that of the *Troilus* and the *Letter of Cupid*: texts that are themselves offered up as transcriptions of literary missives. To read this closing sequence through its voices, rather than its authors, is to realign the dramatic effect of textual transcription in the Devonshire manuscript.

> Muir 43: *Letter of Cupid* (lines 344–50): Cupid's voice
> Muir 44: *Letter of Cupid* (lines 64–77): Cupid's voice
> Muir 45: *Remedy of Love* (lines 239–45): man's misogynist voice, adapted as a voice of praise; woman's voice?
> Muir 46: *La Belle Dame* (lines 717–24): Lamant
> Muir 47: *La Belle Dame* (lines 229–36): Lamant
> Muir 48: *Letter of Cupid* (lines 302–8): Cupid's voice
> Muir 49: *Anelida and Arcite* (lines 308–16): Anelida's voice
> Muir 50–51: *Troilus and Criseyde* (II.337–51): Pandarus's voice

Muir 52–53: *Troilus and Criseyde* (II.778–91): Criseyde's voice

Muir 54: *Troilus and Criseyde* (II.855–61): Antigone's voice

What emerges from this sequence is a dialogue among male and female speakers. Cupid begins the debate, positing what might be thought of as the topic for discussion, the resolution, as it were, for the debate: "Womans herte vnto no creweltye / Enclynyd is . . ." The next two stanzas offer a response. The following selection, from the *Remedy*, presents the claim that it would be impossible to write completely of the good of women. Stanzas 46 and 47, drawn from the laments of Lamant, are markedly in the male voice; Hoccleve's Cupid returns again in stanza 48 to remind us of the deceitfulness of men, while in stanza 49 the voice of the complaining Anelida sustains this critique: "Wher ys the truthe off man?" The male voice returns in stanzas 50–51, now the language of Pandarus adapted to the speaker himself (the Devonshire scribe has altered Chaucer's line "his death" to "my death"). The woman has the last word in the final three stanzas of the sequence, drawn from Criseyde's speeches and Antigone's song.

The central theme of this exchange is honesty and truth in the face of treason. Such issues as the confessing of traitorous behavior and the dissimulating of speech (to speak "so fayre and falsey inward thowght," stanza 44), acts of deceit (stanza 48), slander and false report (stanzas 52–53), and defamation (stanza 54) have both a literary and a social resonance for Devonshire and its readers. On the one hand, they recall the bywords of a courtly making, the preoccupations with deception and fidelity that inform the texture of Henrician verse from Hawes to Wyatt. They are, to some degree, the tropes of love, whether articulated by the broken poet of the *Conforte of Louers*, the beset squire of *Undo Youre Dore*, or by Wyatt's narrator himself who, in the first poem of the Devonshire Manuscript had counseled, "Take heed betime lest ye be spied." But on the other hand, these are the facts of social life. The fear of false report and slander takes on an immediacy in a time when gentry were reporting on each other, when spouses were encouraged to betray, and when letters were intercepted for evidence of sedition. In a world of such interceptory politics, the Devonshire Manuscript's fascination with the makings of the pen takes on a fearful resonance. What was showed "by the meane off penne" were the very acts of sedition that Henry VIII's legislations were enacted to regulate. The emphases on writing, ciphering, and printing; the anxiousness about the signature; the fear of forgery – all grant a powerful political subtext to such familiar Chaucerian ventriloquisms as those of the quaking pen. If all the earth *were* parchment scribable, one might presume, surveillance would be simple.

The correspondence of the Lisle family from the mid 1530s, for example, is rife with examples of the letter-writers' refusal to convey information, with the anxiousness about reporting "news," and with the recognition that the very existence of letters (irrespective of their contents) could be actionable offenses.[59] Informancy was, if not rampant, then at least common enough for the gentry to reserve their words. "Also wyckyd tonges byn so prest / To speake us harme," says Criseyde, now ventriloquized in the penultimate stanza of Devonshire (II.785–86; Muir 53). She may as well be speaking in the voice of Lady Honor Lisle, who recognized the possibility of interception and the threats of arrest. "Here are no news to be written," she cautiously writes to her husband.[60] So, too, John Husee, Lord Lisle's secretary, had to suppress information from a letter whose contents he needed to "declare" to the Lord of the Privy Seal: "Touching news, this bearer will inform your lordship," face to face, it is assumed.[61] As Muriel St. Clare Byrne notes, summarizing the elisions and anxieties of this clutch of letters,

This complete detachment of Lisle and his wife, in their letters, from the fate of his kinsmen, is perhaps the most eloquent comment in the whole correspondence upon the danger of sending news in letters . . . [A]t this point their personal correspondence proves beyond a doubt that they had woken up to the reality of the immediate present. (*The Lisle Letters*, vol. V, p. 279)

But if anyone had been awake to the immediate present, and if anyone could have been sensitive to the Criseydean anxieties of "wyckyd tonges," it would have been Margaret Douglas herself. It has long been suspected that Douglas had been inscribed into the narratives of Devonshire's excerpts. The passage from Book IV put together into the first of the Chaucerian entries of the manuscript (Muir 14) has two lacunae, where, it is presumed, Criseyde's name from the original text has been omitted so that Margaret's name could be inserted (though this name, if it is her name, has been erased from the manuscript).[62] If Thomas Howard represents, to some degree, the Troilan lover, Margaret Douglas is Criseyde, and her identification with a literary figure goes far beyond mere role-playing. From her youth, Margaret Douglas had lived as the object of personal desire and political exchange, and the surviving documents that tell her tale inscribe her in the narratives of inquiry and pimpery that make her a Criseydean figure in the stories of Pandaric life.

The niece of Henry VIII, Margaret spent her life shuttling among the needs of men.[63] First her father, the Earl of Angus, who abducted her in 1528 from her mother and her mother's half-brother, the Scottish King James V. Then, King Henry himself, who after her arrival at the court in 1531 at age sixteen soon placed her in the pandarisms of diplomacy. A letter from Castillon to Francis I of 16 March 1534 succinctly defines

Margaret's place in Henry's scheme. Reporting on discussions of the marriageability of Henry's daughter, Mary, Castillon noted:

He added that there were many other girls in his kingdom, and that he had a niece, daughter of the queen of Scotland, whom he keeps with the Queen his wife, and treats like a queen's daughter, and if any proposition were made for her, he would make her marriage worth as much as his daughter Mary's. I assure you the lady is beautiful, and highly esteemed here; and if Mary is passed over, there is a daughter of the late queen of France and the duke of Suffolk, but still very young, for whom he will readily enter the said alliance. (*Letters and Papers*, VII.13)

Henry plays pander to his niece, as Castillon shares in the pimperies of state alliances: two figures out of Skelton's *Magnyfycence* parading female wares before a marriage-seeking prince. Such panderings were, in the legislations of the King, however, soon to be not just the preferences of the sovereign but the rule of law. "A statute has . . . been passed," noted Chapuys to Charles V in July of 1536, "making it treason to treat for marriage with anyone of the blood royal without the King's consent" (*Letters and Papers*, VII.147), and this was to be Margaret Douglas's undoing. For, in Chapuys's account, Thomas Howard had "treated a marriage *par parolles de present* with the daughter of the queen of Scots and earl of Angus," and such a contract had provoked the Parliament to condemn him to death. Chapuys goes on, after noting the passing of the new statute:

The said personage of the blood royal [i.e., Margaret Douglas] was also to die, but for the present has been pardoned her life considering that copulation had not taken place; and certainly if she had done much worse she deserved pardon, seeing the number of domestic examples she has seen and sees daily, and that she has been for eight years of age and capacity to marry. Since the case has been discovered she has not been seen, and no one knows whether she be in the Tower, or some other prison.

   The King is much mortified 'devant mariage dicelle sa nyece' . . . (*Letters and Papers*, XI.147)

Margaret functions in these narratives not only as the subject of a legal wrangle but as the object of male inquiry. The powerful intrusiveness of Chapuys's letter leaves much tantalizingly unsaid: just how did anybody know that copulation had not taken place; what were the domestic examples she had seen; where is she now? Margaret's body is as paradoxically elusive as it is identifiable, as much the subject of intrusive discovery as it is the object of speculation. She is, in these accounts, the sight and story of the men who make her.

   The love affair between Margaret and Thomas Howard went beyond the speculations of ambassadorial intruders. It became the subject of an official inquiry, and the transcript of his, and his witness's, examination reads like a bizarre legal burlesque of the Pandaric world of *Troilus and Criseyde*.

(1) The lord Thomas examined how long he hath loved the lady Margaret; answers, about a twelvemonth. (2) What tokens he has given her within this twelvemonth – none but a crampring. (3) What tokens he has received of her – none but her 'phisnamye,' painted, and a diamond. (4) When the first communication was of the contract – only since Easter. (5) Who was of counsel – heard that she told it the next day after the contract to lord William's wife that now is, and he lately told it to Hastings, his mother's servant.
2. John Ashley examined how long he hath known any love between the lady Margaret and the lord Thomas says about a quarter of a year.
Thomas Smyth says the same, and that he never carried any tokens between them and never was made of counsel by either party, nor knows nor suspects any who were of counsel except her women. Examined when he first knew there was a contract; says she told him yesterday (*in margin*, 8 July), saying she expected he would be thereupon examined. Being asked whether he had seen him (Lord Thomas) resort unto her when my lady of Richmond was present; he says divers times, insomuch that he would watch till my lady Boleyn was gone, and then steal into her chamber. Examined whether he hath been there with him (lord Thomas); he answers, sundry times, but never heard any communication of any such matter. (*Letters and Papers*, IX.48)

Howard's examination shows us Pandarus as prosecutor. Each question corresponds to the dictates of love taught by the friend of Troilus; each ticks off the prerequisites of courtly dalliance as told in Chaucer's poem. The length of love; the importance of tokens, here, the ring, the portrait, and the jewel; the problem of communication and the idea of a contract between them; and the importance of the "counsel" – all of these features mark the love affair as something deeply Troilan in its outlines. Indeed, much like the relations of Chaucer's lovers, Margaret and Thomas are the object of much debate on the precise legal status of their love: what is precisely the contract "par parolles de present"? Does it constitute a betrothal as such? Certainly Chapuys had it on some authority that the relationship had not been consummated, but how could one know?

The second part of this transcript, however, offers up a different side of the Pandaric. Here, in the examination of one Thomas Smyth, we find Pandarus on trial. He denies having carried any tokens between them or having privy knowledge of their love (i.e., "counsel"), and he avers that he had only recent knowledge of the contract between the two lovers. And yet he admits to the intrusive voyeurisms of the Pandar. He watches, then steals into the chamber; and he clearly spends time with Thomas, too, perhaps as friend, though again, he denies hearing "any communication" of the matter of the contract.

This is a document of legal history, but it is too, a narrative of literary love. The very language of the transcript invokes the key terms of illicit desire. For Thomas Howard to "resort unto" Margaret Douglas is to place him in the role of legendary lover: for example, to make him a Lancelot who, in Malory's words, "began to resort unto Queen Guenever again" after the quest of the Sangrail was over. "But ever his thoughts," Malory goes on, "were privily on the queen, and so they loved together more hotter than they did toforehand, and had such privy draughts together, that many in the court spake of it . . ."[64] To resort to someone is, in the English of the day, to return to someone for private, if not sexual pleasure. By the time of Shakespeare, the term clearly had such currency that it could be the lever of a joke in the *Two Gentlemen of Verona*:

> No man hath access by day to her.
> Why, then, I would resort to her by night.   (III.i.110)[65]

This is the language of covert sexual union, a language that recasts the legal details of the Howard/Douglas affair into the broader arc of a literary liaison. Together with the testimony of Thomas Smyth, it inscribes Margaret in the tale of male spying, contributes to her personal construction as a gazed-upon, manipulated, traded, and maligned Criseyde. "Allas," Chaucer's heroine had lamented in Book V,

> of me, unto the worldes ende,
> Shal neyther ben ywriten nor ysonge
> No good word, for thise bokes wol me shende.
> O, rolled shal I ben on many a tonge!   (V.1058-61)

For Margaret Douglas, already inscribed into the books of law and rolled upon the tongues of kings, ambassadors, and servants, the impersonation of Criseyde has become a mask of life. The chunks of Chaucer at the close of Devonshire do not, I think, provide her with what Elizabeth Heale calls "a language she could put to her own use, both to express a passion for which she was willing to break her duties as daughter and subject and to articulate a value system which, for aristocratic women, might constitute a form of rebellion against the harsh, patriarchal exigencies of their lives."[66] Nor does it enable what Paul Remley calls a voice for "indignation at the treatment of women of her time by hypocritical lovers."[67] Read in the contexts I have offered here, the final stanzas of the Devonshire Manuscript instead write a sad *debat d'amour* on the Criseydean condition. To be subject to, and subject of, the hands, the tongues, the eyes of men is to be subject not just to the ways of loving but the ways of reading. The final leaves of Devonshire query the very nature of the fictive play-acting that may have shaped the Douglas/Howard lives. They illustrate the pitfalls of impersonation, the dangers of being inscribed into the narratives of surreptitious love. For Margaret Douglas, and perhaps for Thomas Howard – living on in letters and in poems, transcribed into the accounts of chronicle, examination, and diplomacy – all the earth is, indeed, parchment scribable.

Personal reading, literary history

What is the literary history inscribed in the Wellys and Devonshire manuscripts? In one sense, it is a clearly authorialized history, a narrative of influence, dissemination, imitation, and response generated by a central writing figure against whom all others should be measured and through whom all past and present texts should be understood. For Wellys, this authorizing figure is Stephen Hawes. I have already detailed how Hawes's distinctive language of impression and engraving characterizes the poetry of Wellys's compilation – how the centos fashioned from his longer poems form the centerpiece of the anthology, how his vision of the courtly lover is transmuted into the anxieties of courtly readings for the following generation. Hawes is the measure for Wellys, so much so that the Lydgatean selections and Chaucerian entries are rewritten or recast to fit the metaphorical or generic paradigms set out in Hawes's work. Hawes is, too, a central figure in the literary economics of de Worde and his successors. As Hawes's sole publisher, de Worde clearly had a vested interest in the circulation of the poet's work, sustaining his presence in early Tudor readerships through reprints and through interventions in the rivalries among Hawes and his fellow writers, Skelton and Barclay. Hawes represents a distinctive early Tudor taste, and the Hawesean flavor of many later amorous allegories and dialogues – as well as his explicit use by later poets such as William Walter and Thomas Feylde – comes to characterize one strain of printed literature during the 1520s and 30s.[68] Wellys's literary sensibilities were shaped by such publications, and his use of printed texts in his anthology reflects an adherence to a set of literary tastes or canons of a previous generation. His identifiable reliance on the pre-Thynne publications of Chaucer and his apocrypha testify to a personalized vision of the literary products of the de Worde circle.[69] His political poems, too, locate his central interests in the early years of the 1520s, a decade or so before the manuscript was written and compiled. Wellys's vision of early Tudor poetry and politics is thus, in a profound way, deeply elegiac. Its conception of court personages is of those dead or disgraced; its notion of court poetry is of the Hawesean allegories and ministrations of the truelove of another lifetime. It is a work of critical nostalgia, a collection that defines the scope of English literary history as something fundamentally past.

By contrast, Devonshire locates its literary history in the immediacies of the local present. Its printed source book, Thynne's Chaucer edition, could have been only a few years past its printing before Thomas Howard (if that is who did it) carved out his selections for the manuscript. So, too, its personal allusions charge the manuscript with the topics of the moment. And, for the Devonshire Manuscript, the central authorizing figure is not some dead *auctor* from a printed book, but the living Thomas Wyatt. I will have much more to say about Wyatt in my next chapter, but it may suffice to say here that his presence in Devonshire does more than contribute to our modern critical conception of the Wyatt "canon" or of the place of the poet in the personal coteries of the Howard–Shelton clique. What it does do is testify to the immediacy of writing, to the very meaning of the pen that is so central a metaphor in the poetry both written for and copied into this anthology. It represents the manuscript as transcript, if not of performance, then of the ongoing life of literary culture. Literary history for Wellys is something read and copied out, something, perhaps like politics or family relations, surreptitiously observed or voyeuristically enjoyed. But, at the very least, it is something that is apart from the anthologist and reader. Devonshire shows us literary history being made. It illustrates the making of an authorial canon, shows us the immediate and personalized uses of a newly printed volume, and reveals the ways in which the pen takes precedence over the print. Both are, in their distinctive ways, acts of ventriloquism and performance. But Wellys's speakers – be they Troilus and Criseyde, or Lob the Fool, anonymous lovers or named members of the families in nearby Stafford – are all distant or all dead. Devonshire's voices are alive. They are the players of the courtly circle, the actors in family relations, figures out of lived current experience.

To this extent, Wellys and Devonshire also embody two different, yet complementary, versions of family Chauceriana and of the relationships between the texts of literary fiction and the personages of domestic life. To put it generally, Wellys inscribes the Pandaric persona into family life. He makes the figures of his local group objects of voyeurism and epistolary interception. He writes the romance of family experience, furthermore, on the most pained and mutilated of the bodies of late medieval English verse. The objects of Wellys's eye are calibrated to recall, I think, those of Chaucer's poem: the horrifically gored Troilus of Criseyde's dream, the heart-torn-out Criseyde of Troilus's, the raped and dis-armed Procne who stands behind Pandarus's uneasy early morning

half-waking fantasy, or – less violently but no less painfully – the
emotionally imprisoned Criseyde who writes to unfetter her heart. There
is a violence to the dreamt and writing bodies of *Troilus and Criseyde*
that finds its way into Wellys's anthology and makes it both a book of
letters and a book of dreams. The erotic love visions of the manuscript,
for all their superficial resemblance to Wyatt's fantasies, are far more
blunt, if not vulgar. They offer visions of excess: "I kyssed hur I bassed
hur owt of all mesure" (36.37), avers one; "I thought I hur vnlasyde"
(37.10), imagines another; and when the poet awakes in a third, he finds
"to wette my selfe Soo woo begone" (46.10). These are the wet dreams of
desire, fantasies both amorous and political. In my dreams, I kiss her; in
my dreams, the head of the world is the Pope.

For Devonshire, the romance of reading is a family romance. We have
long been encouraged to imagine the compilers of the manuscript sitting
around like Chaucer's Greeks, sharing the "romance" books now, not of
Thebes, but of Chaucer himself.[70] With the deep impress of Book II of
the *Troilus* on the compilation, it may not be going too far to imagine the
initial setting of that book as something of a template for impersonation.
When Pandarus enters into Criseyde's house, he finds

> two othere ladys sete and she,
> Withinne a paved parlour, and they thre
> Herden a mayden reden hem the geste
> Of the siege of Thebes, while hem leste.   (II.81–84)

But there is, too, another Troilan paradigm inscribed into the Howard
family. John Skelton had already read its personal relations, and its
patronage, through the stories of Pandaric desire in the *Garlande of
Laurell*, and it is worth returning to his lines to understand the nature of
this family Chauceriana in the early Tudor period. He addresses Lady
Elisabeth Howard, "To be your remembraunceer, madame, I am
bounde" (line 864), and he goes on:

> Goodly Creisseid, fayrer than Polexene,
> For to envyve Pandarus appetite;
> Troilus, I trowe, if that he had you sene,
> In yow he wolde have set his hole delight.
> Of all your bewte I suffyce not to wryght:
> But, as I sayd, your florisshinge tender age
> Is lusty to loke on, plesaunt, demure, and sage.   (*Garlande*, lines 871–77)

While there is some debate about just where this Elisabeth fits into the
Howard family relations, it is most likely that she was the daughter of
Thomas Howard, Earl of Surrey and the second Duke of Norfolk. She
was the sister of the Thomas Howard of the Devonshire Manuscript, the

mother of Anne Boleyn, and the aunt of the poet Surrey.[71] She stands not only at the nexus of family and royal patronage, but, in Skelton's lines, at the heart of Chaucerian male desire. The Howard family is already inscribed into the dynamics of Chaucerian reception. Pandaric desire and Troilan love become the scripts of patronage. The family romance is the romance of the Howard family.

Skelton is the "remembrancer" of Howard beauty, and his phrasing now returns us to the scribal gap between romance and remembrance where Pandarus lives in the reception of his poem. To be a poet or a reader, too, is to be caught within this gap. The Wellys anthology and Devonshire Manuscript show us the world of reading between romance and remembrance. They take Chaucer's poetry – and, indeed, the heritage of medieval English literature at large – not on to the stages of the great, but into the studies of the subservient. They privatize, domesticate, make secret the desires of its characters. Instead of a voice for public counsel or a goad to royal pimpery, Pandarus functions in them as a creature of withdrawal or a figure of private, maximal advice. He has a role in the *debats d'amour* of Devonshire, where he irrupts into strings of personal verse letters or stands as the male advisor to the penmanship of love. He has a role, too, in the work of Humphrey Wellys, as he becomes the model for a surreptitious reading of illicit letters, be they the intercepted missives among friends or the counterfeit love epistles of a "courte Inperyall."

What, in the end, could "envyve" Pandarus's appetite? For Wellys it is the surreption of epistolary interception, of political sedition, of corporeal delectation, of the privy world of privy counselors and the jakes. For Devonshire, it is the romance of family reading: the maximal intrusions and contributions to ongoing conversations or poetic exchanges. The Troilan fantasy of Devonshire is not unique to the inscriptions of the manuscript, but had been part and parcel of the literary and the legal texts both written for, and of, the family. And if we, like Pandarus himself, burst upon these private scenes of reading or peep in on private letters or the conjugalities of love, then we must find, too, in these manuscripts both the romance of remembrance and the remembrance of romance: a testimony to a world of parchment scribable.

5 Wyatt, Chaucer, Tottel: the verse epistle and the subjects of the courtly lyric

> But ware, I say, so gold thee help and speed
> > That in this case thou be not so unwise
> > As Pandar was in such a like deed;
> For he, the fool, of conscience was so nice
> > That he no gain would have for all his pain.
> > Be next thyself, for friendship bears no prize.
>
> (Rebholz, *The Complete Poems*, CLI.73–78)

Much like Pandarus, Wyatt was a master of translation: a courtier advisor who had skillfully negotiated all (or nearly all) the ruses of duplicity, an *interpres* who, quite literally, came between the King and his ambassadors, while at the same time interpreting the writings of Latin satirists and Italian amorists for English coterie readerships. He has been much discussed of late in the environments of sexuality and power, as a player on that Henrician stage so compellingly imagined by Stephen Greenblatt, where the "anxieties, bad faith, and betrayals" of court service provoked the writing of a poetry that paradoxically – or dialectically, in Greenblatt's idiom – critiqued and advanced a career of courtiership.[1] "Wyatt's poetry," Greenblatt concludes, in an interpretation that has influenced a decade-and-a-half of critical response, "originates in a kind of diplomacy, but the ambassadorial expression is given greater and greater power until it intimates a perception of its own situation that subverts its official purpose."[2] It is a poetry that, he avers again, "at its best [is] distinctly more convincing, more deeply moving, than any written not only in his generation but in the preceding century."[3]

Part of my purpose in this study has been to refigure the relations between authorship and literary culture that inform such judgments. On the one hand, I have sought to illustrate the mutual relations among love and politics that would originate not just the poetry of Wyatt but the literary culture of early Tudor England "in a kind of diplomacy." But on the other hand, I have attempted to push back the boundaries of such a culture to see a continuity of reading and response that makes the surreptions of the court, the interceptions of the letter, and the compilations of the manuscript the venues for a deeply moving and convincing kind of writing at least a generation before Wyatt himself. Central to my argument has been the place of Chaucer's *Troilus and Criseyde* in the constructions of these literary and political discourses, and I have sought – in limning the outlines of the early Tudor reading and reception of that work – to understand the reconfigurations of vernacular literary history during the period. Finally, I have claimed not just a topical resonance for these works, but a political environment that shapes the writing and dissemination of both public literature and private letters. I have called this a culture of the Pandaric, an age of regulated reading in which the behaviors of a literary figure found themselves the habits of the state.

Wyatt is obviously a *telos* to this study, and the Satire to Francis Bryan, from whose lines I take my epigraph, is a summa of the poet's courtly and poetic career. Long valued for its ironic compendia of proverbial knowledge and its subtle blend of Horatian form and collo-quial English idiom, this poem has recently been reread as a commentary on the tensions that inhere in courtier poetry itself.[4] It is a poem, in Greenblatt's reading, that risks "subverting [Wyatt's] own moral authority,"[5] one that plays out the irony of offering a verse epistle of advice to someone notorious for duplicity and vice. Indeed, if anyone could fill the role of Pandar to the King in the late 1530s, it would have been Francis Bryan himself. A lifelong courtier, amateur poet, and ambassadorial intriguer, Bryan shows up throughout the chronicles of Henrician pandarism. He was one of the young minions named by the historian Edward Hall as embarrassing himself in France in 1519, riding "disguysed through Paris" with the French King, "throwing Egges, stones and other foolishe trifles at the people," and returning to England full of the "Frence vices."[6] He nonetheless advanced rapidly through the court, marrying one wealthy widow after another, arranging important matches for his sisters, and eventually rising to the position of Chief Gentleman of the Privy Chamber in 1536–38 – a position, in the words of David Starkey, in which he performed "the vilest of services" for the aging King.[7] "He dressed and undressed him; and he probably even . . . wiped the royal bottom."[8] His bawdry earned him the epithet "Vicar of Hell," while his bluntness with the King often met with an equally blunt response. Nicholas Saunders's well-known anecdote offers a telling vignette of this blend of bawdry and familiarity.

On one occasion the King asked [Bryan] what sort of sin he thought it was to know first the mother and then the daughter. To which Bryan replied: 'Exactly the same, sir, as first to eat the hen and then the chicken!' The King laughed heartily and then said, 'You really do deserve your title of my Vicar of Hell.'

It is an episode like this one that leads Starkey, as well as Greenblatt and, most recently, Perez Zagorin, to contextualize Wyatt's Satire in the biographical details of its addressee and the topical environments of courtly life.[9] For Stephen Foley, however, such evidence takes a back seat to what he calls the larger "cultural authority" of the discourses of the poem, notably the proverb, "an ideological function that stands in place of the individual human subjects who speak it."[10] Foley's account of Wyatt's poem is a detailed reading of these deconstructions of the proverb, and he closes with the recognition of the centrality to Wyatt's verse not of living men but of dead literary figures. The allusions to *Troilus and Criseyde*, together with the recastings of Horace and the nods to Persius and Terence, make this poem not only an essay on the pitfalls of courtiership but a retrospective of the literary history of courtly poetry itself. Though Foley nods to the importance of the "discourses of class and economy" operating in the poem, his is a reading more concerned with discourses than social history: a chronicle of the rhetorical slippages that inhere in the genres and the gestures of advisory satire.

Foley's largely formalist reading does not necessarily exclude the biographical desiderata of historicist accounts, and in what follows I propose to read the Satire to Bryan as an essay in the problematics of the literary and the lived. It is a poem that recasts the topicalities of Henrician service through the Chaucerian legacies of amicitial advice. The historical subtext of Bryan's court pandering combines with the Pandaric uses of the proverb to give meaning not just to a local poetic allusion but to the experience of Wyatt reading Chaucer. For the fact is that the Satire is shot through with references to Chaucer's poetry. They are its controlling structural device and its locative poetic principle. Read in the context of its broader Chaucerian frames – especially in the first Satire to John Poyntz, as well as in the shorter lyrics and ballads – this poem stands as a review and retrospection of the place of poetic impersonation in the literary court. Thomas Greene notes that Wyatt's concern with proverbial wisdom and the notion of the "wasting" or decay of verbal meaning "adds a level of linguistic self-consciousness missing in [this poem's] principal subtext, the fifth satire of Horace's second book."[11] I suggest that this linguistic self-consciousness is learned from Chaucer, and that the poem as a whole is both constructed out of and responds to the conditions of the Pandaric impersonations I have sought to define throughout this study. Chaucer and Wyatt stand not simply as source and appropriation but in a complex tension that reflects on the making of the canonicity of English writing and, in turn, on the relations between public poetry and private reading for the late medieval and the early Tudor periods. Wyatt's Chaucerianism extends beyond local allusion and quotation. It is the means by which he defines the key idioms of his verse and the key stances of his selves. The Boethian imagery of beastliness; the philosophical reflections on the doubleness of public speech; the social withdrawal to the bed and private chamber as the place of private reading; and the investment in certain key vocabulary terms, especially the idea of the "counterfeit" in public life and private reading – these are the *loci* of Chaucerian impact on Wyatt's writing, and the Satire to Bryan brings them all together in a stretto of quotation and allusion.

In addition to placing this poem in the arc of Wyatt's writing life and in the contexts of the courtly service of his compeers, this chapter locates its position in the textuality of Wyatt's work. It is a commonplace of Wyatt scholarship to note the instability of his poetic texts: to chart the variations among texts in his own hand and those of others and to mark the changes wrought by Tottel in his normalized and smoothed-out printings of the poetry.[12] Such issues have a meaning that extends beyond the ministrations of the editor. They are a theme of the poems themselves, a critical preoccupation in the making of the reading and the writing subject. The tensions between tongue and pen, voice and script, song and text expose themselves in many of the sonnets, ballads, and short lyrics of the Wyatt canon. And the slippages among them – the mishearing of a word, the miswriting of a syllable – become central not just to the literary but to the political stances Wyatt took throughout his life. The acts of speaking, reading, and transcribing are the constitutive processes of Wyattic self-presentation. To understand his poetry as acts of social and fictive impersonation is to expose both the historicity and textuality of author and audience. Sir Francis Bryan survives not only in the records of affairs of state but in the letters of the 1530s. He comes to live in the epistolarity of the over-heard and surreptitiously exposed. His place in this Satire is of a piece with his place in the discourses of Cromwellian England, and Wyatt's poem may be as much a reading of his addressee's textual presence as it is a reading of those Chaucerian texts that help explain him.

And those texts are epistles. In *Troilus and Criseyde* and in the shorter philosophical and political ballads, letters are the vehicle for personal self-presentation, pleas for patronage, or marks of amicitial relations. The impact of such poetry (and in particular the impact of a poem such as Chaucer's *Truth*) on early Tudor readers lay not simply in its language or its doctrines but its form. For Wyatt, in particular, the verse epistle is the place where he confronts the burden of a literary heritage and the boundaries of public writing. But more generally, it is the means by which the manuscript compiler and the early English printer defined literariness itself. In the verse letter canonical authorship and courtly discourse take shape and, in the process, write the origins of English literary history. The idea of the English lyric voice, as codified by Tottel, is inescapably epistolary: not, in other words the phrasings of unmediated passion or the transcripts of felt experience, but the scripts of carefully constructed desire. These are texts that are always read not just by the intended recipient but by the intruder. The English verse epistle is a poem viewed over the shoulder, a personal missive that addresses itself to an invited and an uninvited reader.

It is this quality of thematized intrusiveness that makes Wyatt's work so complex and anxious and, in turn, that grants it a historical specificity in the invasive readings of Cromwellian surveillance in the later 1530s. Doors are continually opened, chambers entered, bedrooms stalked. Love here, much like in Wellys's anthology, is secret, surreptitious, and intrusive. The line between the amorous and the political blurs itself constantly in Wyatt's lines, as the poet evinces not so much an inwardness as what I would call a sidelong quality. Wyatt's speakers look not so much at the interiorities of subject formation as they look sideways at the invasions of privacy and the intrusions of a lover, a censor, or a reader. The way to read Wyatt, I propose here, is thus as a voyeur himself – as the intruder on the private space of lyric and epistolary writing. It is, I suggest too, the way he was read in the early sixteenth century: for example, by the compilers of the Devonshire Manuscript (wary of discovery and constantly engaged in ciphering and codings of desire); by the annotator to the Egerton Manuscript (who occasionally censors or clears up potential problems in the lines); and by Tottel, who, as it were, invites his readers into the previously closed chambers of court poetry and, for but the price of the volume, will present them with the secret sights of coterie poets.

If this was how the poetry was read, then it was, too, the way the poet was memorialized. If Tottel's volume is a book of letters, it is also something of a book of elegies. The poetry of Henry Howard, Earl of Surrey, that begins the *Miscellany* – indeed, that grants the book its original title – is in many ways a poetry of mourning. Not only in its elegies to Wyatt, but in its long poems on bereft or dying lovers, Surrey's verse returns to the paradigms of *Troilus and Criseyde* to find a resting place for the Chaucerian inheritance. These elegiac gestures, too, may help us come to terms with the constructions of the self and the preoccupations with the verbally unstable throughout Wyatt's poetry and its modern reception. The verse epistle to a friend becomes an act of cultural remembrance; the defense before accusers becomes a performance of self-eulogy; the editorial manipulations of a text become a search for an originary hand. In closing this chapter, and in concluding this study, I propose that the poetry of Wyatt and its critical reception is inherently elegiac. It seeks, vainly, to recover a lost point of origin, a "text" made by the hand of the author, whether that author is a named, historical poet or a fictional epistolarist. Wyatt, Surrey, and Tottel expose not just the laments of Troilan lovers or the losses of Pandaric courtiers, but the elegiac nature of all writing and reading. They recognize estrangements between hand and heart, the pen and pain, or, as Criseyde would put it, "th'entente" and "the lettres space."

A spending hand

Structurally and thematically, Wyatt's Satire to Francis Bryan confronts the courtly legacy of Pandarus. Its first words affirm the Pandaric faith in proverbs, while its final lines address the difficulties of the tongue that is so much the central human organ of the *Troilus*. Within this verbal bracketing, Wyatt locates two specific allusions to Chaucer's go-between (one named, the other anonymous), and at the poem's center lies a statement of the paradox of truth's relationship to public counsel and the split between word and deed that governs that slippage between the moral and the semiotic central to the poet's vision of the language of courtiership.

Spend as you get; a rolling stone gathers no moss. Such aphorisms, banal as much to the sixteenth century as to the modern reader, none-theless are offered as the rock and loam of social counsel.

> these proverbs yet do last.
> Reason hath set them in so sure a place
> That length of years their force can never waste.
>
> (Rebholz, *The Complete Poems*, CLI.4–6)

A faith in the proverbial is the hallmark of Pandarus, who hardly enters into Troilus's bedroom before he comes off spouting such a string of old familiar maxims, gnomes, and classical allusions that Troilus must protest, "thy proverbes may me naught availle" (*Troilus and Criseyde*, I.756).[13] And still, when Pandarus advises Criseyde in Book II, he avers, "Lat this proverbe a loore unto yow be" (II.397). The reliance on proverbs is at the heart of Pandaric *amicitia*, so much so that he turns the word, uniquely in Middle English, into a verb:

> For which thise wise clerkes that ben dede
> Han evere yet proverbed to us yonge,
> That 'firste vertue is to *kepe tonge*'.   (III.292–94)[14]   "to hold your tongue"

And yet, what are these proverbs Pandarus adduces? For so much of his appearance in the poem, proverbs key themselves not just to forms of action or behavior but to talk. If the first virtue is to keep one's tongue then, as he will aver but one stanza later,

> Proverbes kanst thiself ynowe and *woost*　　　　　　　"know"
> Ayeins that vice, for to ben *a labbe*,　　　　　　"blabbermouth"
> Al seyde men *soth* as often as thei gabbe.　(III.299–301)　"truly"

These are the sentiments that infused the fifteenth-century appropriation of Pandaric counsel in such poems as "The Tongue," containing the next three stanzas of the *Troilus* (III.302–22).[15] And they are the sentiments that govern the appropriations of Chaucerian advice in the proliferating manuals of public conduct that deployed the poet's maxims in the early Tudor period. Proverbialism is keyed to verbal conduct, and the keeping of the tongue is one of the great paradoxes of Pandarus's own career. For while his maxims promise secrecy in love, his actions show a man incapable of keeping his tongue; while his advice to Troilus and Criseyde concerns the rectitude of speech and writing, his behavior always shows us someone only barely in control of his own verbal wiles. This is a creature who would file his tongue (II.1681, an idiom significantly shared with Chaucer's Pardoner from the *Canterbury Tales*), and yet who, when humiliated by his failures at the poem's end, stands speechless ("As stille as ston; a word ne kowde he seye," V.1729), and signs off from Troilus's life and Chaucer's poem with a brief, two-stanza invective against Criseyde that ends, "I kan namore seye" (V.1743).[16]

These figurations stand behind Wyatt's own complex exposure of the social function of the proverb and the pitfalls of courtly counsel. At his poem's end, he counsels Bryan, perhaps, to leave courtly service and feel free to speak his mind unfettered by the constraints of a public or a patron.

> Nay then, farewell, and if you care for shame,
> 　Content thee then with honest poverty,
> 　With free tongue, what thee mislikes, to blame,
> And, for thy truth, sometime adversity.
> 　　　　　(Rebholz, *The Complete Poems*, CLI. 85–88)

The realm of the free tongue is the realm of the private and the poor; it is the realm outside the counsels of the courtier; and, too, it is the realm outside Wyatt's own poem. In advising freedom of the tongue, Wyatt himself must close with silence. The paradox of Wyatt's lines lies in the fact that leaving courtly service does not liberate the tongue but close it up. Speech is the courtier's role, and poetry, for Wyatt, is the currency of courtier self-definition. What "proverbs yet do last," as he would put it, are not just the glib banalities of spending hands and rolling stones but, more complexly, the proverbs of the tongue. Proverbial advice is central to courtier counsel and, for that matter, epistolary poetry, and what the Satire to Bryan traces out is the self-fashioning, if not self-canceling, of the Pandaric position.

Wyatt's poem is a string of proverbs. Drawing on English lore and learned maxims, the Satire to Bryan works as a compendium of the proverbial advice deployed in courtiership. It stands as something of a miniature anthology, an Erasmian book of *Adages* writ small. It has been said that there is something of a Newtonian principle of proverbial speech: for every proverb there is an equal and opposite proverb.[17] By seeking to explain everything, proverbs in fact explain nothing, and in these terms no single proverb has the weight of counsel. Rather, the social meaning of a proverb lies in its participation in a system of difference, what one might call – to change the metaphor and the historical resonance – a Saussurian dimension to the proverb. Each utterance in Wyatt's poem has its meaning in the context of the larger structure of advice and each, to some degree, is canceled out by another. Thus, the opening allusion to the rolling stone contrasts with the stability of proverbial wisdom itself. "Reason hath set them in so sure a place." So, too, the very verbal nature of this spoken counsel is challenged by the primacy of writing offered at the poem's opening.

> I thought forthwith to write,
>   Brian, to thee, who knows how great a grace
> In writing is to counsel man the right.   (lines 8–10)

The right of writing is, of course, more than rhyme to Wyatt but a pun that powerfully dismantles the claims of both speech and writing in the poem. Counsel, as Bryan and Pandarus would know, is speech, and Bryan was famous for the bluntness of his speech to Henry. As the anecdotes of Bryan's career show, he was a man more given to the immediacies of talk than the meditations of writing. His was a tongue that took a precedence over the pen, in Starkey's words, "a complex character in which moral laxity was strangely blended with a remarkable and very attractive freedom of speech."[18] Bryan knows that the way to "counsel man the right" is through such speechifying, and, as we read on in Wyatt's poem, we may query the effectiveness of writing anything at all to a man, as the poem states, who "never rests." This is a poem to a reader who could never read it; a complex debate on counsel, speech, and writing, to a man too busy to attend; a poem rich with classical allusion and the subtleties of argument whose central question finds its answer, in

its quoted dialogue, in the bluntness of the barnyard and the rudeness of
scatology.

> Likest thou not this? 'No.' Why? 'For swine so groins
> In sty and chaw the turds moulded on the ground,
> And drivel on pearls, the head still in the manger.'   (lines 18–20)

Bryan's answer also brings Chaucer into Wyatt's courtly discourse,
and provides the poem with the first of its direct allusions to Pandaric
counsel: "Then of the harp the ass do hear the sound" (line 21). Mired in
Bryan's outburst about groining swine and chewing turds and drivel lies
one of the central images of Stoic intellection, passed through Longinus
and Boethius to Chaucer and Erasmus.[19] The *Adages* say much about
the sources and the resonances of this passage for the early sixteenth-
century reader.[20] But Pandarus, as well, had adduced it in the first of his
long advisory harangues of the bedridden Troilus, and his words have
long been seen as standing behind Bryan's.[21]

> 'What! *Slombrestow* as in a *litargie*?   "do you sleep" "lethargy"
> Or artow lik an asse to the harpe,
> That hereth *sown* whan men the strynges *plye*,   "sound" "pluck"
> But in his mynde of that no melodie
> May sinken hym to gladen, for that he
> So dul ys of his bestialite?'   (*Troilus and Criseyde*, I.730–35)

The "bestialite" of *Troilus and Criseyde* – a word that in the Middle
English of the poem connotes ignorance rather than behavior – becomes,
by the early sixteenth century a term of physicalized beastliness.[22]
Indeed, one might well see this powerful semantic shift as central to the
outburst of this section of the poem: a shift from a mental category to a
physical condition, a shift from a metaphor to a reality. Bryan's outburst
is the epitome of beastliness, a string of obscene and blasphemous
utterances that reveal the speaker as an animal and make him something
of the ass to Wyatt's harp. It is, rhetorically, of a piece with Saunders's
story about the courtier's conversation with the King, where Henry's
question about sex becomes Bryan's answer about the barnyard.

How can one have a conversation with, let alone compose a verse
epistle to, an interlocutor such as this? "By God, well said," says Wyatt
after all this drivel (Rebholz, *The Complete Poems*, CLI.28) – a line not
so much spoken in praise of Brian's attitude as it is offered in the spirit of
keeping the conversation going. It is a line, too, resonant of Chaucer, in
particular of the ironies of the narrator of the *General Prologue* to the
Canterbury Tales, who in response to the Monk's dismissal of life lived
only within the "cloystre," can vouch, "And I seyde his opinion was
good" (A, lines 181–83). There is a pervasive Chaucerian quality to this

exchange in Wyatt's poem. The avowals of a blunt self-serving creature of the court (whose condemnations of the cloister and controlling imagery of sty and barnyard, food and physicality, recall the Monk himself) are answered with the agreeable *bonhomie* of the cheerful companion. Wyatt's advice to Bryan follows in this spirit: an impersonation of a craven courtliness, a miming of the basest features of the Pandar that take Bryan's words and turn them, by the poem's close, against themselves.

And against Chaucer, too. In the context of this advisory passage, Wyatt returns to the key Chaucerian conciliar texts to illustrate their wild inapplicability to the ruses of the courtier. It is as if Wyatt is saying that the very paradigms of courtly and poetic counsel fail when put in practice. Or, to put it slightly differently, the Chaucerian inheritance of public poetry dissolves when one turns from a reader to an actor in the stagy politics of courtly life.

> Flee therefore truth.   (Rebholz, *The Complete Poems*, CLI. 34)

In this half-line, Wyatt combines the two most famous of Chaucerian advisory remarks not to augment their power but to cancel them out. The ballad known as *Truth* circulated widely in the fifteenth and the early sixteenth centuries as one of the most famous of Chaucer's public statements.[23] It appears not just singly in the manuscript and early print anthologies of Chaucer's works, but as postscripts to other poems – moral envoys, in effect, that close the version of the *Clerk's Tale* in one early Tudor manuscript anthology (Huntington Library MS HM 140) and the little paraphrase of *Troilus and Criseyde* in Tottel's *Miscellany* over half a century later.[24] It is, too, as Thomas Greene has recognized, one of the central subtexts to Wyatt's own public balladry, and it provided one of the key terms in his lexicon of love and service. With its complex and interlocking connotations of verbal veracity and practical fealty, the word *trouth* centers Chaucer's poem (and, indeed, all his political ballads and epistles) in the uneasy space between private confidence and public performance. It is, as Greene defines it, "the Chaucerian word that organizes Wyatt's moral code." "The word *trouth* gathers into itself most of the various values which in Wyatt are repeatedly threatened with debasement. Its richness of accumulated but beleaguered signification serves to illustrate the ways moral ambiguities turn out to be semiotic ambiguities."[25] In the Satire to Bryan, *Truth* stands as both a source and foil for Wyatt's counsel. Chaucer's ballad opens, "Flee fro the prees and dwelle with sothfastnesse," an injunction that Wyatt had earlier made the touchstone of another Satire on courtliness, this one to John Poyntz:

> Mine own John Poyntz, since ye delight to know
>   The cause why that homeward I me draw
>   (And *flee the press* of courts whereso they go
> Rather than to live thrall under the awe
>   Of lordly looks).
>   (Rebholz, *The Complete Poems*, CXLIX.1–4, emphases added)[26]

Here, Chaucer's moral phraseology becomes a dictum about courtly
service, and the general Boethian maxims that structure *Truth*'s advisory
poetic narrow themselves to the practicalities of political life. The home-
ward move in the Satire to John Poyntz domesticates the spiritual gestures
of Chaucer's ballad, and the thralldom of lordly looks recalibrates the
thralldom of the yoked beast. Chaucer's arguments for steadfastness
against the fickleness of fortune draw on the Boethian imagery of beastliness that also stands behind the lethargy of Troilus. In terms that recall
the Herculean effort of the ascent to the stars from the *Consolation of
Philosophy*, and in terms that resonate ironically with Pandarus's exhorta-
tions to his bedridden friend, Chaucer counsels his reader:

> Forth, pilgrim, forth! Forth, beste, out of thy stal!
> Know thy contree, look up, thank God of al;
> Hold the heye wey and lat thy *gost* thee lede,   "spirit"
> And trouthe thee shal delivere, it is *no drede*.   "without a doubt"
>   (*Truth*, lines 18–21)[27]

For Wyatt writing to Bryan, the injunction to "Flee therefore truth"
represents a powerful rhetorical inversion of both Chaucer's and his own
earlier counsel. These three words yoke together the rhetorical strategy
of *Truth*'s opening together with the moral counsel of its close. They also
pointedly return the reader to the opening address to Poyntz, making the
two Satires not simply two views of the courtly life, but two competing
readings of their Chaucerian subtext. For the narrator of the earlier
Satire, the flight from the press and the embracing of truth provide the
deliverance promised at the close of Chaucer's ballad. For a beastly
Bryan, who would wallow in the stall of vulgar imagery and self-debasing
service, there can be no deliverance. "Flee therefore truth" becomes an
injunction to reject the literary models on which Wyatt had constructed
his courtier poetry. We read these lines, now, not just as a maxim of
behavior but a guide to reading: to flee the very poem that would deliver
one from servitude and service.

Such an account of Chaucer's poem, and its place both in the canon of
Wyatt's poetry and the early sixteenth-century reception of the *Troilus*,
inscribes itself in Tottel's presentation of the ballad. Towards the close of
the *Miscellany*, Tottel prints a poem titled, "A comparison of his loue

wyth the faithfull and painful loue of Troylus to Creside."[28] The narrator begins by noting how, "I read how Troylus serued in Troy" (Rollins, ed., *Miscellany*, p.183, line 22), and then reviews not so much the plot as the emotive content of the first half of Chaucer's poem, concluding with the injunction to his beloved: "And set me in as happy case, / As Troylus with his lady was" (p.185, lines 24–25). Following these verses, Tottel then prints the first three stanzas of *Truth*.[29] He makes a few adjustments to the lines (changing, for example, the penultimate line of the poem to "Weane well thy lust, and honest life ay leade," p.186, line 9),[30] but what is most significant is its headnote. "To lead a virtuous and honest life," he titles it, and he follows this title not with a period but with a comma. It is as if the title is the first part of the poem: to do this, "Flee from the prese." Chaucer's poem is thus already pressed into the service of moral counsel. It stands not as some autonomous ballad of universal advice, but as a specific set of injunctions whose goal is "to lead a virtuous and honest life." And such injunctions are presented on the heels of a poem about the love of Troilus and Criseyde: a poem that presents itself not as a précis but a personalized reading of the story. "I read how Troylus serued in Troy." This is a tale of reading Chaucer's text, an account of how the force of Chaucer's poem can provoke the writing of a verse epistle to the lover. Of course, its verses radically reinterpret *Troilus and Criseyde*. There is nothing here of the betrayal of the woman, the despondency and death of the man, and of the intrigues of the go-between. It is really only the first half of the Chaucerian narrative, and Tottel follows it with *Truth* precisely to complete the moral narrative of *Troilus and Criseyde*.

Tottel's apposition of these texts reflects a notion of Chaucerian production, current in the mid sixteenth century, that associates the *Troilus* and *Truth*. Both had been mainstays of the manuscript and early print identity of Chaucer, and *Truth* in particular had been a central document of personal and courtier appropriations of the poet's moral stance. This little poem appears more frequently than any other short text by Chaucer: twenty-four manuscripts, ranging from personal collections to commissioned anthologies, testify to its circulation across temporal and class boundaries.[31] It was a key text for early Chaucerian printing from Caxton onward, and *Truth*, with a clutch of ballads, closes Thynne's edition of the poet's works.[32] What Tottel does is, in effect, to distill the entire range of Chaucerian writing into two small texts: the one, a personalized reading of his great love poem, the other, an exemplary ballad presented now as a piece of practical maximal advice. The first is private, the second public. The first lives in the study and the chamber, the second in the public world. For Troilus here,

> His chamber was his common walke,
> Wherin he kept him secretely,
> He made his bedde the place of talke,
> To heare his great extremitie.   (Rollins, ed., *Miscellany*, p.184, lines 2–5)

This chambered world is, too, the world of Wyatt's shorter poems, and no doubt much of the language of this Troilan versifying is indebted to the sensibilities of Henrician court verse. It appealed so much to Tottel that he most likely included it in his *Miscellany* for its resonances to Wyatt. Indeed, these lines about Troilus might well apply to the narrator of one of the most famous of Wyatt's poems.

> They flee from me that sometime did me seek
> With naked foot stalking in my chamber.
>   (Rebholz, *The Complete Poems*, LXXX.1–2)

And elsewhere, Wyatt's bed is the locus of intellection and poetic craft, the place of the Petrarchan paradox of love that, too, is at the heart of Troilus's desire.

> The restful place, reviver of my smart,
> The labour's salve, increasing my sorrow,
> The body's ease and troubler of my heart,
> Quieter of mind and my unquiet foe,
> Forgetter of pain, remembering my woe,
> The place of sleep wherein I do but wake,
> Besprent with tears, my bed, I thee forsake.   (LXXI.1–7)[33]

For Francis Bryan, beds and chambers lie far from the realms of service. Here is man who "trots still up and down / And never rests," (CLI.11–12) of whom Wyatt may ask:

> Why dost thou wear thy body to the bones
> And mightst at home sleep in thy bed of down?   (lines 14–15)

And, unlike the once-tamed creatures who would come to Wyatt's chamber, "To take bread at my hand" (LXXX.6), the animals of Bryan's world are neither tame nor wild but merely bought-off. The public life of Byran is, in these details, almost a point-by-point rebuttal of the opening feints of "They flee from me," as the erotic power of the naked foot and the bread-fed creature is transformed into the political debasements of the pimp.

> Else be thou sure thou shalt be far unmeet
>   To get thy bread, each thing is now so scant.
>   Seek still thy profit upon thy bare feet.
> Lend in no wise, for fear that thou do want,
>   Unless it be as to a dog a cheese.   (CLI.40–44)

Read against the Boethian injunctions of Chaucer's *Truth* – "Forth, beste, out of thy stal!" – the world of Bryan's commercial ventures comes off as a glib parody.

> Learn at Kitson, that in a long white coat
> From under the stall without lands or fees
> Hath leapt into the shop;   (lines 47–49)

The classicizing maxims of the Chaucerian ballad find themselves mis-translated into the commercial locales of the shop. Deliverance is here no longer a life in the stars but a life of inheritance. Gold, now, becomes the currency of service: "The good is gold"; "so gold thee help and speed"; "Change that for gold." Truth finds itself, in the Satire's second half, not simply subject or subordinate to craven wealth, but rather mediated by the gold of coin. This is, now, a poem about the counterfeit, a poem about the feignings of fealty.

And, too, it is a poem about the counterfeit in *Troilus and Criseyde*. The mercantilisms of the Satire's second half resonate with the false coinings of the poem – with Pandarus's sly remark to Troilus that he need not "countrefete" a love he feels so passionately (II.1532), and with Troilus's own attempt at the poem's close to "contrefete" himself in disguise to see Criseyde (V.1578). Troilus and Criseyde define themselves against such false creations and the lure of gold. As Troilus says, when he attempts to argue out of the position that Pandarus is a bawd, "But he that gooth for gold or for ricchesse / On swich message, calle hym what the list" (III.400–401). And as Criseyde puts it to the despondent Troilus, in terms that anticipate both the mercantile and the barnyard images of Wyatt's Satire,

> Lo, Troilus, men seyn that hard it is
> The wolf ful and the *wether* hool to have;   "sheep"
> This is to seyn, that men ful ofte, iwys,
> Mote spenden part the remenant for to save;
> For ay with gold men may *the herte grave* "make an impression in the heart"
> Of hym that set is upon coveytise.   (IV.1373–78)

The gold of *Troilus and Criseyde* is thus the mark of fealty, the anti-type of love, desire, friendship, *gentillesse* – in a word, "trouth" – and the aureate temptations and denials of the poet's characters become the foil for Wyatt's Bryan and his Pandarus. "Pandar" does not come out of nowhere at line 75 of the Satire. He has been artfully prepared for: in the string of proverbial dicta that begin the poem; in the complex and allusive verbal tangents that place the poem in relationship to *Troilus* and to *Truth*; and in the stretto of Chaucerian allusions that define courtly behavior against gold. Even such small touches as the reference to the bridled mule have their formal location in the Troilan paradigm.

> Let the old mule bite upon the bridle
> Whilst there do lie a sweeter in thine arm.
> In this also see you be not idle.   (Rebholz, *The Complete Poems*, CLI.65–67)

The bridle is a central image of the *Troilus*. It connotes the blind beast led by human reason, while at the same time evoking the image of the bought Criseyde led off by Diomede. And, at such moments, Chaucer signals the distinction between agency and failure in the same rhyme. Witness Pandarus's amorous advice to Troilus in Book I:

> Now loke that *atempre* be thi bridel,   "restrained"
> And for the beste ay *suffre to the tyde*, "be patient with the passage of time"
> Or elles al oure laboure is *on ydel*,   "in vain"
> He hasteth wel that wisely kan abyde.   (I.953–56)

And compare, too, Diomede's final transport of Criseyde:

> This Diomede, that ledde hire by the bridel,
> Whan that he saugh the folk of Troie aweye,
> Thoughte 'Al my labour shal not ben on ydel,
> If that I may, for somwhat shal I seye,
> For at the werste it may yet shorte oure weye.
> I haue herd seyd ek tymes twyes twelve,
> "He is a fool that wol foryete hymselve".'   (V.92–98)

The *bridle/idle* rhyme in Wyatt locates his advice to Bryan precisely in these Chaucerian moments. It is not so much an allusion or quotation as it is a pointer to the reader – a device for sonically recalling those dramatic passages that may constitute a kind of moral gloss on Wyatt's lines. These passages concern themselves with the reward of service and the role of proverbs in determining a course of action. For Pandarus, the adagial advice to make haste slowly looks forward to Wyatt's own counsel for patience in the service of the prince: just wait, he says to Bryan, and the man you serve will die, leaving you either wealth or widow for your pains. In turn, the counsel to provide "Thy niece, thy cousin, thy sister, or thy daughter" (Rebholz, *The Complete Poems*, CLI.68) for courtly self-advancement takes us back to the Chaucerian contexts of this counsel – not just in the facts of Criseyde as Pandarus's niece, but in Pandarus's language itself.

> Were it for my suster, al thy sorwe,
> By my wil she sholde al be thyn to-morwe. (*Troilus and Criseyde*, I.860–61)

Similarly, Diomede's reflections have a place in Wyatt's poem over and above their sonic resonance. The proverb *he* adduces to explain his

action relocates itself in Wyatt's lines, now explicitly taking us to
Chaucer's poem.

> But ware, I say, so gold thee help and speed
> That in this case thou be not so unwise
> As Pandar was in such a like deed;
> For he, the fool, of conscience was so nice
> That he no gain would have for all his pain.
> Be next thyself, for friendship bears no prize.
>
> (Rebholz, *The Complete Poems*, CLI.73–78)

To know thyself becomes the anti-type of foolishness. And Pandarus,
now fool, becomes the figure of the unwise man "that wol foryete
hymselve." "Be next thyself," Wyatt advises Bryan – not simply, as its
editors have glossed it, "be your own best friend," but rather be close to
yourself, know yourself as closely as possible, do not forget just who you
are.

If, at its close, the Satire to Bryan brings together the Chaucerian
refractions of the moral proverb and the immoral Pandar, it also evokes
their reception and their place in early Tudor literary history. The lines
on Pandar recalibrate Skelton's bitter description of "Pandaer" in
Phyllyp Sparowe. He is, as we recall, a man that "Hath won nothing,"
who lives on, "named as Troylus baud."

> Of that name he is sure
> Whyles the world shall dure.   (*Phyllyp Sparowe*, lines 722–23)

So, too, the afterlives of other figures in the poem hinge on what we
might call an economy of naming: Criseyde, for whom "blemysshed is
her name" (line 712); Troilus, who "hath lost / On her moch love and
cost" (line 714–15). Chaucer's poem is, as I have argued, many things to
Jane Scrope, but what it appears as now is a story of exchanges and
rewards: a story, when read against its reconfigurations in Wyatt's
allusive Chaucerianisms, in which the economy of giving and getting
controls love and love service. Troilus, Jane puts it here, "coulde not
optayne" (line 697), and it is this overarching sense of obtaining that
figures so prominently in Wyatt's Satire to Bryan. The hand may spend,
but the Pandar gets nothing.

What honest name could Bryan then aspire to in such a life? In his
response to Wyatt's counsel, he avers,

> Wouldest thou I should for any loss or gain
> Change that for gold that I have ta'en for best –
> Next godly things, to have an honest name?
> Should I leave that? Then take me for a beast!
>
> (Rebholz, *The Complete Poems*, CLI.81–84)

Throughout this Satire, we have been asked to take him for a beast – to locate both his words and deeds in the Boethianized beastliness of Chaucer's *Truth* and *Troilus and Criseyde* and find his name marked with the literary allusions of Pandarus. This poem comments on the entire literary heritage of the Pandaric: a heritage framed in the Skeltonic refractions of a bawd and go-between, of a figure informing the collusions and counterfeitings of *Magnyfycence*, a figure, too, who shapes the impress of Chaucerian writing on the anthologists and readers of the early sixteenth century. To read this poem against the excerpts in the Devonshire Manuscript or the cento in the Wellys anthology is to locate it in a central problematic of early Tudor culture: how the literary figure stands as model or as measure for the public life. Just what is the effect of reading poetry, and in particular, Chaucerian poetry, on the construction of relationships of court, family, and friendship? Wyatt reflects on these questions through the complex tissue of allusions to Chaucer's work. He makes the subject of this Satire not simply the anxieties of service, but the anxiousness of reading. Even the text of Wyatt's Satire itself becomes "this thing," an object in the economics of amicitial exchange. Recall the oblique idiom of Skelton's *Phyllyp Sparowe*, as Criseyde's betrayal destroys the loving Troilus:

> Yet there was a thyng
> That made the male to wryng.   (*Phyllyp Sparowe*, lines 699–700)

Yet there was something that made the purse make noise, or more figuratively, that caused trouble. The very mercantile metaphor of this portion of the poem reinforces what I have been calling the economy of love in Skelton's telling of the *Troilus*: a sense, now, that pain has its language in the fillings of a purse. For Wyatt, whose "thing" shall be given as a token to his friend, the economies of court service, much like the economies of friendship, is both fickle and elusive.

> In this world now, little prosperity,
> And coin to keep, as water in a sieve.
> (Rebholz, *The Complete Poems*, CLI.90–91)

Not only is the service of the court as transitory as the water in a sieve. The meaning of this poem, too, stands insecurely in the realms of personal ventriloquism, literary allusion, and public epistolography. The poem is the coin, and the value of proverbs – their "prys," to use Chaucer's word for both commercial and linguistic value – like the value of proverbial poetry is but water in a sieve, a little thing to make "the male to wryng."

Lives of Bryan

If Wyatt's Satire is, at least to some degree, about the fashioning of a life against literary models, then it is too about the possibilities of making the lived life the subject of literary discourse. We know so much about Sir Francis Bryan – and what we know is so pointed, so delightfully maximal, anecdotal, and apparently univocal – that critics all too often rise to the temptation of inscribing the "historical" Bryan into Wyatt's literary text. For many recent readers of this poem the palpability of Brian leads to a transparent topicality of reading. The literary addressee is, in brief, nothing other than the historical figure. And yet, such a historical figure is himself the creation – and the self-creation – of the written text. Saunders's anecdotes, for all their historical validity, are carefully constructed moral narratives of courtly life. So, too, Bryan's own self-representation in his letters toys with the public reputation he had garnered. In his letters to Lord Lisle, for example, he plays his role as libertine to represent himself as friend and confidant.[34] Dispatched to Calais as Lord Lisle's deputy, Bryan wrote on 24 October 1533:

Sir, whereas in your last letter I perceive that in Calais ye have sufficient of courtezans to furnish and accomplish my desires, I do thank you of your good provision, but this shall be to advertise to you that since my coming hither I have called to my remembrance the misliving that ye and such other hath brought me to; for the which, being repented, have had absolution of the Pope. And because ye be my friend, I would advertise you in likewise to be sorry of that ye have done, and ask my lady your wife forgiveness. (Byrne, *The Lisle Letters*, vol. I, p.596)

The old companion begs forgiveness. Bryan recalls the "misliving" he shared with Lisle, the exploits of a youth that are now to be forgiven by wives and pardoned by the Pope. And yet, for all of his avowals of a changed life, Bryan cannot but conclude the letter on a curiously leering note. The Pope has come to Calais for the marriage of his niece to the Duke of Orleans, and that niece arrived with a set of gentlewomen and mistresses who "be not as fair as was Lucrece" (vol. I, p.596). Here, in a letter to a friend and patron, Bryan fashions himself not the courtly Vicar of Hell but the reformed rake. It is a letter that begins with memories of a libido and concludes with mention of a marriage. It is a document of *amicitia* framed in the desirings of women, as if what makes friendship here are the shared mislivings with courtesans and the inside jokes about the good looks of the servants of the Pope's niece.

Bryan's place throughout the correspondence of the Lisle family is as complex and self-complicating as it is here. In his epistolary entrances, Bryan appears not simply as a libertine (active or reformed) but as a

friend, and it is the quality of that friendship that is always the subject of
the letter. In contrast to Wyatt's preoccupations with the maskings,
feignings, and collusions of the courtly life, Bryan appears in these
accounts honest, unfeigned, unmasked: in a word, *true*. But nonetheless,
he is in these epistles, as he is in Wyatt's poem, still a creature of the
barnyard and the beastly. From Marseilles he could write that "dead
men be more plenty than quick capons" (vol. I, p.646); from Westminster
he would beg that Lisle send his regards to Lady Lisle's "little dog" (vol.
II, p.30); and from Antibes, in June of 1538, he could remark that "in the
French Court I never saw so many women. I would I had so many sheep
to find my house whilst I live!" (vol. V, p.145).

But perhaps nowhere is Bryan's role as friend and courtier as telling as
in the letter John Husee wrote to Lord Lisle on 20 September 1534 (vol.
II, pp.255–57). This letter, from a private secretary to a master, is one of
a series written late in that month concerning the so-called Whethill
affair – a bit of courtly infighting in which a noblewoman came to court
to sue for the protection of her son and which ultimately came to involve
Henry VIII and Cromwell in a series of deceits and disputations.[35] Bryan
himself had written to Lisle on 1 September advising his friend to get
"some honest man further to open and declare unto the King's Highness
your demeanour towards the said Whethill, with a bill signed with the
hands of them which heard the words betwixt your lordship and him"
(vol. II, p.249). Bryan here is a counselor of writing, a friend who can
advise Lisle that his letters are believed to be "not true" (vol. II, p.249)
and thus get him to forgo the personal communiqués of speech and get
things down on paper. Here is the Bryan of the opening of Wyatt's
Satire, "who knows how great a grace / In writing is to counsel man the
right." In Husee's letter, Bryan figures in a nexus of epistolary intrigue.
The Whethill matter goes on in the realm of letters: first with Whethill's
own delivery of letters, then with Whethill's father sending "a great
Libell," that is a written declaration of intent that Husee has seen "in
articles" (vol. II, p.256). Now Bryan and Henry Norris implore Husee
"to write you that yet all times you should obtemper [i.e., obey] the
King's letters." He goes on:

Further, Mr. Secretary [i.e., Cromwell] marvelled that your lordship should write
to Mr. Norris that in case Whethill had the room your lordship would rather give
up your room and wait upon the King in England than abide; and he said in case
the King had seen that letter it would not a' pleased his Grace. I perceive a man
had need to take heed what he write, but truly both Mr. Norris and Mr. Bryan
are your good lordship's unfeigned friends, wherefore they are both to be highly
thanked and to be remembered. (vol. II, p.256)

Courtly infighting goes on through the exchange of missives. Obedience to King and country constitutes obedience to the King's letter, and the fear of writing – the sense, in the Fall of 1534, that the machinery of Cromwell's epistolary intercessions is already starting to turn – may be overcome by the reliance on true "unfeigned friends" like Norris and Bryan.

Husee goes on:

> I shewed Mr. Kingston according as your lordship commanded me, who denieth that he never spake for Whethill; but I perceive all is not gold that shineth. He taketh the wood sale earnestly, and as far as I can perceive he is not minded the first sale shall stand. What reasoning I had further with him I remit till my coming to Calais. Mr. Treasurer desireth your lordship to remember his wine, and saith that he is yours after the old manner. Also Mr. Bryan willed me to write further to your lordship that you must keep all things secreter than you have used, and saith that there is nothing done nor spoken but it is with speed knowen in the Court. And further he willeth your lordship to take more upon you and be knowen for the King's Deputy there, and not to use company of mean personages, nor to be conversant with some persons which he saith useth daily company with your lordship sounding highly against your honour. I trust your lordship will take no displeasure with me because I write so plainly, as I was desired, but I take God to record, I would your lordship as much good as my own heart. And at my coming I know well Mr. Bryan will advertise you largely of that, with all others. (vol. II, p.256)

All that glitters is not gold. With this familiar proverb, Husee shifts from the details of courtly infighting to the accounts of private purchases. It is a rhetorical move that looks ahead to Wyatt's own displacement of the worth of friendship on the gold of courtly pandering. The mercantile metaphors of the Satire to Bryan resonate with Husee's own investment in a similar arrangement of proverb and economic fact to place Sir Francis Bryan, once again, in the environs of the gold of amicitial service. Yet Husee's letter shows us a Bryan with an honest name, a Bryan whose political and private function is to prove in practice the reliance on the gold of friendship. The intersection between speech and writing here, as in the Satire, becomes the nodal point for defining political sagacity. The need for secrecy in writing – the injunctions against spreading "news" in letters that had become Cromwell's way of regulating rumor and dissent – balances itself against the need for trust in conversation. Bryan is one of Lisle's "unfeigned friends," one whose friendship was not, in the terms of Erasmian courtier duplicity, a mask. Bryan functions in Husee's letter not as the dissolute self-aggrandizing Pandar of the King's court but as a tutor in the arts of amicitial diplomacy. And when Husee himself begs pardon for writing "so plainly," he has Bryan intercede again, not just to "advertise" Husee's coming to Lord Lisle, but in effect, to clear Husee of any mistakes in communication. He stands as the true *interpres*, as the go-between who clears up rumor, intercedes in personal conflict, and passes back and forth between the court and courtier.

Bryan, in brief, lives in the realm of letters. His status as a friend and counselor, just as his status as a libertine, is made in the self-presentations and the intercessions of the secretarial. Bryan's epistolary life (and afterlife, for that matter) provides a new environment in which to understand the nature of Wyatt's Satire. By making him the addressee of a verse epistle, Wyatt reinscribes his erstwhile friend into the discourses of secretive epistolarity in which Bryan himself had been presented at his most "unfeigned." We need do more than just assess the ironies of praising the Vicar of Hell as a model courtier. We need to understand that Bryan is – for all the anecdotal evidence of his glib speech – a creature not of talk but of the text. He is a man, in Husee's version of things, of subtle writings and interpretations. He is Pandaric not just in his voyeuristic sexuality or his associations with the pimpery of courtiership, but in his epistolary intercessions and his mastery of "things secreter" than they have been.

As such a figure, Bryan contrasts, too, with the "privy dissimuled friends" of Husee's next letter. Here, in a long and detailed document about his interview with Cromwell on 21 September, Husee reviews all the key features of political and scribal life under the Chancellor (letter dated 23 September, Byrne, *The Lisle Letters*, vol. II, pp.257–60). There is, from the start, the fear of epistolary interception: "incontinent upon the receipt" of his letter to Cromwell, Husee delivers it directly to him (vol. II, p.257). The letter gets mishandled, lost, denied. Cromwell gets Husee in an after-dinner interview – more like an inquisition, really – about how he controls access to the King and about how Lisle should keep his nose out of affairs that do not matter to him. First, Cromwell tells Husee, in the latter's paraphrase, that Lisle "is led . . . by some which although you take them for your friends are but feigned" (vol. II, p.258). Then, he tells Husee, now in direct quotation, "Well, I would you advised my lord to meddle in no such *lyʒt* matters" (vol. II, p.259, emphases added). Byrne edits Husee's word *lyʒt* (light), which I have retained, to "like."[36] But I believe his wording is quite precise, and resonates with the rhetoric of the "light touches" and the "light handlings" of Henry VIII's minion life and letters. *Light* comes to mean inappropriately intimate or intrusive. The light touches of the minions were, as I had argued, the all-too-familiar gestures of courtiers who had forgotten their subordinate role; and the light handlings of the letters got the King's secret epistles to his lover intercepted and broadcast in London. Husee, here, makes his conversation with Cromwell a conversation that reflects on the very activity of what he does. This is a letter that both concerns and enacts the secrecies of correspondence, a letter that reveals a court in which nothing is secret. Cromwell shows himself, here and throughout the letter, master of rumor. He seems to know everything, from the contents of Lisle's letters to the feelings of his friends. Husee, of course, must share with Lisle his own access to information (he relies on those "that are nigh about Mr. Secretary," vol. II, p.259). And yet, as he begins to close the letter, Husee must remind Lord Lisle "to keep what I writ unto you secret" (vol. II, p.259). He calls attention to the falsehoods passed in letters written about Lisle. And he ends, in a remarkable gesture of self-cancellation, with a bit of advice that locates us once more in both the political realities of the Cromwellian 1530s and the rhetorical feints of Henry VIII's own letters.

> And now that I have opened unto your lordship the circumstance of what I was commanded and what I do know, I trust your lordship will in the premises take pain to be your own secretary, for so it doth behove you to do, and else you may be deceived. And what you write or send, let it be left in my absence with the wife of the Red Lion in Southwark, for I know not how long I shall remain at the Court. (vol. II, p.260)

Closings are openings, presences are absences. The vision of the private secretary counseling his master to be secretary to himself must seem one of the most painful of gestures in the courtly world. Husee's gesture recalls Henry's self-conscious bypassings of secretarial control, first in the early letters to Wolsey and then in the love letters to Anne. As Henry wrote to Wolsey, there were things "which be so secret that they cause me at this time to write to you myself."[37] Now, for Husee, who had entreated Lisle "to keep what I writ unto you secret," the machinery of state intrusion may seem far too great even for him. The writer cancels himself out, closes a letter with the injunction for future letters to be left in his absence, wavers even on his own future presence at the court.

I have dwelled in detail on this collection of letters not only to flesh out the social world of Francis Bryan but to frame that portrait in the politics of epistolarity. The subject of these letters, more than local courtly sparring or political preferment, is the act of letter writing itself – the complex cultural processes by which secretaries are empowered to represent (in all senses of the word) the master. Husee's status as a diplomat for Lisle takes shape in these accounts of friendship, loyalty, and surreption. For the point is that the true unfeigned friend is the secretary, the man who does not dissimulate but must record, with absolute accuracy, the dictations of the master and the language of all other speech and writing. Husee tells stories of friendship constructed out of writing, and when he counsels Lord Lisle to be his own best secretary, it has the rhetorical effect of telling one to be one's own best friend. Recall Wyatt's advice to Bryan: "Be next thyself, for friendship bears no prize."

These letters from the Lisle correspondence provide a dark foil for Wyatt's colloquy with Bryan. They present two versions of the textual construction of the courtly counselor in the realms of epistolary conversation and mercantile metaphorics. Bryan is not the counterfeiter of desire but the one unfeigned friend among mimics of fidelity. His sagacious counsel steers the courtier through the eddies of what has become a kind of state Pandarism: the intrusions of Cromwellian control, the interceptions of missives, the hunting out of seditious speech and writing. These are the contours of a private Bryan, and they contrast with the public figure of the King's court. They provide, therefore, another way of understanding Wyatt's poem: as a meditation on the need for a public face. The intimacies of the verse epistle are, much like those of the prose, always subject to intrusion and interception.

A defense of poetry

And what of Wyatt himself? Soon after Cromwell's fall in 1540, Wyatt's name appeared in papers once suppressed but now examined by the King's authorities.[38] In documents from 1538 they found complaints made by Dr. Edmund Bonner and Dr. Simon Heynes about Wyatt's potentially treasonous associations and remarks. With Cromwell dead, Wyatt could count on no one, at least at first, to counter the charges made by Bonner, in particular, that he had slandered Henry VIII. Though it was generally believed that Wyatt's arrest (on 17 January 1541) was a result of his loss of Cromwell as protector and his sympathy for Lutheran opinions, one of the central accusations was that he had said "that he feared the King should be cast out of a cart's arse and that, by God's blood, if he were so, he were well served, and would he were so."[39] Stephen Foley has made much of this remark and the defense Wyatt prepared (but did not have to deliver) in framing his account of the proverbial in the Satire to Bryan.[40] There are clear verbal resonances between the verse Satire and two prose texts Wyatt wrote in 1541 explaining his remarks and justifying his activities during his ambassadorial service in the late 1530s: *A Declaration . . . of his Innocence . . .* and *Wyatt's Defence To the Iudges after the Indictement and the evidence.*[41] In these documents Wyatt goes to great lengths to affirm his habitual use of proverbs and to argue that Bonner, knowing of this habit, added one that Wyatt did not utter, in order to lend credence to a slanderous story about Wyatt himself. The prose texts and the poem, Foley argues, are "two moments . . . deeply engaged with the larger cultural problems of identity and impersonation" – moments, in other words, when the poet puts on what he himself calls, in the defense, the "garments" of language to project authority before others.[42]

I turn to these prose writings now, to move beyond the moment of the writing and reception of the Satire and understand, more generally, the material quality of Wyatt's writing itself. At the heart of Wyatt's self-defense is concern with proper speaking, writing, and receiving – a concern with language at the syllabic level. The altering of a single syllable, Wyatt argues, "ether with penn or word," can change the entire meaning of an utterance, an argument he marshals to claim that his statement was heard and transcribed inaccurately. Wyatt's *Declaration* and *Defence*, I argue in what follows, are not just statements about proverbial language or engagements with problems of identity and impersonation but, taken together, constitute a manifesto of editorial principles. Their comments on the modes of writing and reading bear directly on the circulation of Wyatt's own verse. They come to equate poem and letter as forms of discourse equally subject to the slippage of the pen or the intrusions of the interceptor. The status of manuscript poems in the age of Wyatt *is* the letter – not just in coterie circles of exchange that defined gentlemanly class against the "stigma" of public and commercial print, but rather as documents that have all the intimacy of the epistle; documents, in short, that work like letters and that, in their transcription and compilation, operate as intercepted letters in the coteries of courtly culture.[43]

Wyatt begins his *Declaration* with a claim of innocence. His central task is to recall, years later, "suche thynges as have passed me . . . by worde, wrytinge, communinge, or receauing" (Muir, *Life and Letters*, p.178). This *Declaration* is not so much an appeal to innocence as a remembrance of letters – an accounting of all the documents passed through his office while at the Emperor's court. Letters upon letters stack themselves in Wyatt's prose.[44] "[L]ettres or wrytnges," he tries to recall, "came to my handys or thorow my handes vnopened" (p.180). He never, he protests, knowingly communicated with a traitor. Those documents he could not verify were, as he put it "ether so secretly handlede or yett not in couerture" that he could not see them (p.181). Some letters, he avers as well, never reached him, in particular, the letters of Mason addressed to Wyatt and the Earl of Essex (p.183). And he goes on to define the province of "an Imbassadoure" as secrecy itself, and to note that "a prince were as good sende nakede lettres and to receaue naked lettres as to be at charge for Recidencers" (p.184).

The *Declaration* concludes, following Wyatt's signature, "This with-owte correctinge, sendinge, or ouerseinge" (p.184), and in the *Defence* that follows it Wyatt develops the activities of correcting, sending, and overseeing into an essay on the nature of reading and writing itself. Reflection on the practice of diplomacy leads to a meditation on intention and expression.

Intelligens concludethe a familiarite or conferringe of devyses to gyther, which may be by worde, message or wrytinge, which the lawe forbiddythe to be had with anye the kinges traytours or rebels, payne of the lyke. Reherse the lawe, declare, my lordes, I beseke you, the meaninge thereof. Am I a traytor by cawse I spake with the kinges traytor? No, not for that, for I may byd him 'avaunte, traytor' or 'defye hym, traytor.' No man will tayke this for treasone; but where he is holpen, counceled, advertysed by my worde, there lyethe the treason, there lyethe the treason. In wrytinge yt is lyke. In message yt is lyke; for I may sende hym bothe lettre and message of chalinge or defyaunce. (p.190)

Just because a man speaks with a traitor does not make him a traitor. Identity lies in intention, in the adherance to codes of conduct or the rules of law. In writing as in speech, the individual's identity should not be confused with that of the addressee. Such statements have, I believe, a profound resonance with Wyatt's own poetic practice. The gist of the verse epistle lies in these tensions between reader and addressee. It establishes a form of "intelligens" between the two. Its understanding demands a rehearsal of the laws of literary discourse, an inquiry into "meaninge" made through verse. But the verse epistle also sets up the conventions of reported speech *as* conventions. It makes quotation the defining mode of writer and addressee – indeed, it makes each poem operate entirely, as it were, within quotation marks. The fiction of the letter, now, is the fiction of the voice. The colloquy between friends is an act of "intelligens" based on "familiarite." The problem, therefore, lies along the line between the poetic and the historical. When is a quotation not a quotation? In the Satire to Bryan, the poem's speaker goes to great lengths to distance himself from the pandering courtier, while at the same time brilliantly ventriloquizing his position in the other's voice. "Am I a traytor by cawse I spake with the kinges traytor? . . . In wryting yt is lyke." Am I a Pandar because I spoke with, wrote to, *wrote as*, the King's Pandar?

How can one defend oneself against words quoted, reported, and transcribed? This is the heart of Bonner's accusation and Wyatt's defense. "And what say my accusares in thes wordes? Do theie swere I spake them trayterously or maliciously? . . . Rede ther depositions, theie say not so. Confer ther depositions, yf theie agre worde for worde" (p.197). The accusations against Wyatt become texts; the texts become subject to conferral, that is, comparison. Such documents are treated here as if they were the objects of an editor: compared, collated, and reviewed for accuracy. Wyatt goes on:

Yf theie mysagre in wordis and not in substance, let vs here the woordes theie varie in. For in some lyttell thynge may apere the truthe which I dare saye you seke for your consciens sake. And besydys that, yt is a smale thynge in alteringe of one syllable ether with penne or worde that may mayk in the conceavinge of the truthe myche matter or error. For in thys thynge 'I fere', or 'I truste', semethe but one smale syllable chaynged, and yet it makethe a great dyfferaunce, and may be of an herer wronge conceaved and worse reported, and yet worste of all altered by an examyner. Agayne 'fall owte' 'caste owte', or 'lefte owte' makethe dyfferaunce, yea and the settinge of the wordes one in an others place may mayke greate dyfferaunce, tho the wordes were all one – as 'a myll horse' and 'a horse myll'. I besyche you therfore examen the matter vnder this sorte. *Confere* theire severall sayinges togyther, *confer* th'examynations vpone the same matter and I dare warrante ye shall fynde mysreportynge and mysvnderstandinge. (p.197, emphases added)

In the specific context of the defense, Wyatt argues that his words have been mistaken. His deployment of the proverb, "I am lefte owte of the cartes ars" (p.198), has been taken out of context, misheard, misreported, and mistranscribed into the environment of royal offense. Instead of saying what he has been accused of saying ("ye shall see the kinge our maister cast out at the carts tail"), what Wyatt claims he said was more like, "I fere for all these menes fayer promyses the kinge shalbe lefte owte of the cartes ars." He recalls that he may have very well said something like that, and may well have invoked this proverbial sentiment on occasion. "But that I vsed it with Bonar or Haynes I neuer remembre; and yf I euer dyd I am sure neuer as thei couche the tale" (p.198).

But in the larger world of Wyatt's discourse, his appeal to memory and intention takes on the flavor of a theory of textual criticism. Comparison of manuscripts – signaled by the Latin verb *conferre* and its past participial form, *collatus* – was the hallmark of the early humanist philological method.[45] I have argued elsewhere that this language of comparison and criticism may have influenced the self-promotions (if not the practice itself) of England's early printers, and Wyatt's appeals in his defense resonate with the terms of contemporary editorial reflection.[46] One need only compare Brian Tuke's Preface to Thynne's 1532 Chaucer edition to see the workings of this language in practice.

as bokes of dyuers imprintes came unto my handes / I easely and without grete study / might and haue deprehended in them many errours / falsyties / and deprauacions / whiche euydently appered by the contrarietees and alteracions founde by *collacion* of the one with the other / wherby I was moued and styred to make dilygent sertch / where I might fynde or recouer any trewe copies or exemplaries of the sayd bookes. (Aii v, emphasis added)[47]

The collation of manuscripts helps what Tuke calls "the restauracion" of Chaucer's works in their authorized form, and this process, he avers, is not just a literary but a political "dewtie" growing out of his "very honesty and loue to my countrey" (Aiii r). Tuke's preface is a statement of national fealty, an appeal to King Henry VIII as patron to exercise his "discrecyon and iugement" and accept the volume as it has been printed.[48] If Wyatt's *Defence* reads as a statement of editorial principles, then Tuke's preface may stand as something of a defense of its own: a plea before a judging King for the authentic value of an author's works and, in turn, for a recognition of the editor's own searching out of falsity and error through the collation of texts.

As in the making of an edition, the slightest slips can change the meaning of a line. "I fere" or "I truste," Wyatt offers, differ only in "one smale syllable." But what a syllable it is. Certainly, such a case is not a random call. *Fear* and *trust* are the two poles of Wyatt's poetic emotion. In the first poem of the Wyatt section of Tottel's *Miscellany*, they are the epicenters of the poet's consciousness of love and requital.

> She that me learneth to love and suffer
> And will that my *trust* and lust's negligence
> Be reined by reason, shame, and reverence,
> With his hardiness taketh displeasure.
> Wherewithal unto the heart's forest he fleeth,
> Leaving his enterprise with pain and cry,
> And there him hideth and not appeareth.
> What may I do when my master *feareth*,
> But in the field with him to live and die?
> For good is the life ending faithfully.
>
> (Rebholz, *The Complete Poems*, X.5–14, emphases added)

Trust is a form of confidence, or, one might say, the expression of a hope of a good outcome. Fear, by contrast, is the opposite of such a hope, and the opposition finds its voice again in one of the ballades:

> It may be good, like it who list.
> But I do doubt. Who can me blame?
> For oft assured yet I have missed
> And now again I *fear* the same.
> . . .
> Assured I doubt I be not sure.
> And should I *trust* to such surety
> That oft hath put the proof in ure
> And never hath found it *trusty*?   (LXXXV.1–4, 15–18, emphases added)

Translated into the oxymorons of Petrarchan love, Wyatt avers else-where: "I fear and hope, I burn and freeze like ice" (XVII.2). In another of the Petrarchan sonnets, he laments "That all my trust and travail is but waste" (XXI.14). "I see that from my hand falleth my trust," he fears at the close of another sonnet (XXII.13), and in a song he begins, "Mistrustful minds be moved / To have me in suspect" (CXXXVIII.1–2). Tottel prints a poem in his Wyatt section which, while rejected from the canon by later editors, nonetheless voices this characteristic instability of hope and faith: "My wastefull will is tried by trust" (Rollins, ed., *Miscellany*, p.59, line 22). And, in yet another of Wyatt's translations from Petrarch, he distills the Italian lexicon of pain – sighing, hope, and desire – into a unique oxymoron of his own:[49]

> An endless wind doth tear the sail apace
> Of forced sighs and *trusty fearfulness*.
> (Rebholz, *The Complete Poems*, XIX.7–8, emphases added)

Finally, in one of the ballads preserved in the Blage manuscript, Wyatt expounds not just on the nature of his trust, but on the very problems of transcription and substitution that are the subject of his *Defence*. Concluding the ballad, whose refrain line had been "Patience, perforce, content thyself with wrong," he offers:

> I burn and boil, without redress.
> I sigh, I weep, and all in vain,
> Now hot, now cold. Who can express
> The thousand part of my great pain?
> But if I might her favour attain
> Then would I trust to change this song,
> With 'pity' for 'patience' and 'conscience' for 'wrong'.   (CXCI.15–21)

Wyatt performs an act of critical self-revision. He suggests changing words for words, locates the change in "trust," and posits a revisionary poetics that makes the language of the song subject always to rewriting, depending on the circumstances of performance.

"My word nor I shall not be variable" (XXX.13). In spite of this protest, Wyatt's words were variable. The very nature of the writing and transmitting of his poetry lies in the variations of the scribe, in the self-cancellations and revisions of the poet, and in the manipulations of the printer. It is, of course, a commonplace of Wyatt criticism to remark on the unstable quality of his verse line, on the idiosyncrasies of his spelling, and on the variations generated by competing manuscript and print editions. The practice of textual criticism runs up against the intractable wall of Wyatt's own texts. As Jonathan Crewe recognizes, modern editions of Wyatt's poetry (as of much early sixteenth-century verse) are in themselves modernizations: recastings of his words and lines. "In quite a fundamental sense," Crewe notes, "to print Wyatt modernized is to censor his work."[50]

My purpose here is not to review systematically those variations that contribute to the instability of Wyatt's texts. Nor is it my goal to restore Wyatt's work to something of its "authorial" or original context. What I do wish to argue is that the problem of textual instability is itself thematized in Wyatt's writings: that it is the underlying subject of the *Declaration* and the *Defence* and that it controls the making and transmission of his verse in a self-conscious and deliberate way. The text is always variable. Shifts in syllable or word are shifts in meaning. Mistaking a phrase, a word, a line, a proverb results in mistaking the intention of the speaker or the writer. As a consequence, all writing is a form of a defense: a constant process of revision and rescription, of rereading and collating, that leads to a governing appreciation of the slippages of language. "I dare warrante ye shall fynde mysreportinge and mysvnderstandinge." Such an injunction is a goad not just to Wyatt's accusers but to all who dare to read him.

Wyatt's work survives always in the mishandlings of others, in the manuscript transcriptions, editorial revisions, scribal alterations, censorships, and challenges of his own and his reader's hands. Modern critics have long supposed that there is something undeniably authentic behind all of these mishandlings. The so-called "Tottelization" of Wyatt, for example, has been understood as a maligning of his lines to regularize them for easy imitation by a later generation of poetic amateurs.[51] And in the scholarship attendant on the other major manuscripts containing his poetry, the impulse has long been to recover an authentic text not only from the local variations of the scribes, but from the larger arc of the compilers. The question of what exactly *is* Wyatt's in these manuscripts, has, I believe, overshadowed the more meaningful question of how each manuscript articulates its principles of *compilatio* – in other words, why certain poems make it into certain manuscripts and whether we may palpably discern an overarching interest (thematic, imagistic, social) in their presence.

I have already suggested some lines of inquiry into this question for the Wellys and Devonshire Manuscripts. For the latter, the concern with secrecy and intrusion motivates the selection of Wyattic and non-Wyattic verse, as Raymond Southall noticed long ago.[52] Its opening text, Wyatt's "Take heed betime lest ye be spied" (Rebholz, *The Complete Poems*, CXVIII) appears only in Devonshire, as do a clutch of poems concerned with the problems of scribal transcription and individual reading. Poems such as "Me list no more to sing" (CXXV), "Lament my loss"

(CLXXVII), "My pen, take pain a little space" (CCVIII), "I see the change" (CCXV), and "Who would have ever thought" (CCXLII), all address the same problems of text and reader as the sequences of poems attributed to Thomas Howard. The plea for correction and emendation – the familiar cliché of the post-Chaucerian tradition – takes on new force in a poem such as "Lament my loss," where the imagery of the quaking pen resonates with the selections from Chaucer's *Troilus* that close the first sequence of Howard's poems in the Manuscript (Muir, "Unpublished Poems," 14).

> Yet well ye know it will renew my smart
> Thus to rehearse the pains that I have passed.
> My hand doth shake, my pen scant doth his part,
> My body quakes, my wits begin to waste.
> 'Twixt heat and cold in fear I feel my heart
> Panting for pain; and thus, as all aghast
> I do remain scant wotting what I write,
> Pardon me, then, rudely though I indite.
>
> And patiently, O reader, I thee pray,
> Take in good part this work as it is meant
> And grieve thee not with aught that I shall say
> Since with goodwill this book abroad is sent
> To tell men how in youth I did assay
> What love did mean, and now I it repent,
> That, noting me, my friends may well be ware
> And keep them free from all such pain and care.
>
> (Rebholz, *The Complete Poems*, CLXXVII.17–32)

What Wyatt, in the *Defence*, called "mysreportinge and mysvnderstandinge" resonates anew with the conventions of the envoy and the fears of the pen. In this ballad, however, the quaking pen has been transferred to the poet's whole body. The sequence of lines 19 to 21 is a veritable anatomy of a Chaucerian idiom: from hand, to pen, to body, to wits, to heart, the insecurities of writer move from the extremities of writing to the inner site of feeling and desire. By the time we get to the line, "I do remain scant wotting what I write," we can see that the narrator's self-ignorance grows from this fundamental separation of the writing hand from the feeling heart.[53] To grant the writer our "goodwill" is not, therefore, simply to share in the topoi of modesty but to recognize that those texts inscribed with quaking pens are, quite simply, textually unreliable.

This question of the unreliable text is both a condition of Wyatt's textual transmission and a theme addressed throughout the poetry. When Wyatt concludes the short poem, "Who would have ever thought," with the lines,

> But note I will this text
> To draw better the next.   (CCXLII.17–18),

what he implies is the possibility of endless rescription. The next poem
will be better drawn; the scribal lessons of the previous will be incorporated in the next. But this will never happen. Wyatt's poems are
continually preoccupied with their own linguistic instability, and with the
inability of the poetic hand to transcribe the intentions of the heart. Even
when the author's own text is presented as a proof, he recognizes that it
may never suffice.

> And with my pen this do I write
> To show *the* plain by proof of sight
>   I see *the* change.
>
> I see the change of wearied mind
> And slipper hold hath quit my hire
> Lo, how by proof in *the* I find
> A burning faith in changing fire.
> Farewell my part. Proof is no liar.
>   I see *the* change.   (CCXV.4–12, re-edited by me, emphases added)

But proof seems hard to come by, and the poem ends with the avowal,
"Never to trust the like again" (line 29). Even the text in the lover's own
hand cannot suffice as proof, cannot, now in the terms of Wyatt's
Defence, efface wholly the fear that lies behind trust. The logic of this
poem hinges on another linguistic instability, the play on *the* and *thee*.
Here, too, the hand has been mistrusted: but not by the Tudor lover but
the modern editor. In the Devonshire Manuscript (where this poem
uniquely appears) the scribe has spelled both words as simply *the* – a fact
Rebholz acknowledges in the notes to his edition, and yet one he ignores
in the editing itself.[54] Thus, he prints line 6 as "To show *thee* plain by
proof of sight" and line 9 as "Lo, how by proof in *thee* I find" (emphases
mine). In Devonshire, the refrain line can mean both "I see the change"
and "I see thee change" – indeed, such a confusion and its resolution is
what charts the reader's progress through the poem, as the first lines of
each stanza repeat the four words of the refrain in new contexts. The
definite article and the second person pronoun are never textually secure.
Here, in a poem on the insecurities of proof itself, a poem on the nature
of change, the modern editor fails to "see the change." What we must
see, as Wyatt's readers, is the constantly changing nature of his verse as it
is always written, and in the process, to expose how both the poems and
their scribes bring out the insecurities of manuscript transmission.

   Let us return to Wyatt's Satires. They are a set, treated as such since
the eighteenth-century appreciations of Wharton and the nineteenth-

century edition of Nott.[55] More recently, they have been located in the occasions of the diplomatic and the personal; have been grounded in certain generic and formal properties; and have been explained as part of the poet's larger engagement with the borrowed forms of classical and Continental satire and the inherited idioms of Chaucerian colloquy.[56] And yet, these are poems that survive in manuscript and early printed contexts in forms slightly different and in arrangements tellingly dissimilar from their modern presentations. Egerton places the first two together (though lines 1–51 of "Myne owne John Poyntz" are omitted), while separating the Satire to Bryan, while Arundel places the poem to Bryan together with "My mother's maids," while separating out "Myne owne John Pointz." Tottel printed the three together, in the order "My mother's maids," "Myne owne John Poyntz," and "A Spending hand," and followed by the Song of Iopas, they conclude the Wyatt section of the *Miscellany*.[57] In addition to these differences of order, not all the Satires survived complete in all their manuscripts. Only the first eighteen lines of "My mother's maids" show up in Devonshire.[58] And the first fifty-one lines of "Myne owne John Poyntz" are missing in the Egerton Manuscript, the one widely believed to be in Wyatt's own hand.

In all their appearances, the poems differ, at times slightly, at times significantly. Much has been made, for example, of the Arundel and Tottel revision of these lines from the Satire to Bryan:

> So sacks of dirt be filled up in the cloister
> That serves for less than do these fatted swine.
>
> (Rebholz, *The Complete Poems*, CLI.22–23)

> So sacks of dirt be filled. The neat courtier
> So serves for less than do these fatted swine.   (Arundel and Tottel)

It has been argued that these revisions were made during the reign of the Catholic Queen Mary, when satires against the monks would have been inexcusable.[59] But there are also revisions which point not to the exigencies of current politics but the demands of literary understanding. The version of "Myne owne John Poyntz" in the Parker Manuscript presents a series of unique readings which, I believe, resituate this poem in the legacy of Chaucer's writing and exemplify those alterations in the word or syllable that Wyatt himself recognized as the heart of the textual condition.

Because the first fifty-one lines of this Satire do not appear in Egerton, it is impossible to recover what Wyatt's "original" text may have looked like. Richard Harrier chose the Arundel Manuscript version of these lines as his base text, while listing variant readings from the others.[60] Ronald Rebholz, by contrast, uses Parker as his copytext and draws on other manuscripts to offer what he considers "readings which appear to have greatest authority according to this family-tree or stemma" of manuscripts as it has been recovered.[61] But Rebholz does not print all the Parker variants (preferring, on occasion, readings from textual lineage of Arundel, Devonshire, and Hill), and I believe his text represents a serious misrepresentation of the language and direction of that version of the poem. Here is his edition of its first twenty-one lines.

> Mine own John Poyntz, since ye delight to know
>   The cause why that homeward I me draw
>   (And flee the press of courts whereso they go
> Rather than to live thrall under the awe
>   Of lordly looks) wrapped within my cloak,
>   To will and lust learning to set a law,
> It is not because I scorn or mock
>   The power of them to whom Fortune hath lent
>   Charge over us, of right to strike the stroke;
> But true it is that I have always meant
>   Less to esteem them than the common sort,
>   Of outward things that judge in their intent
> Without regard what doth inward resort.
>   I grant sometime that of glory the fire
>   Doth touch my heart; me list not to report
> Blame by honour and honour to desire.
>   But how may I this honour now attain
>   That cannot dye the colour black a liar?
> My Poyntz, I cannot frame my tune to feign,
>   To cloak the truth for praise, without desert,
>   Of them that list all vice for to retain.
>   (Rebholz, *The Complete Poems*, CXLIX.1–21)

Now, here is my edition with all the Parker variants restored, with the significant ones highlighted by me.[62]

> Myne owne Ihon poyntz sins ye delite to know
>   The *causes* why that homeward I me drawe
>   (And flee the presse of courtes where so *I* goo
> Rather then to lyue thrall vnder the awe
>   Of lordly lookes) wrapped within my cloke,
>   To wyll and lust lernyng to set a lawe,
> It is not bycause I scorne or mocke
>   The power of them to whome fortune hath lent
>   Charge over us, of ryght to stroke to strike [corrected in
> the   margin as *to strik ye stroke*]
> But trewe it is that I have allwaies ment
>   Lesse to esteme them then the Commune sorte,
>   Of owtwarde thinges that iuge in their intent

> Withowt regard that dothe inwarde resort.
>   I grant somtime that of glorye the fyer
>   Doth touche my harte; *and me lust not repent*
> Blame by honour and honour to desier.
>   But howe may I this honour now attayne
>   That cannot dye the colour of blak a lyer
> My poyntz I cannot frame my *tonge to fayne*
>   To cloke the trewthe for prayse, without desert,
>   Of them that lust all vices to retayne.

While such differences may seem minor, taken together they represent a reconception of the poem's imagery and syntax fundamentally different from any other manuscript, and for that matter, from Rebholz's modern edition. To replace *they* with *I* (line 3) is, as at a very basic level, to remove a syntactical confusion. Just what the *they* refers to is unclear, and editors from Nott to Rebholz have considered it as either metrical filler (the phrase "whereso they go" stuck in to fill the line and make it rhyme, as Muir and Thompson suggest), or as referring more generally to the progress of the court.[63] But at a larger level, the replacement of *they* with *I* locates the speaker in the Chaucerian world of *Truth* – the world of Boethian advice evoked in Wyatt's opening injunction to "flee the press" and not to "live thrall." The substitution makes the speaker more assured, places his movement from the courts to the home, and makes the choice offered in lines 4–6 a first-person decision rather than a second-person counsel. So, too, the seeming misreading in line 15 shifts the balance of rhetorical power in the poem. "And me lust not repent" makes this, in some ways, a more pointedly Wyattic line: one that recalls the close of the ballad "Lament my loss": "and now I it repent" (Rebholz, *The Complete Poems*, CLXXVII.30). Against this reading, the Parker version of the Satire makes Wyatt's lines to Poyntz a palpable revision of that earlier repentance. At stake now is the choice not to repent, a choice that echoes the rhyme scheme of "Lament my loss":

> Take in good part this work as it is *meant*
>   And grieve thee not with aught that I shall say
> Since with goodwill this book abroad is *sent*
>   To tell me how in youth I did assay
> What love did mean, and now I it *repent*.
>   (CLXXVII.26–30, emphases added)

Meaning, intention, and repentance: *meant, intent, repent* – this is the movement of the speaker's thought as traced in Parker's rhymes. And in the substitution of *tongue* for *tune* in line 19, the poem's speaker is restored to his courtly self. Now, we have not the metaphorics of the poet as a tunesmith, but the problematics of the courtier as Pandarus.

Such courtiership hinges, in this poem, on a governing assemblage of reversals that make up the body of the Satire to Poyntz. Wyatt catalogues all of the things he cannot do, and with them, all the reversals that make him the courtier *manqué*. His literary taste, in this regard, is similarly perverse:

> And he that diethe for hungar off gold
> Call him Alexander, and saye that Pan
> Passeth Apollo in musike many a fold;
> Prayes Sir Thopas for a noble tale
> And scorne the storye that the knight tolld;
> Prayse him for counsall that is drunk off ale.
>
> (CXLIX.47–52, re-edited by me)

To take Sir Thopas over Chaucer's Knight is, at a basic level, to misread the *Canterbury Tales*, and with it, the inheritance of Chaucerian litera-ture. The inept, interrupted tellings of the pilgrim Geoffrey are, of course, the joke of *The Tale of Sir Thopas*, and Wyatt augments his own ineptness as reader in the following line. The "him" who is "drunk of ale" is, in this context of Chaucerian allusion, none other than the drunken Miller who erupts into the opening of the pilgrims' contest and subverts the Host's choice of the Monk as tale-teller after the Knight. The references to the drunkenness of the Miller – five times in thirty lines in the *Prologue to the Miller's Tale* – constitute something of an epithet for Chaucer's character; so much so, I believe, that in this context of Wyatt's allusions to the hierarchies of the *Tales* its referent must be the Miller himself.[64] What Wyatt posits here, then, is not so much a bad choice among the offerings of Chaucer's poem as it is a fundamentally inverted reading of the text itself: a reading that is uncourtly and foolish, one that – in the terms of the Satires to Poyntz and Bryan – favors the beastly over the cultivated, be it the animal-like crudeness of the Miller or the monstrous villains of *Sir Thopas*.[65]

By the time we get to the close of the Satire, Wyatt has effectively effaced himself from courtiership and literary history by realigning both the political and poetic priorities of courtly life.

> But here I am in Kent and Christendom
> Among the Muses, where I read and rhyme,
> Where if thou list, my Poyntz, for to come,
> Thou shalt be judge how I do spend my time.
>
> (Rebholz, *The Complete Poems*, CXLIX.100–3)

Enisled in the home counties, Wyatt can only read and rhyme, and he invites Poyntz to be judge of these private poetic efforts. To spend one's time, here, is to read and rhyme: not just to take time reading and writing, but actually to make meters. Spending time constitutes a metaphor for making meter, and if one had any question of this resonance, one need only return to the Parker Manuscript to see what it actually says:

> Thow shalt be judge how I *dispende* my tyme.
>
> (my edition; emphasis added)

Chaucer himself had been chastised for dispending time in the very text Wyatt had taken as primary among the poet's production, *The Tale of Sir Thopas*. Breaking off the tail-rhyme iterations of the poem, Harry Bailly breaks in:

> 'By God,' quod he, 'for pleynly, at a word,
> Thy drasty rymyng is nat worth a toord!
> Thou doost noght elles but despendest tyme.
> Sire, at o word, thou shalt no lenger ryme.
>
> (*Canterbury Tales*, VII lines 929–32)

To invite Poyntz to judge how he *dispends* his time is, in the allusion of the Parker Manuscript, to seek his playful playing of the Host's role to Wyatt's inept Chaucer. Behind this final line now lies the Chaucerian moment of failed poetry: a moment of radical mis-taking of poetic intention and performance. Such a moment is the comic foil for the Satire to Poyntz and, too, for the reflections of the later *Defence*. The dangers of mistaking and mishearing are the dangers of the literary *and* the political career. For the prolix Geoffrey Chaucer of the Canterbury pilgrimage, the verdict is ineptitude and the sentence – or penance, depending on one's sensibilities – is the retreat from poetic performance into the staid securities of prose treatise (the *Tale of Melibee*). For Wyatt, too, the accusations can be answered only in prose treatise. And yet, such a prose tract, such an undelivered oration, may not be the only defense he offers. In a larger sense, the Satires themselves are defenses of poetry. They justify the spending, or the dispending, of time. The "spending hand" of the Satire to Bryan, in this matrix of allusion and self-reference, takes on a meaning now not just of tired proverb but of vivid act. It is a hand of literary making: not a giving but a writing hand "that alway poureth out" the texts that may be read and judged by friend and enemy alike.

> And therewithal this thing I shall thee give –
> In this world now, little prosperity,
> And coin to keep, as water in a sieve.
>
> (Rebholz, *The Complete Poems*, CLI. 89–91)

"Thing," in Chaucer's Middle English, meant poem, as well as object, a meaning picked up later in the sixteenth century by Puttenham, and one that, I believe, stands at the core of Wyatt's closing lines to Francis Bryan.[66] "This thing" is now the poem, and unlike the counterfeitings of the courtier or the false coinings of *Troilus and Criseyde*, it is a coin to keep. And yet, to keep the currency of its meaning – to keep stable its text and prevent all misinterpretations or miswritings – is as futile as keeping water in a sieve.

Mark well this text

"Th'entente is al, and nat the lettres space." Criseyde had recognized the pitfalls of epistolary writing at the close of *Troilus and Criseyde*. A woman writing to be read by men, she falls into that category of mistranscribed and misunderstood female epistolarists who Pandarus had relied on for his counseling of Troilus. Oenene's letter to Paris is subject to Pandaric revision, while Antigone's song and Cassandra's prophecies are subject to competing interpretations. The substitution of the word, the mistake of the syllable, the mismetering of the scribe – these are the theme and practice of the *Troilus*. These are the places where Chaucer defines the nature of manuscript literary culture and the place of the authorial within it. The submission for "correccioun" that closes *Troilus and Criseyde* would become, in the century-and-a-half since its circulation, the defining trope of vernacular authorship.[67] Lydgate, Hawes, Skelton, and Wyatt all indulge in the plea for correction, the sending of the book to readers either more or less able than the writer. Such a condition of the literary, as well as the political utterance, are the subject of one of Wyatt's Songs – one that appears only in Devonshire and that, too, speaks to the concerns of that manuscript as much as it addresses the poet's own anxieties.

> Me list no more to sing
> Of love nor of such thing,
> How sore that it me wring;
> For what I sung or spake
> Men did my songs mistake.   (Rebholz, *The Complete Poems*, CXXXV.1–5)

He goes on to remark on how his songs were "too diffuse" for common folk and laments that it avails little to present truth or, in this poem's terms, "treasure," when it will be only misapprehended.

> Therefore fear not t'assay
> To gather, ye that may,
> The flower that this day
> Is fresher than the next.
> Mark well, I say, this text.   (lines 26–30)

Fear not, he notes, and the opposite of fear here (as elsewhere) is a form of trust. The gathering of flowers is the central image for a kind of reading. The very words *florilegium* and *anthology* mean a bouquet. Texts were culled on the analogy of picking such a bouquet, or of the bee going from flower to flower to make honey out of different nectars.[68] The poem is the flower, as the previous stanza had put it:

> What vaileth the flower
> To stand still and wither?
> If no man it savour
> It serves only for sight
> And fadeth towards night.   (lines 21–25)

What good is a poem if it is never read?[69] Or more to the point, what good is a poem if it is never gathered, never brought into the treasury of the anthology?

> And as for such treasure
> That maketh thee the richer
> And no deal the poorer
> When it is given or lent,
> Methinks it were well spent.   (lines 36–40)

Readers of these verses have traditionally taken "treasure" in line 36 to refer to the body as a means of sexual pleasure and to have understood this poem as a meditation on the ruses of desire and the whims of sexuality.[70] The treasure may connote the body, but it also figures forth the book: the treasury of knowledge, the thesaurus of the word.[71] This is a poem less about the joys of the body than about the pleasures of the text. It is a poem about the uses of poetry, about the ways in which texts are transmitted, read, transcribed, and, perhaps, misunderstood. The poem's meaning lies in its participation in a system of poetic making and reception.

> What vaileth under key
> To keep treasure alway
> That never shall see day?
> If it be not used
> It is but abused.   (lines 16–20)

This is the vision of the key to remembrance, the Chaucerian notion of the book as key that unlocks literary meaning. It is an image of the *arca libraria*, an image central, too, to the contemporary verses of the Wellys Anthology.[72] And, in a final recollection of the older critical vocabulary of Lydgate and Hawes – who wrote of poets cloaking their meanings under "cloudy figures" – Wyatt concludes:[73]

If this be under mist
And not well plainly wist,
Understand me who list
For I reck not a bean;
I wot what I do mean.   (lines 41–45)

Wyatt knows what he means, and what he means here is that poems
unused are abused: that poetry not read, transcribed, gathered, incorporated into compilations or contexts is a poetry that stands still and
withers. But he recognizes, too, that the price paid for such a use is the
potential mistranscription and mistaking of the text. "Mark well, I say,
this text." Not just remark upon it or remember it, but mark it well,
transcribe it right, make marks upon the page that signal understanding
or response.

The consciousness of Wyatt's sense of literary text takes us back to
the *Defence*, back to the Satires, and ultimately back to *Troilus and
Criseyde*, to help us understand the import of the verse epistle in the
makings of an early Tudor literary culture. For it lies in the letter, in
the text marked with the hand, that the character of the individual is
told. The verse epistle, I propose, is the defining genre of an early
modern literary subjectivity. It is the utterance made textual, the
speech transformed into the markings of the hand, the character
transcribed for reader and compiler. Tottel's insight lay in recognizing
this, and he constructs the *Miscellany* as a book of letters. Not only
does he include a preponderance of verse epistles in his volume. His
titles make the poems communications between writer and reader –
acts of private counsel, confessions of desire, injunctions to behavior.
But unlike those in Humphrey Wellys's volume, Tottel's poems are not
the surreptitiously intercepted missives of the court and country. These
are authorized, authoritative texts; models for future making; templates
for the poetaster in all who buy and read the book. Tottel's *Miscellany*
performs now for a paying public that tuition in amorous epistolography that was the heart of Chaucer's impact on the early Tudor
court.

A poem attributed to Wyatt and uniquely printed in Tottel epitomizes
this Troilan transformation of the early Tudor lyric into verse epistle.
Following the long canzone, "So feble is the thread," which Tottel
entitles "Complaint of the absence of his loue" (Rollins, ed., *Miscellany*,
pp.71–74) there appears a short poem printed with the title, "The louer
blameth his loue for renting of the letter he sent her."

Svffised not (madame) that you did teare,
My wofull hart, but thus also to rent:
The weping paper that to you I sent.

Wherof eche letter was written with a teare.
Could not my present paines, alas suffise,
Your gredy hart? and that my hart doth fele,
Tormentes that prick more sharper than the stele,
But new and new must to my lot arise.
Vse then my death. So shal your cruelty:
Spite of your spite rid me from all my smart,
And I no more such tormentes of the hart:
Fele as I do. This shalt thou gain thereby.

(Rollins, ed., *Miscellany*, p.74; Rebholz, *The Complete Poems*, CXXV)

This little text ventriloquizes brilliantly the problems of epistolary self-representation that had motivated amorous writing from Troilus through Henry VIII. The letter's presentation as a "weping paper," where each letter had been "written with a teare," recalls explicitly Pandarus's advice to Troilus on the writing of his first epistle to Criseyde. "Biblotte it with thi teris ek a lite" (*Troilus and Criseyde*, II.1027), he counseled, and Troilus fulfills his friend's instruction when he finishes "And with hise salte teris gan he bathe / The rube in his signet" (II.1086–87). The imagery of cruelty, of the prick in the heart, recalls, too, a dispiriting Troilan moment, here from Book IV when Pandarus counsels the abduction of Criseyde ("It is no rape, in my dom, ne no vice, / Hire to witholden that ye love moost," IV.596–97),[74] and Troilus responds:

'Frend, graunt mercy, ich assente.
But certeynly thow maist nat so me priken,
Ne peyne non ne may me so tormente,
That, for no cas, it is nat myn entente,
At shorte wordes, though I deyen sholde,
To ravysshe hire, but if hireself it wolde.'   (IV.632–37)

And pain, too, had been Troilus's condition in his final letter to Criseyde. He notes the tears which stain the letter (V.1336, 1374), recalls repeatedly the "peyne" in which he suffers, and closes, in terms echoed by Wyatt's own closing lines:

In yow my lif, in yow myght for to save
Me fro disese of alle peynes smerte;
And far now wel, myn owen swete herte!   (V.1419–21)

This poem is a self-position of the Troilan dilemma. It is a dazzling, if brief, act of impersonation, a speaking from the Troilan persona as if it were playing out all the logic of Pandaric instruction. To read it as a poem in the Wyatt canon is to see the poet's hand manipulating, once again, the tropes of Chaucerian writing. It is to witness the appropriation of the verse epistle as the means of lyric subjectivity. "Fele as I do": an injunction, not just for the imagined lady of the letter, but for all the readers of his verse. Reading becomes an act of personal impersonation, of placing the self in the quotations of the lover or the lyricist. To understand the poem is to understand impersonation. "This shalt thou gain thereby." What we gain is the technique of the early Tudor lyric. To some degree, this had been Tottel's purpose: to provide his readers with the templates of poetic imitation. "Feel as I do" becomes, in the project of the *Miscellany*, an injunction to write as I do, and what will be gained is what Tottel offers in the prefatory "Printer to the Reader": "to haue wel written in verse." To read this poem, now, within the Tottel canon is to recognize its close affiliations with the other verse epistles in the *Miscellany*. It is to illustrate the ways in which Tottel constructs the history of early Tudor verse as a history of letters gone awry.

Epistle, epitaph

He had a hand, wrote Surrey,

> that taught, what might be sayd in ryme:
> That reft Chaucer the glory of his wit.
>
> (Rollins, ed., *Miscellany*, p.28, lines 15–16)

The story of this book has been a story of remembrances. The legacy of Chaucer, the repute of Pandarus, the afterlives of Troilus and Criseyde, have fed into a larger narrative about the public and the private and the ways of reading culture. The spectatorial and voyeuristic impulses of courtly life informed the habits of the manuscript compiler and the motives of the printer. The displays of the body shaped the presentations of the book. And the manipulations of that body – whether they be the rhetorical dismemberings of the *blazon* or the displaced marks of a barely stayed King's hand – found themselves transferred onto the interpretive devices of citation and quotation: the excerpts, centos, and shards of Chaucerian writing that become, in essence, blazons of the poet's literary corpus. Surrey's great eulogy to Wyatt may stand at the close of this narrative as a critical anatomy, not just of Wyatt's buried body, but of the traditions of Troilan reception that informed the courtly literature of Henry VIII's reign. A head, a visage, a hand, a tongue, an eye, a heart, a valiant corps. We move, in Surrey's catalogue, through all the parts that make up the poetic body, finding Wyatt, at this eulogy's close, not deep within the earth, but sent to heaven. Indeed, we are left at this poem's end with something more akin to Troilus's own death: a death that takes the lifeless body from the earth up to the stars: "The earth his bones, the heauens possesse his gost" (p.28, line 40). This is as much an epitaph for

Troilus, or indeed, for Surrey himself, as it is for Wyatt, and its inclusion in Tottel marks a central moment in the *Miscellany*'s understanding of the legacies of early Tudor literature.

For, in a sense, the *Miscellany* is a kind of tomb: a resting place for letters, loves, and lives that populated Henry's court. I had suggested earlier that there is something of a voyeuristic quality to reading Tottel, a sense that we have been offered, for the price of bibliographic admission, a peep into courtly privacies. The headings of the poems, combined with their authorial attributions and their topical allusions, constitute a record of a hitherto inaccessible world of private exchanges, of surreptitious meetings, of laments, pains, and desires. Tottel is in some sense, to appropriate the phrasing of Wendy Wall's reassessment of the history of sonnet publication, a "voyeuristic text."[75] It offers up what Tottel himself calls, in his Preface, a collection of "parcelles," little packages sent back and forth and now intercepted and opened by new readers. It is a book that, in Wall's phrasing, "ushered printed texts into the public eye by naming that entrance as a titillating and transgressive act"[76] – only here, it is not the explicit titillations of the woman's body found in, say, Nashe and other Elizabethan writers, but rather the more subtle excitements to be found in exposing what "the vngentle horders vp of such treasure haue heretofore enuied thee" (Rollins, ed., *Miscellany*, p.2). Tottel's Preface presents the texts as something of a treasure, hoarded, kept secret. Its reading is an act, now, of instruction in a skill, an act designed to "purge that swinelike grossenesse" of the unlettered. Indeed, the purgation of such a grossness is itself, at the heart of the vulgar rantings of Sir Francis Bryan in Wyatt's Satire, and to some degree, we may well read Tottel's Preface as guide to the flight from courtly swinishness exemplified by Bryan in that text.

But, central to this Preface, too, is the sense of the loss of poetry. Surrey and Wyatt are the masters of the English style – of what Tottel calls "our tong" – and the syntax of the Preface leads to some compelling ambiguities about the nature of the volume and the status of its elegiac verse.

It resteth now (gentle reder) that thou thinke it not euill doon, to publish, to the honor of the Englishe tong, and for profit of the studious of Englishe eloquence, those workes which the vngentle horders vp of such treasure haue heretofore enuied thee. And for this point (good reder) thine own profit and pleasure, in these presently, and in moe hereafter, shal answere for my defence. (Rollins, ed., *Miscellany*, p.2)

What "resteth now," on first reading, is a referent from the previous sentence: perhaps "our tong," or perhaps the "stile" of Surrey or the "weightiness" of Wyatt's verse. There is a sense that what is resting now are Surrey and Wyatt: that what is resting in the peace of Tottel's volume is the legacy of English verse. As Surrey puts it, in the opening of his eulogy:

> W. resteth here, that quick could neuer rest;
> Whose heauenly giftes encreased by disdayn,
> And vertue sank the deper in his brest.
> Such profit he by enuy could obtain.
>
> (Rollins, ed., Miscellany, p.28, lines 3–6)

The verbal parallels to Tottel's preface are striking. *Rest, profit, envy* – these terms stand as the terms of eulogy, and I suggest that we reread the preface to the *Miscellany* through Surrey's lines to see the volume not just as a printer's ploy for sales or even as a voyeuristic peep into a courtly world, but as a Tudor book of the dead.

For Surrey, whose poetics of the dying self have been explored in challenging detail by Sheldon Zitner and Jonathan Crewe, the book of poems is the book of death, and his reworkings of the Troilan tradition – and, in turn, his insertion of Wyatt into that tradition – center on the elegiac moments of that poem's close.[77] Surrey recasts many of the tropes of *Troilus and Criseyde* through patterns of marked death and elegy, and in this practice he returns us to *La conusaunce damours*. That poem's constellating of the story of Pyramus and Thisbe and the romance of Troilus and Criseyde offered up, I argued in chapter 1, a model for apposing these two sets of lovers in the frames of surreptitious love, encounter, and exchange. In Surrey, such a constellation is far less an issue of domestic life and privacy (as it was, I had claimed, for *La conusaunce*), than it is one of authorial self-representation. And, too, it is a constellation that does not so much affirm as profoundly decenter the relationships of gender and authority in male friendship and literary history.

Nowhere in Surrey's poetry are these terms fraught with such confusion as the other, shorter poem on the death of Wyatt, the one that appears in Tottel before the long eulogy.

> Dyuers thy death doe diuersly bemone.
> Some, that in presence of thy liuelyhed
> Lurked, whose brestes enuy with hate had swolne,
> Yeld Caesars tears vpon Pompeius hed.
> Some, that watched with the murdrers knife,
> With egre thirst to drink thy giltlesse blood,
> Whose practise brake by happy ende of lyfe,
> Wepe enuious teares to heare thy fame so good.
> But I, that knew what harbred in that hed:

> What vertues rare were temperd in that brest:
> Honour the place, that such a iewell bred,
> And kisse the ground, whereas thy corse doth rest,
> With vapord eyes: from whence such streames auayl,
> As Pyramus dyd on Thisbes brest bewail.
>
> (Rollins, ed., *Miscellany*, p.27.23–36)

This too, is an anatomy of poetry, yet here, an anatomy performed not by the rhetoricians but the killer's hand. Just what is that "murdrers knife" doing in this story? The narrative of Caesar and Pompey has about it, in this telling, the status of a violent and dismembering subtext to Wyatt's death. The breasts swollen with envy are the anti-type of Wyatt's own breast, where virtues are tempered. The hypocritical tears of Caesar find themselves transformed into the envious tears shed by those who hear of Wyatt's fame. Pompey's head is apposed to Wyatt's, and the corpse that rests lies in a ground marked, at the poem's close, not so much by political as literary markers. Surrey's sonnet ends with *Troilus and Criseyde* and Pyramus and Thisbe. "Kisse the ground" echoes Chaucer's envoy to his own book: that it may "kis the steppes where as thow sees pace / Virgile, Ovide, Omer, Lucan, and Stace" (V.1792–93). But kissing is the central act of Pyramus and Thisbe in *La conusaunce damours*. They seek a secret place to kiss; resolve themselves to kissing only each side of the wall; when Pyramus finds Thisbe's bloody kerchief, he kisses it; and when Thisbe finds Pyramus's body, she, too, "kyssed / his deedly colde visage."[78]

The closing lines of Surrey's sonnet are, perhaps, some of the oddest and most confusing phrasings of a literary loss in all of elegiac history. As Crewe points out, "this particular scenario, in which times of death, causes and effects, and gender roles seem notably confused, is what we are left with in the Pyramus and Thisbe story with which the poem ends."[79] Emrys Jones, in his gloss on these closing lines in his edition of Surrey's poetry, puts it more succinctly, if more judgmentally: "The allusion is unfortunately quite inapt."[80] But is it? The confusions behind these lines go beyond shifts of gender. The allusion to the *Troilus*, for example, relocates a Chaucerian farewell to the book onto the farewell to the man. And Pyramus, too, mourns not over the dead body of Thisbe, but over the sign of her bloody kerchief. He assumes Thisbe to be dead: kills himself not over a corpse but over a representation of an absent corpse. The Pyramus and Thisbe story is a tragedy of misinterpretation. So, too, is Surrey's sonnet. Envy and hatred led to accusations of treason; few could see the virtues in the man. Wyatt's political career, as distilled in this poem, is a career of mistakings, of misprisons – a career, as figured in Wyatt's own *Defence*, that hinged on the misunderstandings of intention and expressions, of the displacements of small syllables onto great matters. In this environment of misunderstanding, the close of Surrey's poem leads to a mythological logic all its own. After Pyramus thinks Thisbe dead, he kills himself. Only then, when Thisbe finds the corpse, do we hear something of the laments figured at the close of Surrey's poem. Compare those final lines with Thisbe's lament in *La conusaunce damours*:

> She rent and tore / her goodly youlowe heare
> And toke the corps / in her armes twayne
> Desperously / wepynge many a teare
> Amonge the blode / of her louer slayne
> Her bytter teares / lay as thycke as rayne
> And ofte she kyssed / his deedly colde visage
> Styll cryeng / as though she wolde enrage.   (Biii r)

The force of Surrey's diction offers up the opposite of what he claims. Weeping over Wyatt is not Pyramus bewailing over Thisbe but Thisbe weeping over Pyramus. Surrey's language effectively feminizes the act of mourning. It recalls laments over dead men at the tombs of others, brings together the multiple resonances of the lovers' meeting place (Ninus's tomb) and the entombment of the lovers themselves.

Such conflations and confusions also control one of the lesser known, but no less representative of Surrey's poems, the "Complaint of a diyng louer refused vpon his ladies iniust mistaking of his writyng" (Rollins, ed., *Miscellany*, pp.16–18). Here, Surrey confronts the problematics of epistolary love from Chaucer through the coteries of Wyatt and the Devonshire Manuscript.[81] It is a poem of misreading and misunderstanding; a poem of the "cursed pen"; a poem of the killing hand, the writing self, the mourning reader. Its speaker is a shepherd who discovers a bereft lover weeping under a willow tree. Yet what he hears, at first, are not the familiar laments located on the woman's body, or the distressful complaints directed at himself, but a blunt condemnation of the pen.

> Thou cursed pen (sayd he) wo worth the bird thee bare,
> The man, the knife, and all that made the, wo be to their share.
> Wo worth the time, and place, where I so could endite.
> And wo be it yet once agayne, the pen that so can write.
>   (p.16, lines 28–31)

This is a story of betrayal told as an account of letters gone awry. It is a narrative of literary tropes, a tale that takes us back to Chaucer's quaking pen in *Troilus and Criseyde* and to the relocations of desire onto instruments of writing in the post-Chaucerian tradition. It tells of the pitfalls of penmanship, of pens and pains that narrativize the allusive associations in Wyatt's verse.

> Is me befallen a greater losse, than Priam had of Troy.
> She is reuersed clene: and beareth me in hand,
> That my desertes haue giue[n] her cause to break thys faithful band.
>
> (p.17, lines 28–30)

Priam and Troy locate this lover's anguish in the fantasies of Troilan myth, and they place the rejection of the lover on a par with that of Troilus's epistolary rejection by Criseyde. And when the lover of this poem takes his own life, the shepherd thus finds an appropriate "place for such a corse to rest" (p.18, line 20).

> And in my mind it came: from thence not farre away,
> Where Chreseids loue, king Priams so[n]ne, ye worthy Troilus lay.
> By him I made his tomb, in token he was treew.
>
> (p.18, lines 11–13)

Much like the "corse" of Wyatt, this "corse" finds its resting place in a tomb marked by the Chaucerian inheritance. But such a burial involves more than the mimings of a literary tradition. Both this text and the eulogies on Wyatt give voice to an epitaphic Surrey. They enable the self-presentations of the new poet. They create the literary subject through pastoral elegy. Such a creation is, of course, a commonplace of literary history, but Surrey here is burying not just a lover or a poet or a friend (witness, too, the poem written while imprisoned in Windsor, which incorporates a lament for the death of Surrey's boyhood companion and brother-in-law, Henry Fitzroy, and which recalls too, a Troilan past: "my childishe yeres did passe, / In greater feast than Priams sonnes of Troy" [p.12, lines 34–35]). For what we read here is an inhumation of the Chaucerian tradition itself: the celebration, yet entombment, of the loves of Chaucer's heroes and the complaints of his narrators. Surrey scripts an epitaph, not just for Troilus but for *Troilus and Criseyde*.

It may appear that I have left the wiles of Pandarus for the laments of Troilus, and to some degree the elegies of Surrey do locate their energies on the inhumed Troilan body. And yet, I think, this is precisely the point. The Pandaric has been displaced – not on to courtiers or poets but to us. The act of reading Surrey's Troilan poetry, or for that matter, Wyatt's bedroom lyrics, or the whole of Tottel's *Miscellany*, is an act of Pandaric intrusion. We open up the volume to discern its missed missives, intercepted texts, unsent epistles, undelivered eulogies. The legacy of Pandarus lives on, not in the impersonations of the lyricist but in the invasions of the reader. As I suggested at the opening of this book, the modern legacy of Pandarus is scholarship itself. It can be found in the intrusive compilations of mid-Tudor antiquarians and collectors: men, say, like John Stowe, John Leland, and John Bale who assembled bits and pieces of the literary and official documents of England's past. It can be found in the constitutive practices of modern – i.e., nineteenth-century – medieval studies. The editing of family correspondence was to become the defining mode of historical scholarship. The letters of the King and counselors, together with the correspondence of such families as the Pastons, Celeys, Stonors, and the Lisles, would make up the great monuments of Victorian public scholarship – or, one might put it in the terms I have applied elsewhere, Victorian state Pandarism. "The most valuable records, even for general history," wrote John Bruce in the mid-nineteenth century, "are to be found among the records of private and personal experience."[82] What the antiquarians had found in opening these private documents for public display were not only the historical accounts of great and small, but something of a romance of inspection itself: a fascination with discovering the secrets of past families or communities. Such a romance had become, in the hands of mid-century novelists, a glamour of antiquarianism witnessed in Benjamin Disraeli's *Sybil*: "If you want to understand the ups and downs of life, there's nothing like the parchments of an estate."[83] Note, too, public journalism of intrusion, in *The Standard*'s review of the publication of the *First Report* of the Historical Manuscripts Commission: "The whole story of our country as a state, the reputation of her famous men, the motives of her policy, the secret springs and wheels by which her power, from age to age, has been brought into action, are gradually being laid bare."[84] And when we read the letters of the King to his mistress, when we witness recusant compilers or illicit lovers culling from their Chaucers bits and pieces of an amorous epistolarity, when we open the *Miscellany* to find coterie verse and personal elegy – when we do all these things we, too, lay bare the secret springs and wheels of reputation, motive, power. The study of the early Tudor period is, in itself, an act of the Pandaric, and what I have tried to trace out here are the impersonations, guidelines, and the tropes of service and inspection that bequeath from Chaucer's figure both the texture of Henrician court culture and the subtexts of its scholarly remembrance.

Notes

1 PRETEXTS: CHAUCER'S PANDARUS AND THE ORIGINS OF COURTLY DISCOURSE

1   "Nescit dissimulare qui nescit vivere." For the importance of this aphorism in defining courtier behavior, see Perez Zagorin, *Ways of Lying: Dissimulation, Persecution, and Conformity* (Cambridge, MA: Harvard University Press, 1990), p. 8, and "Sir Thomas Wyatt and the Court of Henry VIII: The Courtier's Ambivalence," *Journal of Medieval and Renaissance Studies* 23 (1993): 113–41, especially p. 121. For diplomacy, deceit, and espionage as informing the discourses of sixteenth-century intellectual inquiry, as well as courtiership, see John Archer, *Sovereignty and Intelligence: Spying and Court Culture in the English Renaissance* (Stanford: Stanford University Press, 1993). For the theatrics of dissimulation, and in turn, the outline of the paradigms of what would become the New Historicist inquiry into self-presentation and ruses of official service, see Stephen Greenblatt, *Renaissance Self-Fashioning, More to Shakespeare* (Chicago: University of Chicago Press, 1980).

2   Machiavelli and Castiglione have been long offered as the originary figures in courtier theorizing. See Daniel Javitch, *Poetry and Courtliness in Renaissance England* (Princeton: Princeton University Press, 1978), pp. 18–49; Wayne A. Rebhorn, *Courtly Performances: Masking and Festivity in Castiglione's Book of the Courtier* (Detroit: Wayne State University Press, 1978); David Starkey, "The Court: Castiglione's Ideal and Tudor Reality," *Journal of the Warburg and Courtauld Institutes* 45 (1982):232–39; Frank Whigham, *Ambition and Privilege: The Social Tropes of Elizabethan Courtesy Theory* (Berkeley and Los Angeles: University of California Press, 1984); and John M. Najemy, *Between Friends: Discourses of Power and Desire in the Machiavelli–Vettori Letters of 1513–1515* (Princeton: Princeton University Press, 1993). For a critique of the historiography of Renaissance courtiership, see Victoria Kahn, "Humanism and the Resistance to Theory," in Patricia Parker and David Quint, eds., *Literary Theory / Renaissance Texts* (Baltimore: Johns Hopkins University Press, 1985), pp. 373–96, and *Machiavellian Rhetoric* (Princeton: Princeton University Press, 1994). The importance of Henrician society in determining the tropes of courtly literature has recently been stressed by Peter C. Herman, ed., *Rethinking the Henrician Era: Essays on Early Tudor Texts and Contexts* (Urbana: University of Illinois Press, 1994).

3 Carroz's Letter to Ferdinand of 29 May 1510, which will form a major focus of the second chapter of this book, can be found in G. A. Bergenroth, ed., *Supplement to Volume I and Volume II of Letters, Dispatches, and State Papers Related to the Negotiations Between England and Spain* (London, 1868), pp. 36–44.

4 For Hawes, see A. S. G. Edwards, *Stephen Hawes* (Boston: Twayne, 1983); Alistair Fox, *Politics and Literature in the Reigns of Henry VII and Henry VIII* (Oxford: Blackwell, 1989), pp. 56–72; and Seth Lerer, *Chaucer and His Readers: Imagining the Author in Late-Medieval England* (Princeton: Princeton University Press, 1993), pp. 176–208. For Skelton, see Greg Walker, *John Skelton and the Politics of the 1520s* (Cambridge: Cambridge University Press, 1990); Richard Halpern, *The Poetics of Primitive Accumulation: English Renaissance Culture and the Genealogy of Capital* (Ithaca: Cornell University Press, 1991), pp. 103–35; A. C. Spearing, *The Medieval Poet as Voyeur* (Cambridge: Cambridge University Press, 1993), pp. 268–82; and many of the essays collected in Herman, ed., *Rethinking the Henrician Era.*

5 Greenblatt, *Renaissance Self-Fashioning*, p. 30.

6 From *De conscribendis epistolis*, ed. Jean-Claude Margolin, in *Opera Omnia Desiderii Erasmi Roterodami* (Amsterdam: North Holland, 1971), vol. I, part 2, p. 500; translation by Charles Fantazzi, in J. K. Sowards, ed., *The Collected Works of Erasmus: Literary and Educational Writings*, vol. XXV (Toronto: University of Toronto Press, 1985), pp. 195–96.

7 *De conscribendis epistolis*, ed. Margolin, p. 502: "Semper esto querulus ac petax, et quemadmodum callidae meretrices, variis nominibus ac modis, semper aliquid auferunt ab amatoribus, ita tibi studio sit semper aliquid auferre a principe." Translation from Fantazzi, in Sowards, ed., *The Collected Works of Erasmus*, p. 197.

8 See Stephen Jaeger, *The Origins of Courtliness: Civilizing Trends and the Formation of Courtly Ideals 939–1210* (Philadelphia: University of Pennsylvania Press, 1985). For relations between rhetorical education and courtier feigning, see Javitch, *Poetry and Courtliness*; Rebhorn, *Courtly Performances*; and Whigham, *Ambition and Privilege*. The anxieties provoked by manuals of rhetorical and social behavior in the sixteenth century – and the critical alignments set up to define their influence – have been reviewed and critiqued by Jonathan Goldberg, *Sodometries: Renaissance Texts, Modern Sexualities* (Stanford: Stanford University Press, 1993), pp. 29–62.

9 Jaeger, *Origins of Courtliness*, pp. 126–75.

10 See Richard Firth Green, *Poets and Princepleasers: Literature and the English Court in the Late Middle Ages* (Toronto: University of Toronto Press, 1980); Lee Patterson, "Ambiguity and Interpretation: A Fifteenth-Century Reading of *Troilus and Criseyde*," in his *Negotiating the Past: The Historical Study of Medieval Literature* (Madison: University of Wisconsin Press, 1987), pp. 115–53; C. David Benson, "True Troilus and False Cresseid: The Descent from Tragedy," in Pietro Boitani, ed., *The European Tragedy of Troilus* (Oxford: Clarendon Press, 1989), pp. 153–70; and Anna Torti, "From 'History' To 'Tragedy': The Story of Troilus and Criseyde in Lydgate's *Troy Book* and Henryson's *Testament of Cresseid*," in *ibid.*, pp. 171–98. For details on the textual transmission of the poem, see Barry

Windeatt, ed., *Chaucer: Troilus and Criseyde*, pp. 25–76. For quotations, citations, and allusions to the poem from the beginning of the fifteenth through the middle of the sixteenth century, see Caroline F. E. Spurgeon, *Five Hundred Years of Chaucer Criticism and Allusion* (London: Kegan Paul, 1914), vol. I, pp. 14–95. More such allusions and citations are still being unearthed. See, for example, Francis X. Ryan, SJ, "Sir Thomas More's Use of Chaucer," *Studies in English Literature 1500–1900* 35 (1995): 1–17. Evidence of early reception drawn from marginal annotations to manuscripts is assessed in Julia Boffey, "Annotation in Some Manuscripts of *Troilus and Criseyde*," *English Manuscript Studies 1100–1700* 5 (1995): 1–17.

11   On sources, see C. S. Lewis, "What Chaucer Really Did to *Il Filostrato*," *Essays and Studies* 17 (1932): 56–75; Winthrop Wetherbee, *Chaucer and the Poets: An Essay on Troilus and Criseyde* (Ithaca: Cornell University Press, 1984); David Wallace, *Chaucer and the Early Writings of Boccaccio* (Cambridge: D. S. Brewer, 1985); and the parallel text of *Il Filostrato* printed in Windeatt, ed., *Chaucer: Troilus and Criseyde*. On the debts to Boethius and the moral–philosophical tradition, see John V. Fleming, *Classical Imitation and Interpretation in Chaucer's Troilus* (Lincoln: University of Nebraska Press, 1991). On the lyric quality of the poem, see Thomas Stillinger, *The Song of Troilus* (Philadelphia: University of Pennsylvania Press, 1993). On politics, history, and courtiership, see Lee Patterson, *Chaucer and the Subject of History* (Madison: University of Wisconsin Press, 1991), pp. 84–164.

12   John Stevens, *Music and Poetry in the Early Tudor Court* (London: Methuen, 1961), p. 213.

13   Green, *Poets and Princepleasers*, p. 129.

14   Raymond Southall, *The Courtly Maker* (Oxford: Blackwell, 1964), p. 25.

15   The noun "pander" appears first cited in the *OED* from the satiric *Testament of Papyngo* (1530) by the Scots poet David Lyndsay (ed. Douglas Hamer, *The Works of Sir David Lindsay* [Edinburgh: Blackwood, 1931] vol. I, pp. 56–90). The court, he writes, is full of "Pandaris, pykthankis, custronis, and clatteraris" (line 390). Lyndesay is discussing the "vaine ascens of court" (line 351), noting, in an allusion to one of the great maxims of courtier instability derived from the Boethianism of Chaucer's *Troilus*, "Quho sittith moist hie sal fynd the sait most slider" (line 352). The colophon to the 1538 London edition of John Byddell states that the work was completed in December 1530. On the cultural and literary context of this work, see Carol Edington, *Court and Culture in Renaissance Scotland: Sir David Lindsay of the Mount* (Amherst: University of Massachusetts Press, 1994). The use of the noun "pander" as a general term, however, may have been in currency as early as the mid-fifteenth century. The poem known as the *Chance of the Dice* (preserved in two manuscripts of mid century, Bodleian Library MSS Fairfax 16 and Bodley 638), writes of a joy comparable to that "syn that Troylus wann first Criseyde in Troye" (line 140), and it soon announces: "There is no beter pandare / as I trowe / for al this londe through out / suche be ye knowe" (lines 160–61). See Eleanor Prescott Hammond, "The Chance of the Dice," *Englische Studien* 59 (1925): 1–16.

16   The mid-fifteenth-century scribe and bibliophile John Shirley found Pandarus's whetstone stanza (*Troilus and Criseyde*, I.631–37), which he titled

"Pandare to Trojlus," an apt addition to his personal anthology of Chaucerian verse (Trinity College Cambridge MS R. 3. 20, fol. 361 r). Similarly, Pandarus's advice to Troilus on the dangers of uncontrolled speech found its way into two late fifteenth-century anthologies, Trinity College Cambridge MS R. 4. 20 (fol. 171 v) and Cambridge University Library MS F. 1. 6. In the anonymous *La conusaunce damours* (printed *c.* 1528), he appears as the "trusty frende" without whom Troilus would "Of his lyfe . . . had lyghtly made an ende" (sig. Ci r). And in the excerpts from Chaucer's poem copied into the Devonshire Manuscript in the 1530s (now known to be copied from Thynne's 1532 edition), Pandarus's proverbializing and advisory stanzas predominate. For identification of these texts, see Ethel Seaton, " 'The Devonshire Manuscript' and its Medieval Fragments," *RES*, ns 7 (1956): 55–56; Richard C. Harrier, "A Printed Source for 'The Devonshire Manuscript'," *RES*, ns 11 (1960): 54. For interpretations of this Chaucerian material, see Paul Remley, "Mary Shelton and her Tudor Literary Milieu," in Herman, ed., *Rethinking the Henrician Era*, pp. 40–77; Helen Baron, "Mary (Howard) Fitzroy's Hand in the Devonshire Manuscript," *RES*, ns 45 (1994): 318–35; Elizabeth Heale, "Women and the Courtly Love Lyric: The Devonshire MS (BL Additional 17492)," *Modern Language Review* 90 (1995): 296–313. I discuss this material in chapters 4 and 5 of this book.

17 Gervase Matthew, *The Court of Richard II* (London: John Murray, 1968), p. 68.

18 The phrase constitutes the title of chapter 3 of *Renaissance Self-Fashioning*.

19 For the former, see Lerer, *Chaucer and His Readers*. For the latter, see Stephen Orgel, *The Illusion of Power* (Berkeley and Los Angeles: University of California Press, 1975); Greenblatt, *Renaissance Self-Fashioning*; and Steven Mullaney, *The Place of the Stage: License, Play, and Power in Renaissance England* (Chicago: University of Chicago Press, 1988).

20 C. S. Lewis, *English Literature in the Sixteenth Century, Excluding Drama* (Oxford: Clarendon Press, 1954); H. A. Mason, *Humanism and Poetry in the Early Tudor Period* (London: Routledge and Kegan Paul, 1959).

21 Greenblatt, *Renaissance Self-Fashioning*, especially the famous maximal critique on pp. 136–37: "Entertainments in the court of Henry VIII were perhaps less lighthearted than Lewis' charming account suggests; conversation with the king himself must have been like small talk with Stalin." Further dismantlings of Lewisian literary history along these lines include Jonathan Crewe, *Trials of Authorship: Anterior Forms and Poetic Reconstruction from Wyatt to Shakespeare* (Berkeley and Los Angeles: University of California Press, 1990); Goldberg, *Sodometries*; Stephen Merriam Foley, *Sir Thomas Wyatt* (Boston: Twayne, 1990); and Peter C. Herman, "Introduction," in *Rethinking the Henrician Era*, pp. 1–15.

22 Goldberg, *Sodometries*, pp. 29–61.

23 See Lerer, *Chaucer and His Readers*, pp. 176–208, and Antony Hasler, "Allegories of Authority in Early Tudor Poetry," PhD thesis, University of Cambridge (1995).

24 See David Carlson, *English Humanist Books: Writers and Patrons, Manuscript and Print, 1475–1525* (Toronto: University of Toronto Press, 1993).

25 Marshall McLuhan, *The Gutenberg Galaxy* (Toronto: University of Toronto Press, 1962); Elizabeth Eisenstein, *The Printing Press as an Agent of Change* (Cambridge: Cambridge University Press, 1979). For a critique of the techno-determinism of the approach associated with McLuhan and Eisenstein, see Michael Warner, *The Letters of the Republic: Publication and the Public Sphere in Eighteenth-Century America* (Cambridge: Harvard University Press, 1990), pp. 4–9. For the revisionisms of the French school of *l'histoire du livre*, see the representative recent collection, Roger Chartier, ed., *The Culture of Print*, trans. Lydia Cochrane (Princeton: Princeton University Press, 1989). I have discussed these issues in detail in my review of Carlson, *English Humanist Books*, in *The Huntington Library Quarterly* 56 (1993): 399–408.

26 See Lisa Jardine, *Erasmus, Man of Letters: The Construction of Charisma in Print* (Princeton: Princeton University Press, 1993). For approaches to the variety of homoerotic possibilities in Renaissance pedagogy and friendship, see the essays in Jonathan Goldberg, ed., *Queering the Renaissance* (Durham: Duke University Press, 1994).

27 See Goldberg, *Sodometries*, pp. 29–61.

28 See H. A. Mason, *Editing Wyatt* (Cambridge: Cambridge Quarterly Publications, 1972); Rebholz, ed., *Sir Thomas Wyatt: The Complete Poems*; Arthur Marotti, *Manuscript, Print, and the English Renaissance Lyric* (Ithaca: Cornell University Press, 1995).

29 David Starkey, "The King's Privy Chamber, 1485–1547," PhD thesis, University of Cambridge (1973); "Representation through Intimacy," in Ioan Lewis, ed., *Symbols and Sentiments* (London: Academic Press, 1977), pp. 187–244; "Intimacy and Innovation: The Rise of the Privy Chamber, 1485–1547," in Starkey, ed., *The English Court: From the Wars of the Roses to the Civil War* (London: Longman, 1987), pp. 71–118; "Court and Government," in Christopher Coleman and David Starkey, eds., *Revolution Reassessed: Revisions in the History of Tudor Government and Administration* (Oxford: Clarendon Press, 1986), pp. 29–58.

30 See Michel Foucault, *Discipline and Punish: The Birth of the Prison*, trans. Alan Sheridan (Harmondsworth: Penguin, 1982), pp. 3–69.

31 Louis Montrose, "The Elizabethan Subject and the Spenserian Text," in Parker and Quint, eds., *Literary Theory / Renaissance*, pp. 303–40.

32 Goldberg, *Sodometries*, pp. 29–61; *Writing Matter: From the Hands of the Renaissance* (Stanford: Stanford University Press, 1990).

33 For a review of Elton's publications and their impact, see Christopher Coleman, "Professor Elton's 'Revolution,'" in Coleman and Starkey, eds., *Revolution Reassessed*, pp. 1–12.

34 G. R. Elton, *The Tudor Revolution in Government* (Cambridge: Cambridge University Press, 1953).

35 This is Coleman's paraphrase, "Professor Elton's 'Revolution,'" p. 2.

36 Elton, *Policy and Police: The Enforcement of the Reformation in the Age of Thomas Cromwell* (Cambridge: Cambridge University Press, 1972).

37 As, for example, in a study such as Fox, *Politics and Literature in the Reigns of Henry VII and Henry VIII,* or in the studies of topical allegory and political context by Walker, *John Skelton and the Politics of the 1520s,* and

Plays of Persuasion: Drama and Politics at the Court of Henry VIII (Cambridge: Cambridge University Press, 1991).

38 I appropriate this phrase, with grateful acknowledgment, from the reader's report on the original submission of this book.

39 Critics from a variety of schools have called attention to Pandarus's epistolary machinations. For those working in the so-called exegetical tradition of medieval studies, see Chauncy Wood, *The Elements of Chaucer's Troilus* (Durham: Duke University Press, 1984), pp. 143–53, and John V. Fleming, *Classical Imitation and Interpretation in Chaucer's Troilus.* For a feminist critique of the Chaucerian project (and its masculinist critics), see Carolyn Dinshaw, *Chaucer's Sexual Poetics* (Madison: University of Wisconsin Press, 1989), pp. 28–64. For work inspired by the psychoanalytic inheritance, see A. C. Spearing, *The Medieval Poet as Voyeur*, pp. 120–39, and the two essays of Sarah Stanbury, "The Voyeur and the Private Life in *Troilus and Criseyde*," *SAC* 13 (1991): 141–58, and "Women's Letters and Private Space in Chaucer," *Exemplaria* 6 (1994): 271–85.

40 See Norman Davis, "The *Litera Troili* and English Letters," *RES*, ns 16 (1965): 233–44.

41 See Martin Camargo, *The Middle English Verse Epistle* (Halle: Max Niemeyer, 1993).

42 See Stanbury, "Women's Letters and Private Space," p. 280.

43 See Najemy, *Between Friends*, pp. 18–57.

44 On the sources, contemporary relations, and aspects of the composition of *De conscribendis epistolis*, see Sowards's introduction to *Collected Works*, vol. XXVI, pp. li–lix; and Fantazzi's introduction to his translation, pp. 2–9. See, too, the extensive review of sources and analogues in Kurt Smolak, ed. and trans., *De conscribendis epistolis: Anleitung zum Briefschreiben, Erasmus von Rotterdam, Ausgewählte Schriften*, vol. VIII (Darmstadt: Wissenschaftliche Buchgesellschaft, 1980), pp. ix–lxxvi; Judith Rice Henderson, "Erasmus on the Art of Letter Writing," in J. J. Murphy, ed., *Renaissance Eloquence* (Berkeley and Los Angeles: University of California Press, 1983), pp. 331–55; and Jardine, *Erasmus.*

45 Najemy, *Between Friends*, p. 42.

46 Desiderius Erasmus, *Libellus de conscribendis epistolis* (Cambridge: Siberch, 1521), fol. 1 r, quoted and translated in Jardine, *Erasmus*, p. 151 and p. 267 n. 13.

47 For the historical and theoretical implications of the history of "character," see Goldberg, *Writing Matter*, and Jardine, *Erasmus*, pp. 31–38.

48 Jardine, *Erasmus*, p. 151.

49 P. G. W. Glare, ed., *The Oxford Latin Dictionary* (Oxford: Oxford University Press, 1982), s.v., *committo*. Note, in particular, the uses in Quintilian's *Institutiones oratoriae*: to commit adultery (VII.2.11), to commit parricide (VII.2.2), to commit incest (VII.10.19). For the association of committing something to writing and committing a social transgression, see Ovid's story of Byblis' potentially incestuous love of her brother in *Metamorphoses* IX.526–665. She writes a letter to him on a wax tablet, and when her brother rejects it, laments: "quid, quae cleanda fuerunt, / tam cito commisi properatis verba tabellis?" (*Met.* IX.586–87; "Why was I in such

haste to commit to tablets what should have been concealed?"). Text and translation from Ovid, *Metamorphoses*, ed. and trans. F. J. Miller (Cambridge: Loeb Library, 1916).

50 Glare, *Oxford Latin Dictionary*, s.v., *expromo*. For a distinctive use of the word in an epistolary context that may well stand behind Erasmus's own formulation, see the opening of Cicero's letter, *Ad familiares* V.12: "Coram me tecum eadem haec agere saepe conantem deterruit pudor quidam paene subrusticus; quae nunc expromam absens audacius; epistula enim non erubescit" ("Often, when I have attempted to discuss this topic with you, face to face, I have been deterred by a sort of almost boorish bashfulness; but now that I am away from you I shall bring it all out with greater boldness; for a letter does not blush"). Text and translation from Cicero, *Letters to his Friends*, ed. and trans. W. Glynn Williams (Cambridge: Loeb Library, 1958–60).

51 See Henderson, "Erasmus on the Art of Letter Writing." Fantazzi notes that "similar sentiments are expressed in a letter written in Paris in the spring of 1500 to an unnamed person," conjectured to be Adolph of Burgundy (in Sowards, ed., *Collected Works*, vol. XXV, p. 4).

52 See Starkey, "Representation Through Intimacy"; the opening chapters of J. J. Scarisbrick, *Henry VIII* (Berkeley and Los Angeles: University of California Press, 1968); and Skiles Howard, " 'Ascending the Riche Mount': Performing Hierarchy and Gender in the Henrician Masque," in Herman, ed., *Rethinking the Henrician Era*, pp. 16–39.

53 See Foley, *Sir Thomas Wyatt*, especially pp. 57–79, and Jardine, *Erasmus*, pp. 26–53.

54 Spearing, *Medieval Poet as Voyeur*; Stanbury, "The Voyeur and the Private Life"; Geraldine Heng, "The Woman Wants: The Lady, Gawain, and the Forms of Seduction," *Yale Journal of Criticism* 5 (1992): 101–34.

55 Sigmund Freud, *Three Essays in the Theory of Sexuality*, in *The Standard Edition of the Complete Psychological Works of Sigmund Freud* (London: Hogarth, 1953–74), vol. VII, pp. 149–50. This text, and its larger critical reception, is central to Spearing's attempt to historicize voyeurism as a social practice into a literary theme for medieval narratives (see *Medieval Poet as Voyeur*, p. 3).

56 Jean-Paul Sartre, *Being and Nothingness*, trans. Hazel E. Barnes (New York: Philosophical Library, 1956), p. 277. Spearing discusses this passage in the *Medieval Poet as Voyeur*, p. 10.

57 Roland Barthes, "Right in the Eyes," in his *The Responsibility of Forms: Critical Essays on Music, Art, and Representation*, trans. Richard Howard (New York: Hill and Wang, 1985), p. 241. Stanbury discusses a portion of this passage in relationship both to Sartre's pretext in *Being and Nothingness* and to Troilus's gaze when he first sees Criseyde.

58 Norman K. Denzin, "The Voyeur's Desire," *Current Perspectives in Social Theory* 13 (1993): 139–58, this quotation from p. 140.

59 See Renato Rosaldo, "From the Door of His Tent: The Fieldworker and the Inquisitor," in J. Clifford and G. E. Marcus, eds., *Writing Culture* (Berkeley and Los Angeles: University of California Press, 1986), pp. 77–97: "the fieldworker's mode of surveillance uncomfortably resembles Michel

Foucault's Panopticon, the site from which the (disciplining) disciples enjoy gazing upon (and subjecting) their subjects" (p. 92; quoted in Denzin, "Voyeur's Desire," p. 154 n. 2).

60 Natalie Z. Davis, *Fiction in the Archives: Pardon Tales and Their Tellers in Sixteenth-Century France* (Stanford: Stanford University Press, 1987), p. 5.

61 Fox, *Politics and Literature*.

62 Walker, *Plays of Persuasion*, p. 87.

63 Gordon Kipling, *The Triumph of Honour: The Burgundian Origins of the Elizabethan Renaissance* (The Hague: University of Leiden Press for the Sir Thomas Browne Institute, 1977), and "Henry VII and the Origins of Tudor Patronage," in Guy Fitch Lytle and Stephen Orgel, eds., *Patronage in the Renaissance* (Princeton: Princeton University Press, 1981).

64 Walker, *Plays of Persuasion*, p. 88.

65 Carlson, *English Humanist Books*.

66 Wendy Wall, *The Imprint of Gender: Authorship and Publication in the English Renaissance* (Ithaca: Cornell University Press, 1993), pp. 172, 177.

67 Paul Saenger, "Silent Reading: Its Impact on Late Medieval Script and Society," *Viator* 13 (1982): 367–414; "Books of Hours and the Reading Habits of the Late Middle Ages," in Roger Chartier, ed., *The Culture of Print*, pp. 141–73; and *Space Between Words: The Origin of Silent Reading* (Stanford: Stanford University Press, forthcoming).

68 Saenger, "Books of Hours," p. 147.

69 Saenger, "Silent Reading," p. 412.

70 *Ibid.*, p. 413.

71 I have discussed the *Toison D'Or* and Saenger's uses of its arguments from a somewhat different perspective in *Chaucer and His Readers*, pp. 183–84. For the impact of this text on early Tudor household management and courtly practice, see Kipling, "Henry VII," pp. 118–19.

72 Quoted and translated in Saenger, "Books of Hours," pp. 167–68 n. 76.

73 *Ibid.*, p. 150.

74 Paul Zumthor, *Le masque et la lumière* (Paris: Seuil, 1978), portions of which have appeared in translation as "From Hi(story) to Poem, or the Paths of Pun: The Grands Rhéthoriquers of Fifteenth-Century France," *New Literary History* 10 (1979): 231–63; this quotation is from p. 243.

75 Material in this paragraph summarizes critical interpretations, evidence, and arguments offered in my *Chaucer and His Readers*, pp. 182–91, with references and bibliography on pp. 275–79.

76 On this section of the *Conuercyon* (lines 113–58), see the edition of Gluck and Morgan, eds., *Stephen Hawes: The Minor Poems*, and their discussion on p. 147. The shaped portion of verse appears in de Worde's edition, sigs. Aiii v–Aiii r; a reproduction of these pages may be found in my *Chaucer and His Readers*, p. 191.

77 See Eamon Duffy, *The Stripping of the Altars: Traditional Religion in England, 1400–1580* (New Haven: Yale University Press, 1992), p. 107.

78 These examples are from, respectively, John Bellamy, *Crime and Public Order in England in the Later Middle Ages* (London: Routledge and Kegan Paul, 1973), p. 182, and William Harrison, *An Historical Description of the Iland of Britaine*, printed as the introductory material to Raphael Holinshed,

Chronicles of England, Scotland, and Ireland (originally published in 1584; reprinted, London, 1807), vol. I, p. 311.

79 On the "textualization" of the marked or mutilated criminal, see Michel Foucault, *Discipline and Punish: The Birth of the Prison*, p. 34, and Michel de Certeau, *Practice of Everyday Life*, trans. Steven Rendall (Berkeley and Los Angeles: University of California Press, 1984), pp. 139–41.

80 Bellamy, *Crime and Public Order*, p. 185.

81 See John A. F. Thomson, *The Later Lollards 1414–1520* (Oxford: Oxford University Press, 1965), p. 231, and Sarah Beckwith, "Ritual, Church, and Theater: Medieval Dramas of the Sacramental Body," in David Aers, ed., *Culture and History 1350–1600* (Detroit: Wayne State University Press, 1992), pp. 65–89, especially p. 72.

82 Randall McGowen, "The Body and Punishment in Eighteenth-Century England," *Journal of Modern History* 59 (1987): 651–79, this quotation from p. 666.

83 George Osborne, *The Civic Magistrate's Right of Inflicting Punishment* (London, 1733), pp. 8–9, quoted in McGowen, "Body and Punishment," p. 666. For the move from public punishment to private incarceration, see the discussions in McGowen; Stephen Wilf, "Imagining Justice: Aesthetics and Public Executions in Late Eighteenth-Century England," *Yale Journal of Law and the Humanities* 5 (1993): 51–78; and John Bender, *Imagining the Penitentiary* (Chicago: University of Chicago Press, 1987).

84 Harrison, *Historical Description*, vol. I, pp. 311–12.

85 See Richard van Dülmen, *Theater of Horror: Crime and Punishment in Early Modern Germany*, trans. Elizabeth Neu (Oxford: Polity Press, 1990). For some specifics in Henrician England, see Elton, *Policy and Police*, pp. 383–425.

86 See, for example, Gail M. Gibson, *The Theater of Devotion* (Chicago: University of Chicago Press, 1989). For the development of Eucharistic theology and the theatrics of the Mass, see Miri Rubin, *Corpus Christi* (Cambridge: Cambridge University Press, 1993).

87 Duffy, *Stripping of the Altars*, p. 106.

88 For the thematics of vision in the Corpus Christi Plays, see David Mills, "The 'Behold and See' Convention in Medieval Drama," *Medieval English Theatre* 7:1 (1985): 4–12, and the discussion in Greg Walker, *Plays of Persuasion*, pp. 11–13, especially his remarks in n. 17 concerning the "stress upon the physical, observable, presentation of spiritual truths" in the Cycle Plays, in particular, that "the audience is asked to judge the veracity of the message expounded on the strength of their own observation. Hence characters repeatedly refer to what the audience has seen, does see or will see."

89 For a fuller development of these observations, see my essay, " 'Representyd now in yower syght': The Culture of Spectatorship in Late-Fifteenth-Century England," in David Wallace and Barbara Hanawalt, eds., *Bodies and Disciplines: Intersections of Literature and History in Fifteenth-Century England* (Minneapolis: University of Minnesota Press, 1996), pp. 29–62.

90 Sydney Anglo, *Spectacle and Pageantry in Early Tudor Policy* (Oxford: Clarendon Press, 1969). See, too, the discussions in Greenblatt, *Renaissance*

Self-Fashioning, Walker, *Plays of Persuasion*, and Bill Readings, "When Did the Renaissance Begin? The Henrician Court and the Shakesperian Stage," in Herman, ed., *Rethinking the Henrician Era*, pp. 283–302.

91 Howard, "'Ascending the Riche Mount,'" p. 29.

92 Stephen Orgel, *The Jonsonian Masque* (New York: Columbia University Press, 1965), p. 7.

93 Starkey, "Representation through Intimacy," and "Intimacy and Innovation."

94 Patricia Fumerton, *Cultural Aesthetics: Renaissance Literature and the Practice of Social Ornament* (Chicago: University of Chicago Press, 1991).

95 Starkey, "Intimacy and Innovation," pp. 74, 78.

96 See H. M. Smyser, "The Domestic Background in *Troilus and Criseyde*," *Speculum* 31 (1956): 297–315; Spearing, *Medieval Poet as Voyeur*, pp. 120–36; Stanbury, "The Voyeur and the Private Life."

97 See Dominique Barthélemy and Philippe Contamine, "The Use of Private Space," in George Duby, ed., *A History of Private Life II: Revelations of the Medieval World*, trans. Arthur Godhammer (Cambridge, MA: Harvard University Press, 1988), the section titled "The Bed," pp. 489–99, a section rich with visual and literary illustrations of late medieval domestic life. It is pointed out here that the word *chambre* could refer to the "matched ensemble" of "canopy, curtains, headboard, bedspread, and wall hangings" (pp. 494–95).

98 For discussion of this passage in relationship to its recognized source in Geoffrey of Vinsauf's *Poetria Nova*, see Donald R. Howard, *The Idea of the Canterbury Tales* (Berkeley and Los Angeles: University of California Press, 1976), pp. 134–37.

99 John Fyler, "The Fabrications of Pandarus," *Modern Language Quarterly* 41 (1980): 115–30.

100 See A. C. Spearing, in *Chaucer: Troilus and Criseyde* (London: Arnold, 1976), p. 55, and my discussion in chapter 4.

101 See the discussion in Spearing, *Medieval Poet as Voyeur*, pp. 177–93, and my arguments in chapter 2.

102 The popularity of the *Legend* is attested by its circulation in twelve manuscripts; by its frequent mention and citation in the works of such Chaucerian imitators as Lydgate and Hawes; and by its inclusion in Thynne's 1532 edition of Chaucer's *Works* (whose text indicates the circulation of manuscripts that no longer survive). One manuscript anthology, Cambridge University Library Ff. 1. 6, offers only the legend of Pyramus and Thisbe (lines 706–923 in Chaucer's poem). Chaucer's version is based on Ovid's *Metamorphoses*, IV.55–166; a version of the story by Gower (*Confessio Amantis* 3.1331–1494) is often considered related to Chaucer's, though it is unclear precisely what that relationship is (see the notes in the *Riverside Chaucer*, p. 1067).

103 All quotations from this poem are taken from the unique copy preserved in the British Library. Though its debts to Chaucer's version of the Pyramus and Thisbe story have never been discussed in detail, and though its literary context remains obscure, there are brief references to its place in the post-Chaucerian tradition in C. David Benson, "True Troilus and False Cres-

seid," p. 168, and Julia Boffey, "Richard Pynson's Book of Fame and the Letter of Dido," *Viator* 19 (1988): 351n. 45 (she notes that the "version of the story of Pyramus and Thisbe . . . is clearly modelled on the appropriate section of the *Legend of Good Women*"). For the range of meanings of the word "conusaunce," see the *OED*, s.v., *cognizance*, which notes that the origins of the term lie in the Anglo-French legal discourse of "taking judicial or authoritative notice" or the "hearing and trying of a case." See the citation from 1532, W. H. Turner, *Select Records of Oxford*, 38: "The Chancellor . . . shall have connusance of plees." The sense defined as "knowledge as attained by observation or information" has no sixteenth-century citations in the *OED*; yet there are several entries in the *MED* (s.v., *conissaunce*, def. 1a) that point to this meaning in the Middle English period. It is clear, too, that the earlier French and legal uses of the word carry with them the distinctive sense of information obtained by inquiry (*MED*, s.v., *conissaunce*, defs. 3a, b, with citations in legal French).

104 For some of these broader cultural changes that may inform the new emphases of this poem, see Steven Ozment, *When Fathers Ruled: Family Life in Reformation Europe* (Cambridge, MA: Harvard University Press, 1983), especially pp. 25–49. Though interested primarily in Lutheran Europe, Ozment's work provides many contemporary references to attitudes towards marriage and parental responsibility that are reflected in *La conusaunce damours*. Note, for example, this statute from Augsburg of 1537: "Children are not to be forced against their will into a marriage they find unpleasant and undesirable; parents should take the greatest care to respect and advance what is to the profit and well-being of their children's persons and possessions" (quoted on p. 39). For a study of relations between privacy and domesticity in mid-sixteenth century England, see Lena Cowen Olin, *Private Matters and Public Culture in Post-Reformation England* (Ithaca: Cornell University Press, 1994).

105 "Of the death of the same sir. T. w.," quoted from Rollins, ed., *Tottel's Miscellany*, p. 27.33–36. The phrase "And kisse the ground" was noted by Rollins as recalling the envoy of *Troilus and Criseyde*, V.1791, "And kiss the steppes" (*Tottel's Miscellany* vol. II, p. 154).

106 See Crewe, *Trials of Authorship*, pp. 48–78, especially pp. 75–76, and Martine Braekman, "A Chaucerian 'Courtly Love Aunter' by Henry Howard, Earl of Surrey," *Neophilologus* 79 (1995): 675–87.

107 Vives praises the moral ending of the play in his *De causis corruptarum artium* (1531), but he condemns it in *De institutione foeminae Christianae* (1524, dedicated to Katherine of Aragon and her daughter, Mary) as part of a list *de pestiferis libris*. Vives's Latin text was translated by Richard Hyrd (a protégé and tutor of Thomas More's daughters) in 1541, where the play becomes one of "those ungracious bokes" and Celestina becomes "the baude, mother of naughtynes." See Richard Axton, ed., *Three Rastell Plays* (Cambridge: D. S. Brewer, 1979), pp. 15–16.

108 See my discussion in chapter 2.

109 *Calisto and Melibea*, printed in Axton, ed., *Three Rastell Plays*, pp. 70–96. For a discussion of its publication and its place in the reception of *La Celestina*, see Axton's introduction, pp. 15–20.

110 Roberto Gonzáles Echevarría, *Celestina's Brood: Continuities of the Baroque in Spanish and Latin American Literature* (Durham: Duke University Press, 1993), this quotation from p. 11.

111 *Ibid.*, pp. 11–12.

112 Note, for example, Criseyde's remark at the close of the poem: "'Allas,' quod she, 'the pleasance and the joie, / The which that now al torned in-to galle is" (V.731–32).

113 Elton, *Policy and Police*, p. 397.

114 Statutes of the Realm, 27 Henry VIII.2, Act concerning the forgyng of the Kinges signe manuell signet and Prevye seale (1535–36).

115 Quoted in Walker, *Plays of Persuasion*, p. 218; see pp. 217–18, for the impact of this legislation on public literacy and political drama.

116 Statutes of the Realm, 33 Henry VIII.14, quoted and discussed in Edward Wilson, "Local Habitations and Names in MS Rawlinson C. 813 in the Bodleian Library, Oxford," *RES*, ns 41 (1990): 12–44, this discussion on pp. 41–42.

117 Muriel St. Clare Byrne, *The Lisle Letters*, 6 vols. (Chicago: University of Chicago Press, 1980), vol. V, p. 280.

118 What also seems at stake for the control of information was the actual physical concealment of offenders themselves. Part of the Act of Proclamations of 1539 avers that concealment itself was grounds for conviction: "if any person or persones offending contrarie to this acte doe willingly and contemptuouslie withdraw absent eloyne [i.e., alone] or secretlie hide hymselfe within any parte of this Realme" then they will be judged guilty.

119 Bryan is quoted in a letter by John Husee to Lord Lisle, dated 20 September, 1534. Printed in Byrne, *Lisle Letters*, no. 260, vol. II, p. 256.

2 THE KING'S PANDARS: PERFORMING COURTIERSHIP IN THE 1510s

1 Revels Books of Richard Gibson, Records of the Exchequer, reprinted in H. N. Hillebrand, *The Child Actors, University of Illinois Studies in Language and Literature* 11 (Urbana: University of Illinois Press, 1926); pp. 1–356, this material on pp. 324–25. Suzanne Westfall notes that "Cornish and the children performed *Troilus and Pandar* in Latin," but offers no substantiation for this claim (*Patrons and Performance: Early Tudor Household Revels* [Oxford: Clarendon Press, 1990], p. 41). For other references to the performance of this play and others as part of these Twelfth Night celebrations, see Ian Lancashire, *Dramatic Texts and Records of Britain* (Toronto: University of Toronto Press, 1984), pp. 129–31.

2 C. W. Wallace, *The Evolution of the English Drama up to Shakespeare*, *Shakespeare Jahrbuch Supplement* 4 (Berlin: G. Reimer, 1912), p. 38; Hillebrand, *Child Actors*, pp. 54–56; Greg Walker, *Plays of Persuasion: Drama and Politics at the Court of Henry VIII* (Cambridge: Cambridge University Press, 1991), p. 16, and more generally, pp. 15–24; Westfall, *Patrons and Performance*, p. 47, and more generally, pp. 28–48; W. R. Streitberger, "William Cornish and the Players of the Chapel," *Medieval English Theatre* 8 (1986): 1–20.

3 Walker, *Plays of Persuasion*, pp. 15–17.

4   See A. C. Spearing, *From Medieval to Renaissance in English Poetry* (Cambridge: Cambridge University Press, 1985), pp. 224–77; Susan Schibanoff, "Taking Jane's Cue: *Phyllyp Sparowe* as a Primer for Woman Readers," *PMLA* 101 (1986): 832–47; John Scattergood, "Skelton's *Garlande of Laurell* and the Chaucerian Tradition," in Ruth Morse and Barry Windeatt, eds., *Chaucer Traditions* (Cambridge: Cambridge University Press, 1990), pp. 122–38; Seth Lerer, *Chaucer and His Readers: Imagining the Author in Late-Medieval England* (Princeton: Princeton University Press, 1993), pp. 193–208.

5   On the textual circulation and literary reception of *Phyllyp Sparowe*, see Scattergood, ed., *Complete English Poems*, pp. 405–6, and the concluding section of this chapter.

6   See A. C. Spearing, *The Medieval Poet as Voyeur* (Cambridge: Cambridge University Press, 1993), p. 135 and p. 293 n. 21, and my discussion of this material in chapter 4.

7   David Starkey, "Representation Through Intimacy," in Ioan Lewis, ed., *Symbols and Sentiments* (London: Academic Press, 1977), pp. 187–224, especially pp. 203–13; and "Intimacy and Innovation: The Rise of the Privy Chamber, 1485–1547," in Starkey, ed., *The English Court: From the Wars of the Roses to the Civil War* (London: Longman, 1987), pp. 71–118.

8   Starkey, "Representation Through Intimacy," pp. 206–7; Specific references to these events are, respectively, as follows: *The Letters and Papers (Foreign and Domestic) of the Reign of King Henry VIII*, eds. J. Brewer and J. Gairduer (London, 1862–1920), I.474 (a paraphrase of Carroz's letter to Ferdinand, which I discuss in detail later in this chapter); on Norris, Starkey cites G.-A. Crapelet, *Lettres de Henry VIII à Anne Boleyn* (Paris, 1835), p. 184, and *Letters and Papers*, VI.193, on his status as bawd between the King and Anne. Starkey also cites the testimony of the sixteenth-century historian John Leland on the service of Anthony Denny.

9   In reviewing the performances at Twelfth Night, Gibson first outlines the "Troilus and Pandar" play and concludes that the actors were dressed "a kordyng to ye intent or purpoos aft weche Camedy playd . . ." The grammar of Gibson's sentences, however, is very difficult to construe, and I take "weche Camedy" to refer to the Troilus play (text in Hillebrand, *Child Actors*, p. 324).

10 Alistair Fox, *Politics and Literature in the Reigns of Henry VII and Henry VIII* (Oxford: Blackwell, 1989), pp. 229–31.

11 Information in this paragraph is drawn from G. W. Bernard, "The Rise of Sir William Compton, Early Tudor Courtier," *English Historical Review* 81 (1979): 754–77.

12 *Ibid.*, pp. 753–57.

13 *Ibid.*, p. 773.

14 Edward Hall, *Hall's Chronicle* (London: 1809, reprinted New York: AMS Press, 1965), originally published as *The Vnion of the Two Noble and Illustre Famelies of Lancastre and Yorke* (London: 1548). This quotation is from p. 513. Future references will be cited by page number in the text.

15 J. J. Scarisbrick, *Henry VIII* (Berkeley and Los Angeles: University of California Press, 1968), p. 20.

16 Ovid, *Ars Amatoria*, ed. and trans. G. P. Goold (Cambridge, MA: Harvard University Press, 1973).

17 For a review of these texts and traditions, see Lee Patterson, "Ambiguity and Interpretation: A Fifteenth-Century Reading of *Troilus and Criseyde*," in his *Negotiating the Past: The Historical Study of Medieval Literature* (Madison: University of Wisconsin Press, 1987), pp. 132–38.

18 Trans. Charles Fantazzi, in J. K. Sowards, ed., *The Collected Works of Erasmus: Literary and Educational Writings*, vol. XXVI, Toronto: University of Toronto Press, 1985), pp. 195–96.

19 Ed. J. C. Margolin, in *Opera Omnia Desiderii Erasmi Roterodami* (Amsterdam: North Holland, 1971), vol. I, part 2, pp. 499–500.

20 Skiles Howard, "'Ascending the Riche Mount': Performing Hierarchy and Gender in the Henrician Masque," in Peter C. Herman, ed., *Rethinking the Henrician Era: Essays on Early Tudor Texts and Contexts* (Urbana: University of Illinois Press, 1994), p. 29.

21 For details, see Greg Walker, "The Expulsion of the Minions Reconsidered," *The Historical Journal* 32 (1989): 1–16.

22 Jonathan Goldberg reviews the dismissal of the minions as an episode of sexual anxiety at Henry's court: "Were Henry's minions, those men closest to his body, sexually close?" (*Sodometries: Renaissance Texts, Modern Sexualities* [Stanford: Stanford University Press, 1993], p. 48).

23 OED, s.v., *perceive*, def. 5, citing More's *Confutations of Tyndale*, 1526.

24 See the representative discussion in Elaine Tuttle Hansen, *Chaucer and the Fictions of Gender* (Berkeley and Los Angeles: University of California Press, 1993), pp. 141–87.

25 Louis Montrose, "The Elizabethan Subject and the Spenserian Text," in Patricia Parker and David Quint, eds., *Literary Theory / Renaissance Texts* (Baltimore: Johns Hopkins University Press, 1985), p. 312.

26 *Ibid.*, p. 314.

27 Carroz's Spanish text, and an English translation, are printed in G. A. Bergenroth, ed., *Supplement to Volume I and Volume II of Letters, Dispatches, and State Papers Related to the Negotiations between England and Spain* (London, 1868), pp. 36–44; references will be cited by page number in my text. To my knowledge, this letter has never been fully discussed, nor has it been reprinted or retranslated since Bergenroth's edition of 1868. It has, however, often served as the basis of historical paraphrase on the events of the period: see *Letters and Papers*, I.474, and Garrett Mattingly, *Catherine of Aragon* (Boston: Little Brown, 1941), pp. 140–46 (who also offers an imaginative portrait of Carroz himself).

28 Goldberg, *Sodometries*, p. 33.

29 Scarisbrick, *Henry VIII*, p. 7.

30 For a narrative of the tensions between the two men, see Mattingly, *Catherine of Aragon*, pp. 137–46.

31 As on pp. 41–44 of Bergenroth, ed., *Supplement*.

32 The details of Katherine's pregnancies and miscarriages have been clarified by Sir John Dewhurst, "The Alleged Miscarriages of Catherine of Aragon and Anne Boleyn," *Medical History* 28 (1984): 49–56.

33 The translation of Diego Fernandez's letter is quoted in *ibid.*, p. 50, from

Bergenroth, ed., *Supplement*, p. 34 (that is, from the document immediately preceding Carroz's letter of 29 May).

34 All quotations from the play are from Fernando de Rojas, *Comedia o Tragicomedia de Calisto y Melebea*, ed., Peter E. Russell (Madrid: Clásicos Castalia, 1991), and will be cited by page number in the text. The English translation is the seventeenth-century version by Joseph Mabbe, generally agreed to be the one that captures fully the flavor of the play's idiom, *Celestine or the Tragick–Comedie of Calisto and Melibea*, ed. Guadalupe Martinez LaCalle (London: Tamesis, 1972), cited by page number in the text.

35 See the review of criticism and the discussion in Roberto Gonzáles Echevarría, *Celestina's Brood: Continuities of the Baroque in Spanish and Latin American Literature* (Durham: Duke University Press, 1993), with the summary remark, "Celestina stands for language, the quintessential mediator" (p. 12).

36 See the discussions of Olga Lucía Valbuena, "Sorceresses, Love Magic, and the Inquisition of Linguistic Sorcery in *Celestina*," *PMLA* 109 (1994): 207–24, especially p. 221 n. 17.

37 For the dates, circumstances of composition and publication, and broad historical contexts of Hawes's works, see A. S. G. Edwards, *Stephen Hawes* (Boston: Twayne, 1983). For bibliographical and editorial details, see the edition of Gluck and Morgan, *Stephen Hawes: The Minor Poems*, from which all quotations from the *Conforte of Louers* are taken here.

38 See the discussions of this poem in Edwards, *Stephen Hawes*, pp. 77–87; Spearing, *From Medieval To Renaissance*, pp. 255–61; Fox, *Politics and Literature*, pp. 56–72.

39 David Carlson, "Reputation and Duplicity," *ELH* 58 (1991): 261–81.

40 André had been appointed historiographer and "poeta laureatus" to Henry VII by 1490; Skelton had received the laureation from English and European universities and, by the ascension of Henry VIII, consistently presented himself as poet laureate. For details on these references, see my *Chaucer and His Readers*, p. 272 n. 46. Spearing also considers Hawes's remarks here to be allusions to the success of Skelton and André at the new King's court (*From Medieval to Renaissance*, p. 255).

41 See Edwards, *Stephen Hawes*, pp. 2–4.

42 "Representation Through Intimacy," p. 198.

43 Fox, *Politics and Literature*, pp. 56–72, developing arguments originally presented in "Stephen Hawes and the Political Allegory of the Confort of Lovers," *English Literary Renaissance* 17 (1987): 113–38.

44 *Sodometries*, p. 39.

45 Hawes's advisory lady begins by counseling him "Dyspayre you not / for it auayleth nought," (line 150), an echo of Pandarus's inaugural strategy at *Troilus and Criseyde* I.779–80: "Quod Pandarus, 'allas, what may this be, / That thow dispeired art thus causeles?' " Her remarks in the following line, "Ioye cometh after / whan the payne is gone," are noted by Gluck and Morgan as echoing *Troilus and Criseyde* I.952, "And also ioie is next the fyn of sorwe." The maxim in the *Conforte*, "Clymbe not to fast / lest sodenly ye slyde" (line 157) resonates, too, with Pandarus's Boethian advice to get off

Fortune's wheel. It is worth noting that this line also comes to stand as something of a maxim for courtier ambition in later satiric verse. See Lyndsay's remark in the *Testament of Papyngo*, "Quho sittish moist hie sal fynd the sait most slider" (line 352; see my discussion in chapter 1, n. 15).

46 See, for example, Carolyn Dinshaw, *Chaucer's Sexual Poetics* (Madison: University of Wisconsin Press, 1989), esp. p. 82; Hansen, *Chaucer and the Fictions of Gender*, esp. pp. 150ff.

47 *Renaissance Self-Fashioning, More to Shakespeare* (Chicago: University of Chicago Press, 1980), pp. 124–25.

48 See Lawrence D. Kritzman, *The Rhetoric of Sexuality and the Literature of the French Renaissance* (Cambridge: Cambridge University Press, 1991), pp. 97–111.

49 Nancy J. Vickers, "Diana Described: Scattered Woman and Scattered Rhyme," *Critical Inquiry* 8 (1981): 265–79; Kritzman, *The Rhetoric of Sexuality*, pp. 97–111.

50 Kritzman, *The Rhetoric of Sexuality*, pp. 97, 99.

51 Edwards briefly discusses Hawes's references to the word "pastime" in the poem, though without their apposition to "conforte" (*Stephen Hawes*, pp. 82–83).

52 I quote from the edition in Scattergood, ed., *Complete English Poems*, though I have also consulted Paula Neuss, ed., *Magnificence* (Baltimore: Johns Hopkins University Press, 1980), whose introduction (pp. 1–64) offers a useful review of textual, historical, and critical contexts.

53 Both Fox, *Politics and Literature*, pp. 236–40, and Walker, *Plays of Persuasion*, pp. 60–101, locate the play's historical environment in the minion controversy of 1519, challenging earlier attempts at dating the play to 1515–16 (that is, as marking the beginning of Skelton's satires against Wolsey).

54 The difficulties, both textual and interpretive, in this passage are reviewed by Neuss, ed., *Magnificence*, pp. 103–4. She suggests that Clokyd Colusyon wears a double-layered garment, but there is some possibility that "cope" in line 601 refers to an ecclesiastical vestment. Neuss's text, however, differs markedly from Scattergood's. She attributes line 601 to Counterfet Countenaunce and punctuates it, "What is this? He weareth a cope!" Her punctuation of the entire passage also differs from Scattergood's. At line 605 she prints the text as it appears in the surviving early prints of the play: "Tush, it is Sir John Double-Cloak," instead of emending to "Double-Cope" as R. L. Ramsay did (ed., *Magnyfycence*, EETS ES 98 [London: Oxford University Press, 1908]) and as Scattergood follows.

55 The *OED* considers the word *travesty* to have entered English only in the seventeenth-century borrowings of the French word *travesti*, initially in Florio's translation of Montaigne (s.v., *travesty*). The French word, however, is itself a loan from Italian, where it appears in Boccaccio and Machiavelli, and it is clear from the lexica that the word did form part of the European vernacular vocabulary of disguise, theatricality, and duplicity. See Carlo Battisti and Giovanni Alessio, *Dizionario Etimologico Italiano* (Firenze: G. Barbera, 1957), s.v., *travestire* (with citations to Machiavelli and Boccaccio); *Trésor de la Langue Française*, vol. XVI (Paris: Gallimard,

1994), s.v., *travestir* (which offers the earliest French usage from 1543, *transvesti*, "déguise, qui a pris le costume d'une autre condition").

56 Mary S. Gossy, *The Untold Story: Women and Theory in Golden Age Texts* (Ann Arbor: University of Michigan Press, 1989), p. 42.

57 Mabbe, *Celestine*, p. 137; *Calisto y Melebea*, p. 244. This passage is discussed in Gossy, *The Untold Story*, p. 43.

58 *De institutione foeminae Christianae*, cited in Richard Axton, ed., *Three Rastell Plays* (Cambridge: D. S. Brewer, 1979), p. 16.

59 Ed., *Magnificence*, p. 93.

60 "That can my husband say, / Whan we kys and play / In lust and in lykyng. / He calleth me his whytyng, / His mullyng and his mytyng, / His nobbes and his conny" (*Elynour Rummynge*, lines 220–25). See, too, the opening of part three of the poem, "In stede of coyne and monny / Some brynge her a conny" (lines 244–45), where the wordplay on *coyne* and *conny* may resonate with the lines from *Magnyfycence*. The *OED* cites the first passage from *Elynour Rummynge* as the earliest appearance of *cony* as a term of endearment for women, but cites the first appearance of its "indecent" uses as 1591 (s.v., *cony*, def. 5a, b).

61 Ed. *Magnificence*, p. 94.

62 Scattergood, ed., *Complete English Poems*, p. 438. Neuss, ed., *Magnificence*, p. 93, argues that the word "resayte" (normalized in her edition to "receipt") means "a *written* acknowledgement here" (her emphasis).

63 R. A. Shoaf, *Dante, Chaucer, and the Currency of the Word: Money, Images, and Reference in Late Medieval Poetry* (Norman: Pilgrim Books, 1983), p. 115.

64 All quotations, cited by line number, are from the edition in Axton, *Three Rastell Plays*.

65 See the discussion in Walker, *Plays of Persuasion*, p. 71.

66 *MED*, s.v., *sad*. For the role of this word in the moral, philosophical, and social contexts of Chaucer's works, see Michaela Paasche Grudin, "Chaucer's *Clerk's Tale* as Political Paradox," *Studies in the Age of Chaucer* 11 (1989): 63–92, esp. pp. 88–91. Note, too, the title given to *Why Come Ye Nat to Courte?* in the complete edition of Skelton's *Workes* published by Marshe in 1568: "The relucent mirror for all Prelats and Presidents, as well spirituall as temporall, *sadly to loke upon* . . ." (emphases added; quoted in Scattergood, ed., *Complete English Poems*, p. 482).

67 See my discussion in *Chaucer and His Readers*, pp. 113–14.

68 The only modern edition of the poem is William Edward Mead, ed., *The Squyr of Lowe Degre* (Boston: Ginn, 1904). It survives in three versions: one, a fragmentary copy of de Worde's print, *c*. 1520; a complete copy of Copeland's edition, probably from the late 1550s; and a short version of the story from the seventeenth-century Percy Folio Manuscript, British Library MS Additional 27879. I quote from the edition of de Worde when possible (line numbers in my text prefaced by W), and from Copeland only when his is the surviving copy (line numbers prefaced by C). A review of these bibliographical issues, together with a collection of early references to the poem, appears in Mead's edition, pp. xi–xiii. Derek Pearsall considers the poem's composition roughly contemporary with its earliest publication, and

– in spite of locating it in a study of "medieval" poetry – Spearing finds its topical allusions to be "evidence for thinking of the *Squyr* as an early Tudor work." See Pearsall, "English Romance in the Fifteenth Century," *Essays and Studies* ns 29 (1976): 66, and Spearing, *Medieval Poet as Voyeur*, p. 297 n. 13. Carol Meale excludes the poem from her discussion of de Worde's printing of romance, as it seems to fall into the category of "those which survive only in later manuscript copies or in printed form" ("Caxton, de Worde, and the Publication of Romance in Late Medieval England," *The Library*, sixth series 14 [1992]: 285).

69   Spearing, *Medieval Poet as Voyeur*, pp. 177–93. Kevin Kiernan, "*Undo Your Door* and the Order of Chivalry," *Studies in Philology* 70 (1973): 345–66 sensitively calls attention to the vigorous sexual wordplay and narrative burlesques of the poem.

70   Though the Hungarian setting has been ignored by critics, it is interesting that in Hall's account of the Twelfth Night revels of 1516, part of the strange disguises of the actors include "the mens apparell of thesame suyte made lyke Iulys of Hungary" (Hall, *Chronicle*, p. 583), suggesting perhaps some topical significance for the poem's setting.

71   See, for example, the king's speech to his daughter at lines 739–852.

72   See Peter T. Hadorn, "The Westminster Tournament of 1511: A Study in Tudor Propaganda," *Research Opportunities in Renaissance Drama* 31 (1992): 25–45. Hadorn summarizes the Tournament as presenting "a chivalric romance with a coherent narrative plot" (p. 25), where aspirants tilt and joust before the Queen. Hadorn describes the central event of the Tournament in terms that resonate, to my mind, with the plot of the *Squyr of Lowe Degre*: "In this symbolic interaction between knight and Queen, the monarch's mere presence is capable of releasing the knight from bondage. The message is clear: unless the knight can be at court where he can loyally serve in the presence of the monarch, he is no better than a hermit exiled to prison" (p. 31).

73   These quotations are from Bernard, "The Rise of Sir William Compton," pp. 776–77. Compare the remarks of Frank Whigham, *Ambition and Privilege: The Social Tropes of Elizabethan Courtesy Theory* (Berkeley and Los Angeles: University of California Press, 1984), p. 5: "elite identity was a mode of being that could be acquired, taken on in adulthood – a commodity . . . that could be bought."

74   Laura Kendrick, *Chaucerian Play* (Berkeley and Los Angeles: University of California Press, 1988), pp. 5–19.

75   Gail M. Gibson, *The Theater of Devotion* (Chicago: University of Chicago Press, 1989), pp. 154–55. This phrasing also appears in one of the late fourteenth-century lyrics from the manuscript of John Grimestone (National Library of Scotland MS Advocates 18. 7. 21, dated 1372), based on the medieval exegetical interpretation of the Song of Songs: "Undo þi dore, my spuse dere/ Allas! wy stond I loken out here?" See J. A. Burrow and Thorlac Turville-Petre, *A Book of Middle English* (Oxford: Blackwell, 1992), p. 250.

76   *Ludus Coventriae*, ed. K. S. Block, EETS ES 120 (London: Oxford University Press, 1922), p. 109. These are the opening ten lines of the play. Quoted in Gibson, *Theater of Devotion*, p. 154; emphases here are mine.

77 Gibson, p. 154.
78 *Ibid.*
79 *Medieval Poet as Voyeur*, p. 190.
80 The following discussion adapts and abbreviates a longer and more technical analysis of this woodcut and de Worde's editions from my essay, "The Wiles of a Woodcut: Wynkyn de Worde and the Early Tudor Reader," *The Huntington Library Quarterly* 59 (1996).
81 Edward Hodnett, *English Woodcuts, 1480–1535* (London: Bibliographical Society, 1935), number 1009 (p. 278), and the revision of this description in *English Woodcuts, 1480–1535: Additions and Corrections* (London: Bibliographical Society, 1973), p. 65.
82 Sig. Giii, before line 1961. The picture is reproduced in W. E. Mead, ed., *Stephen Hawes, The Pastime of Pleasure*, EETS OS 173 (London: Oxford University Press, 1928), p. 77. The one surviving copy of the 1509 edition now in the British library is defective, though it does have the page with the woodcut surviving. The unique copy of the 1517 edition is in the Pierpont Morgan Library, and is reproduced in facsimile in Frank J. Spang, ed., *The Works of Stephen Hawes* (Delmar: Scholars's Facsimiles and Reprints, 1975). For the publishing history of the *Pastime*, see Edwards, "Poet and Printer in the Sixteenth Century: Stephen Hawes and Wynkyn de Worde," *Gutenberg Jahrbuch* (1980).
83 *The IIII Leues of a Truelove* survives in two copies, one in the British Library (which I have examined on microfilm), the other in the Huntington Library (which I have examined personally). The edition was originally dated 1530? by the original *STC*. The *RSTC* redates it as provisionally 1510. By comparing the typefaces used in the *IIII Leues* with the analysis of de Worde's types provided by Frank Isaac, *English and Scottish Printing Types, 1501–1535* (Oxford: Bibliographical Society, 1930), pp. 1–3, I believe that this publication should be dated in the second half of the 1510s, thus making the *Troilus*, the *Conforte of Louers*, and the *Squyr of Lowe Degre* all contemporary with it.
The relationship between the *IIII Leues* and the *Quatrefoil of Love* was first noticed by N. F. Blake, "Wynkyn de Worde and the *Quatrefoil of Love*," *Archiv für das Studium der neueren Sprachen und Literaturen* 206 (1969): 189–200, who is largely concerned with de Worde's alterations of the poem's Northern alliterative vocabulary. For an edition of this earlier poem, see Israel Gollancz and Magdalene M. Weale, *The Quatrefoil of Love*, EETS OS 195 (London: Oxford University Press, 1935).
84 De Worde's critical awareness and his sensitivity to the physical contexts in which his books appeared have been stressed by Edwards, "Poet and Printer": 82–88; and "From Manuscript to Print: Wynkyn de Worde and the Printing of Contemporary Poetry," *Gutenberg Jahrbuch* (1991): 143–48; and by Meale, "Caxton, de Worde, and the Publication of Romance."
85 See Edwards, "Poet and Printer."
86 Scattergood, ed., *Complete English Poems*, p. 412, note to lines 677–723.
87 Schibanoff, "Taking Jane's Cue," p. 835.
88 *Ibid.*, pp. 835, 839.

89 These words, by the way, are reset differently in the *IIII Leues* print, indicating that de Worde did not simply run off the same cut for that poem.

90 See the discussions in Gluck and Morgan, eds., *Stephen Hawes: The Minor Poems*, pp. 160–62; Edwards, *Stephen Hawes*, pp. 81–82.

91 Gluck and Morgan, p. 161, for texts and discussion.

92 *Ibid.*, p. 160.

93 See the discussion in Fox, *Politics and Literature*, pp. 42–45.

94 *Ibid.*, p. 44.

95 Carlson, "Reputation and Duplicity," p. 271.

96 Edwards, "Poet and Printer," and "From Manuscript to Print."

97 Edwards, "Poet and Printer"; "An Allusion to Stephen Hawes, c. 1530," *Notes and Queries* 224 (1979): 397; "Nevill's *Castell of Pleasure* and Stephen Hawes," *Notes and Queries* 226 (1981): 487; and *Stephen Hawes*, pp. 88–97. See, too, Mary C. Erler, *Robert Copeland: Poems* (Toronto: University of Toronto Press, 1993), p. 141.

98 Quotations from the *IIII Leues* are from the copy in the Huntington Library, cited by signature. Numbers following refer to the line numbers in the edition of the *Quatrefoil* by Gollancz and Weale. Because de Worde (or his source) garbled the stanzaic patterning of the *Quatrefoil*, occasionally misplacing, for example, the short bob lines of the bob-and-wheel sections of the stanzas, the lineation in de Worde's text does not correspond to that of the edition of the *Quatrefoil*. For comparisons, see Blake, "Wynkyn de Worde and the *Quatrefoil of Love*."

99 For some speculations on de Worde's motivations, and the status of Northern poetry in London reading circles, see Blake, "Wynkyn de Worde and the *Quatrefoil*." One of the *Quatrefoil*'s surviving manuscripts is BL MS Additional 31042, a personal anthology assembled by the Lincoln antiquary Robert Thornton. On the details of this manuscript and its relations to late medieval English literary cuture, see John J. Thompson, *Robert Thornton and the London Thornton Manuscript* (Cambridge: D. S. Brewer, 1987).

100 On the religious traditions of the *quatrefolium*, see Siegfried Wenzel, *Verses in Sermons: Fasciculus Morum and its Middle English Poems* (Cambridge, MA: Medieval Academy of America, 1978), pp. 158–60.

101 *Canterbury Tales*, A line 3692.

102 Ed. J. R. R. Tolkein and E. V. Gordon, revised by Norman Davis (Oxford: Oxford University Press, 1967), line 612. See the note on this line in this edition, p. 92.

103 *OED*, s.v., *true-love, true-love knot*, which cites several early sixteenth-century appearances of the word, suggesting its association with rings, brooches and other gifts. It also quotes a historical text from 1877, W. Jones, *Finger-ring*: "true-love knots were common (on rings)."

104 Space does not permit a comprehensive review of the late medieval poetry of trueloves, but a good place to begin would be the poetry compiled by Humphey Wellys in Bodleian Library Rawlinson MS C.813. Many of the poems of this manuscript contain references to seeking, finding, and presenting truelove tokens, and some of them offer what I believe to be specific verbal allusions to the *IIII Leues*. For evidence and arguments developing this belief, see my "Wiles of a Woodcut."

105 I am grateful to Mary Robertson, Curator of Manuscripts at the Huntington Library, for advice on this inscription.
106 Meale, "Caxton, de Worde, and the Publication of Romance," p. 294.
107 Schibanoff, "Taking Jane's Cue," p. 839.

3 THE KING'S HAND: BODY POLITICS IN THE LETTERS OF HENRY VIII

1 David Starkey, "Court and Government," in Christopher Coleman and David Starkey, eds., *Revolution Reassessed: Revisions in the History of Tudor Government and Administration* (Oxford: Clarendon Press, 1986), p. 47. See, too, Jonathan Goldberg, *Writing Matter: From the Hands of the Renaissance* (Stanford: Stanford University Press, 1990), pp. 118, 260–63.
2 Starkey, "Court and Government," pp. 49–50, citing *Letters and Papers* III. ii. 1399, 1429; XIV. ii. 149, 153, 163.
3 Starkey, "Court and Government," p. 50, citing *Letters and Papers* I. ii. 1960; IV. ii. 4409.
4 See the discussion in Muriel St. Clare Byrne, *The Letters of King Henry VIII* (New York: Funk and Wagnalls, 1968), p. xv, with an excellent example being the recast letter of instruction to Wyatt and Hoby, dated 16 October 1538 (printed in Byrne, pp. 202–10). This letter notes that Hoby took with him "the King's letters of his own hand-writing" (p. 202), though these do not survive.
5 Letter of July 1518, quoted and discussed in Richard Rambuss, *Spenser's Secret Career* (Cambridge: Cambridge University Press, 1993), p. 135 n. 23. The text of the letter is printed in Byrne, *Letters*, pp. 43–44. Surviving holographs to Wolsey are printed and discussed in Byrne, *Letters*, pp. 23 (1514), 28 (1525?), 43 (July 1518), 76–78 (July 1528), 79–80 (July 1528), 81 (July–August 1528).
6 Henry wrote a long letter to Tunstall in March, 1539, concerning the status of auricular confession (Byrne, *Letters*, pp. 256–58).
7 Lorna Hutson, *The Usurer's Daughter* (London: Routledge, 1994), p. 3.
8 Byrne, *Letters*, p. 43.
9 *Ibid.*, pp. 76–78, Letter of July 1528. The closing salutation I quote is from the subsequent letter of July 1528 (*ibid.*, pp. 79–81), in which Henry also notes, "Howbeit your Legacy herein might, peradventure, *apud Homines* be a Cloak, but not *apud Deum.*"
10 And not, as Byrne notes, find in them "the most sincere and candid of Henry's utterances that has been recorded," *ibid.*, p. 76.
11 Quoted in John Scattergood, ed., *John Skelton, Complete English Poems*, p. 488, but I quote from the recent edition of Douglas H. Parker, *Rede Me and Be Nott Wrothe* (Toronto: University of Toronto Press, 1992), lines 3016–18.
12 Lisa Jardine, *Erasmus, Man of Letters: The Construction of Charisma in Print* (Princeton: Princeton University Press, 1993), p. 31.
13 *Ibid.*, p. 33.
14 With the exception of the few letters to Wolsey, the letter to Tunstall, and the letters to Anne Boleyn, the only other surviving correspondence in Henry's hand is a postscript to a letter to Katherine Parr of 8 September

1544 (signed, "Written with the hand of your loving husband, Henry R";
Byrne, *Letters*, pp. 367–68).

15 Note, in particular, the advice on writing letters in *Ars amatoria* I.455–68.
For the corporealization of epistolary love, see the account of Byblis's
potentially incestuous love of her brother in *Metamorphoses* IX.526–665,
especially this account of her letter writing: "Protinus inpressa signat sua
crimina gemma, / quem tinxit lacrimis (linguam defecerat umor)" (*Met.*
IX. 566–57, "Straightway she stamped the shameful letter with her seal
which she moistened with her tears (for moisture failed her tongue)." From
Ovid, *Metamorphoses*, ed. and trans. F. J. Miller (Cambridge: Loeb Library,
1916). *Amores* XV – an erotic elegy to the lover's ring that informs a lineage
of medieval and Renaissance lyrics – similarly marks its letter with the fluids
of the body ("idem ego, ut arcanas possim signare tabellas, / neve tenax
ceram siccaque gemma trahat / umida formosae tangam prius ora puellae –
tantum ne signem scripta dolena mihi," 15–18; "Likewise, to help her seal
her secret missives, and to keep the dry, clinging gem from drawing away the
wax, I should first touch the moist lips of my beautiful love – only so that I
sealed no missive that would bring me pain."). Tears blot the letter of Briseis
to Achilles in *Heroides* III ("quascumque adspicies, lacrimae fecere lituras,"
3; "Whatever blots you see, her tears have made"). From Ovid, *Heroides and
Amores*, ed. and trans. G. P. Goold (Cambridge: Loeb Library, 1977). These
texts, together with their complex medieval encrustings of commentary and
response, have long been seen as standing behind Pandarus's epistolographic
instructions to Troilus in Book II. See the discussion in John V. Fleming,
Classical Imitation and Interpretation in Chaucer's Troilus (Lincoln: University of Nebraska Press, 1991), pp. 161–63. For accounts of these traditions in
vernacular literary epistolography, see Peter Dronke, *Women Writers of the
Middle Ages* (Cambridge: Cambridge University Press, 1984), pp. 88–97; on
the letter "as a material representation of the lover–writer," see Sylvia Huot,
From Song to Book (Ithaca: Cornell University Press, 1987), p. 150.

16 Jardine, *Erasmus*, p. 31.

17 See Forrest Tyler Stevens, "Erasmus's 'Tigress': The Language of Friendship, Pleasure, and the Renaissance Letter," in Jonathan Goldberg, ed.,
Queering the Renaissance (Durham: Duke University Press, 1994), pp. 124–
40.

18 Letter from Erasmus to Servatius Rogerus (*c.* 1488), in *The Collected Works
of Erasmus: The Correspondence of Erasmus*, trans. R. A. B. Mynors and D.
F. S. Thomson, volume I (Toronto: University of Toronto Press, 1974),
p. 20, quoted and discussed in Stevens, "Erasmus's 'Tigress,'" p. 139 n. 4.

19 Letter to Servatius Rogerus (*c.* 1487), in *Correspondence*, vol. I, p. 14,
quoted and discussed in Stevens, "Erasmus's 'Tigress,'" p. 137.

20 *De conscribendis epistolis*, trans. Charles Fantazzi, in J. K. Sowards, ed., *The
Collected Works of Erasmus: Literary and Educational Writings*, vol. XXV
(Toronto: University of Toronto Press, 1985), p. 37, quoted and discussed in
Stevens, "Erasmus's 'Tigress,'" p. 134. In fact, the entire quotation from
which this phrase appears concerns ways in which the letter writer may
ingratiate himself with his recipient. "In this regard it could also be added
that letters exchanged between young men, boon companions, and lovers

should be framed in a more winning manner [*In hoc argumento poeterit et illud admoneri, blandiorem oportere fingi epistolam, quam adolescens adolescenti, congerro congerroni, amans scribit amanti*]. In this way the person persuading will inspire more confidence by frankly avowing and condemning his own mistake, and he will evoke the memory of past sensual pleasures [*voluptatem memoriam*] in such a way as to reveal that his mind shrinks from the mere recollection." (Latin text from *De conscribendis epistolis*, ed. Jean-Claude Margolin, in *Opera Omnia Desiderii Erasmi Roterodami* [Amsterdam: North Holland, 1971], vol. I, part 2, p. 252).

21   See *OED*, s.v., *study, chamber*, and the discussions of this material in the following chapter. For the shifting connotations of "hand," note the changes in the definitions of *manus* in successive editions of Thomas Elyot's *Dictionary*. In the first edition (London: Berthelet, 1538), the definition reads in its entirety: "*Manus*, a hande, a grapul to fasten shippes together, somtime it signifieth a multitude of men in the ayde of one, sometyme power, sometyme writynge, also the nose or snoute of an olyphant." In the revised edition of 1545 (titled *Bibliotheca Eliotae Eliotis Librarie* [London: Berthelet, 1545]) this definition is kept, but additional idiomatic uses of the word *manus* are added. Then, in the edition of 1548 (with the same title as the 1545 edition), the definition itself changes as follows: "*Manus*, a hande, a mans hande in writynge, a writynge, a subscription, with ones owne hande. also a grapull to fasten shypis together. sometyme it signifieth a multitude of men in the aide of one; sometyme power. also the nose or snoute of an olifant." I believe the shift in this definition, with the new emphasis on the act of the writing hand and its products, is a consequence of the administrative and cultural changes worked through Henry's realignments of the secretariat, the use of his own hand as an icon of royal power, and the broader shifts in the teaching and uses of handwriting.

22   David Starkey, "Intimacy and Innovation: The Rise of the Privy Chamber, 1485–1547," in Starkey, ed., *The English Court: From the Wars of the Roses to the Civil War* (London: Longman, 1987), pp. 74, 78.

23   Stephen Merriam Foley, *Sir Thomas Wyatt* (Boston: Twayne, 1990), p. 34, citing David Loades, *The Tudor Court* (Totowa: Barnes and Noble, 1987), p. 63.

24   From *Household Ordinances* (London: Society of Antiquaries, 1790), p. 153, quoted in Foley, *Sir Thomas Wyatt*, p. 34.

25   The history of this correspondence's reception has been sketched by Jasper Ridley, *The Love Letters of Henry VIII* (London: Cassell, 1988), and traced more extensively by Theo Stemmler, *Die Liebesbriefe Heinrichs VIII. an Anna Boleyn* (Zurich: Belser Verlag, 1988). My quotations in French and English from the letters will be from Stemmler's edition (silently accepting his emendations and expansions of abbreviations); all translations from the French will be from Ridley. For a full account of the correspondence in the political and cultural environments of the late 1520s, see Retha M. Warnicke, *The Rise and Fall of Anne Boleyn* (Cambridge: Cambridge University Press, 1989), pp. 76–99; for a reading of the correspondence in the context of Henry's appropriations of the tropes of courtly love, see E. W. Ives, *Anne Boleyn* (Oxford: Blackwell, 1986), pp. 102–10, and Theo

Stemmler, "The Songs and Love-Letters of Henry VIII: On the Flexibility of Literary Genres," in Uwe Baumann, ed., *Henry VIII in History, Historiography and Literature* (Frankfurt am Main: Peter Lang, 1992), pp. 97–112. Still of value is the collection of translations and linking narrative provided by Byrne, *Letters*.

26 The archival order of the letters in the Vatican Library was decided, apparently, by an anonymous cataloguer in the sixteenth or seventeenth century and has nothing to do with the order in which they might have been written. This numbering, however, was used by the printer J. Churchill in his original edition of the letters (London, 1714) and in their 1745 republication in the *Harleian Miscellany*. Attempts at placing them in chronological order were made by J. Brewer and J. Gairdner, eds., *The Letters and Papers (Foreign and Domestic) of the Reign of King Henry VIII* (London, 1862–1920), vol. IV (hereafter cited as *Letters and Papers*). Subsequent editors and commentators have derived their own ordering, though usually with reference to the standard Harleian numbers (though attempting to date the letters, Ridley publishes his translations in the old Harleian order). Though it is usually assumed that the correspondence began in the summer of 1527, Warnicke believes that Henry only began to write to Anne after their forced separation in 1528 (*Rise and Fall*, pp. 76–79).

27 The letters clearly had been intercepted in the summer of 1528 (see below). It is presumed that they were stolen, as a group, sometime in 1529, possibly by (or with the collusion of) Lorenzo, Cardinal Campeggio who had arrived in England to supervise the inquiry into Henry's dissolving marriage to Katherine of Aragon. See the discussion in Warnicke, *Rise and Fall*, pp. 76–77, though Ridley suggests that this version of events was concocted by William Oldys, in his preface to the Harleian printing, out of a later eighteenth-century anti-papalism.

28 Byrne, *Letters*, p. 368.

29 *Ibid.*, p. xviii.

30 *Ibid.*, p. xvii.

31 *Ibid.*, p. xviii, a curious phrasing in the context of the original edition of this work, published in 1936, the year of Edward VIII's brief reign and constitutional crisis precipitated by the person he called, in his radio broadcast of December 1936, "the woman I love."

32 Goldberg, *Writing Matter*, pp. 260, 237, respectively.

33 Foley, *Sir Thomas Wyatt*, p. 38.

34 The letter was placed first by the original Vatican cataloguer. Byrne considers it the first written (*Letters*, p. 54), as does Ridley. Stemmler places it fifth in his sequence (though he garbles his own ordering in the comparative table of editions on p. 18). Warnicke constructs a unique sequence of letters, arguing that the French correspondence was not written to inaugurate the relationship but rather to revive it after a disagreement (*Rise and Fall*, pp. 77–78, and see her list of correspondences on pp. 273–74 nn. 14–34).

35 "Si epistolae carent veris affectibus neque vitam ipsam hominis repraesentant, iam epistolae nomen non merentur." Quoted and translated in Jardine, *Erasmus*, pp. 151, 267 n. 14.

36   Foley, *Sir Thomas Wyatt*, p. 36.

37   *Ibid.*, p. 37.

38   This paragraph summarizes materials presented in the following: Roy Strong, *Artists of The Tudor Court* (London: Victoria and Albert Museum, 1983), pp. 34–44; Strong, *The English Renaissance Miniature* (London: Thames and Hudson, 1983), pp. 12–44 (especially pp. 27–29); John Rowlands, *Holbein* (Boston: Godine, 1985), pp. 89–90.

39   Strong, *English Renaissance Miniature*, pp. 41–42. For an excellent color reproduction of this object, see Theo Stemmler, *Die Liebesbriefe*, p. 79.

40   Reproduced in color as Plate III, p. 18, in Strong, *Artists of the Tudor Court*; for issues of dating and technique, see the discussion on pp. 36–37, though Strong notes, "It is unusual in showing the hands" (p. 37).

41   For the Margaret Roper portrait, see the reproduction, Plate 43, p. 48, in Strong, *English Renaissance Miniature*, and the discussion in *Artists of the Tudor Court*, p. 47 (where it is not reproduced). For the Charles Brandon portrait, see the color reproduction, Plate 28, p. 106, in Rowlands, *Holbein*, and the discussion in Strong, *Artists of the Tudor Court*, p. 51 (where it is reproduced in black-and-white on p. 50).

42   Foley, *Sir Thomas Wyatt*, p. 37.

43   Jardine, *Erasmus*, pp. 27–53. Note, too, the remarkably modeled hands in Holbein's sketches for the Erasmus portraits; reproduced in Paul Hamlyn, *The Drawings of Holbein* (London, 1966), Plate XLV, and discussed (and dated to *c.* 1523) on p. 39.

44   Reproduced in color in Rowlands, *Holbein*, Plate 19, p. 98.

45   For discussion of the picture's origin and provenance, see *ibid.*, pp. 137–38.

46   Reproduced in black-and-white in *ibid.*, Plate 80, and discussed on p. 139.

47   Ridley, *Love Letters*, V, Stemmler, *Die Liebesbriefe*, VI; Ridley, *Love Letters*, XI, Stemmler, *Die Liebesbriefe*, VII; Ridley, *Love Letters*, XII, Stemmler, *Die Liebesbriefe*, X. For reproductions of these signatures, see the accompanying facsimiles in Stemmler's edition.

48   Ridley, *Love Letters*, VIII, Stemmler, *Die Liebesbriefe*, II. The motto has long been undecipherable. Stemmler reassesses traditional transcriptions and proposes a new reading: B. N. A. I. de . A. O. Na. V. e. r. Stemmler deciphers this inscription as "A An(n)a Bov(lleyne) de Enri" (*Die Liebesbriefe*, p. 152).

49   These quotations are drawn from the *OED*, s.v., *secretary*, sb. 2, in texts dated 1440 and 1450, respectively.

50   This is Letter XVI in Ridley, *Love Letters*. The original Vatican compiler placed it eighth, making it one of the first letters in English, but Byrne and Ives place it fourteenth and Warnicke thirteenth. There seems to be a general consensus that it was written sometime in the late summer of 1528.

51   See Ridley, *Love Letters*, p. 65.

52   The impress of a Hawesean vocabulary on Henry's letters may be apparent, too, in the King's use of the phrase "rude lettre" in two of the French epistles (Stemmler, *Die Liebesbriefe*, III and IV, Ridley, *Love Letters*, IV and II, respectively); indeed, I think this is not a French phrase at all, but an English idiom (and thus comparable, for example, to Henry's use of such words as "picture," instead of the French "peinture," in the letter offering Anne the

bracelet; and of a piece, too, with his search for French equivalents of English clichés, see my discussion of his phrase "racine en ceure," below). Compare the lines from Grande Amoure's farewell to La Belle Pucelle in the *Pastime* with the language of Stemmler, *Die Liebesbriefe*, III / Ridley, *Love Letters*, IV, where Grande Amoure asks his beloved to consider "What payne I suffre by grete extremyte / And to pardone my of my rude wrytynge" (*Pastime*, lines 2546–47).

53 Lawrence D. Kritzman, *The Rhetoric of Sexuality and the Literature of the French Renaissance* (Cambridge: Cambridge University Press, 1991), p. 97.

54 *Ibid.*, p. 99.

55 Jansen and Jordan, eds., *The Welles Anthology*, item 4, lines 17–20.

56 Note, for example, the display of epstolary clichés in item 55 of Wellys's manuscript, a poem that concerns itself, much like Henry's early letters, with defining the proper rhetorical relations between writer and reader and, too, the proper terms of address. The poem begins "With greate humylyte I your gentylnes / and with dew reuerens lowly I me recommende" (55.1–2), terms that recall the appeal to recommendation of the King's letters. Note, too, the interest in defining the lover as the "spetyall frende" in the refrain lines of the poem (a key problem in the King's adjudication between "mestres et amye"), and finally the first line of its final stanza, "noo more to yow now att thys tyme" (55.29), a commonplace of epistolary closure that Henry deploys throughout his letters to Anne (and, one might add, his letters to Wolsey, too).

57 The text, made up of stanzas drawn from Hawes's *Pastime of Pleasure*, together with one stanza from his *Conforte of Louers*, is printed in Jansen and Jordan, eds., *The Welles Anthology*, as item 13, pp. 117–24. Citations of this poem follow the numeration and lineation in this edition.

58 Henry uses the phrase "vous sans aultre racine en ceure," which Stemmler traces to this Chaucerian idiom (Stemmler, *Die Liebesbriefe*, VI, and his note on p. 152; the translation is garbled in Ridley, *Love Letters*, V).

59 Ives, *Anne Boleyn*, p. 103.

60 The possibilities of wordplay would have been recognized in Henry's day. See, for example, Thomas Elyot's entry in his *Dictionary* (London: Berthelet, 1538): "*Sapio, sapui, sapere*, to taste or sauour, to fele, to be wise, to haue a right opinion." For the panoply of early French uses, see Walther von Wartburg, *Französisches Etymologisches Wörterbuch* (Bonn: F. Kopp, 1928–), vol. XI, pp. 193–201, s.v., *sapere*.

61 I can find no examples of the spelling *encorps* in the standard lexica of medieval and sixteenth-century French.

62 For something of this Rabelaisian verbal quality – and for the sense of Christological and Eucharistic play that informs Henry's letter – see Florence M. Weinberg, *The Wine and the Will: Rabelais's Bacchic Christianity* (Detroit: Wayne State University Press, 1972), and François Rigolot, "Rabelais, Misogyny, and Christian Charity: Biblical Intertextuality and the Renaissance Crisis of Exemplarity," *PMLA* 109 (1994): 225–37.

63 Goldberg, *Writing Matter*, pp. 70–75.

64 *Ibid.*, p. 73.

65 See Marcelle Thiébaux, *The Stag of Love: The Chase in Medieval Literature* (Ithaca: Cornell University Press, 1974).

66 See the summary of critical positions in R. A. Rebholz, ed., *Sir Thomas Wyatt: The Complete Poems*, pp. 343–44; Stephen Greenblatt, *Renaissance Self-Fashioning, More to Shakespeare* (Chicago: University of Chicago Press, 1980), pp. 145–50; Jonathan Crewe, *Trials of Authorship: Anterior Forms and Poetic Reconstruction from Wyatt to Shakespeare* (Berkeley and Los Angeles: University of California Press, 1990), pp. 36–45; Foley, *Sir Thomas Wyatt*, pp. 98–99.

67 Crewe, *Trials of Authorship*, p. 38. See, too, the discussion of Wyatt's Petrarchism and the constructions of Renaissance subjectivity in Thomas M. Greene, *The Light in Troy* (New Haven, Yale University Press, 1982), pp. 242–63, especially pp. 261–62.

68 Stephen Foley calls attention to John Leland's description of Wyatt's signet ring (*Sir Thomas Wyatt*, p. 97). In one of the memorial Latin poems published in his *Naeniae*, Leland noted that the poet wore a ring bearing the carved likeness of Julius Caesar, "a notable token for sealing up his letters" ("occludendis signum spectabile chartis").

69 It is worth comparing Henry's later English letter to Anne (Ridley, *Love Letters*, VI, Stemmler, *Die Liebesbriefe*, XVI, datable to September 1528), which closes: "No more to yow at thys present, myne awne darlyng, for lake off tyme, but that I wolde yow were in myne armes or I in yours, for I thynk it long, syns I kyst yow. Writtyn affter the kyllyng off an hart, att XI off the kloke, myndyng with god grace tomorow mytely timely to kyll Another. By the hand off him, whyche I trust shortly shall be yours" (text from Stemmler's transcription). This letter similarly conflates the figure of the hand as killer, writer, and lover. Its English idioms may, furthermore, play out the long-standing wordplay on *hart/heart* in the context of the literary hunt of love and importance placed on body parts throughout the letters. But unlike the earlier French letter, this one does not offer up the hart as a gift. Its structure of remembrance lies not in the claim to eat the animal – and thus share in something of a spiritual typology of devotion – but rather in the King's own "myndyng" of the clock and in the regulation of his recreations. The killing of the hart thus functions in the logic of male entertainment and control, not in the dynamics of gift-giving and seduction.

70 See Ives, *Anne Boleyn*, pp. 16–19, 128. For George Boleyn's appointment as Esquire of the Body, see *Letters and Papers*, IV.4779.

71 Quoted in Muriel St. Clare Byrne, *The Lisle Letters*, 6 vols. (Chicago: University of Chicago Press, 1981), vol. I, p. 149.

72 For the Wilton matter, see Ridley, *Love Letters*, p. 58, and the extended note in Stemmler, *Die Liebesbriefe*, p. 153, with reference to M. D. Knowles, "The Matter of Wilton in 1528," *Bulletin of the Institute of Historical Research* 31 (1958): 92–96.

73 I quote from the two letters to Wolsey, printed in Byrne, *Letters*, pp. 76–78, 79–80.

74 The letter is printed in *ibid.*, p. 81, and in Ridley, *Love Letters*, p. 69. Byrne dates it as July–August 1528, but Ridley considers it "Written about 17 June 1528."

75 *Hall's Chronicle*, p. 598.

76 Jonathan Goldberg, *Sodometries: Renaissance Texts, Modern Sexualities* (Stanford: Stanford University Press, 1993), pp. 48–49.
77 Henry clearly means *buck*, a uniquely English word, though his spelling suggests that he is confusing it with the French word *bouc*, meaning he-goat. See *OED*, s.v., *buck*, sub. 1, and Edmond Huget, *Dictionnaire de la Langue Française du Siezième Siècle* (Paris: E. Champion, 1925–73), s.v., *bouc*.
78 See Edward Wilson, "*The Testament of the Buck* and the Sociology of the Text," *RES* ns 45 (1994): 157–84. The poem is titled as such in Wellys's manuscript, and as *Wyl Bucke His Testament* in Copeland's print (*RSTC* 15118.5, dated *c.* 1560). It also appears as a paste-in in British Library MS Cotton Julius A. v., in a hand datable to, perhaps, a generation after Wellys (Wilson, "*The Testament of the Buck*," p. 158).
79 Wilson, "*The Testament of the Buck*," p. 177.
80 The poems are printed in Jansen and Jordan, eds., *The Welles Anthology*, as follows: on Lob (17, with, by the way, its remarkably knowledgable line, "Thow was nother Erasmus nor Luter"); on Ryse and his wife (18, 19); "The Testament of the Buck" (20); a series of erotic lyrics and medical recipes (21–29); an excerpt from Skelton's *Why Come Ye Nat to Courte?* (30); a sequence of verse epistles concluding with a cento of stanzas drawn from *Troilus and Criseyde* (31–38); the poem on the death of Buckingham (39). Wilson has demonstrated in detail how Wellys grouped poems around shared topical and thematic interests. See "Local Habitations and Names in MS Rawlinson C. 813 in the Bodleian Library, Oxford," *RES* ns 41 (1990): 12–44. On the codicological contexts of the "Testament of the Buck," see Wilson, "*The Testament of the Buck*," p. 181.
81 Thiébaux, *The Stag of Love*, p. 35.
82 *Letters and Papers*, IV.4649
83 Warnicke, *Rise and Fall*, p. 77; Ridley, *Love Letters*, pp. 17–18.
84 Warnicke, *Rise and Fall*, p. 84.
85 See my discussion in chapter 4.
86 Jansen and Jordan, eds., *The Welles Anthology*, p. 124.
87 Act in Restraint of Appeals (24 Henry VIII, c. 12), reprinted in G. R. Elton, *The Tudor Constitution: Documents and Commentary*, 2nd edn. (Cambridge: Cambridge University Press, 1982), pp. 353–58. For the vexed question of just when Henry began to think of England as an empire – for the historical precedents and for Cromwell's role in the decision – see Walter Ullmann, "This Realm of England is an Empire," *Journal of Ecclesiastical History* 30 (1979): 175–204; John Guy, "Thomas Cromwell and the Intellectual Origins of the Henrician Revolution," in Alistair Fox and John Guy, eds., *Reassessing the Henrician Age* (Oxford: Clarendon Press, 1986), pp. 151–78; Dale Hoak, "The Iconography of the Crown Imperial," in Dale Hoak, ed., *Tudor Political Culture* (Cambridge: Cambridge University Press, 1995), pp. 54–103.
88 See the account in Hoak, "Iconography," p. 54 (who quotes from Hall's remarks and Udall's script), and the narrative in Warnicke, *Rise and Fall*, pp. 123–27.
89 Colyns's manuscript, now British Library Harley MS 2252, began to be compiled probably shortly after 1517, and he continued to make entries until

his death in 1539. This poem appears on fols. 155 r–v of the volume. It is printed in Ewald Flügel, *Neuenglisches Lesebuch* (Halle: Niemeyer, 1895), pp. 165–67; this quotation from 166.27–30. Colyns's work is the subject of a study by Carol Meale, "The Compiler at Work: John Colyns and BL MS Harley 2252," in Derek Pearsall, ed., *Manuscripts and Readers in Fifteenth-Century England* (Cambridge: D. S. Brewer, 1983), pp. 82–103, and Ulrich Frost, *Das Commonplace Book von John Colyns* (Frankfurt am Main: Peter Lang, 1988). Meale argues that the poem on Anne is inserted into a larger section of the manuscript dealing with political satire and topical commentary ("The Compiler at Work," pp. 86–87); Frost briefly discusses the literary antecedents of the ballad (*Das Commonplace Book*, pp. 301–3).

90   For the 1536 Act (27 Henry VIII, c. 2), see the text as reprinted in Elton, *Tudor Constitution*, p. 64.

91   G. R. Elton, *Policy and Police: The Enforcement of the Reformation in the Age of Thomas Cromwell* (Cambridge: Cambridge University Press, 1972), p. 397. My discussion in chapter 4 treats some of this material in greater detail.

92   31 Henry VIII, c. 14, Act abolishing diversity in opinions, in Elton, *Tudor Constitution*, pp. 399–401.

93   33 Henry VIII, c. 14, quoted and discussed in Wilson, "Local Habitations," pp. 42–43.

94   See the facsimile, transcription, and translation in Jansen and Jordan, eds., *The Welles Anthology*, pp. 1–3, and for a somewhat different reading, Wilson, "Local Habitations," pp. 14–15.

95   See, for example, those poems that enjoin the secrecy and anonymity of the lovers, often with the phrasing that the writer should not reveal his name (3.45–48, 5.29–30, 33.43–44, 47.65–66).

96   For more on the familial, social, and political environments of Wellys and his manuscript, see my discussion in the following chapter.

97   G. A. Bergenroth, *et al.*, eds., *Calendar of State Papers: Spanish* vol. V, part 2, pp. 127–28.

98   Walker, *Plays of Persuasion: Drama and Politics at the Court of Henry VIII* (Cambridge: Cambridge University Press, 1991), p. 21 and n. 41.

99   Thomas Elyot, *Pasquil the Playne* (London: Berthelet, 1533), A4 r, reprinted in facsimile in Lillian Gottesman, ed., *Four Political Treatises . . . . by Sir Thomas Elyot* (Gainesville: Scholars' Facsimiles and Reprints, 1967).

4 PRIVATE QUOTATIONS, PUBLIC MEMORIES: *TROILUS AND CRISEYDE*
AND THE POLITICS OF THE MANUSCRIPT ANTHOLOGY

1   A. C. Spearing, *Chaucer: Troilus and Criseyde* (London: Arnold, 1976), p. 55. See, too, his remarks in *The Medieval Poet as Voyeur* (Cambridge: Cambridge University Press, 1993), pp. 133–35.

2   *Medieval Poet as Voyeur*, p. 135. See, too, Sarah Stanbury, "The Voyeur and the Private Life in *Troilus and Criseyde*," *SAC* 13 (1991): 243–63, and Evan Carton, "Complicity and Responsibility in Pandarus's Bed and Chaucer's Art," *PMLA* 94 (1979): 47–61.

3   *Medieval Poet as Voyeur*, p. 293 n. 21.

4 See Windeatt's textual notes to these lines, *Troilus and Criseyde*, p. 299, referring to the scribal alterations in BL MS Harley 4912 (Windeatt's MS H5).

5 G. R. Elton, *Policy and Police: The Enforcement of the Reformation in the Age of Thomas Cromwell* (Cambridge: Cambridge University Press, 1972).

6 John Shirley was clearly much taken with the whetstone stanza of the poem (I.631–37), copying it twice into his personal anthologies: once, heading it "Pandare to Trojlus" in a sequence of moral colloquies (TCC MS R. 3. 20, p. 361), another time (Huntington Library MS EL 26. A. 13, fols. 2b-3a), heading it as "Gower," and following it with the first stanza of the *Cantus Troili* (headed "Troilus") and a stanza from Walton's verse translation of the *Consolation of Philosophy* (headed "Boese"). Two late fifteenth-century manuscripts also preserve three stanzas copied from Book III of the poem, where Pandarus offers advice on discretion in keeping one's love secret (III.302–22). In one of these selections (TCC MS R. 4. 20, fol. 171b), Pandarus's stanzas stand, with some slight verbal modifications, as a freestanding poem against boasting and lies. In the other, from the Findern Anthology, these three stanzas are placed inside a longer seven-stanza poem cobbled together out of pieces of Lydgate's *Fall of Princes*. For an edition of this latter poem, see Frederick J. Furnivall, ed., *Odd Texts of Chaucer's Minor Poems*, Chaucer Society First Series, vol. XXIII, part I (London: Trübner, 1871), pp. xi–xii. For the Shirley texts, see Henry Noble Mac-Cracken, "More Odd Texts of Chaucer's *Troilus*," *Modern Language Notes* 25 (1910): 126–27.

7 Edward Wilson, "Local Habitations and Names in MS Rawlinson C 813 in the Bodleian Library, Oxford," *RES* ns 41 (1990): 12–44, these remarks from p. 23.

8 See E. A. Bond, "Wyatt's Poems," *The Athenaeum*, 27 May 1871, pp. 654–55; Raymond Southall, "The Devonshire Manuscript Collection of Early Tudor Poetry, 1532–41," *RES* ns 15 (1964): 142–50, and *The Courtly Maker* (Oxford: Blackwell, 1964), pp. 15–25; Julia Boffey, *Manuscripts of English Courtly Love Lyrics in the Later Middle Ages* (Cambridge: D. S. Brewer, 1985), esp. pp. 7–9, 69–70, 81–86; Paul G. Remley, "Mary Shelton and Her Tudor Literary Milieu," in Peter C. Herman, ed., *Rethinking the Henrician Era: Essays on Early Tudor Texts and Contexts* (Urbana: University of Illinois Press, 1994), pp. 40–77; Elizabeth Heale, "Women and the Courtly Love Lyric: The Devonshire MS (BL Additional 17492)," *Modern Language Review* 90 (1995): 296–313.

9 The excerpts were first identified by Ethel Seaton, "'The Devonshire Manuscript' and its Medieval Fragments," *RES* ns 7 (1956): 55–56; their source in Thynne was discovered by Richard C. Harrier, "A Printed Source for 'The Devonshire Manuscript,'" *RES* ns 11 (1960): 54; Southall, "Devonshire Manuscript," added to and qualified these identifications. These texts, together with many others not published in the editions of Wyatt and Surrey, were edited by Kenneth Muir, "Unpublished Poems in the Devonshire Manuscript," *Proceedings of the Leeds Philosophical Society, Literary and Historical Section* 6 (1947): 253–82. My quotations in this chapter will be from this text, keyed to Muir's numbering of poems.

10   See Muir, "Unpublished Poems"; Remley, "Mary Shelton"; and Helen
     Baron, "Mary (Howard) Fitzroy's Hand in the Devonshire Manuscript,"
     RES ns 45 (1994): 318–35.
11   Southall, "Devonshire Manuscript," p. 150.
12   See Mary Thomas Crane, *Framing Authority: Sayings, Self, and Society in
     Sixteenth-Century England* (Princeton: Princeton University Press, 1993).
     For the social contexts of earlier medieval anthologies – with special
     reference to the relationships of class and status involved in the making and
     commissioning of anthologies of vernacular literature in the fourteenth and
     fifteenth centuries – see Julia Boffey and John J. Thompson, "Anthologies
     and Miscellanies: Production and Choice of Texts," in J. J. Griffiths and
     Derek Pearsall, eds., *Book Production and Publishing in Britain, 1375–1475*
     (Cambridge: Cambridge University Press, 1989), pp. 278–315.
13   See Lisa Jardine, *Erasmus, Man of Letters: The Construction of Charisma in
     Print* (Princeton: Princeton University Press, 1993).
14   *Framing Authority*, p. 4.
15   *Ibid.*, p. 5.
16   Charles Rosen, *The Romantic Generation* (Cambridge, MA: Harvard Uni-
     versity Press, 1995), p. 111.
17   The first stanza of this poem is modeled on *Pastime*, lines 2052–58.
18   See the notes to this poem in Jansen and Jordan, eds., *The Welles Anthology*,
     pp. 93–94, and their general discussion of the erotic verses in the manuscript,
     pp. 22–29.
19   P. J. Frankis, "The Erotic Dream in Middle English Lyrics," *Neuphilolo-
     gische Mitteilungen* 57 (1956): 228–37.
20   Jansen and Jordan, eds. *The Welles Anthology*, pp. 15–16, 22–29, and their
     brief analysis of poem 12 in the manuscript, which they associate with
     Wyatt's courtly songs (pp. 116–17).
21   For the transcription and grammar of this phrase, see *ibid.*, pp. 95–96.
22   Edward Wilson notes: "For in this manuscript poems do not just occur, they
     are arranged . . . [I]n the case of Humphrey Wellys we have a man with a
     legal training, an administrator of such competence that he avoided dismissal
     for recusancy, to whom the careful, organizational task of compilation was
     not foreign . . . In the Rawlinson manuscript we see not the happenstance of
     the commonplace book, with the intercalation of many literary kinds, but
     rather a concentration on, and physical separation of, two principle genres,
     the lyric and the political prophecy . . . To look for order and purpose is not
     to go against the grain of Wellys's mind." ("Local Habitations," pp. 23,
     30–31).
23   Versions of this poem appear in six other manuscripts. For information on
     its circulation, dating, textual variants, and historical context, see Jansen and
     Jordan, eds., *The Welles Anthology*, pp. 96–100.
24   The following discussion implies that Wellys knew Skelton's work well and
     that there is some conscious understanding of the resonances of the poetry in
     his manuscript with the language of Skelton's poetry. There is an excerpt
     from *Why Come Ye Nat to Court?* in the anthology (item 30, a copy of the
     poem with lines 30–840 excised), indicating that Wellys had access to an
     early manuscript (it was not printed until Kele's edition of *c.* 1545). The

appearance of this text suggests that Wellys had ties to the courtly and the London circles in which Skelton's poems circulated – as did John Colyns, whose commonplace book (MS Harley 2252) contains copies of Skelton's *Speke Parrot* and *Colyn Clout*. See John Scattergood, "The London Manuscripts of John Skelton's Poems," in Felicity Riddy, ed., *Regionalism in Late Medieval Manuscripts and Texts* (Cambridge: D. S. Brewer, 1991), pp. 171–83. Scattergood argues not only that the Wellys and Colyns manuscripts represent informed courtly and metropolitan literary taste (and thus naturally include Skelton), but that Skelton himself wrote for an audience exemplified by these compilers: "it seems fairly clear that Skelton was influenced in his choice of poetic forms and modes by what he thought might appeal to his London audience. Many of his lyrics are of the same type and genre as those which appear in Rawlinson C. 813" ("London Manuscripts," p. 181). Scattergood goes on to illustrate some similarities between the poetry of this manuscript and Skelton's *Phyllyp Sparowe* (in circulation by 1509). As I suggest here, associations between the poetry of Wellys's anthology and *Magnyfycence* (in print by 1530) may further place this manuscript in the environment of Skeltonic erotic satire.

25 See Gluck and Morgan, eds., *Stephen Hawes: The Minor Poems*, p. 161.

26 This quotation corresponds to *Pastime* lines 1751–57, 3867. For a complete list of the sources of this poem in the *Pastime*, see Gluck and Morgan, eds., *The Minor Poems*, p. 301.

27 Material in this paragraph is drawn from the account of Wellys's life in Wilson, "Local Habitations."

28 Elton, *Policy and Police*, p. 383.

29 *Statutes of the Realm* 31 Henry VIII (1539) c. 14, stating that any person shall be declared a heretic who "by worde writing ymprintinge cypheringe or in enye otherwise doe publishe preache theach say affirme delcare dispute argue or hold any opinion" deemed contrary to the articles of this act (this portion of the Act abolishing diversity of opinions, is not printed in Elton's excerpt, *The Tudor Constitution: Documents and Commentary*, 2nd edn. [Cambridge: Cambridge University Press, 1982], p. 401). Note, too, the language of 28 Henry VIII (1538) c. 10, the act extinguishing the authority of the bishop of Rome, citing penalties for anyone who, after 1536, "shall, by writing, ciphering, printing, preaching, or teaching, deed or act" defend the authority of the Pope (modernized text from Elton, *Tudor Constitution*, p. 366).

30 Wilson, "Local Habitations," p. 28.

31 *Ibid.*, p. 30. See *OED*, s.v., *study*, def. 8a, "A room in a house or other building, furnished with books, and used for private study, reading, writing, or the like." Note, in particular, the quotation from *c.* 1430, *Life of St. Katherine*: "He . . . passed from chambre to chambre tyle he come yn to hir secreet study where no creature vsed to come bot hir self allone." In def. 8b, the *OED* cites the definition from Elyot's Dictionary, 1538, "*Armarium*, a study where bokes are laide." See, too, *OED*, s.v., *settle*, def. 3, and the quotation from 1596, Nashe Saffron Waiden: "To Rdr. D. His Booke . . . I hauing kept idle by me in a by settle out of sight amongst old shooes and bootes almost this two yere."

32 Jansen and Jordan note that the concern with secrecy and anonymity in many of the poems in the manuscript is a feature that "seems to be unique to the Welles poet" (*The Welles Anthology*, p. 28).

33 See the excerpt from *The Chance of the Dice* as printed in Caroline F. E. Spurgeon, *Five Hundred Years of Chaucer Criticism and Allusion* (London: Kegan Paul, 1914), vol. I, pp. 44–45. For the late medieval reputation of Criseyde generally, see Gretchen Mieszkowski, "The Reputation of Criseyde, 1155–1500," *Transactions of the Connecticut Academy of Arts and Sciences* 43 (1971): 71–153.

34 My text is from Wilson, "Local Habitations," who offers a better transcription of the manuscript than Jansen and Jordan do. I have also examined the manuscript on microfilm and present here some emendations of my own (mostly of capitalization and punctuation).

35 *Ibid.*, pp. 24–25; Jansen and Jordan, eds., *The Welles Anthology*, pp. 1–7.

36 "Local Habitations", p. 44.

37 Jansen and Jordan, eds., *The Welles Anthology*, p. 102.

38 The following discussion of this cento develops and qualifies my earlier interpretation in *Chaucer and His Readers, Imagining the Author in Late-Medieval England* (Princeton: Princeton University Press, 1993), pp. 214–17.

39 This account of the textual tradition of these phrasings corrects my earlier interpretation in *ibid.*, pp. 215–16.

40 For example, the reading "all my Sorowe" at 38. 12 is the Caxtonian reading of II. 845, as is the reading "vnto" for "to" at 38. 25, corresponding to II. 564. The garblings in 38. 27–28 may draw on Caxton's reading of II. 567, "as lyef as."

41 Remley, "Mary Shelton," p. 55.

42 Wilson, "Local Habitations," p. 31.

43 See Heale, "Women and the Courtly Love Lyric," especially her remarks on pp. 306–7 on the "fondness of this copyist for plundering medieval poems."

44 Muir considered these three sets of entries to be all in the hand of Thomas Howard. He also clearly believed Howard to have been the author of them ("Unpublished Poems," pp. 254–56).

45 Remley, "Mary Shelton," pp. 57, 56.

46 Baron, "Mary (Howard) Fitzroy's Hand." Baron labels this hand TH2, though she hedges somewhat on the absolute identification of the hand as Howard's (calling it "Thomas Howard?"). For a complete review of earlier scholarship on the hands, together with a table of all identifiable hands in the manuscript, see pp. 324–33. Specific attributions to the TH2 hand are on p. 332.

47 For a reading of this sequence through the topicalities of the Howard/Douglas romance, see Heale, "Women and the Courtly Love Lyric," pp. 304–6.

48 *OED*, s.v., *report*, def. 2b: "An account brought by one person to another, esp. of some matter specially investigated." See, too, def. 3a, *make report* – to give information.

49 See *OED*, s.v., *term*, legal uses, def. 4b; See too *MED*, s.v., *terme*, 4f, "terme of lyf"; Paston letters citation from *c.* 1437, as a prison sentence.

50 *OED*, s.v., *case*, def. 6, first citation as legal case from 1523; but see too 1552 entry.

51 See *MED*, s.v., *quake*, for citations.

52 The sources for these lines have not been previously identified.

53 Compare these lines from the *Temple of Glas*: "Nou at my laarge, nou feterid in prisone / Nov in turment, nov in souerein glorie, / Nou in paradise and nov in purgatorie" (lines 648–50).

54 The impact of the *Temple of Glas* on late medieval courtship has long been seen as evidenced in the letter of John Paston III to his brother, dated 17 February 1472: "Brother I comande me to yow and praye yow to loke vppe my Temple off Glasse, and send it me by the berer heroff" (Norman Davis, ed., *The Paston Letters and Papers of the Fifteenth Century* [Oxford: Clarendon Press, 1977], vol. I, p. 447). This request has been interpreted in the context of John III's wooing of Anne Hault, and his need for Lydgate's poem has been understood as a request for a textbook in the arts of courtiership. For Ethel Seaton, the letter is evidence for a cultural position to this poem akin to that of Tottel's *Miscellany* a century later: "He probably wanted it just as Slender wanted his 'Book of Songs and Sonnets' to woo another Mistress Anne" (*Sir Richard Roos* [London: R. Hart-Davis, 1961], p. 376). See, too, the discussion in Derek Pearsall, *John Lydgate* (Charlottesville: University of Virginia Press, 1970), p. 18, and Julia Boffey, *Manuscripts of Courtly Love Lyrics*, p. 86.

55 The section is written in Baron's TH2, Harrier's B, "a legible and consistent secretary hand but not of professional refinement" (Richard C. Harrier, *The Canon of Sir Thomas Wyatt's Poetry* (Cambridge, MA: Harvard University Press, 1975), p. 38.

56 IV.13–14, with the Cosin variants provided by Windeatt, ed., *Chaucer: Troilus and Criseyde*, p. 349.

57 See the discussion in Heale, "Women and the Courtly Love Lyric," pp. 302–3.

58 *Ibid.*, p. 307.

59 See the discussions in Muriel St. Clare Byrne, ed., *The Lisle Letters*, 6 vols. (Chicago: University of Chicago Press, 1981), vol. I, p. 9, vol. II, p. 197, vol. III, pp. 246–47, 250–52, 566–69. For a telling anecdote on the interception of letters and the intrusions of Cromwellian surveillance into personal communication during the mid 1530s, see Elton, *Policy and Police*, p. 336.

60 Letter dated 8 November 1538, in Byrne, ed., *Lisle Letters*, vol. V, p. 276.

61 Letter dated 8 November 1538, in *ibid.*, vol. V, p. 277

62 See Remley, "Mary Shelton," p. 72 n. 57.

63 For a distillation of the events of Margaret Douglas's life, drawn from materials collected in *Letters and Papers*, see Heale, "Women and the Courtly Love Lyric," pp. 288–89.

64 Sir Thomas Malory, *Le Morte Darthure*, XVIII.1, ed. Janet Cowan (Baltimore: Penguin, 1968), vol. II, p. 373.

65 Ed. Clifford Leech (London: Methuen, 1969).

66 Heale, "Women and the Courtly Love Lyric," p. 313.

67 Remley, "Mary Shelton," p. 56.

68 See A. S. G. Edwards, "Poet and Printer in the Sixteenth Century: Stephen Hawes and Wynkyn de Worde," *Gutenberg Jahrbuch* (1980): 82–88; "From Manuscript to Print: Wynkyn de Worde and the Printing of Contemporary

Poetry," *Gutenberg Jahrbuch* (1991): 143–48; "An Allusion to Stephen Hawes, c. 1530," *Notes and Queries* 226 (1981): 487.

69 I have pointed out in greater detail some of these allusions and contexts for Wellys's volume in "The Wiles of a Woodcut: Wynkyn de Worde and the Early Tudor Reader," *The Huntington Library Quarterly* 56 (1996).

70 Such is the tenor of Southall's account in *The Courtly Maker*.

71 See Scattergood's note to this section of the *Garlande*, *Complete English Poems*, p. 505. The complex relations among the Howard family members are usefully laid out in the genealogical table in Rosemary O'Day, *The Longman Companion to the Tudor Age* (London: Longman, 1995), pp. 234–35.

5 WYATT, CHAUCER, TOTTEL: THE VERSE EPISTLE AND THE SUBJECTS OF THE COURTLY LYRIC

1 Stephen Greenblatt, *Renaissance Self-Fashioning, More to Shakespeare* (Chicago: University of Chicago Press, 1980), pp. 115–56, this quotation from p. 136.

2 *Ibid.*, p. 156.

3 *Ibid.*

4 *Ibid.*, pp. 133–36. David Starkey, "The Court: Castiglione's Ideal and Tudor Reality, Being a Discussion of Sir Thomas Wyatt's *Satire Addressed to Sir Francis Bryan*," *Journal of the Warburg and Courtauld Institutes* 45 (1982): 232–39; Stephen M. Foley, *Sir Thomas Wyatt* (Boston: Twayne, 1990), pp. 72–79; Perez Zagorin, "Sir Thomas Wyatt and the Court of Henry VIII: The Courtier's Ambivalence," *Journal of Medieval and Renaissance Studies* 23 (1993): 113–41.

5 Greenblatt, *Renaissance Self-Fashioning*, p. 135.

6 Edward Hall, *Hall's Chronicle* (London: 1809; reprinted New York: AMS Press, 1965), p. 597.

7 Starkey, "The Court," p. 236.

8 *Ibid.*, p. 237.

9 *Ibid.*, pp. 235–38; Greenblatt, *Renaissance Self-Fashioning*, pp. 133–36; Zagorin, "Sir Thomas Wyatt and the Court," pp. 139–40.

10 Foley, *Sir Thomas Wyatt*, p. 72.

11 Thomas M. Greene, *The Light in Troy* (New Haven: Yale University Press, 1983), p. 262.

12 See Richard Harrier, *The Canon of Sir Thomas Wyatt's Poetry* (Cambridge: Harvard University Press, 1975); H. A. Mason, *Editing Wyatt* (Cambridge: Cambridge Quarterly Publications, 1972); Jonathan Crewe, *Trials of Authorship: Anterior Forms and Poetic Reconstruction from Wyatt to Shakespeare* (Berkeley and Los Angeles: University of California Press, 1990), pp. 23–26; Wendy Wall, *The Imprint of Gender: Authorship and Publication in the English Renaissance* (Ithaca: Cornell University Press, 1993), pp. 23–30; Arthur Marotti, *Manuscript, Print, and the English Renaissance Lyric* (Ithaca: Cornell University Press, 1995), pp. 212–19.

13 Pandarus's penchant for proverbs has been analyzed by Karla Taylor, "Chaucer's Use of Proverbs," in Stephen A. Barney, ed., *Chaucer's Troilus: Essays in Criticism* (New Haven: Archon, 1980), pp. 277–96; Chauncey M.

Wood, *The Elements of Chaucer's* Troilus (Durham: Duke University Press, 1984), pp. 143–53.

14 *MED*, s.v., *proverben*, which cites this passage as the only example of the word used as a verb.

15 Printed in F. J. Furnivall, ed., *Odd Texts of Chaucer's Minor Poems*, Chaucer Society First Series, vol. XXIII, part I (London: Trubner, 1871), pp. xi–xii.

16 See Donald R. Howard, *The Idea of the Canterbury Tales* (Berkeley and Los Angeles: University of California Press, 1976), p. 368.

17 Jay Schleusener, *"The Owl and the Nightingale*: A Matter of Judgment," *Modern Philology* 70 (1973): 185–89.

18 Starkey, "The Court," p. 236.

19 The proverb has an ancient history. See the account in Erasmus, *Adages*, I. iv. 35, "Asinus ad lyram," in J. K. Sowards, ed., *The Collected Works of Erasmus, Adages*, trans. Margaret Mann Phillips, annotated by R. A. B. Mynors, vol. XXXI (Toronto: University of Toronto Press, 1982), pp. 344–45. Chaucer most likely got it from Boethius, *Consolation of Philosophy*, I. pr.4. 2–3. See the note to *Troilus and Criseyde*, I. 731, in the *Riverside Chaucer*, p. 1029.

20 Erasmus interprets it as "a hit at people who lack judgment through their ignorance," and offers a string of classical references that stress the public and political applicability of the adage (*Collected Works*, vol. XXXI, pp. 344–45).

21 See Rollins, ed., *Miscellany*, vol. II, p. 220, who also adduces Lydgate's use of the proverb in *The Churl and the Bird* as relevant to Wyatt's phrasing; and Rebholz, *Sir Thomas Wyatt, The Complete Poems*, p. 451.

22 *MED*, s.v., *bestialite*, citing this passage from *Troilus and Criseyde* as the first usage.

23 For the circulation of the poem in fifteenth-century manuscripts and early sixteenth-century printed editions, see Ralph Hanna III, "Authorial Versions, Rolling Revision, Scribal Error? Or the Truth about *Truth*," *SAC* 10 (1988): 23–40. For its impact on late medieval moral versifying, especially in the poetry of Lydgate, see A. S. G. Edwards, "Lydgate Manuscripts: Some Directions for Future Research," in Derek Pearsall, ed., *Manuscripts and Readers in Fifteenth-Century England* (Cambridge: D. S. Brewer, 1983), pp. 15–26.

24 For *Truth* as a Lydgatean envoy to the *Clerk's Tale*, see the discussion in Seth Lerer, *Chaucer and His Readers, Imagining the Author in Late-Medieval England* (Princeton: Princeton University Press, 1993), pp. 100–5. For the ballad's role in Tottel's *Miscellany*, see my discussion in this chapter, below.

25 Greene, *Light in Troy*, p. 254.

26 Compare, too, Rebholz, *The Complete Poems*, LXXXIV.1–3: "If thou wilt mighty bee, flee from the rage / Of cruel will and see thou keep thee free / From the foul yoke of sensual bondage." See Rebholz's note, p. 399, on the Boethianism of this poem, and Patricia Thompson, "Wyatt's Boethian Ballade," *RES* ns 15 (1964): 262–7. See, too, the discussion in Helen Cooper, "Wyatt and Chaucer: A Reappraisal," *Leeds Studies in English* 13 (1982): 115.

27 See *Consolation of Philosophy*, III. m. 12, for the source of this injunction in the story of Hercules.

28 Rollins, ed., *Miscellany*, pp. 183–85.

29 Though modern editions print a fourth stanza, the envoy to Chaucer's friend Vache, this final stanza surivives in only one manuscript (British Library MS Additional 10340). Fifteenth- and sixteenth-century readers knew it as a three-stanza poem. Tottel's edition does not exactly correspond to any manuscript or printed text of Chaucer's poem. Rollins finds it agreeing most closely with Thynne's 1532 edition, and he catalogues the variants between them (vol. II, p. 296).

30 This is a unique reading. For the complete collation and list of variants, see the edition in George B. Pace and Alfred David, eds., *The Variorum Edition of the Works of Geoffrey Chaucer*, vol. V, part 1, *The Minor Poems* (Norman: University of Oklahoma Press, 1982), p. 64, note to line 20.

31 See Hanna, "Authorial Versions."

32 Pace and David comment: "The printing of *Truth* has been continuous from Caxton on" (*Minor Poems*, p. 53 n. 1). The early publication history of *Truth* is as follows: Caxton, *c.* 1477, *Temple of bras* (fols. 21 v–22 r); de Worde, *c.* 1515, *Prouerbes of Lydgate* (Aiii v); Pynson, *The boke of fame*, 1526 (Ei v); Thynne, Chaucer's Works, 1532 (Vvv4 r–v). The publications of Caxton and de Worde are collections of shorter Chauceriana (Caxton's contains the *Parliament of Foules*, *Gentillesse*, *Fortune*, *Scogan*, and *Truth*; de Worde's contains excerpts from Lydgate's *Fall of Princes* plus *Fortune* and *Truth*). Pynson's book is considered to be part of a larger, three-part publication project of the complete Chaucer works (though this volume contains, in addition to the dream poems and shorter ballads, five non-Chaucerian pieces). See Pace and David, eds., *The Minor Poems*, pp. 30–32, 52–58.

33 The bed, too, is the place of private reading. Compare Chaucer's *Book of the Duchesse* (lines 44–61, 231–69) where the narrator reads himself to sleep with the story of Cyex and Alcione from the *Metamorphoses*. It has been argued that this representation of reading in bed is a Chaucerian innovation in the traditions of medieval dream poetry (see the note to lines 44–45 in the *Riverside Chaucer*, p. 967).

34 All quotations from *The Lisle Letters* are from Muriel St. Clare Byrne's edition (Chicago: University of Chicago Press, 1981), 6 volumes.

35 For a brief account of the affair, see Byrne, *The Lisle Letters*, vol. II, p. 8, and the sequence of letters and commentary at vol. II, pp. 249–61.

36 See vol. II, p. 259 n. 1.

37 Letter to Wolsey, July 1518, in Muriel St. Clare Byrne, *The Letters of King Henry VIII* (New York: Funk and Wagnalls, 1968), p. 43.

38 See the account in Kenneth Muir, *The Life and Letters of Sir Thomas Wyatt* (Liverpool: Liverpool University Press, 1963), pp. 172–78; Zagorin, "Sir Thomas Wyatt and the Court," pp. 122–23, 132–33; Foley, *Sir Thomas Wyatt*, pp. 76–77.

39 Muir, *Life and Letters*, p. 186.

40 Foley, *Sir Thomas Wyatt*, pp. 76–78. See, too, Zagorin, "Sir Thomas Wyatt and the Court," pp. 133–35; and Alistair Fox, *Politics and Literature in the Reigns of Henry VII and Henry VIII* (Oxford: Blackwell, 1989), pp. 279–80.

41 The two texts are preserved in British Library MS Harley 78, fols. 5–15, and edited by Muir, *Life and Letters* (*Declaration*, pp. 178–84; *Defence*, pp. 187–209). The reasons why Wyatt did not deliver these speeches remain unclear, though Zagorin argues that Wyatt "went through the motions of confession and petitioning for mercy in order to save his life and regain his freedom" ("Sir Thomas Wyatt and the Court," p. 135).

42 Foley, *Sir Thomas Wyatt*, p. 77.

43 See J. W. Saunders, "The Stigma of Print: A Note on the Social Bases of Tudor Poetry," *Essays in Criticism* 1 (1951): 139–54, and Marotti, *Manuscript, Print, and the English Renaissance Lyric*, pp. 209–11.

44 See the repeated remarks on letters sent and received, Muir, *Life and Letters*, pp. 179–80.

45 See Anthony Grafton, *Defenders of the Text* (Cambridge, MA: Harvard University Press, 1990), pp. 47–75, and Paolo Trovato, *Con ogni diligenza corretto: La stampa e le revisioni editoriali dei testi letterari Italiani (1470–1570)* (Bologna: Il Mulino, 1991), especially pp. 93–96.

46 Lerer, *Chaucer and His Readers*, pp. 166–69.

47 I quote from the facsimile edition, ed. Derek Brewer, *Geoffrey Chaucer, The Works, 1532 . . .* (Menston: Scolar, 1969). The *OED* cites this passage as the first appearance in English of the word "collation" used in textual criticism (s.v., *collation*, def. 3). To *collate*, *confer*, and to *compare* are linked together in the example offered next by the *OED*, a 1568 reference to H. Campbell, ed., *Love Letters of Mary Queen of Scots*, App. 52: "The originals . . . were duly *conferred* and *compared* . . . with sundry other lettres . . . in *collation* whereof no difference was found" (emphases added). The *OED* also notes, s.v., *confer*, def. 4: "to bring into comparison, compare, collate (exceedingly common from 1530 to 1650)," and offers a citation from 1533 as its first appearance.

48 See W. A. Sessions, "Surrey's Wyatt: Autumn 1542 and the New Poet," in Peter C. Herman, ed., *Rethinking the Henrician Era: Essays on Early Tudor Texts and Contexts* (Urbana: University of Illinois Press, 1994), p. 175: "What Brian Tuke had indicated in his preface to Thynne's 1532 edition of Chaucer – as obvious a place as any to locate the inception of the idea of a new language – the later Tottel and Puttenham knew absolutely: the power of language was nothing if it did not center primarily on that source of all power and finance, the court."

49 See Rebholz's note, *The Complete Poems*, p. 349.

50 Crewe, *ibid.*, p. 22.

51 See the discussions in Crewe, *Trials of Authorship*, pp. 23–26, and Wall, *Imprint of Gender*, p. 29.

52 Raymond Southall, *The Courtly Maker* (Oxford: Blackwell, 1964), p. 25.

53 Recall, too, Skelton's indictment of Wolsey and King in *Why Come Ye Nat to Courte?*: "He sayth the kynge doth wryte, / And writeth he wottith nat what" (678–79).

54 Rebholz, *The Complete Poems*, p. 522.

55 See Greenblatt, *Renaissance Self-Fashioning*, p. 131.

56 See the discussion in Rebholz, *The Complete Poems*, pp. 437–38.

57 For Egerton (British Library MS Egerton 2711), see Richard Harrier, *The*

Canon of Sir Thomas Wyatt's Poetry; for Arundel (The Arundel Harrington Manuscript, Arundel Castle), see Ruth Hughey, ed., *The Arundel Harrington Manuscript of Tudor Poetry* (Columbus: Ohio State University Press, 1960); for Tottel, see Rollins, *Tottel's Miscellany*.

58   Rebholz, *The Complete Poems*, p. 445.

59   Noted in *ibid.*, p. 451, and discussed in Hughey, *Arundel Harrington Manuscript*, vol. II, p. 184.

60   Harrier, *The Canon of Sir Thomas Wyatt's Poetry*, pp. 170–72, though it is unclear from Harrier's discussion what the relationship is between arguments and editorial practice. Even though he prints a version of the poem's opening based on Arundel, he nonetheless states that, after a long and detailed textual argument, "One may conclude, then, that the first 51 lines should be based on C [i. e., the Parker manuscript] and emended from A and D [Arundel and Devonshire]" (p. 170). Kenneth Muir and Patricia Thompson take Devonshire as their base text, though offering variants from Parker (*Collected Poems of Sir Thomas Wyatt* [Liverpool: Liverpool University Press, 1969], pp. 88–91).

61   Rebholz, *The Complete Poems*, p. 438. The Parker manuscript is Corpus Christi College Cambridge MS Parker 168, an assembly of texts relating to ecclesiastical and public affairs in Tudor England. It contains one other Wyatt poem in addition to the Satire, "Like as the Birde" (Rebholz, *The Complete Poems*, XC). For a description of this manuscript, see Harrier, *The Canon of Sir Thomas Wyatt's Poetry*, pp. 78–79. For a full discussion of the textual relations among the various manuscripts of this poem, see Harrier, *The Canon of Sir Thomas Wyatt's Poetry*, pp. 168–72, who argues that the Devonshire text, rather than Parker (Harrier's MS C) "is probably the best source for lines 1–51" (p. 168).

62   Edited from the microfilm of the manuscript.

63   See the summary of critical positions in Rebholz, *The Complete Poems*, p. 439.

64   *Canterbury Tales* A, lines 3120, 3128, 3138, 3145, 3150.

65   I have argued that the monstrosity of the villains in the *Tale of Sir Thopas* represent the monstrously rude Host in the *Prologue* to that *Tale*. See "'Now holde youre mouth!': The Romance of Orality in the *Canterbury Tales*," in Mark Amodio, ed., *Oral Poetry and Middle English Literature* (New York: Garland, 1994), pp. 185–205.

66   *OED*, s.v., *thing*, def. 13, "an individual work of literature or art," citing Chaucer, *Canterbury Tales* A, line 325 and *Squire's Tale* F, line 78, as the earliest usages, and citing Puttenham, *Art of English Poesie* III. xxii. But *MED*, s.v., *thing*, def. 7c, cites a range of usages from late Old English through 1500. The use of the word *thing* connoting a written text as a gift (Wyatt's sense) is nicely brought out in the passage from Scrope's translation of the *Epistle to Othea* (*c.* 1440), quoted in the *MED*: "This book translated haue I . . . Please you, ryght hiȝ prince, to take of this thynge The poure effecte of my litell connyng."

67   *Troilus and Criseyde* V.1856–59. For the sources behind this request for authorial correction, and a commentary on the genre of submission, see J. S. P. Tatlock, "The Epilog of Chaucer's *Troilus*," *Modern Philology* 18 (1921):

115–18. For imitations of Chaucer's plea for correction, see the entires in the *MED*, s.v., *correccioun*, def. 1; *correcten*, def. 1, and the collection of Caxton quotations from the prologues to his printed editions, assembled in *OED*, s.v., *correct*, *correction*. Skelton often plays off the Chaucerian envoy, submitting books for perusal and emendation in ways that undermine the the humility topos. See, for example, *Phyllyp Sparowe*, lines 1245–46; the multiple envoys that close *Speke Parott*; the envoy to the *Garlande of Laurell* (esp. line 1575); and *A Replycacion* (line 391). All of Hawes's poems close with some version of the Chaucerian envoy, though he enjoins forms of emendation, rather than correction, as his plea.

68 See G. W. Pigman III, "Versions of Imitation in the Renaissance," *Renaissance Quarterly* 33 (1980): 1–32, especially pp. 4–9.

69 Compare Petrarch's remark (*Ad Familiares* 1. 8. 28) on gathering and imitating: "Take care that what you have gathered does not long remain in its original form inside of you: the bees would not be glorious if they did not convert what they found into something different and something better" (quoted in Pigman, "Versions of Imitation," p. 7).

70 See the account in Rebholz, *The Complete Poems*, p. 431.

71 Though the *OED* does not cite an appearance of the word *thesaurus* in a lexicographical context until 1568 (s.v., *thesaurus*), the French *trésor* and Italian *tesoro* connoted treasuries of words or knowledge as early as the mid thirteenth-century treatise of Brunetto Latini (*Il Tesoro*, and in French translation, *Le Livre du Trésor*). The word *trésor* was also used in 1541 to refer to a collection of biblical terms. See *Trésor de la Langue Française* vol. XVI (Paris: Gallimard, 1994), s.v., *trésor*.

72 See, for example, 45. 7–10 in the Wellys Anthology, quoted and discussed in chapter 4, above, pp. 137–40.

73 Hawes often deploys the idiom of poetic allegory as "cloudy," drawing on Lydgate's sense of the darkness or obfuscating quality of allegorical writing. See, for example, the opening of the *Conforte of Louers*: "The gentyll poetes / vnder cloudy fygures / Do touche a trouth / and cloke it subtylly" (lines 1–2). Similar phrasings appear in the *Example of Vertue* (lines 901–3), *Conversion of Swerers* (lines 11–14), and the *Pastime of Pleasure*, lines 32–35, (where the practice is explicitly attributed to Lydgate), 715–21, 932–45, and (resonant with Wyatt's phrasing) 981–87: "In an example / with a mysty cloude / Of couert lykenesse / the poetes do wryte / . . . As I here after / shall the trouthe soone shewe / Of all theyr mysty / and theyr fatall dewe."

74 Windeatt considers this a variant reading (preserved in four manuscripts), printing for line 596, "It is no shame vn-to ʒow, ne no vice." He considers that "the cruder reading may reflect Chaucer's translation process here" (p. 385). The *Riverside Chaucer* prints *rape, in my dom*, arguing that the other readings are either scribal errors or Chaucer's own revision (p. 1173). An example of scribal bowdlerization may be the reading *jape in my dom*, preserved in Cambridge University Library MS Gg. 4. 27 and Huntington Library MS HM 114.

75 Wall, *The Imprint of Gender*, p. 25.

76 *Ibid.*, p. 172.

77 Sheldon P. Zitner, "Truth and Mourning in a Sonnet by Surrey," *A Journal*

of English Literary History 50 (1983): 59–80; Crewe, *Trials of Authorship*, pp. 48–78.

78 The quotations are, respectively: "O envuious wall certes thou dost amysse / If thou wylt nat suffre / that we may / Ioyne our bodies / suffre us to kysse" (Aiiii v); "On eche syde / they kyst the wall swetely" (*ibid.*); "And on the kerchef / with face pale and tryst / He loked ofte / and it right swetely kyst" (Bii v); "Her bytter teares / lay as thycke as rayne / And ofte she kyssed / his deedly colde visage" (Biii r).

79 Crewe, *Trials of Authorship*, p. 76.

80 Emrys Jones, ed., *Henry Howard, Earl of Surrey, Poems* (Oxford: Clarendon Press, 1964), p. 125.

81 See Martine Braekman, "A Chaucerian 'Courtly Love Aunter' By Henry Howard, Earl of Surrey," *Neophilologus* 79 (1995): 675–87.

82 John Bruce, preface to the *Verney Papers* (London: Camden Society, 1853), quoted in Roger H. Ellis, "The Royal Commission on Historical Manuscripts: A Short History and Explanation," in *Manuscripts and Men: An Exhibition of Manuscripts, Portraits, and Pictures . . . to Mark the Centenary of the Royal Commission on Historical Manuscripts, 1869–1969* (London: Her Majesty's Stationery Office, 1969), pp. 1–39, this quotation on p. 1.

83 Quoted in Ellis, "Royal Commission," pp. 4–5.

84 *The Standard* 4 April 1970, quoted in *ibid.*, p. 13.

Index

Cambridge Studies in Renaissance Literature and Culture

General editor
STEPHEN ORGEL
Jackson Eli Reynolds Professor of Humanities, Stanford
University